Privacy's Blueprint

WOODROW HARTZOG

Privacy's Blueprint

The Battle to Control the Design
of New Technologies

||| Harvard University Press

Cambridge, Massachusetts, and London, England   2018

Second printing

Library of Congress Cataloging-in-Publication Data

Names: Hartzog, Woodrow, 1978– author.
Title: Privacy's blueprint : the battle to control the design of new
    technologies / Woodrow Hartzog.
Description: Cambridge, Massachusetts : Harvard University Press, 2018. |
    Includes bibliographical references and index.
Identifiers: LCCN 2017039954 | ISBN 9780674976009 (hardcover : alk. paper)
Subjects: LCSH: Privacy, Right of—United States. | Design and technology—
    United States. | Data protection—Law and legislation—United States.
Classification: LCC KF1262 .H37 2018 | DDC 342.7308 / 58—dc23
LC record available at https://lccn.loc.gov/2017039954

For Jen, Will, and Romy,
with love and gratitude

Contents

Preface

Modern discussions of privacy can give rise to worry, but I did not write this book as a privacy and technology fatalist. Quite the opposite. This book is the culmination of both the first part of my academic career as well as my lived experience on the important role that privacy plays in our lives. I have worked for a library, a television station, a restaurant, a university newspaper, a law firm, an advocacy group, and several educational institutions. At every step I have seen how necessary privacy is and how challenging it can be to balance privacy with other important, competing values. And, if I'm being honest, this book was at least partially motivated by the blessed obscurity of the awkward growing pains of my youth.

While my experiences and prior work informed the values I highlight and the theory I propose in this book, I do not mean for this theory to be the final or only word at the intersection of privacy and design. Theories are meant to evolve; they are meant to interact with other theories, to be criticized, reinterpreted, and, with any luck, eventually contribute to a momentum that improves our world.

Portions of this book were adapted from parts of the following articles: "The Indispensable, Inadequate Fair Information Practices," *Maryland Law Review* 76 (2017): 952–982; "The Feds Are Wrong to Warn of 'Warrant-Proof' Phones," *MIT Technology Review,* March 17, 2016; "The Internet of Heirlooms and Disposable Things," *North Carolina Journal of Law and*

Technology 17 (2016): 581–598 (coauthored with Evan Selinger); "Taking Trust Seriously in Privacy Law," *Stanford Technology Law Review* 19 (2016): 431–472 (coauthored with Neil Richards); "Increasing the Transaction Costs of Harassment," *Boston University Law Review Annex,* November 4, 2015 (coauthored with Evan Selinger); "Social Media Needs More Limitations, Not Choices," *Wired,* April 2015; "Surveillance as Loss of Obscurity," *Washington and Lee Law Review* 72 (2015): 1343–1387 (coauthored with Evan Selinger); "The FTC and the New Common Law of Privacy," *Columbia Law Review* 114 (2014): 583–676 (coauthored with Daniel J. Solove); "Reviving Implied Confidentiality," *Indiana Law Journal* 89 (2014): 763–806; "The Value of Modest Privacy Protections in a Hyper Social World," *Colorado Technology Law Journal* 12 (2014): 332–350; "The Case for Online Obscurity," *California Law Review* 101 (2013): 1–50 (coauthored with Fred Stutzman); "The Fight to Frame Privacy," *Michigan Law Review* 111 (2013): 1021–1043; "Obscurity by Design," *Washington Law Review* 88 (2013): 385–418 (coauthored with Fred Stutzman); "Social Data," *Ohio State Law Journal* 74 (2013): 995–1028; "Website Design as Contract," *American University Law Review* 60 (2011): 1635–1671; "The Privacy Box: A Software Proposal," *First Monday* 14 (2009); and "Promises and Privacy: Promissory Estoppel and Confidential Disclosure in Online Communities," *Temple Law Review* 82 (2009): 891–928. In some cases, I have used only selected passages from the articles. In many cases, the text and argument of the articles have been significantly reworked. I give special thanks to Neil Richards, Evan Selinger, Daniel Solove, and Fred Stutzman for allowing me to adapt some of our coauthored material for this book.

Privacy's Blueprint

Introduction:
Designing Our Privacy Away

SOMETIMES even your best efforts are no match for technology. In the fall of 2012, Bobbi Duncan, then a student at the University of Texas at Austin, was outed as a lesbian to her father in part by the design choices of the social network site Facebook. Duncan did her best to keep posts about her sexuality hidden from her father by adjusting her privacy settings. But Facebook's discussion groups were not designed to ensure that the intent of an individual's privacy settings was respected. So when the creator of a Facebook group for UT's Queer Chorus added Duncan to the group, Facebook automatically posted a note to all her Facebook "friends," including her father, without checking with her first. The design default allowed her to be added to the group in a public way without her permission.

Facebook's decision to design its site this way had real consequences. Duncan told the *Wall Street Journal* that a few hours after her "friends" were notified that she had been added to the group, her father began leaving her angry voicemails. "No no no no no no no," Duncan remembers telling a friend. "I have him hidden from my updates, but he saw this. He saw it." Duncan became estranged from her father and fell into depression for weeks. "I couldn't function," she said. "I would be in class and not hear a word anyone was saying. . . . I remember I was miserable and said, 'Facebook decided to tell my dad that I was gay.'"[1]

Bobbi Duncan is hardly the only person whose secrets have been betrayed by design. Hackers exploited the design of the social media service

Snapchat. The service, which set time limits on how long posts by users were visible to recipients, was configured in such a way that third-party applications could access the service (despite third-party access being prohibited in Snapchat's terms of use). Predictably, hundreds of thousands of pictures and videos taken by users were intercepted by hackers through a third-party application and, after a few days of bragging and bluster, were finally posted online in a thirteen-gigabyte dump. Snapchat blamed its users for using insecure applications, but it was Snapchat that let its users down; the company was the entity in the best position to protect its users. There are ways to ensure that only authorized software can interact with Snapchat's servers, like rigorous client authentication in addition to standard user authentication. Yet Snapchat left access to its servers insecure and merely buried a warning about third-party "add-on" apps in the dense, hidden, and confusing terms of use that it knew no user would read.

Design also protects our privacy in profound and unappreciated ways. Search engines like Google, Bing, and DuckDuckGo are designed to respect the robots.txt file, which is stored on web servers and instructs search engines to ignore web pages. YouTube provides a face-blurring tool that lets you hide the identities of video subjects before uploading. Before it shut down, the anonymous posting mobile app Yik Yak applied a "full name" filter to obscure the identities of those being referenced. And, of course, the privacy settings for social media like Facebook, when designed and configured properly, let users control who sees their posts.

Tech design that affects our privacy is now so pervasive that we barely even notice it. We usually don't think about the fact that phone companies have designed the phones we all carry in our pockets to be ideal surveillance devices, tracking our every move and sharing our location with third parties. The privacy policies on websites and mobile apps are usually long, dense, and designed to be as unobtrusive as possible. This helps avoid scrutiny. Have you ever noticed that sometimes the little checkbox next to the marketing preferences on apps and websites is already selected for you? That is no accident. Companies know defaults are sticky—we are more likely to give websites and apps permission to collect our personal information if we have to opt out of such sharing rather than opt in.

Technologies are being designed to identify department store shoppers by their faces, to spy on a partner's computer habits without a trace, to cause users to overshare on social media, to collect information from your email messages and web browsing activities, and to connect your underwear (!) to the Internet. Even seemingly innocuous design decisions can unintentionally affect our privacy. Because URLs are a commonly tracked piece of information, the ostensibly innocent choice to structure a URL according to the content of a web page, such as http://www.webmd.com/popular-herpes -treatments.html instead of, say, http://www.webmd.com/198897/makes it easier to learn a user's browsing history and private health information.

Then there are the design decisions necessary to secure our data. The year 2014 was dubbed the Year of the Data Breach, but it turned out we were just getting warmed up.[2] We saw more massive, high-profile data breaches in the following years. Organizations like health insurers Anthem and Blue Cross Blue Shield, surveillance firm Hacking Team, password manager Last Pass, wireless communications operator T-Mobile, the Internal Revenue Service, U.S. Army National Guard, and credit reporting agency Equifax all had their data compromised. The massive breach by the federal Office of Personnel Management could be one of the most damaging data breaches to national security of all time.

And these are just the problems with software, servers, and databases. Everyday objects are now privacy threats. We have become drunk on our ability to give anything Wi-Fi access. Barbie dolls, baby monitors, coffee makers, refrigerators, clothes, watches, and cars—we have connected it all. Each new device in this Internet of Things provides a new target for hackers and incrementally risks exposing more of our personal information. For example, with minimal help from a screwdriver, an Internet-connected doorbell was so poorly designed as to give out its owner's Wi-Fi password to anyone nearby.[3] Successful hacks on Internet-connected baby monitors are so common that someone created a search engine enabling people to browse images of sleeping babies from hacked webcams.[4]

Twitter accounts like Internet of Shit (@internetofshit) show just how mad we have become. They feature a never-ending parade of dubious decisions to take an object—*any* object—and put a chip in it. Now light switches, cooking pans, stuffed animals, basketballs, headbands, water bottles, rectal thermometers, and more are all connected to the Internet and our mobile devices.[5] Japanese security researchers have already hacked a Bluetooth-controlled toilet, enabling them to flush it and squirt water at people.[6] A literal Internet of shit.

Data breaches don't have to hit giant corporations to be devastating. The adultery facilitation service Ashley Madison suffered a massive hack, revealing the names of those who had used the service, including even those who never actually had an affair. Many victims who were identified suffered depression and lost their families. For example, New Orleans pastor and seminary professor John Gibson committed suicide after he was identified by the hackers as an Ashley Madison user.[7] In his suicide note, he talked about his depression and shame over being identified. There are few areas in which tech design matters more for our privacy than data security.

In the midst of all this, the U.S. government is contemplating forcing designers to weaken one of the most important technologies protecting our privacy, encryption. The government wants technology companies to give it a "back door" or "golden key" that will allow it to bypass protected systems. But crippling encryption would make our privacy more vulnerable. Here again, design is everything. Apple has encrypted its iPhones, making them inaccessible to anyone without the log-in PIN or fingerprint. The company resisted the FBI's request to cripple its failsafe protective device on iPhones, which essentially bricks the phone after a limited number of failed log-in attempts. Not all digital technologies are designed like this. Microsoft stores the encryption key to Windows 10 in the cloud and decrypts users' information when it receives an authorized government demand for data.[8]

The problem is not that companies are evil. While some in industry act perniciously, the designers and executives that I have spoken with tell me they care very much about the privacy of their users and customers. Their designs and actions often reflect this. Many privacy professionals, like chief privacy officers and chief information officers, are tireless privacy design advocates. They are instrumental in ensuring that the privacy "on the books" is implemented "on the ground" in our digital products and services.[9]

The problem is that there are overwhelming incentives to design technologies in a way that maximizes the collection, use, and disclosure of personal information. The predominant Internet business model is built on collecting as much user data as possible and selling it or using it to target and persuade users. The value of personal data has led most companies to adopt a "collect first, ask questions later" mentality. This mentality incentivizes design choices that marginalize users' interests in opacity and control over how their data is collected and used. Design can be leveraged in subtle ways to get more, more, more. Although there are many great examples of privacy-protective design, the market is awash in privacy-corrosive technologies.

Even worse, there are few market incentives to invest in good, secure design because users cannot readily tell which apps and software are secure and privacy protective and which are not.[10] So companies are often comfortable ignoring or even indulging in privacy-corrosive and insecure design and hoping for the best. In short, the design of information technologies is failing us, and our privacy is at risk because of it.

Is there anything to be done? The phrase *privacy by design* has become very popular. But industry too often misuses it as a marketing slogan rather than a meaningful plan for privacy controls. Although the concept is broad, privacy by design is often used to refer to self-regulatory measures taken by companies. Other times it is equated mainly with "good data security" rather than a more holistic approach to what privacy by design pioneer Ann Cavoukian has referred to as "baking privacy" into all aspects of organizational and technological design.

A chorus of industry voices champions the promise of privacy by design, but the conversation ends when the role of law and regulators is raised. The cry is heard loud and clear: industry vigorously opposes government regulations of the design of its products. Opponents of tech regulations contend that there are no bad technologies, only bad users. They say "tech doesn't hurt people, people hurt people." We already have effective privacy laws that prevent harmful collection, use, and disclosure of personal information, these opponents say.

I disagree. Privacy law around the world is deficient because it ignores design. Lawmakers have attempted to establish limits on the collection, use, and distribution of personal information. But they have largely overlooked the power of design. They have discounted the role that design plays in facilitating the conduct and harm privacy law is meant to prevent. Design pitches and picks privacy winners and losers, with people as data subjects and surveillance objects often on the losing side.

Bad design can undermine data protection by distorting user expectations and obscuring privacy harms. A study by the Pew Research Center found that most adults do not believe online service providers will keep their data private and secure. When the design of technology consistently violates users' expectations—and companies' promises—about how data will be shared, users are tempted to give up on privacy. Many privacy laws only protect people who have reasonable expectations of privacy. Design can alter those expectations and, in doing so, erode our cultural reserves of privacy. Exposure and vulnerability become the norm that is difficult to change.

In a world of social media, search engines, and the Internet of Things, most threats of privacy harm are not obvious, like the clear physical danger posed by faulty automobile airbags. Instead, they are incremental. Click by click, our privacy is slowly being eroded. While major privacy failures grab the headlines, the most significant corrosive force on our privacy is often barely noticeable, like death from a thousand cuts. And because most information privacy harms are small and dispersed among many people, courts and lawmakers fail to recognize them.

Even when it is conceded that some regulation of disruptive new technologies might be necessary, regulation is delayed lest we impede innovation. Progress is at stake, and regulation would impede that progress. To the opponents of a legal response, regulations aimed at the design of technologies are too paternalistic. Government regulators are cast as ill suited to the task. Their expertise in technology is perceived as too limited, and opponents argue that much will be lost at the hands of regulators. They ask, "Why should government bureaucrats with no technical expertise tell tech companies how to design their products and services?" Imagine a regulator knowing better how to architect systems than the high-priced engineers at Apple. Nonsense, opponents say.

Lawmakers are in a difficult position. If courts and regulators prohibit too much collection, use, or disclosure of information, they will frustrate commerce, free expression, and our ability to freely interact with others. Overregulating design is dangerous. But so is ignoring it, and an important balance must be struck. Perhaps because of this delicate equilibrium and industry opposition, privacy law has been largely silent on the design of information technologies. This silence is regrettable.

This is a book about the technology design decisions that affect our privacy. It's about going beyond scrutinizing what gets done with our personal information and confronting the designs that enable privacy violations. And it's about how everyone—companies, lawmakers, advocates, educators, and users—can contribute to and interact with the design of privacy-relevant technologies. At base, I am critiquing the structure of our technologies and the rules for that structure. I will explore why privacy is eroding and how the deck is being stacked to ensure privacy's degradation. What we have now is a blueprint for disclosure and exposure. But it doesn't have to be that way.

My argument boils down to one simple idea: the design of popular technologies is critical to privacy, and the law should take it more seriously. Law and policy makers can do so through *recognition* and *guidance*. Lawmakers and courts should better recognize how design shapes our privacy. Torts, contracts, consumer protection, and surveillance laws can all better reflect how design influences our perceptions and actions with respect to our information. Privacy law should guide the design of information technologies to protect our privacy. The law must set boundaries and goals for technological design. Doing so will improve our ability to trust others and interact in the world with an acceptable risk of exposure. But the law must be careful to broach design in a way that is flexible and not unduly constraining. In short, I'm arguing for a design agenda for privacy law.

The design of information technologies is far more important than lawmakers have acknowledged. Technology design should be a fundamental component of privacy law, and this in turn will make it a key aspect of industry policy and practice. Now is the time to act. Many important technologies are still relatively new. Old technologies are being redesigned all the time. We can mitigate lock-in effects, which keep certain designs and technologies around long after they should have been replaced, and still right the ship. But so far we have no principled way to approach using law to encourage or mandate technology designs that protect our privacy. What we need is a blueprint for the next wave of privacy protections for users of digital products and services.

This book develops such a legal blueprint—a framework to fill privacy law's design gap. It is designed to help legislators, regulators, judges, designers, executives, privacy advocates, and others in industry and civil society properly assess privacy design parameters and ideals for common information technologies. I focus on websites, apps, browsers, drones, malware, facial recognition technologies, and anything connected to the Internet that affects our privacy. While design concepts such as data architecture and auditing technologies are also critical for our privacy, this book is primarily about the design of technologies that are used by consumers and about the people whose privacy is at stake. Scrutiny for consumer-facing products and services is enough for one book.

A logical approach to design can answer pressing questions in the privacy debate. How far can governments go in crippling privacy-protective technologies like encryption? Should surveillance technologies be designed to be undetectable? What technical safeguards should companies be required to use to protect their users' data? What should be the limits of nudging, default settings, and structured choice on social media? Should companies be allowed to create manipulative software interfaces that encourage users to disclose information they otherwise would not? What kinds of obligations should be associated with the "wiring up" of everyday objects to be part of the Internet of Things?

This book is also directed at exploring *why* design is so critical for our privacy in the modern age. Media scholar Marshall McLuhan is said to have asserted, "We shape our tools and thereafter our tools shape us."[11] Design decisions establish power and authority in a given setting. They influence societal norms and expectations. When people say they *use* modern information technologies, what they are really doing is *responding* to the signals and options that the technology gives them. We can only click on the buttons that we are provided. Each design decision reflects an intent as to how an information technology is to function or be used.

At base, the design of information technologies can have as much impact on privacy as any tort, regulation, or statute regulating the collection, use, or disclosure of information. Design can be an incredible force to protect cherished privacy-related values like trust and autonomy. In some contexts, design is capable of protecting personal information more efficiently than laws targeting the actions of data collectors and controllers. Privacy design principles can protect people from exploitation. But design can also undermine our privacy, security, and safety; it can make us more vulnerable, less safe, and more transparent in ways that can disadvantage us.

Instead, if companies commit themselves to protecting privacy through design, they can earn the trust of users. Trust is the essential ingredient for commerce, intimacy, and any other avenue for human flourishing that requires other people. So if we want to improve commerce, our relationships, and our search for self, we need better privacy design.

This is a book for anyone interested in privacy, technology, and policy. While the blueprint I develop in this book is primarily focused on law and policy, it is meant to be useful to executives, designers, advocates, students, and anyone interested in the future of privacy and technology. We all have a role to play in the design of information technologies. For example, companies that seek to earn user trust might benefit from the blueprint's user-centered approach to design parameters and the way it leverages concepts like transaction costs and mental models that shape user expectations. Privacy advocates can take advantage of concepts developed in this book like "obscurity lurches" and "abusive design" to rebut common myths surrounding value-neutral technologies and the misguided notion that there is no privacy in public. Advocates can use the blueprint to find common ground with companies and governments to help create international standards and detailed guidelines.

Finally, we users can educate ourselves on how design affects our privacy. The companies asking us to trust them with our data are responsible for protecting our privacy and security, but there are also things we can do to mitigate the harm of design and use it for good. When we are mindful of design, we can mitigate the harm from confusing and manipulative user interfaces and adverse defaults. We can also proactively obscure ourselves or our data from surveillance from search technologies. We can work with companies to protect our information from hackers. We can demand better. And if push comes to shove, we can fight back with the help of the law. If we all work together on design, better information technologies can be created and used for the benefit of all.

A design agenda has great value. It can redirect some of the focus of privacy law from costly ex post facto remedies for limited categories of information to broadly effective ex ante protection for the full slate of privacy interests in personal information. It can also provide an additional perspective for companies seeking to earn people's trust. It can even be an educational tool for all who care about their privacy and want to know what to look for in the design of the devices they use. Most important, privacy law's blueprint will help us control information technologies before they control us.

A Note on Privacy

Before I roll out a blueprint for privacy, I want to clarify what I mean by the term *privacy*. Privacy is an amorphous and elusive concept, which is surprising given its central role in the law and our daily lives. It's one of those concepts that we all intuitively recognize and crave. Yet when pressed to articulate what privacy *is* we are stumped. No one definition has stuck, though the failure is not for lack of trying. Nearly every attempt to define privacy winds up being too specific to apply generally or too general to be useful.

For example, privacy has been conceptualized as "the ability to control information," "the right to be let alone," "limited access to the self," "boundary regulation," secrecy, intimacy, autonomy, and freedom. All of these framings are right, and all of them are wrong, at least in certain contexts. For example, thinking of privacy solely in terms of control is a poor fit for noted problems with public surveillance and the privacy interests inherent in private activities like sexual freedom. Secrecy is a poor fit for information we consider private, yet share with others we trust or in contexts where discovery is unlikely, like that old blog post about your misspent youth that you shared with only a few friends.

Helen Nissenbaum has encouraged us to move away from a specific definition of privacy, instead arguing that what we consider to be private is entirely a function of norms defined by the context of information flows. When the governing norms are broken, the contextual integrity of that information has been violated, and we experience a breach of privacy. Daniel Solove has given up on trying to find one single definition of privacy and argues instead that privacy is best thought of as a related group of problems that share common traits, similar to Ludwig Wittgenstein's notion of family resemblances.

A useful path was proposed by Neil Richards, who conceptualizes privacy as the question of the *rules* and *norms* that govern *action* or *inaction*

related to our personal information.[12] I agree with Solove that privacy is best thought of as an umbrella term that can be used to invoke a range of problems but should then be jettisoned in favor of more specific concepts when possible. In this book, I'll tether privacy and design to notions of trust, obscurity, and *autonomy*, though many different values are implicated.

My point is that it's important to focus on the specific concepts, problems, and rules of privacy rather than dwelling on a broad notion of it. Privacy should be valued for its utility. Privacy is critical because it is a necessary precondition for humans and democracy to flourish. Privacy provides the necessary breathing room for the play, inquiry, and discovery necessary to figure out who we are and who we want to be.[13]

A Note on Design

Because this is a book about design, I would like to take a moment to clarify what I mean by the term. *Design,* like *privacy,* is an elusive term. It can mean many different things. One broad definition is to "create, fashion, execute, or construct according to plan."[14] People can design any creation, including a political strategy, an organizational structure, or the arrangement of furniture in a living room. With respect to technologies, the design process is diverse. Words like *design, engineering,* and *coding* carry cultural connotations and specific meaning in particular contexts. The design process differs between groups, too. Engineers design things in a somewhat formal, objective, and requirements-driven environment. Designers who create user interfaces, interactions, and other parts of the user experience work in a slightly more generative, open-ended way to incorporate a contextual understanding of users and solutions to multiple goals.

I use the term *design* very broadly in this book to refer to the work of engineers as well as other designers such as those who do product design, graphic design, user interface and user experience design. I do not wish to enter the fray over what counts as "real" design, engineering, or computing. Rather, I use the term to refer to the entire universe of people and processes that create consumer technologies and the results of their creative process instantiated in hardware and software. Good design cannot happen without the participation and respect of all stakeholders, including engineers, artists, executives, users, and lawyers.

This book is focused on the function rather than the aesthetics of design. For example, user interfaces are important for privacy not because they are visually appealing but because they can channel user choice and shape user expectations. In short, I use the term *design* to mean how a system is architected, how it functions, how it communicates, and how that architecture, function, and communication affects people.

Within law the concept of design is liberally used to describe the planned creation of statutes, regulatory schemes, lawmaking bodies, and virtually any intended result of a legal rule or action. If a rule is executed according to plan, it was "by design." But within privacy and its related policy, the notion of design has taken on relatively new meaning. Over the past twenty-five years or so, the term *privacy by design* has come to be an important part of the international privacy dialogue. Most students of privacy policy understand privacy by design to mean a proactive ex ante approach to considering and protecting privacy in the development of a group (like a business), action (like information collection), or thing (like a technology). The opposite of privacy by design is responding to a privacy harm after it has occurred.

Privacy by design continues to be developed in specific contexts. Ann Cavoukian, the former information and privacy commissioner of Ontario, launched a highly influential initiative named Privacy by Design (PbD). The initiative is designed to help companies protect privacy by embedding it into the design specifications of technologies, business practices, and physical infrastructures. I do not wish to simply mimic PbD or any other privacy design framework in this book. Instead, I offer the blueprint as a distinct framework for law and policy in the same spirit as PbD and similar programs and as a way to extend its ultimate goals of improving privacy design. As I will discuss in Chapter 2, the relationship between privacy and design includes more than just the PbD model. Entire fields of literature, standardization bodies, advocates, and businesses are dedicated to sound privacy through design.

This book is situated within the larger privacy and design movement, but at its heart it is a book about consumer protection and surveillance. It's about technologies used by and upon us in everyday life. So when I use the term *design* in this book, I'm talking about the creation of tools to understand and act on current conditions. When I argue the law should incorporate design concerns to protect privacy, I am specifically referring to the design of hardware and software used by consumers and the processes that create them. By focusing on users, I wish to highlight not just the way that design makes people vulnerable to *companies,* but also how design makes people vulnerable to *other users* of a company's products or services.

In focusing on hardware and software, I draw from fields that prioritize human values in design, such as the "value sensitive design" movement, which "seeks to provide theory and method to account for human values like fairness, dignity, justice, and many others in a principled and systematic manner throughout the design process."[15] Philosophically, *Privacy's Blueprint* draws from explorations on the politics of artifacts, notions of technology as delegates of their makers, and the affordances offered by technologies. These approaches focus on how technologies embody the goals and values of those whose tasks they perform. Privacy law should incorporate this wisdom.

In a broader sense, I draw inspiration from the insights of psychology professor Don Norman, whose seminal book *The Design of Everyday Things* illustrates how important design is in our everyday lives and how to get it right for users of common things. Norman has written that people should design objects to have visible clues as to how they work.[16] He argues that well-designed objects do not need instruction manuals; users should intuitively know how to use them. Consider these two kinds of doors:

You probably can easily identify which door is the "pull" door and which door is the "push" door. That's because the "push" door doesn't give you the option to pull on a handle. Handles are for pulling. Panels are for pushing. Even better, the location of the handle and panel tell a person on which side the door opens. These constraints and signals help people form a mental model of how a door is supposed to work. Norman's insights into how affordances, constraints, and mapping dictate conceptual models that direct behavior are quite useful. They can help hardware and software designers ensure privacy-protective design. They can also help lawmakers determine which design decisions undermine our privacy expectations and ability to create or exist in privacy-protective environments.

This book's focus on artifacts, hardware, and software is a slightly narrower scope than what is often meant by the term *privacy by design,* which includes things like organizational structure and the duties of employees within a company. Yet a focus on artifacts and interfaces is enough for one book, with thousands of facets that present related yet distinct issues. This book is primarily concerned with technologies that are visible to people as users or targets of technologies, like Facebook's user interface or the privacy settings on the mobile app game Candy Crush Saga. However, some consumer technology design decisions, like Apple's encrypted iPhones or Snapchat's insecure application programming interfaces are invisible to users, yet they still leave us vulnerable because we rely upon the technologies they are a part of. This book concerns both visible and invisible design decisions for consumer technologies. But it leaves for another day the incredibly important issues with "back end" data technologies such as biased and discriminatory algorithms and predictions based on big data.[17] Developing a legal blueprint for the design of consumer and surveillance technologies is challenging enough, even if it is just a small part of a larger movement dedicated to the ex ante protection of privacy.

The Layout of This Book

This book is divided into three parts. In the first part I make the case for a design agenda for privacy law. In Chapter 1, I show how design is everything, and how it is value loaded. A common view of technology is that it is value neutral. People often argue that technology can be used for prosocial or antisocial ends, but the technology itself isn't inherently good or bad. In other words, "there are no bad technologies, only bad technology users." This view leads to the common argument that we should regulate uses of technology, not the technology itself. Chapter 1 will critique that view. Design is everywhere; design is power and design is political. There is nothing value neutral about information technologies. Values are deeply embedded into the design of technology. People do not simply use technology freely for whatever aims they want to achieve. Instead, technology shapes how people use it. Technology shapes people's behavior and choices—and even their attitudes. Privacy law currently ignores one of the most important ways power is distributed and exercised in our world.

In Chapter 2, I highlight the design gap in modern privacy law and policy and make the case for a design agenda to fill it. I argue that most modern privacy regulatory regimes can be distilled down to three simple rules, and design is marginalized in all of them: follow the Fair Information Practices, do not lie, and do not harm. Each of these three rules fails to seriously consider the design of consumer technologies. I will show how lock-in effects for technology make it critical to get design right from the beginning; otherwise we could be stuck with dangerous design for decades. A design agenda can improve the impact of privacy law. Nobody reads privacy policies, but all users are affected by design. Good design rules can also ease the burden of conduct-based privacy laws. Lawmakers and judges can learn from the serious impact of design in other contexts, such as that of cars, airplanes, buildings, pharmaceuticals, technologies implanted in our bodies, and even everyday consumer products. The good news is that the groundwork for a privacy design agenda has already been laid. Now it is time to embrace it.

In Part II of the book, I develop a design agenda for privacy law, which I call Privacy's Blueprint. The blueprint has three parts: values, boundaries, and tools. In Chapter 3, I articulate the *values* that lawmakers and courts should focus on when shaping design through privacy law. Design primarily communicates signals and hinders or facilitates tasks. These functions affect two critical components of privacy: relationships that involve exchanging information and the transaction costs associated with finding, using, and sharing information. My theory of privacy and design is that relationships and transaction costs primarily implicate three privacy-related values: trust (the act of making oneself vulnerable to others), obscurity (the value associated with people or their data being hard or unlikely to be found or understood), and autonomy (freedom from external interference). These three values are intertwined. Autonomy is furthered as a design value when privacy law nurtures technologies that protect our ability to trust and maintain obscurity. Trust and obscurity are complimentary values: trust protects our information within relationships, and obscurity protects us when there is no one to trust.

In Chapter 4, I propose *boundaries* for lawmakers to set: design rules and goals that nurture trust, obscurity, and autonomy. Outer boundaries for design are needed because of the pull that other industry incentives have on the design process. Values become corrupted. I argue that lawmakers should generally prefer flexible standards instead of specific rules when setting boundaries in privacy-related design. Drawing from product safety and consumer protection law, I propose that lawmakers should set standards to discourage three kinds of design: deceptive design, abusive design, and dangerous design. These three kinds of design often overlap and collectively facilitate lies, exploitation, and harm.

In Chapter 5, I explore the *tools* lawmakers and courts can use to further good design. Lawmakers should use their full range of tools, but should do so proportionally. These tools vary in strength from soft to moderate to robust. Soft responses include facilitating industry standards, developing guides, and funding privacy design research. They do not impose a penalty for exceeding the boundaries of privacy design, but rather facilitate achieving the goals of Privacy's Blueprint. Moderate responses include promissory design mandatory notice or process. They provide a penalty for exceeding design boundaries, but only moderately burden the design of technologies. Robust responses include approaches like liability for harm caused by design and certification regimes. Soft responses should be used early and often. Moderate responses should be used more judiciously when soft responses are not enough. Finally, robust responses should be used to confront the most serious privacy design problems. Lawmakers should seek balance and fit when choosing the appropriate legal response to deceptive, abusive, or dangerous designs or when supporting a particular privacy design goal. Moreover, lawmakers must use these tools for constant renewal. Companies benefit from the ability to change software and make it better—even after a product has already been distributed to consumers. The same mindset for ongoing improvements should be true with privacy design; there is no static compliance. Privacy design, just like making improvements in efficiency and aesthetic design, is a continuous process: never done, never perfect.

In Part III of the book I apply Privacy's Blueprint to the most privacy-significant information technologies. In Chapter 6, I explore how the design of social media shapes your online experiences, making you vulnerable or safe. I demonstrate how layout, forced choices, and defaults are designed to get you to share your personal information online more than ever before. I also show how the design of user interfaces can serve as a privacy promise, instead of those long, unreadable privacy policies. I end the chapter demonstrating the role that design does and should play in limiting online harassment and abuse of others.

In Chapter 7, I analyze the design of what I call hide and seek technologies—search engines, browsers, deletion tools, spyware, drones, license plate readers, and facial recognition technologies. I argue that surveillance is about obscurity and transaction costs and I review critical design features from technologies designed to seek, recognize, spy, and hide. In this chapter I argue that lawmakers should better scrutinize designs that dramatically reduce the cost of finding, recognizing, or watching people. These designs should also be reasonably safe. In the least, the design of surveillance technologies must be justified by their overriding benefits to society, especially including those made vulnerable through surveillance. Conversely, law and policy makers should foster "hiding" technologies, those that allow people to preserve or increase the transaction costs to find or understand people and data. This includes embracing, not crippling technologies like encryption, antisurveillance masks, ad blockers, and other obscurity-preserving technologies.

In Chapter 8, I confront the role of design in the Internet of Things (IoT). The decision to "wire up" an item should carry greater legal consequence. While privacy law has taken the *Internet* part of the IoT seriously, it has ignored how the nature of a *Thing* affects our privacy and security. Some things are disposable. Others are meant to be handed down over generations. Yet privacy law and our rhetoric seemingly treat all such things as if they were just another computer. The IoT vulnerabilities affect our trust, obscurity, and autonomy in different ways than do computers. Privacy and data security law should better recognize the distinction.

I conclude by arguing that this blueprint should be used to ensure that information technologies work for everyone, not just the companies deploying them. When we can trust the design of technologies, we will disclose more personal information in a safe, sustainable, and useful way. Commerce, relationships, and democracy can all thrive. Technologies will continue to improve. We just need a plan. This book endeavors to give us one.

PART ONE

THE CASE FOR TAKING DESIGN
SERIOUSLY IN PRIVACY LAW

1

Why Design Is Everything

YOU ARE IN TOTAL CONTROL. At least, that's the story you've been told. You get to choose what you share online, whom you share it with, and how it is shared. Tech companies are bending over backward to give you more perceived control over your personal information. It is no wonder the common narrative is that victims of privacy breaches only have themselves to blame. But the truth is this: all the focus on control distracts you from what really affects your privacy in the modern age. The most important decisions regarding your privacy were made long before you picked up your phone or walked out of your house. It is all in the design.

Design affects how something is perceived, functions, and is used. Technologies are great examples of the power of design. Consider this marketing photo depicting the user interface for the media service Snapchat:

The selectable "seconds" connected to a clock icon, the Send button, and the photo carefully cropped to show only nude skin all suggest that this software is designed to allow users to temporarily share intimate or suggestive photos.[1] All of this is conveyed without an explicit promise or disclaimer—just design. New users would be justified in thinking that naughty photos, or "Snaps," would completely disappear.

Except that's not how it works. The Snaps simply become invisible to recipients. Copies of the photo still exist. Most modern phones are designed to let users take screenshots—a tactic that is regularly used to "capture" Snaps. Data forensics experts are able to recover copies of photos still lingering in storage. There is even third-party software that allows users to save Snaps before they disappear. That's how nineteen-year-old student Zeeshan Aqsar saved a nude photo sent by a fifteen-year-old schoolgirl via Snapchat, which he then used to blackmail her for more photos and money.[2] Like many Snapchat users, the young girl thought the photo she sent would disappear. As previously mentioned, Snapchat initially failed to ensure that only its own software client could access its application programming interface. Design could have been leveraged to better shape users' expectations and make saving photos more difficult. For a while, it was not.

Even when design is not shaping our perceptions of a technology, it is in the background, shaping what happens to us. Users usually cannot tell what kinds of personal information the websites and apps they visit are collecting. Every website and mobile application collects some kind of arguably personal data, such as Internet protocol (IP) addresses, browser type, and even browsing activities. Did you know that when you click on a link, your browser tells the website that you just loaded where you came from? For example, if you are reading a blog about sexual fetishes and click on a link to a book on Amazon, the online merchant would know which salacious website you were reading before you clicked that link. This information is contained in what is known as the hypertext transfer protocol (HTTP) referrer header. We are awash in invisible data streams. Modern information technologies are specifically designed to collect more, more, more.

In this chapter I'll show how design affects your privacy. I'll make three simple points. First, privacy-relevant design is everywhere. It's part of every action we take using our phones, laptops, and tablets. It's also a force upon us as we interact in the physical world. The best way to spot privacy-relevant design is to look for the ways in which technologies *signal* information about their function or operation or how technologies make tasks easier or hárder though *transaction costs.* Signals and transaction costs shape our mental models of how technologies work and form the constraints that guide our behavior in particular ways.[3]

Second, I'll show that design is power. Every design decision makes a certain reality more or less likely. Designers therefore wield a certain amount of control over others. Because people react to signals and constraints in predictable ways, the design of consumer technologies can manipulate its users into making certain decisions. Design affects our perceptions of relationships and risk. It also affects our behavior: when design makes things easy, we are more likely to act; when design makes things hard, we are more likely to give up and look elsewhere. The power of design makes it dangerous to ignore.

I will conclude this chapter by setting up a conflict at the heart of this book: the misconception that design is neutral. A popular argument in technology law circles is that the creation of technologies that are used in harmful ways is less deserving of legal scrutiny than the act of collecting, using, or sharing another's personal information. Those who see great promise in "big data" often argue in favor of rules regulating use of data rather than limitations on the ability to collect personal information.[4] Critics of legal action against companies for having poor data security liken it to the government punishing victims of burglary.[5] Advocates of immunity for services that host harmful content point to the fact that they are just the messenger.[6] By calling attention to the most immediate or proximate source of privacy harm, companies downplay how design affects our privacy. Those seeking to avoid scrutiny for the things they build often critique calls to regulate design by arguing that design is neutral.[7] They're wrong. Design is never neutral. It is political. And it should be a key part of our information policy.

Design Is Everywhere

This book is concerned with the design of two particular kinds of consumer technologies: those used by people and those used directly upon them. Most of the technologies we use *mediate* our experiences. Browsers, mobile apps, social media, messaging software, and the like all act as media through which we find and consume information and communicate with others. Meanwhile, surveillance technologies like license plate readers, drones, and facial recognition software are used upon us. We don't interact with these kinds of technologies, yet they have a profound effect on our privacy.

You can see the impact of design on our privacy almost everywhere you look. In the physical world, doors, walls, closed-circuit television, modesty panels for lecture hall tables, and any countless number of other design features shape our notions of privacy. Structural protections, such as our homes, create "reasonable expectations of privacy," which is the law's touchstone metric. Structure can also erode our privacy when it facilitates surveillance and information misuse. There is a reason bathroom stalls in the workplace are not made of transparent glass, yet many conference room walls are. All the better to see you with, my dear. And any book on privacy and design must make at least a passing, obligatory reference to the most famous of privacy-related structures: the panopticon.

Philosopher and social theorist Jeremy Bentham designed the panopticon as a prison comprising a circular structure with a guard tower at its center, thus allowing a single guard (or a small group of guards) to observe all the prisoners at any given time.[8] The design obscures the view of the guard tower from the cells, and prisoners cannot know when they are being watched or whether a guard is even present; as a result, they are compelled to act as though they are always being watched. This design has become a metaphor, pioneered by philosopher Michel Foucault, for the modern surveillance state and the cause of surveillance paranoia.[9]

Design is just as critical to our privacy in online, mediated environments. For example, app developer GoldenShores Technologies designed the Brightest Flashlight app to collect a mobile user's geolocation data.[10] There is no particular reason a flashlight app needs geolocation data to function. It's a flashlight app. It just needs access to a flash. Yet because "data is the new oil" the company couldn't resist the opportunity made available by the architecture and capabilities presented by the little surveillance devices we all keep in our pockets. GoldenShores probably designed the app to collect our location data because it could and because it was financially advantageous for it to do so. The Federal Trade Commission (FTC) alleged that GoldenShores' design did not comply with its privacy promises and that the company was engaged in an unfair and deceptive trade practice. In Chapter 4, we will revisit this complaint as an example of how lawmakers might better consider privacy-related design.

Compare GoldenShores' design decision with that of tech media outlet Gizmodo, which configured its services to not store the IP addresses of those who visit its website. In explaining the company's decision, Annalee Newitz writes, "if we received [a] subpoena tomorrow, demanding that we hand over personally-identifying information about you because you went into comments and spilled some corporate secrets about Apple—well, we couldn't. Our technical systems team couldn't. We don't log that data, period. And we chose to set up our commenting system that way because we want to protect your right to speak freely and anonymously."[11] Gizmodo's decision demonstrates how design can advance privacy-related values like obscurity and anonymity. These values are furthered by making certain things easier or more difficult to accomplish—or, in the case of Gizmodo, impossible. Of course, engineering plausible deniability cuts both ways, as it can protect wrongdoing as well as provide a space for free expression and human flourishing. In any event, the design here is consequential and value laden.

Apple has designed its encryption system for mobile devices to similarly protect the information on its phones. Because of its design choices, Apple cannot disclose the information of those using its encrypted devices.[12] The decision reflects a commitment to secure, private communications and technology use. That commitment can also be seen in Apple's decision in early 2016 to resist the FBI's request for a customized operating system that would cripple a security failsafe keeping the government from accessing the phone of a terrorism suspect in the shootings in San Bernardino, California.[13] This dispute also demonstrates the very real cost of protective design, which can frustrate law enforcement and intelligence agencies in their duties, reduce cybersecurity in some instances, and facilitate harassment and abuse. For example, law enforcement might be unable to obtain information important in solving a crime. Intelligence agencies might miss important information. Yet these designs protect people's most personal communications and personal information from abuse of process by government and direct attack from hackers. They provide the freedom and autonomy necessary for human development, commerce, infrastructure management, and our own national security.

Because we use digital technologies every day, we tend not to think about the role of design. It's just always there. To understand why design is so important, let's first explore the function of design.

What Does Design Do?

Broadly speaking, particular designs of technologies *communicate* information and *enable* (or *hinder*) activities. Often, design does both, as when labels on online clickboxes and drop-down menu options channel user choice. Password requirements are great examples. Consider a company's practice of securing sensitive electronic documents like paystubs and tax forms with a password. When employers protect PDFs with a password, they simultaneously *hinder* access by ensuring only those who were given the password can view the file, and they also communicate to recipients that the contents of the file are not for general consumption. While the exact nature of what is being communicated is open to interpretation, the design choice of an authentication requirement sends a signal that this information is not for just anyone. Design can act as a medium, communicating *on behalf of* both designers and users. It can also act *upon* users, constraining or enabling them in particular ways. By focusing on signals and barriers, we can see how design affects people and begin to understand the values at stake.

Design Provides Signals

Imagine that you just rented a laptop from a consumer electronics store while yours is in the shop. You boot up your rental and see this pop-up window[14]:

You recognize these kinds of pop-up windows because they are common with new pieces of software. (This is not your first computer, after all.) The window has the famous Microsoft logo and some keys that represent security and access. You also see what would appear to be the product key,  which is a signal that this software is legitimate. The prompt asks routine questions about personal information. There's even an official-looking requirement for you to check that "Under penalty of law, I verify this information is accurate." Serious stuff. Every aspect of the design of this pop-up window communicates to you that Microsoft has created this interface to facilitate activating the software on your laptop.

The problem is that this window is a lie. It was not created by Microsoft but by a software company called DesignerWare. It is part of a pernicious piece of spyware called PC Rental Agent to be used by companies that rent laptops.[15] The software gives companies the ability to track laptops and disable them if renters are late in making their payments. This particular window is part of the software's "detective mode," which can log user keystrokes and hijack the laptop's webcam to record anyone in view.

The pop-up window is a false front. The registration window registers nothing. Instead, it captures all of the personal information entered into the prompt boxes and transmits it back to DesignerWare and to the store renting the laptop. This is no hypothetical. In one of the few instances of privacy law taking design seriously, the FTC alleged this software to be a deceptive practice based on the representations made via the fake registration screen.[16]

I give this example to demonstrate that one of the principal functions of design is to *communicate*. It provides signals to people. The communication can be a message from the designer, information from or about other users, information about how the technology functions, what a user's options are, or simply an aesthetic choice. In the case of the fake registration page, the communication is evident. The designers used text and graphic design to signal authority, security, and protection to manipulate users into sharing their personal information.

Sometimes design communicates in subtler or even subconscious ways. For example, Apple made the decision that the background color for free text messages sent between two iPhones would be a soothing blue, whereas text messages between an iPhone and another type of phone that counted against your text limit would be a harsher green.[17] This difference in color communicated several very subtle messages, including when a user would be charged for texts (communicating with a competitor's phone). The distinction might also mean that texting with people who use a competitor's phone is slightly more irritating than people who have calmer, blue buttons. The green color also communicates that the recipient's phone is not an iPhone.

Through signals, design helps define our relationships and our risk calculus when dealing with others. Design affects our expectations about how things work and the context within which we are acting. Consider the padlock icons that are ubiquitous online. We seem them in our browsers, on our phones, and on social media. They're everywhere.

The padlock icon is one of the most well-known privacy-related design signals, and it is used whenever a company or designer presumably wants to convey some sense of security or protection—like its real-life counterpart, which limits access to rooms and boxes to those with the key. In the case of my Internet browser, the padlock icon lets me know when there's a certificate in place to provide encrypted HTTPS communications versus standard HTTP (the S stands for "secure").[18] HTTPS protects against eavesdropping and "man-in-the-middle attacks," whereby attackers secretly insert themselves between actors who think they are communicating directly to each other. The padlock icon on Twitter represents a "protected" account, which requires users to approve followers before accessing the profile. The padlock on Facebook is the button that directs the user to Facebook's privacy settings.

Each padlock icon invites reliance upon a technology or service. It signals safety. In the case of Twitter and Facebook, the locks can affect peoples' expectations regarding their relationship with a company. Technology users rely upon signals such as this to shape our expectations regarding what companies are going to do with our personal information. As I'll discuss later in this chapter, when signals like padlock icons and privacy settings cause us to perceive a low risk of harm for disclosing information, we are more likely to disclose more because we are comfortable with the perceived odds that we will be negatively affected by sharing.

Design Affects Transaction Costs

When design hinders or facilitates action, it affects the transaction cost of a certain activity. In economic theory, transaction costs refer to a range of expenses required for participating in market exchanges.[19] But the concept can be expanded to cover the expense required to do anything. For example, time and effort are valuable resources. We often evaluate how desirable possibilities are by calculating how much time they will take or how much effort we'll need to spend to accomplish them.

Consider the practice of putting bars on the window of a house. Bars do not make it impossible to burglarize a home. A burglar with sufficient motivation could get a steel file or even more high-powered machinery to remove the bars. But this usually doesn't happen, because the cost of doing so is too high. Filing the bars down would take far too long and machines that can cut steel are too loud, visible, and expensive. Bars don't provide perfect security. They are just good enough for most houses and stores. Online examples are usually not this dramatic, of course. Instead, transaction costs almost imperceptibly guide choice and expectations online.

Transaction costs play a key role in the design of digital technologies. User interface design and user experience design focus on ease of use. For example, in Facebook's early days, there was no central news feed that aggregated all of your friends' activities in one location. Facebook users had to visit the profile of each friend if they wanted to see their posts and activity. The news feed made it easier for people to see what their friends were up to because they didn't have to go through the exercise of first thinking of a friend they wanted to look up, entering that friend's name into the search bar, and navigating to their profile to find them, then repeating the process for each friend. Design made this task *easier*.

In fact, the entire data economy is founded on design that makes tasks easier. Digital data itself is the result of design that makes the recall of information easier because it is preserved in a persistent, searchable state at marginal cost. Because of databases and communication technologies, the sum of humankind's knowledge is available within seconds to anyone with an Internet connection and the proper log-in credentials. This has largely replaced having to travel to libraries and other research areas around the world—that is, assuming you even knew what you were looking for. Talk about making things easier!

Design can also make tasks *more difficult*. For example, Amnesty International helped design a digital "mutant" font for Internet users who wanted to make sure their writing was read by humans only rather than computer bots. Many people using the Internet would prefer to be invisible to online trackers, which seek out and process text through the shape of characters or the source of a font. To accommodate those people, Mutant Font's design includes "small graphic interventions that will block machines from viewing its shapes. It comprises seven different fonts that generate thousands of codes to confuse tracking. Its algorithm is also shuffled every 24 hours to impede automatic scanning."[20]

As you can see, the graphical interventions make this text harder to read. And th e fact that it changes on a regular basis serves to confuse bots that are trying to read what you ve written.

The practical effect of the "mutant font" design is to make the task of widespread processing of data more difficult. Those who seek to track others must dedicate human resources and time, which is more difficult than deploying software bots that can track others without fatigue and at low cost. Sometimes design can make certain tasks practically impossible. For example, the strength of encryption is measured by how long it would take a theoretical attacker to guess all the possible key combinations or passwords until the right one is found (known as a "brute force" attack). At one point experts estimated that it would take a supercomputer around one *billion* billion years (that's a billion billions!) to crack the 128-bit Advanced Encryption Standard key.[21]

Even very slight costs can discourage certain behavior. Facebook again serves as a good example here. The social media service has a reply feature for its private messages, but no forwarding feature.[22] While you could cut and paste your private conversation with one of your friends into a separate message box for other users, that takes more time and effort than simply pressing a Forward button and typing in a name. It is a transaction cost. While the cost might be slight, it adds up over time and works as a nudge against sharing. It also shows how design practically protects the obscurity of these conversations.

Design is capable of other things, of course. It creates aesthetic value, for example. Do you remember how ugly everyone's home pages were in the early days of the World Wide Web? Bad design. But design's most important feature with respect to information and privacy is that it provides signals to people and affects transaction costs.

How to Identify and Think About Design

Few people have clearly articulated the importance of design in our day-to-day lives better than psychologist Don Norman. In his lauded book *The Design of Everyday Things* Norman explains why design is so important for the things we use. He also shows how to design objects in a user-friendly way. "Well-designed objects are easy to interpret and understand," he notes. "They contain visible clues to their operation. Poorly designed objects can be difficult and frustrating to use. They provide no clues—or sometimes false cues. They trap the user and thwart the normal process of interpretation and understanding."[23]

Norman bases his theory of design on the way humans process visual and tactile clues. He theorizes that the fundamental principles of designing for people are to "(1) provide a good conceptual model [allowing users to mentally simulate an object's operation] and (2) make things visible."[24] He argues that the keys to these two principles were in the visible structure of objects, specifically their *affordances, constraints,* and *mappings*.

According to Norman, *affordances* are "the perceived and actual property of the thing, primarily those fundamental properties that determine just how the thing could possibly be used." Affordances "provide strong clues to the operations of things. Plates [on doors] are for pushing. Knobs are for turning. Slots are for inserting things into. Balls are for throwing or bouncing. When affordances are taken advantage of, the user knows what to do just by looking: no picture, label, or instruction is required."[25] The concept of affordances, which was pioneered by psychologist James Gibson, is quite useful in understanding technological design as well.[26] On web pages, boxes are to be checked, down arrows are to be clicked to see more, and the cursor shifting to a pointy finger indicates a mouse click or hyperlink.

Mapping refers to "the relationship between two things, in this case between the controls and their movements and the results in the world."[27] Norman's example is that when steering wheels are turned clockwise, cars turn right. Mapping helps drivers understand the relationship between the control (the steering wheel) and the result (turning). It is easy to learn how to steer a car because the wheel is visible, a clockwise motion is closely related to the desired outcome of a right turn, and the motion provides immediate feedback. Mapping is also crucial for information technologies.

Cursors on the screen mimic the movements of your mouse or touchpad. Knobs, switches, and icons all rely upon mapping to tell us how to use an interface.

Constraints are the final key to good user design. Norman writes, "The physical properties of objects constrain possible operations: the order in which parts can go together and the ways in which an object can be moved, picked up, or otherwise manipulated. Each object has physical features— projections, depressions, screw threads, appendages—that limit its rela- tionships to other objects, operations that can be performed with it, what can be attached to it, and so on." Social norms—what Norman calls "cul- tural conventions"—act as a constraint as well; he observes, "Because of these natural and artificial constraints, the number of alternatives for any particular situation is reduced, as are the amount and specificity of knowl- edge required within human memory."[28] Encryption and password prompts, for example, are technological design constraints that prevent third parties from accessing information. Affordances and constraints can work to- gether in design to clearly guide users to the proper course of action, even when they are encountering an object for the first time.

Norman articulates seven principles for using design to make tasks sim- pler and more intuitive:

1. Use both knowledge in the world and in your head (in other words, be thoughtful and do research).
2. Simplify the structure of tasks (for example, require users to take fewer steps).
3. Make things visible (i.e., make an object's use obvious from its visual elements, and make important design elements obvious).
4. Get the mappings right (i.e., make tasks performed on or with the object correspond intuitively with their results in the world).
5. Exploit the power of constraints, both natural and artificial.
6. Design for (human) error.
7. When all else fails, standardize (i.e., use universally recognizable signals).[29]

This insight is not just useful for designers. It can help everyone understand when and why design has failed us or is exploiting us.

We're all familiar with at least one design feature that makes human error more likely: the Reply All button, which can cause us to send an email to a number of people rather than just the one we intend it for. The Reply All and other accidental email disasters have claimed more than their fair share of victims. The most memorable such incident in my mind is the unfortunate young law student who meant to send an email update to his best friend about his summer internship at a prestigious law firm: "I'm busy doing jack shit. Went to a nice 2hr sushi lunch today at Sushi Zen. Nice place. Spent the rest of the day typing e-mails and bullshitting with people. . . . I should really peruse these materials and not be a fuckup. . . . So yeah, Corporate Love hasn't worn off yet. . . . But just give me time."[30] Unfortunately, the summer associate had accidentally emailed the firm's entire underwriting group. Bad times. There are hundreds of thousands of similar Reply All and listserv disaster stories. Yet they still keep happening. While we can always be more careful online, errors of this frequency point to a design flaw. Companies are failing to design software to help avoid obvious human error. Sometimes companies learn from their mistakes. Thankfully, relatively new features like pop-up warnings and better layout have been introduced to mitigate the scourge of the Reply All button.

We can analyze privacy design failures the same way. In 2012, computer scientists from Columbia University conducted a usability study of the privacy settings on Facebook. The results were disturbing: they found that "overwhelmingly, privacy settings do not match [users'] sharing intentions." Social media users are not sharing or hiding information the way they think there are. What's worse, "a majority of participants indicated that they could not or would not fix the problems. The prevalence of such errors—every participant had at least one incorrect setting—suggests the current approach to privacy controls is deeply and fundamentally flawed and cannot be fixed. A completely different approach is needed."[31] At worst, this version of Facebook's privacy settings may have been intentionally confusing to encourage more sharing. At best, Facebook got the mapping wrong—the settings users were asked to choose from did not correspond logically with their intentions. This study echoes the findings of many researchers that design is a major obstacle to managing our online privacy.[32]

All of this research leads us to two conclusions. First, design is incredibly important. The hardwiring in our brains makes us susceptible to design, which affects us at every turn. Technological design can determine how we communicate and share information, how often we use a particular technology, and how we relate to the businesses and other entities we deal with online. It can make us feel in control or it can frustrate us to the point of giving up—and it can trick us. Second, design is difficult to get right. It requires methodical consideration of how we interact with the things around us and what we expect from those interactions. Design must anticipate human error and respond to feedback. In short, technology needs to be designed for *people*. People that design for a living get this. Researchers rigorously study design, and companies invest heavily in it. Companies have every incentive to use the power of design to their advantage. Yet, as we will see, privacy law has failed to take design seriously.

Design Is Power

If the first truth of design is that it is everywhere, the second truth of design is that it is also a form of power. Power has been defined as "the capacity or ability to direct or influence the behaviour of others or the course of events."[33] Given how design can shape our perceptions, behavior, and values, *power* and *design* often feel like synonyms. Design is power because people react to design in predictable ways. This means that with the right knowledge, design can impose some form of order on chaos.

I want to emphasize that I'm not arguing that design completely dictates our privacy and that nothing else is relevant. Such an extreme argument is a misguided form of technological determinism, which is the idea that technology makes cultures what they are and is the exclusive key to change.[34] But technology does affect us in powerful and tangible ways.

Governments and industry have long known that design is critical to accomplishing basically any significant endeavor. They have always leveraged design to achieve particular ends. This is evident from wide-scale city planning efforts that facilitate the movement of cars and people via traffic circles, grid systems, and road dimensions. It can also be seen in something as small as a park bench, with armrests spaced evenly across the bench to prevent people from lying flat and sleeping on it.

Entire bodies of literature have been dedicated to understanding and harnessing the power of design in policy and industry. The entire field of engineering involves leveraging design to accomplish something. Architects match design with purpose in order to make "structure express ideas," in the words of Frank Lloyd Wright.[35] Urban planners use design to accomplish the goals of a city, improve public welfare, and protect the environment. But the study of design goes far beyond the construction of cities, buildings, and machines. Researchers also explore design's social effects.[36] Rooms built to expose occupants to natural lighting can increase workplace performance.[37] Elevator banks have reflective surfaces to give you something to look at while you wait for an elevator, which can reduce anxiety and anger. The walk from your airplane to the baggage claim area is intentionally long because you are less conscious of the time it takes to claim your baggage if you are walking rather than standing and waiting.[38] Placebo buttons—buttons that do nothing and exist entirely to make you feel better—are everywhere. The "door close" button on the elevators? Probably fake. Crosswalk button? Probably fake. Your office thermostat? Probably fake. I was surprised too.[39]

Economics professor Richard Thaler and law professor Cass Sunstein have pioneered the concept of "nudging," which leverages design to improve people's lives through what Thaler and Sunstein call "choice architecture." Choice architects are people who have "the responsibility for organizing the context in which people make decisions." A nudge is "any aspect of the choice architecture that alters people's behavior in a predictable way without forbidding any options or significantly changing their economic incentives."[40] Designers and engineers are choice architects. Thaler and Sunstein give numerous examples of design nudges, including alarm clocks that run away from you, forcing you to chase them to turn them off (and thus ensure you are awake), increasingly grouped white lines on dangerous curves to make drivers feel as though they are going faster (and thus reflexively slowing themselves down), and smiling and frowning emoticons on power bills to encourage people to use less energy. Nudging through choice architecture does not give designers total control over people. However, it can give designers control at the margins.

Design is powerful because we as people are more easily manipulated than we'd like to think. We often fail to act in our own self-interest. We like to think of ourselves as rational and autonomous actors, but the fact is that we are not. Decades ago, psychologists Daniel Kahneman and Amos Tversky began to unravel the leading "rational actor" model of human decision making by demonstrating the mental shortcuts (rules of thumb known as heuristics) and biases that dominate our mental process and judgment. They hypothesized that while sometimes we call upon a reflective system of logic and reasoning to form judgments, more often we use rules of thumb to automatically form judgments without the cognitive burden of measured, contemplative thought. In his foundational book *Thinking Fast and Slow* Kahneman called the fast, instinctive, and emotional method System 1, and the more deliberative and logical method System 2. System 1 is the one we use most but, unfortunately, it's the troublemaker. It frequently guides us to make decisions that are less than optimal.

While we might not be "rational" in the sense that we often fail to act in our own self-interest, we are pretty consistent. Behavioral economists and psychologists have demonstrated that people have a consistent bias in making routine judgments.[41] For example, we have a tendency to be influenced by irrelevant numbers, often the first ones that come to mind (a process known as the anchoring effect). When trying to gauge the probability of some event happening, we rely far too much on the information that is the easiest to recall in our minds, rather than the most relevant information (a process known as the availability heuristic). We have a tendency to be far more optimistic than we should be, even in the face of contrary evidence (a process known as optimism bias). We regularly keep investing in things even though it's a bad idea, or "throw good money after bad," just because we instinctually want to avoid regret over how much we've already spent (a process known as the sunk cost fallacy). As we will see later in this chapter, we change our attitudes about things based solely on the way facts are presented, even if the facts stay the same (a process known as framing). We consistently choose a "smaller-sooner" reward rather than a "larger-later" one because it will occur earlier in time (a process known as hyperbolic discounting).[42] We also tend to search for, interpret, favor, and recall information in a way that confirms our preexisting beliefs and give less consideration to alternatives that do not (a process known as confirmation bias).[43] Because these effects are consistent and predictable, design can be adjusted to leverage all of these biases at a designer's will.

Design shapes our privacy perceptions, which in turn shape how we use and respond to technologies. Because privacy is so difficult to pin down and the harms are so diverse and often remote, we crave privacy guidance. Design gives it to us. In summarizing the robust literature around privacy and decision making, Alessandro Acquisti, Laura Brandimarte, and George Loewenstein note that three themes have emerged from the literature that explain our vulnerability to design and other external forces that shape how we disclose personal information and make choices regarding our privacy.[44]

First, people are *uncertain* about the nature of privacy trade-offs and about what kinds of trade-offs they prefer. Information asymmetries keep people from properly assessing risk, and even when privacy consequences are clear, people are uncertain about their preferences. Second, our privacy preferences are almost entirely *context dependent*. As Acquisti and colleagues note, "The same person can, in some situations, be oblivious to, but in other situations be acutely concerned about, issues of privacy."[45] Finally, our privacy preferences are incredibly *malleable*—that is, they are subject to influence from others who have better insight into what will make us act.

So while people may be unaware of the forces that modulate their privacy concerns, companies that rely upon personal information are not. Acquisti and colleagues found evidence of the manipulation of subtle factors that activate or suppress privacy concern "in myriad realms, such as the choice of sharing defaults on social networks, or the provision of greater control on social media, which creates an illusion of safety and encourages greater sharing."[46]

Our uncertainty, malleability, and dependence upon context all work together. We might be so dependent upon context because of how uncertain we are about the outcomes of sharing personal information. We need lots of clues to give us a hint as to what to do. And our privacy preferences and behaviors are malleable and subject to influence because we are so dependent upon context. Because our privacy intuitions are so malleable, we are vulnerable to those who would manipulate context to their own advantage.

Enter design. Recall Norman's theory of good design being a function of mental mapping, technical and normative constraints, and affordances. The concept of affordances—the fundamental properties that determine how a thing can be used—is useful because it gives us a framework for understanding how people interpret and then interact with an object or environment. James Gibson has theorized that although we all interact with the same objects and environment, our abilities and limitations cause us to perceive these things differently. People perceive cliffs as dangerous; birds perceive cliffs as irrelevant, or as great places to build nests.

Affordances can be negative or positive, depending upon how they are perceived, and they can also be seen as subject to change. Stairs can be carved into a steep hill to provide a walkable surface. Yet stairs themselves are a negative affordance for those who use wheelchairs. Whether an affordance is true or false, perceptible or hidden, also affects how people interact with objects and environments. Hidden affordances do people no good. Checkboxes allowing people to opt out of information collection are worthless when they're tucked away at the bottom of a screen where they can't be easily seen. False affordances can trick people into relying on protections and escape routes that do not exist. Because people often rely on affordances, an opt-out checkbox that actually does nothing is worse than no affordance to opt out at all.

Language can also be incorporated into design to shape our perceptions, and the way we receive a message may be just as important as the message itself. Even if the substance of a communication remains constant, the presentation of that substance can significantly affect how we perceive it. In communications, sociology, psychology, and related disciplines, this concept is known as framing.[47] Framing theory holds that even small changes in the presentation of an issue or event can produce significant changes of opinion.[48] For example, older studies have shown that some people are more willing to tolerate rallies by controversial hate groups when such rallies are framed as an exercising of free speech rather than a disruption of the public order.[49]

Consider two questions: Do companies with data use policies protect your privacy? And, do companies with privacy policies protect your privacy? While these questions are constructed differently, they are essentially asking the same thing. But the choice of which question to ask could predetermine the answer. In 2005, Joseph Turow led a research effort uncovering that 59 percent of people falsely believe that websites with a privacy policy cannot sell personal information without consent.[50] Meanwhile the term *data use policy,* as used by Facebook and others, carries no implicit marker or promise of respect for privacy.

Judges, lawmakers, and the public all use and are influenced by frames.[51] According to Robert Entman, "To frame is to *select some aspects of a perceived reality and make them more salient in a communicating text, in such a way as to promote a particular problem definition, causal interpreta-*

tion, moral evaluation, and/or treatment recommendation for the item described," and framing offers a way to articulate the "power of a communicating text." By increasing the salience of certain bits of information, frames enhance the probability that receivers will interpret the information in a certain way, discern a particular meaning, and process it accordingly.[52]

While frames do not guarantee an influence on audience thinking, frames that comport with the existing schemata in a receiver's belief system can be particularly effective.[53] Kahneman and Tversky have offered what is now likely the most well-known example of how framing works by highlighting some features while omitting others. In an experiment, the researchers asked test subjects to consider the following hypothetical:

> Imagine that the U.S. is preparing for the outbreak of an unusual Asian disease, which is expected to kill 600 people. Two alternative programs to combat the disease have been proposed. Assume that the exact scientific estimates of the programs are as follows:
> If Program A is adopted, 200 people will be saved. . . .
> If Program B is adopted, there is a one-third probability that 600 people will be saved and a two-thirds probability that no people will be saved. . . .
> Which of the two programs would you favor?

Here, 72 percent chose Program A. Kahneman and Tversky followed this experiment with another that offered mathematically *identical options* to treating the same situation, but the programs were framed in terms of *likely deaths* rather than *lives saved:*

> If Program C is adopted, 400 people will die. . . .
> If Program D is adopted, there is a one-third probability that nobody will die and a two-thirds probability that 600 people will die.

With this alternative framing, 22 percent chose Program C, even though 72 percent of the previous experimental group selected Program A, Program C's mathematical twin.[54] In short, the alternative framing resulted in what was essentially a reversal of the percentages.

The frame in this experiment determined whether most people noticed a problem and how they understood and remembered it. The frame also determined how people evaluated and chose to act on the problem.[55] Perhaps one of the most important functions of frames is that by calling attention to particular aspects of a described reality they, by construction, direct attention away from other facets. This logical sleight of hand means the power of most frames lies in that what they omit as well as include. Omissions of things like definitions of problems, explanations, evaluations, and recommendations might be just as important as what a frame includes in guiding the audience.[56]

Design and language work together to make frames that affect our perceptions of how a technology works and, ultimately, decisions that affect our privacy. For example, contrary to the common assumption in both the literature and popular culture that people have stable, coherent preferences with respect to privacy, Leslie K. John, Alessandro Acquisti, and George Loewenstein have found that "concern about privacy, measured by divulgence of private information, is highly sensitive to contextual factors," including design.[57] In a series of experiments, John and colleagues manipulated the design of interfaces to make privacy concerns more or less salient to certain participants. In each experiment, participants provided identifying information (email addresses) and then indicated whether they had engaged in a series of sensitive, and in some cases illegal, behaviors.

In one experiment the researchers found that participants were more likely to divulge sensitive personal information in a survey with a more frivolous, less professional design than in one with a more formal interface. John and colleagues write, "The study was inspired by news stories about postings on the Facebook group '20 reasons why a girl should call it a night' in which young women voluntarily post compromising pictures of themselves—pictures that, in most other contexts, they would be mortified to share."[58] The researchers were interested in whether the frivolous nature of the site encouraged self-revelation and suppressed concern for privacy. They tested people's responses to two different designs of online surveys that asked people for very sensitive disclosures such as, "Have you ever smoked marijuana (i.e., pot, weed)?" The first design was intended to downplay privacy concerns. It titled the survey "How BAD are U??" and looked lighthearted.

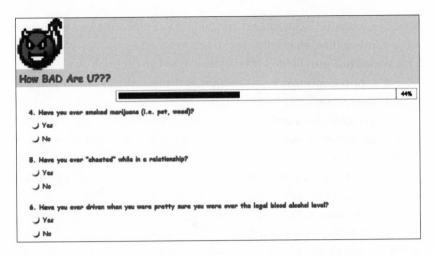

The second control design set the survey within a professional context and was titled "Carnegie Mellon University Survey of Ethical Standards." This was less frivolous in appearance and was thus hypothesized not to minimize privacy concerns in the same way as the more frivolous interface might.

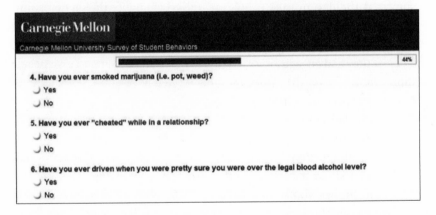

Relative to the nonfrivolous interface, participants in the frivolous-looking survey that asked identical questions were on average 1.7 times more likely to admit to having engaged in risky behaviors. The researchers found that "a participant in the [frivolous-looking survey] was on average 2.03 times more likely to admit to having 'ever taken nude pictures of [him]self or a partner.' People, it seems, feel more comfortable providing personal information on unprofessional sites that are arguably particularly likely to misuse it." The authors conclude, "By illustrating that disclosure of private information is influenced by contextual factors that have little, if any, normative justification, the current research casts serious doubt on whether individuals may be able to navigate this complexity according to their best interests."[59]

Once design affects our perceptions, it begins to shape our behavior. Once it shapes our behavior, it can be used to control us because it shapes what we perceive as normal. And once norms are established, they are difficult to change. Studies have explored how framing and design affect our privacy-related behavior. In multiple experiments in 2014, researchers changed the design, framing, and presentation of online privacy choices to users. For example, one group was exposed to "privacy settings" while another was exposed to "survey settings." They found that "[a]cross three experiments, the choice of the privacy protective options for objectively identical choices ranged from 17% to 55% depending on choice framing."[60]

The researchers concluded that given the value of personal information, it would be surprising if companies did not strategically leverage framing to get people to disclose more. And market forces are unlikely to help consumers much here, because people are unlikely to notice the subtle manipulations like the ones studied by the researchers. Furthermore, people are unlikely to notice the impact of those manipulations on their behavior. We just are not that self-aware. Even when design purports to give people more "control" over their information, we often have a false sense of security leading to risky personal disclosures.[61]

These studies are just the tip of the iceberg for understanding how design affects our privacy perceptions. Defaults, malicious interfaces, intentionally not ringing "privacy alarm bells," and a host of other design choices can all be used to manufacture personal disclosures. Acquisti, Brandimarte, and Loewenstein argue that policy approaches that rely exclusively on informing or empowering people will not work. Even "control" and "transparency," two hallmarks for privacy protection, are demonstrably vulnerable and in many cases radically insufficient when used apart from other principles of data protection. They argue that "People need assistance and even protection to aid in balancing what is otherwise a very uneven playing field."[62] Design can create power disparities, but it can also better distribute power within relationships. The authors conclude, "To be effective, privacy policy should protect the naïve, the uncertain, and the vulnerable. It should be sufficiently flexible to evolve with the emerging, unpredictable complexities of the information age."[63]

Design Affects Our Values

We are what we create, so we must be very careful with what we create.[64] Design reflects the values of its creators and can either support or undermine human values more generally.[65] In Langdon Winner's work on the politics of artifacts, he tells the story of Robert Moses, expert builder of roads, parks, bridges, and other public works from the 1920s to the 1970s in New York. Moses designed overpasses "to specifications that would discourage the presence of buses on his parkways."[66] Stripped of context, this decision seems odd. But when you consider the fact that minorities and the poor in this community and time disproportionately relied upon buses for transportation, this design is revealed as malicious: "According to evidence provided by Moses' biographer, Robert A. Caro, the reasons [for the low overpasses] reflect Moses' social class bias and racial prejudice. Automobile-owning whites of 'upper' and 'comfortable middle' classes, as he called them, would be free to use the parkways for recreation and commuting."[67] No buses, no poor people. (Or at least fewer poor people, given the transportation hardship).

If true, Moses's values were reflected in those bridges, and their design undermined larger human values of openness and equality, to say nothing of efficient transportation. In some contexts, we should pay even more attention to the values furthered by design because of lock-in effects. Winner writes, "For generations after Moses' death and the alliances he forged have fallen apart, his public works, especially the highways and bridges he built to favor the use of the automobile over the development of mass transit, will continue to shape that city. . . . As New York planner Lee Koppleman told Caro about the low bridges, . . . 'The old son-of-a-gun had made sure that buses would *never* be able to use his goddamned parkways.'"[68]

Like that of bridges, technology design can be imbued with social values. Consider the infamous wearable technology Google Glass; envisioned as the first major wearable ubiquitous computing device, it was released in 2012 to widespread criticism (fans of the device came to be known by some as Glassholes).[69] The technology essentially looked like eyeglasses with a small computer and lens slightly covering one eye. Ideally, Google Glass was a way for people to look at a screen without using their hands.

But one design decision may have been too much for us all to handle. Google included a camera on Google Glass. It would have been useful without a camera, but the public has become accustomed to being able to take a picture at any moment, and image sensors are quite useful. It turns out the camera may have been a bridge too far. People need time to adjust to new technologies. Without a camera, we might have been able to wrap our minds around always having little computers in front of our eyes. But a somewhat surreptitious camera—one that could snap a photo at any moment without the user having to hold up a conspicuous device— represented surveillance and a threat to our privacy and autonomy.

Anyone in range of a Google Glass device was put on notice of being watched. Conversations that were casual and free were subject to preservation and mass publication within seconds. The camera embodied everyone's worst fears about surveillance in the modern world.[70] The visible indicator light meant to alert bystanders that the device was recording and the company's lack of support for facial recognition apps for Google Glass could not save its reputation as a privacy-invasive technology.[71] Compare this with the cameras on smartphones. Adding a camera to a phone happened more gradually, which has made the adjustment to living in a world where people are constantly taking and sharing pictures a little easier. Smartphones also live in pockets, purses, and bags and require at least some effort to take out and use. Google Glass shows how both design and culture work together to shape how technologies are used and whether they are accepted. It also shows how design implicates values.

Design Is Political

For the past few years I have spoken with people in industry, academia, government, and civil society about the importance of privacy-related design. In these talks I've heard one argument come up repeatedly: the notion that it is users, not technologies, who are to blame for privacy violations. When I tell people the thesis of this book, sometimes they respond with some form of the argument, "There are no bad technologies. Only bad technology users."

According to this line of thought, it is not technology itself that matters but people—and the social and economic system they exist in. We are accustomed to thinking of tools that can be used well or poorly, for good or for evil, or somewhere in the middle of all of that.[72] This instrumentalist conception of technology is regularly used in ethics and policy discussions about the appropriate use of a technology to focus attention on the actor using the technology rather than the technology itself. For example, intellectual property law gives a pass to technologies with "substantial non-infringing uses."[73] The idea is to not blame the technology when it's really the user that's causing the harm. In this light, technologies are largely innocent bystanders.

This concept of neutral technologies might seem intuitive. Why blame technologies for harms carried out by people? After all, technologies are just tools. They are not self-executing; they require someone (or many people) to bring their intended purpose to fruition. In order to operate your car, you must ignite the engine, press the gas pedal, and turn the steering wheel. Your computer requires you to push the power button, move and click the mouse, and depress letters on your keyboard to make words. Autonomous technologies are still reliant upon designers and operators for initial execution. Even simple, docile objects like your refrigerator must be positioned and plugged in to keep your food cold. Given this subservient role of technology, it is not surprising that a dominant strain of "technological neutrality" exists in policy, industry, and our social lives.

The technological neutrality argument is evocative of a slogan sometimes used by gun rights activists: "Guns don't kill people. People kill people."[74] Technological neutrality arguments have political appeal and have been used effectively to shift lawmakers' focus away from technologies and toward bad actors using those technologies. But this sort of technological neutrality argument gives short shrift to the political and practical power of technology. Every single technology instantiates values by virtue of its design that makes certain realities more or less likely.

At this point you might be thinking, whatever happened to personal responsibility? Indeed, in the absence of a default setting, iPhones do not save someone else's explicit photos on their own. Facial recognition software that is used to find and harass people cannot reflect on its own wrongdoing. These technologies merely serve the people who make harmful decisions.

One way to downplay the importance of design is to call attention to the many different theoretical ways a technology could be used. People can use drones to film birds rather than peep through windows. People can let intimate Snaps they receive fade into the ether instead of saving and posting them to pornography and revenge websites. Framed this way, people's harmful uses of technology seem much more blameworthy than the design of the technology itself.[75]

But it's not that simple. Consider the Pinhole Spy Toothbrush Hidden Camera. The toothbrush is designed with no wires, a long battery life, no external memory card, and a very small lens to make it look as much like a regular electric toothbrush as possible. The website selling this spycam markets it as ideal for illegal behavior and, in an astonishing display of hubris, disclaims that "we are not responsible if this camera is used for illegal activities, this is a home security camera and should be treated as such, with responsibility."[76]

Of course, this technology could be used many different ways and for many legitimate ends. People could use it to brush their teeth. They could use it to take video of their family vacation on the beach. They could use it as a doorstop or play catch with it. Or perhaps they could just mount it on their mantel for aesthetic purposes.

But of course, all those uses are ridiculous. To suggest otherwise is to ignore how this technology embodies behavior-shaping values. To paraphrase Evan Selinger, the design of the toothbrush indicates the preferred ends to which it "should" be used—namely, surveilling others in secret. People aren't likely to spend $230 on a simple toothbrush, toy, or sculpture. And using a toothbrush camera to record your family vacation would just be awkward; better and cheaper cameras that won't make you look like a weirdo are available. The design of this technology facilitates bathroom voyeurism, pure and simple. There is nothing neutral about it.

To be sure, the notion of technological neutrality can be useful. It can help us avoid uncritically blaming objects and technologies for problems without taking into account the social and economic system in which such technologies are embedded. Winner argues that ideas like this, which have been referred to as the "social determination of technology," serve as a "needed corrective to those who . . . fail to look behind technical things to notice the social circumstances of their development, deployment and use. This view provides an antidote to naive technological determinism—the idea that technology develops as the sole result of an internal dynamic, and then, unmediated by any other influence, molds society to fit its patterns."[77]

But we must not overinvest in the belief of technological neutrality. Winner argues, "taken literally, [the social determination of technology] suggests that technical *things* do not matter at all." He instead suggests that artifacts are laden with *politics*—that is, "arrangements of power and authority in human associations as well as the activities that take place within those arrangements." Sometimes, the design or arrangement of a specific technical device or system "becomes a way of settling an issue in a particular community."[78] Winner notices that "we usually do not stop to inquire whether a given device might have been designed and built in such a way that it produces a set of consequences logically and temporally *prior to any of its professed uses*" and contends, "If our moral and political language for evaluating technology includes only categories having to do with tools and uses, if it does not include attention to the meaning of the designs and arrangements of our artifacts, then we will be blinded to much that is intellectually and practically crucial."[79]

He is right. When we fail to pay proper attention to the design of technologies, we end up focusing too much on human conduct. We ask too much of ourselves and others to overcompensate for design that pulled or pushed us in a direction adverse to our interests. We blame ourselves and others for being clumsy or mechanically incompetent. Norman has noticed people's tendency to think they are at fault when they fail in using an everyday object.[80]

On social media, we even have a term for our own "privacy fails"; we call it "oversharing."[81] The Internet is littered with articles like "The 30 Absolute Worst Facebook Overshares" and "Facebook Overshare: 7 Things You Might Not Realize You're Telling the World."[82] These posts describe tales of lost virginity, menstrual awkwardness, kidney stones (including pictures!), sexually transmitted diseases, and almost any other explicit details that one might simply rather not know about someone else. Even random clicks—for example, "liking" someone's photo that was posted three years ago (revealing you might be spending a little too much time "Facebook stalking" someone)—can be considered oversharing.

These obvious examples make it seem like only idiots and people with no dignity overshare. But that's not true. If we consider oversharing to simply be "sharing more than we should" or "sharing more than we would in offline, nonmediated settings," we all overshare regularly. As I will discuss in Chapter 6, social media are disclosure-manufacturing machines. Their entire purpose is to facilitate sharing early and often. For some social media, the more personal the information, the better. It is common for those of us with social media accounts to share our birthdays, illnesses, travel plans (i.e., when we will be away from home), intimate thoughts, and pictures of us in our skimpy swim trunks and bikinis. And sometimes we forget who can see our posts or we simply make a mistake. It's okay to admit it. No one has perfect judgment.[83]

And when people overshare, we almost always say they are to blame. For example, in an article titled "You're as Much to Blame for Facebook's Privacy Woes as Mark Zuckerberg," columnist Farhad Manjoo calls out social media users as the cause for their own privacy concerns, noting, "You should approach Facebook as cautiously as you would approach your open bedroom window" and, regardless of your privacy settings, "you should imagine that everything that you post on Facebook will be available for public consumption forever."[84] This is the only failsafe for sharing on social media. Manjoo also had a column titled "How To Stay Private on Facebook in One Easy Step" that consisted of only two words: "Quit Facebook."[85] To Manjoo, oversharing is ultimately your fault. To prevent it, just shut up. You are not forced to post anything, after all.

This user-fault mentality is also prominent in the context of nonconsensual pornography, sometimes called revenge pornography. As Danielle Citron writes in her book *Hate Crimes in Cyberspace,* "Revenge porn victims have told me that the overwhelming response to their struggles is that they are responsible for their nude photos appearing online." She quotes the operator of the revenge porn site Texxxan.com, who told the press, "When you take a nude photograph of yourself and you send it to this other person, or when you allow someone to take a nude photograph of you, by your very actions you have reduced your expectation of privacy."[86]

Putting aside the self-eroding and problematic nature of the notion of a "reasonable expectation of privacy," this myopic focus on only the most proximate and direct causes of harm ignores the entire structure and context that facilitated it. Of course, sometimes people are careless in their interactions with others. Other times they are betrayed by trusted confidantes, or their actions were just enough to tip delicately balanced scales.

We've all seen a scenario in movies or television where an out-of-control car comes to a stop, dangling perilously on the edge of a cliff, when one of the passengers leans forward slightly, causing it to go over. As any first-year law student will tell you, the person leaning over may have technically "caused" the fall, but she is not the only one at fault.

The notion that human choice, and not design, is what matters most in protecting our privacy is firmly entrenched in U.S. law. In this way, privacy law reflects a kind of neutral or even protectionist approach to technology. Courts generally refuse to hold technology companies liable in tort for unsecure computer code.[87] The four privacy torts all restrict people's conduct—people cannot publicly disclose another's private facts, intrude upon another's seclusion, commercially misappropriate another's name or likeness, or depict another in a false light. Surveillance law in the United States prohibits unauthorized interception of communications but has little to say about the design of surveillance technologies (with one notable exception for spyware, which we will return to in Chapters 5 and 7). With exceptions for data security, statutory regimes like the Family Educational Rights and Privacy Act, the Gramm-Leach-Bliley Act, and the Health Insurance Portability and Accountability Act largely focus on people keeping a confidence but ignore the tools of disclosure.

Even in our day-to-day lives, we often fall prey to the myth of technological neutrality and miss how technological design affects us. Consider the password. Many data breaches are the result of an attacker successfully figuring out someone's password. This has led to the standard advice that we've all heard: "Select a long and complex password. Use upper and lower case, letters and numerals, and special characters. Commit it to memory. Change it frequently. And do this for every account you have."

Most people don't do this. How could they? The most popular passwords are still words like "password" or other simple things that even a bad hacker can crack in seconds. People reuse their passwords, write them down on sticky notes next to their computers, or carry them in scraps of paper in their wallets. And people don't change their passwords very often.

And when accounts with poor passwords are breached, our first reaction is often to blame the user: "This idiot used the password 12345." When my own personal email account was compromised by a spammer a few years ago, I blamed myself. I had used a relatively short, recycled password, and I knew better. I was embarrassed because I write about privacy and data security for a living. How could I be so dense?

What I didn't think about at the time was how design helped precipitate the breach. The system has set us all up to fail. Our memories can handle at most a few long and complex passwords, but not a lot of them and not if they must be changed frequently. According to one study, consumers have an average of twenty-four online accounts. For those who use the Internet more robustly, that number is much higher. It's just too much to handle, so it's no surprise that people fail to follow good password protocol.[88]

If we say "Systems don't facilitate data breaches, people do," we obscure the orchestration of design choices that give people little practical say in the matter. Several different design decisions could have been made to anticipate human limitations and predictable error. For example, designers could have required two-factor authentication, the essence of which is simple: in order to log in, you must have something you know (usually a password), as well as one additional factor, usually something you have (usually your cell phone). Additional factors could be mixed and matched to avoid relying on the sole password. Under a "two-channel" authentication scheme, companies would not authenticate users until they actually hear back from them on the second channel (such as the cell phone) dedicated to authentication. Other factors can include having a friend vouch for you or sign your name. None of these are foolproof (and some are certainly better than others), but generally two factors are much better than one for important accounts.

I am not saying that people should be able to do anything they want online and avoid the consequences of their behavior. That is a ridiculous notion. We should all act reasonably online. We should not be reckless. When we are, we must accept the consequences of our actions. But we must move past the notion that the *only* thing that matters in the privacy debate is collection, use, and disclosure of personal information. The current trajectory of privacy law and discourse cannot continue to marginalize the role of design. Design picks data winners and privacy losers.

This is true even when we cannot characterize outcomes as "intended" or "unintended," which are often oversimplified categories. Winner notes that sometimes "the very process of technical development is so thoroughly biased in a particular direction that it regularly produces results counted as wonderful breakthroughs by some social interests and crushing setbacks by others."[89] Consider the data collection infrastructure that feeds the phenomenon we know as *big data,* an amorphous term usually best thought of as shorthand for powerful data analytics. Scientists rejoice over big data. It holds the potential to answer previously unanswerable questions regarding our health and well-being. Insurers and advertises also love big data. It can allow for better, more efficient personal profiles and more profitable decisions regarding who gets coverage and what ads we see. But big data is also dangerous to those being profiled. It can be used to give us all scores—similar to credit scores—for nearly any aspect of our lives.[90] While the scored society promises many advantages, it also threatens to be a ruthlessly efficient discrimination machine that can curtail our autonomy, disproportionately burden minority communities, and demand ever more personal information to feed the beast. In the world of big data, more is always better.

Winner writes that for most technologies, "it is neither correct nor insightful to say, 'Someone intended to do somebody else harm.' Rather one must say that the technological deck has been stacked long in advance to favor certain social interests, and that some people were bound to receive a better hand than others."[91] To properly understand the role design plays in our privacy, we must understand how, why, and for whom the deck has been stacked.

Design Should Be Policy

Because design can allocate power to people and industries, it is inherently political. Advocates for technological innovation often say "the law should stay out of technology." This is sometimes perceived as a call for neutrality, leaving market forces and norms to shape technology. There are often very good reasons why the law should not directly address the design of technology, but such a decision is not neutral. To not address design is to sanction the power of creators to determine the context in which people make decisions. Most of the time this is the right path. The law usually should not dictate the minutiae of design. It would be a nightmare if every little design choice for every digital technology was micromanaged and had to be preapproved by some regulator.

But there is a difference between zealously *dictating* design and *addressing* it. The law can be responsive to the power of design by articulating boundaries, guidance, and goals. The law can simply better recognize the role that design plays in shaping our privacy expectations and reality. It is an ethical lapse to ignore design altogether under the auspices of neutrality. Because design and architecture affect every choice we make, even silence matters.

Others argue that controlling design itself is ethically problematic, because, stripped bare, design regulations are attempts to manipulate people into making particular choices. In addressing the ethics of nudging, Cass Sunstein writes, "When people make decisions, they do so against a background consisting of choice architecture. A cafeteria has a design, and the design will affect what people choose to eat. The same is true of websites. Department stores have architectures, and they can be designed so as to promote or discourage certain choices by shoppers (such as leaving without making a purchase)."[92] This architecture will affect people's choices even if the effect is not intended by designers. For example, people have a tendency to buy things they encounter first, so even if you are not trying to sell a lot of a sweater vests, putting them at the entrance to your store will probably move more vests than if you tuck them away in some corner.

We cannot avoid choice architecture. As Sunstein notes, "Human beings (or dogs or cats or horses) cannot wish [choice architecture] away. Any store has a design; some products are seen first, and others are not. Any menu places options at various locations. Television stations come with different numbers, and strikingly, numbers matter, even when the costs of switching are vanishingly low; people tend to choose the station at the lower number, so that channel 3 will obtain more viewers than channel 53."[93] A website has a design, and that design will affect how users will navigate the site and how long they will stay. When lawmakers and judges ignore design they implicitly endorse the status quo and the unchecked use of power.

Consider default rules and settings, which are the preselected choices that will take effect anytime a person does nothing or fails to select an option. Sometimes it is impossible to avoid creating a default. Consider the on / off toggle button that is so common on our smartphones:

There are only two possible choices here: *on* or *off*. Designers must choose to preselect the default position for the button. This choice cannot be avoided, because even some halfway choice in a binary decision would basically function as *off*. Because we know defaults are sticky and it would take the user's scarce resources of time and attention to change the setting, the default decision reflects a value. If the default for location tracking and sharing were set to *on*, we should expect the exact location of many more phone users to be tracked and shared. Many of us might not mind, but political dissidents and those seeking refuge from domestic abuse might be jeopardized by this default. The danger of defaults is acute when people are unaware of them or when the panel of selections looks like this cascading array of options:

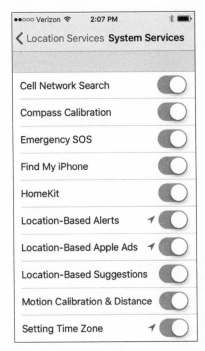

The default for many social media services is set to maximize sharing at the expense of discretion. For example, at one point the mobile payment service Venmo publicly shared its users' transactions by default.[94] The process for users to limit access to all of their transactions is not very intuitive. The Default Audience setting only affects the visibility of the charges and payments initiated by the user. The transactions initiated by friends who have not changed the default privacy setting will still be shared publicly. To obscure all transactions, a user must hunt down and change the inconspicuous Transactions Involving You setting.[95] These kinds of defaults matter. According to a 2015 study from Kaspersky Lab, 28 percent of social media users neglect privacy settings and leave all of their posts, photos, and videos accessible to the public.[96] There are hundreds of buttons under the hood of our technologies. Each default setting affects our choices.

And we users are severely outmatched. Technology users operate as isolated individuals making decisions about things we don't know much about, like the risk of disclosing information and agreeing to confusing legalese. We're up against the brightest graduates from Ivy League schools who spend their days figuring out how to get us to disclose personal data.

It's like we are disorganized little tribes fighting against an organized army. Large tech companies claim to be running thousands of A / B tests at a time, and these tests compare two different versions of an interface to see which one works better. How many of those tests are about maximizing how much personal information can be extracted from people? This is why progressive new laws like Article 25 of the European Union's new General Data Protection Regulation titled "data protection by design and by default," which requires that core data protection principles be integrated into the design and development of data technologies, are so important.[97]

A regulator's choice to address design or to ignore it is also a kind of default, which comes with its own set of consequences. This is actually what the law does—it provides the default rules for how we deal with each other. Even if a government claims to be firmly committed to free markets, private property, and keeping regulation out of technology, it cannot simply refrain from acting—or, in Thaler and Sunstein's word, "nudging." Even a free market, competition-based system requires a legal framework. As Sunstein writes, "the rules of contract (as well as property and tort) provide a form of choice architecture for social ordering." Design can, of course, maintain freedom of choice where it is important, and it can also consciously pursue neutrality in important ways. But, Sunstein notes, "choice architecture itself is inevitable, which means that it is pointless to object to it on ethical grounds."[98]

In fact, ethics compel lawmakers to take design seriously. Designers facilitate morality because the decisions they make in creating an object have morally relevant outcomes. Philosopher Peter-Paul Verbeek notes that technologies facilitate morally "good" and "bad" outcomes; speed bumps, for example, "help us make the moral decision not to drive too fast near a school." Technologies help shape our actions and experiences, and in so doing facilitate our ethical decisions. For example, social media design can nudge us to increase our civic participation or to heckle or harass others. According to Verbeek, because technologies are "bursting with morality," we must develop an ethical framework to conceptualize the moral relevance of technology.[99]

Lawmakers must acknowledge that the law inevitably influences design. Once lawmakers, policy creators, and judges realize that choice architecture is unavoidable and that the design of systems has moral implications, they have a choice to make: they can keep the status quo and basically ignore the design of technologies when addressing privacy law, or they can confront the important ways design shapes morally relevant outcomes. Lawmakers are justified if, upon assessing the effect of design on desired outcomes, they intentionally decline to address design in their laws and regulations and instead preserve the status quo. But failure to act out of a desire for neutrality or pure randomness is not justified, because such outcomes are impossible. Because of the great capacity for design to facilitate human flourishing or inflict suffering, no principal justifies refusing to form a deliberate legal framework, be it permissive or intervening, over the design of technologies. We cannot ethically ignore design.

In this chapter we explored how design affects our privacy because it is everywhere, it is powerful, and it is political. In other words, it is a force that should not be ignored by policy makers. In Chapter 2, I will make the case that privacy-related design deserves much more attention in law and policy.

2

Privacy Law's Design Gap

EVERYWHERE YOU LOOK, privacy law is a bit of a work in progress. The United States system of privacy law is basically a kludge. In 1890 when Samuel Warren and Louis Brandeis searched for a legal remedy for invasions of privacy caused by affordable "instant" cameras and an increasingly inquisitive press, they failed to find anything that would work. So they proposed something new—a right to be let alone.[1] This right was always supposed to be an add-on to the existing hodgepodge of remedies based in notions of confidentiality, property, and reputation. It spurred a revolutionary patchwork of laws and regulations that is nimble and malleable but lacks cohesion. We've been holding it together with duct tape ever since.

Other countries, like those within the European Union and much of Asia, have adopted a more omnibus approach to modern privacy issues, usually in the form of a human rights framework and centralized data protection regime. But this approach to privacy has its own issues. Because privacy is a diverse and contextually dependent concept, data protection regimes often over-rely on notions of "consent" to justify data collection, use, or disclosure. These regimes can be a little myopic and inflexible. They hew closely to the Fair Information Practices (FIPs)—a set of principles for responsible information collection and use that was proposed in the 1970s and has been taking root ever since. (They have also been highly influential in the U.S. data protection regime.) The FIPs are remarkably resilient and useful as an international touchstone for best practices. But as we will see, they only address responsible practices for information in databases. They do not cover the universe of modern privacy problems, which come from large institutional threats as well as small, dispersed ones. The motivations behind privacy violations are also varied.

The benefit of the U.S. patchwork approach to privacy is that it is agile and can be responsive to new problems. The problem with a patchwork approach, however, is that things are bound to fall through the cracks. Even worse, lawmakers focus so intently on the details of complex, sector-specific statutes and regulations that they often fail to see the forest for the trees. Big, important concepts that are right in front of us, like the design of consumer information technologies, fail to become a part of the privacy patchwork because there is no mechanism or unifying notion helping us keep an eye on the big picture. The failure to confront design allows companies to use design to circumvent the purpose of privacy laws. Design tricks like manipulative and confusing website design or evasive surveillance devices can be technically legal yet leave people ignorant, deceived, confused, and hurt.

The common wisdom of regulators and users about what makes good design is misguided. It shares the same major weakness as every privacy regime in the world: the fetishization of control. By ostensibly giving users every conceivable option and every possibly relevant piece of information, companies can claim their designs are user- (and privacy-) friendly. But that's often wrong. Plentiful prestructured choices can overwhelm us or distract us from critically examining the options we *haven't been* given. This makes design a particularly useful tool to practically circumvent the goals of privacy rules.

In these contexts, choice becomes an illusion of empowerment or a burden. Instead of blindly seeking to empower people with control over their information choices, regulatory schemes should seek to ensure that the design of consumer technologies is presenting the most optimal and sustainable choices, affordances, and constraints for users. Privacy law should also seek to ensure that users have accurate mental models about how technologies work. As it stands now, most privacy regimes are largely silent about the relationship between design, choice, and the other various goals of personal information rules.

In this chapter, I will highlight privacy law's design gap and make the case for a design agenda for privacy law and policy—what I call a blueprint.

First, I will argue that for the purposes of this book, modern privacy regulatory regimes can be distilled down to three simple rules: follow the Fair Information Practices (FIPs), do not lie, and do not harm. There is a design gap in the way that these rules are applied around the world, and particularly in the United States. Each rule fails to seriously consider the design of consumer technologies. As a result, design is used to frustrate or circumvent these rules. The potential for privacy-friendly design is squandered.

In the second part of the chapter, I make the case for a design agenda for privacy law. Taking design seriously is no cure-all, but it can help remedy some of the limitations of privacy law. People don't read terms of use, and they may not be aware of privacy laws, but every single person that uses an app or device must make a mental map about how a technology works and reckon with a technology's constraints and affordances.

Right now lawmakers and courts are almost singularly focused on one aspect of the modern privacy dilemma—the particulars of how others collect, use, and share information. But privacy is implicated by more than just conduct; it is also impacted by design. Lawmakers are not using all of the tools available to them, and courts are not taking a broad enough view of how people understand and use technology. They can shore up the deficiencies of modern privacy regimes by taking design more seriously.

I end this chapter by showing how the groundwork for Privacy's Blueprint has already been laid. The law takes design seriously in many other contexts, such as with cars, airplanes, buildings, pharmaceuticals, advertisements, technologies implanted in our bodies, and even everyday consumer products. Furthermore, entire disciplines and industries are dedicated to figuring out what constitutes sound privacy design. We just need to take advantage of it.

The Three Main Rules of Privacy Law Have a Design Gap

Privacy law can be overwhelming. There are so many different rules. The U.S. system breaks privacy into areas like torts, contract, evidentiary privileges, the law of surveillance, consumer protection, and statutory regimes in specific contexts like health, education, and financial information; there's little rhyme or reason to this structure. It is the result of lawmakers and courts simply tacking on laws one at a time to tackle problems as they arise. Other countries may have a centralized system, but it is no less com-

plex. For example, countries within the European Union (EU) commonly
view privacy issues with two distinct lenses: human rights and data protection. Values like dignity are elevated over notions of seclusion and
freedom. While the EU has a more omnibus approach, it still has many
subparts and splinters such as specific rules about tracking "cookies" and
the "right to be forgotten," which can make this system seem as byzantine
as the U.S. privacy regime.

However, amid these conglomerations of laws, virtually every privacy
and data protection regime in the world seems to embrace the three basic
ethics just mentioned: following the FIPs, not lying, and not harming. Yes,
of course I'm being overly reductive. And privacy law should and probably
will eventually encompass more than this. But these three rules are the current soul of privacy law. I'll use these three ethics as an organizing scheme
to show the shortcomings of privacy law when it comes to design.

The FIPs suffer from the myopic mantra of user control, which allows
companies to leverage design to overwhelm people. The FIPs also fail to
directly address design. Privacy laws that follow the *do not lie* ethic too
often succumb to a sort of rote formalism that ignores human limitations
on cognition and allows companies to use design to bury and obscure
privacy-relevant information. Finally, privacy laws built around the *do not
harm* ethic have narrowed the definition of privacy harm so much that
technologies that facilitate incremental, dispersed, and structural harm escape scrutiny.

Rule 1: Follow the Fair Information Practices

One of the most amazing things about a concept as diverse and squishy as
privacy is that people have come to a general consensus on the basic rules
involving personal data. The dominant privacy and data protection model
in the world is based on the Fair Information Practices. The FIPs are the
closest thing the world has to a privacy touchstone.[2] Paula Bruening has
called them "the common language of privacy."[3] These influential principles originated from a report from the U.S. Department of Health, Education and Welfare in the1970s. The Organisation for Economic Co-operation
and Development revised the principles in an internationally influential
document that continues to serve as the bedrock foundation for privacy
regulatory schemes and public policy.

The influence of the FIPs can be seen in data protection regimes across the world: in Australia, Canada, the European Union, and many Asian countries.[4] The FIPs also substantively contour U.S. privacy statutes like the Health Insurance Portability and Accountability Act (HIPAA) and the U.S. Federal Trade Commission's regulation of privacy through its authority to police unfair and deceptive trade practices.

The FIPs implore data collecting entities to:

limit the amount of personal data they collect, and collect personal data with the knowledge or consent of the data subject (the Collection Limitations Principle)

ensure that the data collected is relevant to the purposes for which it will be used and is accurate, complete, and up to date (the Data Quality Principle)

specify the purposes for which data is collected (the Purpose Specification Principle)

obtain consent to use and disclose personal data for purposes other than those specified at the time of collection (the Use Limitation Principle)

take "reasonable security safeguards" to protect data (the Security Safeguards Principle)

be transparent about their data collection practices and policies (the Openness Principle)

allow individuals to access the data collected from them, to challenge the data, and to have inaccurate data erased, rectified, completed, or amended (the Individual Participation Principle)

be accountable for complying with the principles (the Accountability Principle).[5]

These principles focus on how information is collected and used. Lawmakers most commonly implement them through concepts of control, notice, and consent to protect privacy. The FIPs have proven remarkably resilient, even as they are increasingly challenged by new concepts like big data and automation. They recognize the power of electronic databases filled with personal information.

The problem is that lawmakers tend to paint every privacy and data-related problem with the FIPs brush. By structuring privacy frameworks this way, the path for improvement seems fixed: just add more FIPs. Data breach? Time to up those safeguards. Are people upset about what you're collecting or sharing? You must not have turned the "purpose specification" dial up enough. It's as though the answer to every privacy problem is simply to "FIP harder."

FIP-based regimes recognize the power disparities created by personal data and the need for organizational restraint and individual control. But they offer limited protection from the privacy-obscuring tactics of today's consumer technologies. The FIPs are the blueprint for the threats of the 1970s, when only governments and the largest corporations could collect data.

People are too often "protected" by a threadbare, formalistic, or meaningless technical legal compliance with the FIPs that overwhelms individuals with information and choices instead of substantively protecting them. It would be impracticable to read even a small fraction of the privacy notices we're asked to consent to or to forgo using the services we rely on because we disagree with their policies. While control over personal information theoretically empowers user autonomy, in practice our FIP-based legal framework can convert concepts like "consent" and "control" into meaningless formalities. The FIPs can be weakened by design because they don't focus on how technology actually *affects* people.

The FIPs are not focused on design; they are decontextualized goals, like "openness" and "data quality." Phrases like "security safeguards" and "means of openness" in the FIPs show where design might compliment privacy policy. Passwords and online portals are security and transparency solutions, respectively, that leverage design. But because the FIPs do not give any specific technology mandates or guidance, and because there is no mandate to examine how people actually perceive and interact with consumer technologies, privacy law has largely glossed over design. So while the FIPs are quite useful for problems with data and databases, we must dig deeper to fill privacy law's design gap.

I should emphasize at this point that I'm not arguing we should abandon the FIPs; they operationalize important values like dignity and autonomy, and they are invaluable as a common guide for data-related practices. A design agenda should still strive to be FIP-friendly. But the FIPs are not the best blueprint for privacy design policy and certainly should not be the only guide for lawmakers.

Instead we should make people the center of a design agenda—particularly how they are affected by and react to design. We can learn from Don

Norman here, who has said that whether design is good or bad is a function of *affordances, constraints,* and *mappings.*[6]

These variables should be the locus for privacy law's design agenda. As I will explain in Chapter 4, they map nicely onto much of product safety law and consumer protection law. When thinking about good privacy design, the question "Did you follow the FIPs?" is not really useful, as concepts like "openness" and "protection" are open to so many different interpretations. It would be far more useful to ask, "How would a person be expected to use or respond to this technology? What sort of mental model would most users form for how this technology works? What sort of affordances does this technology offer? What sorts of constraints would enable safe and sustainable use?"

Another major problem with the FIPs is that they myopically contemplate responsibilities for one particular kind of actor: a person or entity collecting information into a database. But, of course, many different kinds of people and entities can affect the privacy of data subjects, including other *users* of technology. Consider the organizer of the University of Texas Queer Chorus Facebook group (discussed in the Introduction to this book) who accidentally outed Bobbi Duncan, a member of the group, or those who use commercially available publishing tools, facial recognition technologies, drones, and license plate readers in public for voyeuristic thrills, revenge, or other malicious purposes.

Design facilitates privacy harms in these circumstances by forming mental models, setting constraints, and offering affordances in favor of negligent or malicious actors who are adversarial to data subjects but aren't necessarily data collectors. But the FIPs don't naturally raise the question of how potentially bad actors will react to technologies. For example, the FIPs are largely silent on whether companies that design drones, spycams, and apps for use by third parties bear any responsibility for protecting those who will be surveilled. Design principles can better contemplate the universe of actors and forces that control information flows and influence decisions.

The Overtaxing of User Control: Manufacturing Consent

Let me be blunt: privacy regulators and designers have made a mistake by hinging virtually everything on the notion of control. Regulators and industry seemingly view control as a synonym for privacy protection. This is a problem because control is a critical finite resource for people. Yet both privacy design and FIP-based data protection regimes treat control as if it were a bottomless well.

In theory, the goal of the FIPs is to empower data subjects. To empower in this context means to put in control—to ensure that data subjects have knowledge of a data collector's activities and give consent for certain practices. Knowing companies' data practices and requiring them to seek your consent for any material thing they want to do sounds good in theory; it ostensibly helps people decide for themselves how to weigh the costs and benefits of the collection, use, or disclosure of their information.

Control has become the archetype for data protection regimes. It is the first right articulated in the U.S. White House's proposed Consumer Privacy Bill of Rights.[7] Control was also a major component of the Federal Trade Commission's report *Protecting Consumer Privacy in an Era of Rapid Change*.[8] "Consent" is the linchpin of the EU's entire General Data Protection Regulation. It legitimizes most kinds of data collection, use, and disclosure.[9]

In fact, control over information is often floated as the very definition of privacy itself. The great privacy scholar Alan Westin has defined privacy as "the claim of individuals, groups, or institutions to determine for themselves when, how, and to what extent information about them is communicated to others."[10] Others, including Charles Fried, Arthur Miller, Richard Parker, and Ferdinand Schoeman all conceptualize privacy in terms of control.[11] Countless popular press articles and books are aimed at helping us "take control" of our privacy online.[12] Indeed, some technology companies seem to be making a good faith effort to gradually increase and simplify user control where appropriate.

Control is an industry favorite privacy tool as well. To hear tech companies tell it, the answer to all modern privacy problems is just to give users more control. Facebook has stated, "Our philosophy that people own their information and control who they share it with has remained constant,"[13] and Facebook founder and CEO Mark Zuckerberg notes, "What people want isn't complete privacy. It isn't that they want secrecy. It's that they want control over what they share and what they don't."[14] Microsoft CEO Satya Nadella summarizes his company's focus on user control by stating, "Microsoft experiences will be unique as they will . . . keep a user in control of their privacy," adding that the company will "[a]dvocate laws and legal processes that keep people in control."[15] Google has written, "Google builds simple, powerful privacy and security tools that keep your information safe and put you in control of it."[16] There is seemingly no privacy problem for governments or technology companies that more user control cannot fix. Just chuck some more control at it.

In theory this is a laudable goal, but in practice it hasn't worked out so well. There are two problems with elevating control. First, control doesn't scale. The sheer number of choices that inundate users under a control regime is overwhelming to the point of futility. Second, the other FIPs become subservient. The fixation on control sidelines other important principles, such as limiting data collection in the first place.

Neil Richards and I have cautioned against over-relying on the notion of control to protect privacy.[17] We call this misguided allegiance to control the Control Illusion, and it dominates privacy policy as well as public discourse. When the Federal Trade Commission (FTC) first started to regulate privacy in the late 1990s, it adopted a basic control scheme for businesses dubbed "notice and choice." People were said to have "control" over their information when they were notified about a company's information collection, use, and disclosure practices and given a choice to opt out (usually by not using the service). If people did not opt out, then companies were free to act in any way consistent with the notice given to consumers. The most salient example of this notice and choice regime is the ubiquitous privacy policy: that dense, unreadable, boilerplate text tucked away in some corner of practically every website and application on the Internet. Through notice and choice, "control" is leveraged to become little more than a mechanism optimized to manufacture your permission to collect, use, and share your data.

There are many jokes about whether anyone reads privacy policies, but these jokes rest on the undeniable truth that meaningful control over information is almost impossible to scale. One study by Aleecia McDonald and Lorrie Cranor has found, for example, that if ordinary Internet users were to quickly read every privacy policy they encountered over the course of a year, it would take each person seventy-six working days to do so.[18] Another exploration by leading privacy and technology journalist Julia Angwin has revealed that it is practically impossible to opt out of pervasive surveillance by governments and companies without practically opting out of society and human contact itself.[19]

The control we get from modern privacy regulations is like a distributed denial of service (DDoS) attack on our brains. (The DDoS attack is an attempt to make an online service unavailable by overwhelming servers with traffic from multiple sources and thus crashing them.) From the second you boot up any device, you're gifted with "control" over information in the form of privacy policies, terms of use, and pop-up banners—for each and every website or app you visit or use. Eventually your eyes gloss over and that control does you little good. Your critical faculties just crash, and you give up.

When pressed on this point, federal regulators concede the futility of notice and the absence of real choice about the pervasive collection of personal data. The White House Privacy and Civil Liberties Oversight Board recognized as much in its long-awaited report on privacy and surveillance.[20] In a 2014 report on big data, the U.S. President's Council of Advisors on Science and Technology (PCAST) also repudiated the Control Principle, stating, "The framework of notice and consent is also becoming unworkable as a useful foundation for policy."[21] Even the FTC has realized the limits of notice and choice.[22] Yet despite the acknowledgment that notice and choice cannot do the work we ask of them, the mantra of user control persists.

I am not trying to belittle the idea of control. Quite the opposite. Control is essential; a 2015 Pew Research Center study found that 93 percent of people think it's important to control access to their personal information, and 90 percent care about the type of information that's collected about them.[23] The problem is that regulatory systems treat control as if it were an infinite resource. It's a little like the problem of your passwords: you may be able to remember a few, but it is almost impossible to remember them all. I am arguing that control is far too precious for companies and lawmakers to overleverage it. Control can enable autonomy, but it is not the same thing as autonomy. Any sound approach to privacy in furtherance of autonomy must ensure the right amount of control and structured choice for people. The problem comes when the pursuit of control becomes the *main* or *only* way companies address privacy.

At best, prioritizing "control" of our personal information over other goals, like enforcing trust obligations and minimizing data collection, is fool's gold. At worst, it's a trap. Psychologist Barry Schwartz argues in *The Paradox of Choice* that while autonomy and freedom of choice are critical human values, too many choices and too much control can actually overwhelm and confuse us.[24] Maurice Godelier has described "consent in all forms" as the "strongest and most effective force in guaranteeing the long-term maintenance of power" where the "dominated acquiesce in their own domination."[25] Idris Adjerid, Alessandro Acquisti, and George Loewenstein call upon this notion to argue that choice mechanisms without supplemental protections are likely to mislead consumers, quelling their privacy concerns without providing meaningful protection.[26] People feel falsely empowered by opportunities to restrict the collection and use of their personal information. Meanwhile, in practice, design works in the background ensuring that we actually continue to allow broad, and potentially harmful, access to our data.

Even when control is effective, it can act to shift the burden of responsibility for protecting privacy to people who are less equipped to handle it. We are awash in a dizzying array of data, and virtually every transaction requires us to disclose personal information to someone. Control over personal information might sound attractive in isolation; who doesn't want more power over things that affect our lives? But with this power comes a practical *obligation*. If you do not exercise that control, you are at risk. Companies can take your inaction as acquiescence.

So while you might remember to adjust your privacy settings on Facebook, what about Amazon, Candy Crush Saga, Cortana, Fitbit, Google, Instagram, Netflix, Snapchat, Siri, Twitter, your smart TV, your robot vacuum cleaner, your Wi-Fi-connected car, and your child's Hello Barbie? A 2015 Pew Research Center study found that mobile apps can seek over 235 (!) different types of permissions from smartphone users, with the average app asking for around five different permissions to access and use data.[27] Will you even be able to figure out what all of the settings mean or where they are, much less remember to look for them? Is there even a remote possibly you will be able to be consistent with your choices? Or will this all just devolve into blindly clicking buttons or just accepting the default? And all this is just for the initial setup. When the settings and permission options change, as they often do, you'll need to log back in and change them again. Lather, rinse, repeat. For every online service you use. For the rest of your life.

In the aggregate, the weight of too much structured control will crush us. It will leave us bewildered and hopeless and agreeable to anything. Privacy policies become antiprivacy policies because companies know we will never read them. The default settings for privacy controls are permissive, because companies know that we do not usually change them. Retails stores tracking your devices only let you opt out online instead of in the store because they know you probably will not remember or take the effort to do so later.[28] Control is a vital but scarce resource. It is easily diluted. Adversarial design can make the downsides to control worse. Prioritizing control hides the power imbalances inherent in our modern mediated lives. Privacy regimes should seek to preserve control for when it can be the most effective, and leave the rest to other concepts, like privacy-friendly design.

Rule 2: Do Not Lie

Privacy law in the United States tolerates many different kinds of snoops and publishers. It tolerates gossips, paparazzi, peepers (so long as they are "in public"), trolls, and data black boxes. But one thing privacy law will not tolerate is a liar. Prohibitions on deceptive representations and omissions are the foundation for data protection law in the United States.

As the Internet began to blossom in the mid- to late 1990s and people began to surf the web and engage in online commercial activity, privacy became an obvious concern because a significant amount of personal data could be gathered. Data security was another major concern, as many people were reluctant to use the Internet out of fear that their data could be improperly accessed.

Few laws directly addressed privacy in these contexts. Efforts to adapt the privacy torts to modern data collection and uses largely failed. Industry favored a self-regulatory regime, which consisted largely of the FIP-inspired "notice and choice" approach. For the "notice" part, companies began to include privacy policies on their websites—especially commercial ones. The privacy policy was typically a special page that users could read by clicking a link at the bottom of a website's homepage. These policies described the various ways in which websites collected, used, and shared a visitor's personal information, as well as the various ways that information was protected. For the "choice" part, users were given some kind of choice about how their data would be collected and used, most commonly in the form of an opt-out right, whereby companies could use data in the ways they described in the privacy policy unless users affirmatively indicated they did not consent to these uses.

These privacy policies have now become part of the intractable wall of text on every website and app known as terms of use and sometimes called boilerplate for its nonnegotiability. These dense and usually unreadable documents that set the rights and obligations between the website and the user actually pass as binding contracts most of the time. It is a stretch to call them contracts in the classical sense, which theoretically embodied a "meeting of the minds." Yet companies use these agreements to manage risk by "informing" users about the various permissions they must give websites in exchange for service.

There are lots of privacy laws, but the most commonly encountered online privacy regulatory instrument has to be the contract. There is a contract for virtually every website and mobile app. I visited hundreds (possibly thousands) of websites while doing research for this book; I can't think of a single one that didn't have a terms of use agreement and a privacy policy.

Privacy law generally mandates one simple rule for contracts, privacy policies, and marketing: you can say anything you want about your information practices, but whatever you say has to be the truth. Under *do not lie* privacy laws, the harm comes from being deceived by the surveillance and data practices of others rather than from the invasive or hurtful nature of personal information collection, use, or disclosure.

The most prominent example of the *do not lie* approach is the FTC's regulation of deceptive trade practices. A deceptive trade practice is defined as a "misrepresentation, omission or other practice that misleads the consumer acting reasonably in the circumstances, to the consumer's detriment."[29] The FTC primarily relies upon theories of deception when alleging privacy violations. The agency brings most of its privacy-related enforcement actions against companies that violate their own privacy policies or fail to disclose their data collection and use practices. The *do not lie* ethic also shows up in statutes like the Truth in Lending Act, the Gramm-Leach-Bliley Act, the HIPAA, and state data-breach notification laws. These laws require mandatory disclosure of important privacy-related items. Behind all of these statutes lies the notion that companies must shoot straight with data subjects about their privacy.

The Notice Trap: When Notice Becomes Rote (Rotice?)

Privacy law treats notice as an instrument of truth.[30] Notice is one of the main privacy-related obligations that makers of consumer technologies face in the United States.[31] In fact, notice is quite attractive to regulators.

Lawmakers like mandated notices as regulatory instruments because it costs companies very little and preserves a fair bit of freedom for companies to experiment and design as they wish in the name of innovation. Notice regimes are also compatible with heterogeneous consumer preferences. Instead of setting a ceiling or floor for companies about how data is collected or used, customers that have notice theoretically can decide for themselves whether a company's practices are palatable.

For lawyers, the place for notice is in a privacy policy and the terms of use—the dense, unreadable block of text we all vaguely know we "agree" to but otherwise ignore. For designers, terms of use can be like the elephant in the room: designers can construct an environment that acknowledges the impact of the terms, or they can ignore them, oblivious to any contradictions that might arise between the messages conveyed by design and by contract. For example, mobile applications could notify users that they collect geolocation data with a pop-up screen that requires affirmatively clicking OK before using the app. Alternatively, designers could choose to have such notices left in boilerplate contracts they know no user will read.

When privacy law ignores design, it allows notice to become rote and ineffectual. Design can be used to obscure notice and exploit our limited ability to understand what is being conveyed.[32] Yet privacy law still prioritizes technical compliance over meaningful disclosure when demanding notice. When there is a data breach and companies must inform you that your data has been compromised, they can tell you via a letter mixed in with your regular junk mail. You might throw it away without reading it.

Even if notice were provided in the form of a pop-up box, we are conditioned to thoughtlessly click away. For example, if you go to a popular website hosted in the United Kingdom or another European country, you're likely to see a pop-up ad that reads something like "By using our service you agree that we and our partners may use cookies for personalisation and other purposes." The first time you see this, you might read it. You might even click on the hyperlink that leads to the full, dense cookies policy. But after a while, these sorts of pop-ups fail to be meaningful.[33]

I don't mean to imply that privacy policies are not useful. They can be effective accountability mechanisms that force companies to audit their data troves, assess risk, and implement safeguards.[34] They can provide meaningful transparency and regulatory hooks where none previously existed. In this sense, the longer the privacy statement, the better.[35] They're just not very good at notifying users. The central conceit of the *do not lie* ethic is to empower people to interact with others with full knowledge of what they are getting into. But because privacy law has failed to take design seriously, people are regularly confused, deceived, and manipulated in information relationships.

Rule 3: Do Not Harm

Privacy law looks for concrete harm. Those bringing a claim against allegedly negligent data collectors must prove some kind of (usually financial) harm that has resulted from the company's poor data practices. An unfair act or practice under the Federal Trade Commission Act is one that "causes or is likely to cause substantial injury to consumers which is not reasonably avoidable by consumers themselves and not outweighed by countervailing benefits to consumers or to competition."[36] The U.S. Supreme Court opinion in *Spokeo Inc. v. Robins* held that only "concrete" privacy injuries can be legally cognizable (though what constitutes a "concrete" injury remains an open question).[37] The EU General Data Protection Regulation provides remedies for those who have "suffered damage as a result of an unlawful processing operation."[38]

The problem is that many modern privacy problems are not concentrated, outrageous, or concrete enough to be considered the kind of "harm" required to invoke a particular legal remedy. The disclosure and intrusion torts require conduct that is "highly offensive to a reasonable person." People whose information has been hacked usually must demonstrate some kind of financial or even physical harm to recover, and doing so is very difficult; most data breach lawsuits are dismissed for failure to demonstrate harm.[39] Surveillance victims often have to prove some kind of adverse effect from being watched. In *Clapper v. Amnesty International,* the U.S. Supreme Court denied standing to plaintiffs who feared the government was monitoring them and who spent money on measures to avoid the surveillance.[40] The court held that in order to sustain a claim the plaintiffs needed more than mere speculation that they were under governmental surveillance. According to the court, "allegations about possible future injury are not sufficient" to establish injury.

There are many good reasons to demand a showing of harm from those who claim their privacy has been violated. Emotional harms are difficult to demonstrate, and courts fear that some people might exaggerate or just make them up. People might be able to recover for trivial or fake privacy violations. If you open the floodgates too much, courts and administrative agencies would drown in complaints. So courts have turned the harm dial up to 11 to ensure that only the most realized or, in the words of Daniel Solove and Danielle Citron, only the most "visceral and vested" privacy complaints are heard.[41]

This is a shame. It is true that data harms are often remote, diffuse, risk oriented, or difficult to ascertain. But they are real. Yet the law is reluctant to recognize the adverse effects from data breaches that do not immediately result in identity theft or financial harm, or indiscreet disclosures that are already known by some but not all, as was the case with Bobbi Duncan.

Some adverse effects from lost privacy stem from the inability to negotiate boundaries, trust others, and asses risk rather than some innate financial or extreme emotional harm. When we lose privacy we are forced to watch our back, cover our tracks, and self-censor. Collectively, these burdens can be significant. When the law fails to recognize privacy harms, it saddles the victims with the full burden of protecting themselves, recovering from breaches, and preventing future harms from past breaches. As the harms aggregate, the costs to victims compound. Meanwhile, those who cause privacy harm have little incentive to change their behavior or invest in protections for data subjects because the law ignores the harm.[42]

Harm thresholds in privacy law often result in ill-fitting theories of harm. When privacy is violated, we inevitably sense that there is a problem but cannot easily articulate a clear, cognizable, and individualized injury. This dissonance between actual privacy harms and those addressed in the law paints us into a corner. To describe the harms we're experiencing, we rely on words like *creepy* that sound compelling at first but crumble under the law's scrutiny (as there is no remedy for creepiness).[43]

The U.S. privacy torts' limited conceptualization of harm (or wrongful conduct that would virtually guarantee harm) makes them a difficult fit for most modern privacy problems. The tort of appropriation was not designed to protect against the sale of personal information. The tort occurs when one "appropriates to his own use or benefit the name or likeness of another."[44] Other privacy torts are also of little applicability. The tort of public disclosure of private facts, for example, creates a cause of action when one makes public through widespread disclosure "a matter concerning the private life of another" in a way that "(a) would be highly offensive to a reasonable person, and (b) is not of legitimate concern to the public."[45] Because many uses of data by companies do not involve widespread disclosure and do not involve data that would be highly offensive if disclosed, the tort is often of little use. As a result, few cases involving the privacy torts are brought in situations involving problems with the industrial collection and use of personal data. While tort law recognizes the harm from data collection and breach of trust in limited contexts, it has been remarkably reluctant to fully develop these theories of harm for the modern, mediated world.[46]

Harm is rightfully a central concern in privacy law. We just need to take a broader view of the harm we want to protect against and consider different approaches to mitigating it. Traditional harm thresholds that focus on physical damage, mental anguish, and pecuniary loss fail to capture many of the reasons humans value privacy in the first place. Yet harm remains a key gatekeeper for private action. One way to balance these concerns would be to increase scrutiny of the instrumentalities of privacy harm and focus on ex ante strategies designed to minimize or mitigate the harm before it happens. Enter design.

The Case for Privacy's Blueprint

To address privacy law's design gap, we need a plan. To begin, self-regulation alone is not going to cut it. There are simply too many incentives for companies to design consumer technologies in ways that are adversarial to our modern privacy values. Additionally, the time to act on design is now, before lock-in effects make changing entrenched bad design more difficult. Finally, focusing on design has distinct advantages over focusing on actors' collection, use, or disclosure of information. For example, design protections are often modest and more politically palatable than burdensome restrictions on the collection and use of valuable data. A blueprint for privacy law can better prevent harms from occurring in the first place because it is an ex ante regulator bearing on everyone who uses and is subject to the effects of a technology. Finally, taking design more seriously in privacy law and policy can relieve the need for other, more restrictive privacy laws that threaten free speech and autonomy.

Self-Regulation Alone Is Not Enough

A few years ago, if you walked into Facebook's headquarters in Menlo Park, California, you would see posters on the walls in a large font: "MOVE FAST AND BREAK THINGS." Facebook has since changed its mantra, but these words still serve as the operating ethos for much of Silicon Valley: innovate at all costs. This mentality has problems. Because technologies don't exist in a vacuum, sometimes the things that get broken when companies accelerate the innovation loop are people. And some companies have a bigger tolerance for the damage than others.

One of the principal objections I've heard to a design agenda for privacy law is that companies already do a good job policing themselves, so the law shouldn't micromanage design. Many argue that there are already robust self-regulatory efforts in place, like the Privacy by Design movement (though its originator, Ann Cavoukian, has long advocated for robust privacy laws). There is a wealth of literature dedicated to getting privacy and security design right.[47] Self-regulation advocates often argue it is laughable to think that the government knows more about how technologies should be built than companies completely dedicated to building things that will be attractive to consumers. Industry efforts are indeed essential for good privacy design, but they are not sufficient.

As I will discuss below, industry design standards and the supporting academic literature on good privacy design are indispensable to keep regulatory efforts grounded in reality. Cavoukian's Privacy by Design movement, Batya Friedman's work on value sensitive design, Lorrie Cranor's work on effective notice, and other similar approaches have harnessed the wisdom of engineers, attorneys, technologists, executives, data scientists, and graphic and user interface and user experience designers to provide guidance that is both practical and useful. Any company dedicated to good privacy design that claims it cannot find good direction is either disingenuous or has not searched very hard. Companies must desire and commit to do right by people's privacy through design. Without such dedication, Privacy's Blueprint would devolve into a meaningless exercise in technical compliance undermined by practical loopholes.

But industry efforts by themselves are not enough. Companies have powerful (if conflicting) incentives to exploit design to their advantage with minimal risk. Data is fuel for industry, and good design might inhibit what is collected and how it can be used. Manipulative and leaky design can net companies more data. Add to the mix the fact that pernicious design is difficult for people to recognize—it is often opaque and sometimes completely invisible. This is a recipe for exploitation.

Bad design can obscure privacy violations. Chris Hoofnagle has chronicled how data brokers attempted to design tools to hide privacy violations from consumers, noting that "after California prohibited retailers from asking customers their home addresses during credit card transactions, data brokers created tools that allowed retailers to infer this same information by merely asking for a telephone number. When requesting the phone number was prohibited, data brokers encouraged retailers to collect the ZIP code, which also could be used to identify the customer's home address." This cat-and-mouse game is common because companies that collection personal information often, in the words of one data broker, want to avoid "losing customers who feel that you're invading their privacy." Hoofnagle argues that "businesses say that what consumers do matters more than what consumers say about privacy. Yet, even where consumers seek privacy or choose not to disclose data, businesses use systems to undo their efforts to protect personal information."[48]

Industry has a long history of avoiding architectural regulations by blaming the user rather than the design of a technology. Take the public debate about car safety in the 1950s and 1960s, a focus of Hoofnagle's book on the U.S. Federal Trade Commission and privacy. Fearful about the impact of safety design requirements, the automobile industry "tried to focus public policy on the driver—the 'nut behind the wheel' instead of making major investments in car safety."[49] Massive numbers of people were behind the wheels of cars, yet safe automobile design was not a top priority.

Today things are different. The fatality rate per one hundred million miles traveled today is only 1.1, versus 5.5 in 1966. What happened? According to Hoofnagle, a "revolution in thinking about safety occurred. Cars are equipped with seat belts, air bags, and, importantly, accident avoidance technology such as automatic traction control." Some of this is attributable to better traffic safety enforcement, drunk driving laws, and graduated licensing. People must, of course, drive reasonably. But, as Hoofnagle writes, "the conversation no longer ends by blaming the 'nut behind the wheel.' Hundreds of thousands of Americans are alive today because public policy has focused on the structure and safety of the automobile instead of just blaming the driver."[50] And this shift is at least partially due to the lawsuits, regulations, and fines—that is, rules and enforcement—that motivated manufactures to adopt safer designs.

The way automobile companies blamed the driver is echoed by technology companies that leverage the illusion of control to blame technology users. "After all," some companies argue, "You did click 'I agree,' right? What else are we supposed to think other than you agree to our information collection practices? We spelled it out for you."

But consumers are poorly situated to discover and hold companies accountable for many kinds of harmful design. When you download a mobile application from Apple's App Store, do you really have any idea whether the app is providing reasonable data security or whether the user interface is specifically designed to manipulate you into revealing more than you otherwise would? Would you be able to think of alternative privacy-friendly designs you would rather see? While people might be able to remain vigilant with respect to one mobile app, we cannot keep it up for every technology we come across. Most privacy design problems are not apparent, so to discover them would take great time, effort, and concentration. We all have obligations and pursuits beyond protecting our privacy.

I research issues like these for a living (and for fun!), and yet often find myself glossing over problematic design choices in my day-to-day use of technologies. I care about these issues and try to be conscientious about what I disclose. Yet the last time I was asked to update my phone's operating system, I could not click "I agree to the Terms of Use" fast enough. These agreements are regularly over fifty pages long![51] When companies rely upon dense, boilerplate legalese to serve as "consent" for privacy-invasive practices, they are insulting our time, resources, and autonomy. No one's personal information should be extracted via sleight of hand under the auspices of a well-functioning market.

Although many major technology companies have publicly committed to privacy-sensitive technologies and practices, the digital ecosystem is large and diverse. Companies have widely divergent incentives to self-regulate. Large companies plan far into the future and are reliant upon consumer goodwill for long-term sustainability. But smaller start-ups may be incentivized to collect as much data as possible by tweaking designs to engage in what Neil Richards and I call a kind of digital strip mining. Smaller unscrupulous companies can use legitimate, popular platforms like app marketplaces and artificial intelligence technology to try to exploit people for short-term gain. For example, in October 2015 Apple removed 250 apps from its store after it discovered that a widely used advertising network was using the apps to siphon off private information such as account names, user IDs, and email addresses in breach of Apple's policies.[52] Recall from Chapter 1 the flashlight app that collected geolocation data simply because it could. Even popular apps like Angry Birds and Words with Friends receive low marks from privacy watchdogs for intrusive design aimed at monitoring and obtaining data.[53]

Even established and widely trusted companies often mess up and unwisely err on the side of designing for data collection. Computer maker Lenovo has been criticized for preloading malware that creates a security vulnerability and hidden surveillance software ("hiddenware") that some say pushes the boundary of trust.[54] Google's infamous Buzz software allowed other people to see the users' most frequently emailed contacts.[55] The incentives to collect as much information as possible align with the ability to use design to extract personal information with little or no resistance.

Finally, an exclusive self-regulatory approach to privacy design is not the best way to generate trust between data subjects and data collectors. As I will discuss in Chapter 3, trust is at the heart of technology and privacy. Without trust, humans cannot and will not use technology to flourish. Self-regulatory efforts can only do so much to build trust. Users will feel safer knowing that companies' promises are backed up by legal rules.

Self-regulation is an important part of the privacy puzzle, but industry should not be left to its own devices. Of course, some interventions are more important than others, but a completely hands-off approach to design will leave us all at risk. Instead, policy makers should embrace a coregulatory approach. They should leverage the wisdom of industry, advocates, and academics to create a blueprint of boundaries and goals that will keep privacy design as liberated as possible while still protecting people.

Lock-In Effects Make a Blueprint Urgent

Decisions are being made now that will impact our privacy long into the future, and this makes the need for a privacy design blueprint urgent. Once the basic designs of information technologies are set, we are stuck with them for a while. This phenomenon is sometimes called a lock-in effect or path dependency. Lock-in happens when barriers to change cause the cost of altering design to outweigh the benefits of modification. For example, it is very difficult to change a technology that many other technologies rely upon to operate, like the transmission control protocol / Internet protocol that makes Internet traffic possible. We see lock-in effects everywhere. The next time you're talking to a designer or engineer, try proposing that we change the QWERTY keyboard layout, the voltage of the U.S. power grid, or the fact that all of our power lines are above ground. Then wait for them to stop laughing. None of these designs are optimal anymore, but it would be nearly impossible to change them.

Lock-in effects for privacy design are worrisome for two reasons. First, individual designers have disproportionate power to dictate the long-term implications of technologies. Jaron Lanier notes, "It takes only a tiny group of engineers to create technology that can shape the entire future of human experience with incredible speed. Therefore, crucial arguments about the human relationship with technology should take place between developers and users before such direct manipulations are designed." The law takes particular interest in concentrations of power, and often acts to mitigate related risk in areas involving civil rights, consumer protection, intellectual property, and antitrust. We should care about individual decisions that can affect large groups of people. Lanier adds, "The fateful, unnerving aspect of information technology is that a particular design will occasionally happen to fill a niche and, once implemented, turn out to be unalterable."[56]

Second, lock-in effects are worrisome because they linger even if the design choice is suboptimal or could be improved upon for privacy purposes. Think of all the design choices that impact our privacy that we are basically stuck with now. When the Internet was in its infancy, the domain name system replaced Internet protocol addresses as the functional phone numbers of the Internet, which has been incredibly helpful because it allows people to easily memorize a simple uniform resource locator (URL) like www.WebMD.com instead of 208.93.170.15. But domain names and their associated URLs reveal things about us, like the types of websites we like, our search terms, and the specific kind of pages we read. All smartphones and tablets have cameras and GPS capability. E-book reader software has advanced surveillance tools to provide detailed feedback about our reading habits to vendors and publishers. The third-party ad targeting network, which relies upon personal information and sometimes delivers malware to people's computers, is now the built-in revenue model for huge chunks of the Internet ecosystem. Ethan Zuckerman has called advertising the "original sin of the Internet";[57] he is optimistic that a new revenue model will emerge, but the lock-in effects will be difficult to overcome.

Lock-in effects have plagued the Internet since its inception. Dave Farber, referred to as the Grandfather of the Internet because of his ground-breaking work in distributed computing and his mentorship of those who would build the Internet, has suggested that the design of the Internet is fundamentally insecure, but we're largely stuck with it: "The network was not built to be secure," he notes. "You have to remember the Internet was an experiment. It was hard enough building it without worrying about security. We knew there were some serious flaws, early on. But it's like any other system: once you lay the groundwork there are very few opportunities to change it."[58]

Lock-in effects are exacerbated by the lack of diversity in the tech community. Most of the technologies people use every day were largely designed by white men.[59] When only one perspective gets embedded in design, we are all impoverished. Our technologies glitch and struggle to work for everyone, like the facial recognition technology that rejected a man of Asian descent's passport photo because it mistakenly interpreted his eyes as closed.[60] A more diverse group of designers, executives, and policy makers is necessary to ensure that the full range of perspectives is brought to bear on how technologies are created and used.

Yet there is still hope for other technologies. Important privacy protections can still be built into automated cars. We do not have to connect every single device, from our dolls and diapers to our refrigerators and baby monitors, to the Internet. Biometrics like thumbprint readers and facial recognition technologies have not yet become the authentication method of choice (though that's changing quickly). Even existing technologies like user interfaces can be improved. If we act wisely and with purpose, we can ensure that the design of these technologies, which we will be stuck with for a while, is sound.

Design Protections Can Be Modest (And That's a Good Thing)

Let's get this out of the way right now: design is no panacea. Structural constraints often only mitigate harmful behavior without preventing it. For example, Snapchat's modification of its application programming interface to prevent third-party apps will not completely prevent people from saving Snaps. People can still capture images through their phone's screenshot function or by using another camera. But without third-party apps, saving Snaps becomes harder to scale because it is dispersed and, in the aggregate, labor intensive.

In this way design can act as a sort of modest privacy protection. The value of such protections is often lost on lawmakers and advocates for both technological freedom and privacy. Privacy advocates sometimes find relatively weak or incomplete privacy protections to be "watered down," while critics of privacy regulations point to the failure of complete protection as evidence that a particular law is unjustified. For example, many criticized California's SB 568, known as the "Online Eraser" law. Among other things, this 2015 law gives residents under the age of eighteen a limited right to delete personal information that they, as registered users of sites and networks, post online or on a mobile app. One effect of the law is to encourage social media companies to ensure a "delete" button for juveniles in California.[61] The law acted as a type of indirect design regulation because it established a minimal requirement for online social technologies.

SB 568 was criticized by some for being overprotective because they did not see social media posts shared with others as implicating privacy. Advocates of commercial and technological innovation argued that the law wasn't effective enough to justify its existence. Some privacy advocates criticized the law as too limited to protect teenagers because of exceptions like excluding reposts by others from protection. By failing to extend the right of deletion to third parties posting about minors, many kinds of harmful posts (like gossip and harassment) fall outside the law's scope. Damned if you do; damned if you don't.

This kind of dual criticism is often present in modern privacy debates. The result is that the value of modest privacy protections for socially shared information is often overlooked. The limitations in SB 568 represent deference to free speech principles while giving users the option of erasing heaps of problematic disclosures that no one found interesting enough to share.

The marginalization of perceived "weak" protections for socially shared information is misguided. Criticisms of such protections are often based on a misperception that it is futile or unnecessary to protect information that is shared with other people. But sharing information within trusted relationships or with little to no risk of harm is not the same thing as broadcasting it to everyone on purpose. Lawmakers should focus more on the middle ground between intimate secrets and our most widely broadcast selves.

Modest and incremental privacy protections might be one of the most effective ways to protect semiprivate information while balancing competing values like free speech, innovation, transparency, and security. Privacy cannot coexist with other conflicting values if we attempt to provide absolute protection at all times. In many contexts, modest protections might fit better in larger legal regimes. For example, the EU's so-called Right to Be Forgotten originally required only de-indexing information from search engines, not complete takedowns on the part of the original content host. As a result, websites remained accessible but not searchable—a relative balance of free speech and privacy interests.

The cumulative effect of modest protections can be quite robust. The digital age requires a more granular, diverse, and contextual conceptualization of privacy. Modest design protections can fulfill this need by filling out the spectrum of available remedies to reach information that has been disclosed to some, but not all.

Design Affects Everyone

While design is no cure-all, it can be more effective than laws, terms of service, or organizational policies that restrict activity. Design affects every user; not everyone reads the terms of use or is aware of privacy laws, but every single person that uses an app must reckon with the constraints of technology.

Privacy threats can come from parties that aren't bound or deterred by terms of use and privacy laws. For example, it would be nice if the rules, agreements, and guidelines designed to prevent online harassment were sufficient to curb improper behavior, right? Fat chance. Wrongdoers are not always so easily deterred. Sometimes these approaches are about as effective as attacking tanks with toothpicks. Consider hackers. Practically speaking, the Computer Fraud and Abuse Act, a broadly written anti-hacking statute in the United States, is probably not the most significant deterrent for malicious hackers. Rather, it is the rules and commercial motivations that compel good data security and minimization efforts—process and design—that protect us. Good data security, among other things, strategically increases the transaction costs associated with external hacking and insider snooping. Good data minimization procedures and tech specifications help ensure that there is comparatively little data to be compromised. In other words, design requirements can shore up the deficiencies of rules that only affect some of the relevant parties in a given context.

Scholars have argued for years that design is (or at least should be) an important part of privacy regimes because of its power to affect human behavior at scale. Julie Cohen argues that privacy as a shelter for the processes of play is dependent upon the structural dimensions of the physical space and networked architectures.[62] Mireille Hildebrandt argues for a "legal protection by design" that includes a democratic participation in the design of digital data-driven technologies that shape our lives and our rules for behavior.[63] In the 1990s Joel Reidenberg argued that fair data protection rules could be enforced through technical design mechanisms that coexist with privacy policy. "Technological capabilities and system design choices impose rules on participants," he observed. "The creation and implementation of information policy are embedded in network designs and standards as well as in system configurations. Even user preferences and technical choices create overarching, local default rules."[64] Reidenberg proposed that "in essence, the set of rules for information flows imposed by technology and communication networks form a 'Lex Informatica' that policymakers must understand, consciously recognize, and encourage."[65]

Lawrence Lessig popularized this notion that "code is law" in the late 1990s, arguing that such architecture as software code is a regulatory force on people that is similar to laws, norms, and the market.[66] Lessig noted that "code presents the greatest threat to liberal or libertarian ideals, as well as their greatest promise. We can build, or architect, or code cyberspace to protect values we believe are fundamental, or we can build, or architect, or code cyberspace to allow those values to disappear. There is no middle ground. There is no choice that does not include some kind of *building*."[67] In the chapter on privacy in his influential book *Code and Other Laws of Cyberspace*, Lessig argued in favor of technologies as a way to provide choices about how our information is used and shared, limit information collection, and secure our data—all notions captured by the FIPs.

Design Is Proactive, Not Reactive

Good design protects against privacy harms before they even happen. Compare this to privacy law's current focus on conduct and harm. By definition, people have to wait until they have actually suffered before they can seek redress. If given the choice, we should seek to keep harms from happening at all. Even when relief is available to victims, it cannot make them "whole." The law strives to get as close as it can through money damages and injunctions, but most people who suffer harm would likely prefer to avoid the injury in the first place.

Privacy harms regularly go unaddressed even when explicitly prohibited. There is a litany of reasons why, not the least of which are threshold harm requirements and wrongdoers that cannot be located or reached through U.S. law. Sometimes privacy harms may go undetected even by their victims, but that doesn't mean the victims aren't being harmed. Other times harms like identity theft can be so remote that they can't be connected to the breach. All of this combines to create an environment where "reactive" laws focused on conduct and harm do not function well enough as deterrents. People and companies are often willing to accept the risk of pushing the boundaries of what they are allowed to collect and share, because a huge chunk of dubious activity is likely to go legally unchallenged.

Adding a proactive protection like design to privacy law will help fill these gaps. Design-based protections can require companies to protect against reasonably anticipated third-party harms. Technology users will not have to worry as much about hiring an attorney or suffering only to receive a paltry recovery, because they will not become victims. Design cannot do everything, but it can dissuade would-be wrongdoers if the transaction cost is high enough.

Design Relieves the Pressure from Conduct-Based Privacy Laws

Earlier in this chapter I discussed how privacy law was obsessed with conduct and harm, at the expense of more structural notions like design. One benefit of privacy law taking design more seriously is that it need not continue to contort itself to address privacy problems that do not fit into the traditional conduct / harm mold. By diversifying privacy law's approach, policy makers can let certain remedies and regimes address the problems they are best equipped for and let design pick up the slack.

For example, once design is taken seriously in privacy law, we can finally all admit to each other that the four U.S. privacy torts (intrusion, disclosure of private facts, misappropriation of name or likeness, and false light) are useful only in the most exceptional circumstances. Even better, maybe we can all agree that this is a good thing. We have asked so much of tort privacy in part because there was no alternative. When all you have is a hammer, everything looks like a nail. (Ironically, the privacy torts were created because there was nothing else in the law that would work to address these privacy problems). But the four privacy torts were problematic from the start. If allowed to roam free, the torts represent serious threats to free speech and autonomy. As Neil Richards, Diane Zimmerman, and others have argued, the four privacy torts have been rightfully curtailed in the interest of civil liberties, speech, commerce, and democracy.[68]

Not all privacy-relevant tort law should be curtailed, however. Torts like breach of confidentiality that look to promises and relationships of trust instead of privileging certain facts about someone in all contexts are not as developed as they should be. The tort of negligence is impressively flexible and capable of responding to certain design defects in technologies. As I'll discuss in Chapter 5, design can play an important role in tort law as a response to deceptive, abusive, and dangerous design. But generally, it is best if we keep the privacy-related torts from becoming the first line of defense.

Private causes of action for privacy violations should be exceptions to the general rule of compliance. The problem, of course, is that modern privacy harms are not exceptional; they're common. They are more incremental than many of the classic privacy harms such as Peeping Toms, to be sure. But modern privacy harms in the collection, use, and dissemination of personal information are consistent and frustratingly routine. Every day we have thousands of actions taken upon our personal information. Like a death from a thousand cuts, each one in isolation is probably not enough to raise the alarm; otherwise we would do little else but read privacy policies and sue companies all day. But collectively, these small incursions can overwhelm us.

By looking to design rules to help protect people's privacy, lawmakers could refocus their conduct-based rules on more clear-cut and justified restrictions on people's speech and conduct. The law could become more tolerant of human mistakes and errors in judgment, focusing instead on truly deceptive, abusive, and harmful acts. We would all have a little bit more breathing room to disclose, collect, and share information within the constraints of well-designed, protective media. This breathing room for information practices and human interaction motivated the free speech movement of the 1960s starting with *New York Times v. Sullivan* and is a key component of human flourishing. Scholars like Julie Cohen, Erving Goffman, Neil Richards, and many others have noted that we need space from scrutiny to experiment and make mistakes if we are to improve. Focusing on structure rather than individual action is one way to provide this space for everyone involved in the collection, use, and sharing of personal information.

We have tied ourselves into knots focusing on individual acts that violate privacy. (What did you *collect?* How did you *use* this data? Whom did you *share* it with?) We have hit diminishing returns with this approach. Instead, let us shift our focus so that we can accept the strengths and limitations of individualized and conduct-based privacy laws and leave the rest to design.

Finding the Right Balance for Design in Policy

At this point you may be thinking, "If design is so important, why has the law largely ignored it?" The answer is not just the myth of neutral technologies. Courts and lawmakers are leery of going overboard. They feel that designers are in the best position to know what constitutes good design and if the courts and the law muck up the process with too many regulations, companies will produce fewer or inferior products. There is some wisdom in this mind-set. But too much deference creates an environment where industry encourages designers to abuse their expertise and inside knowledge by presenting industry's preferred outcomes as ones demanded by the technology.

The central challenge for privacy design policy is finding the sweet spot between under- and overregulation. Too few boundaries would fail to prevent technologies meant to abuse, betray, and exploit people. Too many boundaries might unduly impede technological progress, stifle commerce, and wrongfully curtail individual autonomy. If we fail to get the balance right, we will be worse off. For example, Caller ID and Facebook's news feed were once both criticized as privacy invasive, yet now they are considered indispensable features of phones and social media. Burdensome design regulations can prohibit new entrants to the market and force existing tech companies out of business.

There's good reason to be cautious of overzealous regulation of the design of technologies. Civil rights organizations focused on technology, like the Electronic Frontier Foundation (EFF), have long pushed back against the overregulation of technology and its uses to ensure freedom and access to developing technologies. Advocates for innovation have argued against adopting the "precautionary principle" in regulating technology, the belief that new innovations should be curtailed or disallowed until their developers can prove that the technology will not harm people. Instead, innovation advocates sometimes argue in favor of "permissionless innovation," which is the notion that "experimentation with new technologies and business models should generally be permitted by default."[69] One reading of this concept is that, in general, we should not use worst-case scenarios to guide public policy. Progress requires that we tolerate some risk of harm. Designers need to be able to experiment if they are to determine the best path forward, and this requires learning from mistakes and failures. If the law is completely intolerant of risk, we will be very reluctant to try anything new. Yet too often industry wants the freedom to experiment on the public without accepting the responsibility for the harm they cause.[70] Therefore, while it is important to design rules that are tolerant of some risk taking, the burden of that risk and subsequent failure should be better allocated to those at fault.

Bad design laws can be adverse to human values. In Chapter 7 we will explore the U.S. government's push to compel technology companies and encryption designers to create back doors that would allow the government to bypass encryption. In addition to being logistically unworkable, some of these requests would cripple the very infrastructure people rely upon for safe, protected communications every day. The balance between safety and privacy is quite difficult to achieve, but we can do better than compromising critical security for arguably speculative gains.

Any privacy design agenda should adequately ensure the freedom for companies to take reasonable risks, learn from mistakes, and account for other regulatory pressures like social norms and market forces. A blueprint should also provide a structure to identify, balance, and advance competing values. A clunky, broken piece of technology that offers robust privacy protections is worthless if no one is going to use it or no one can afford it. If there is a way to make a technology useful and also safe and sustainable, we should encourage it. A privacy-protective technology is similarly compromised if it dramatically erodes other goals like expression or property. Designers must have the freedom to balance many values.

A design agenda should also have a broad view of the risks and relevant actors. Obvious bad actors are a justifiable and common target of privacy law: the jealous ex-boyfriend who publishes nonconsensual pornography online, the peeper using a drone to spy on your house, the data broker who sells your information to anyone who asks, or the hacker who downloads private photos from your cloud storage. To be sure, these actors are an important piece of the puzzle. But in addition to malicious spies, spiteful Internet trolls, and morally bankrupt organizations, there are well-intentioned people and generally upstanding companies who accidentally jeopardize the privacy of others in both dramatic and incremental ways. Privacy law should find the appropriate way to handle accidental as well as malicious threats to privacy. While salacious exposures grab all the headlines, the most common threat to our privacy happens innocuously, piece by piece. And nobody discloses more of your personal information than you do yourself. Current privacy law can be unforgiving about the fact that we are regularly our own worst enemy even in the best of circumstances.

None of this happens in a vacuum. It happens in context: people interact through mediated environments and use technologies designed to extract, use, and share personal information. Sometimes these technologies are great. In those cases, lawmakers and courts might want to focus on conduct rather than design. For example, we should not ban all cameras just because they can be used to capture private moments. Yet some technologies, like undetectable spyware, do more harm than good.

Perhaps the strongest argument in the case for Privacy's Blueprint is that we're already halfway there. If policy makers decide to take design seriously, they will not have to reinvent the wheel or rely upon their own expertise. There is a robust and sustainable discipline dedicated to sound privacy design. It would be a mistake to overlook the wisdom of those already committed to leveraging technological design to protect our privacy.

Additionally, the law has long regulated various aspects of the design of technologies. The lessons learned from design regulation in other areas inform the design blueprint proposed in this book.

The Limits of Design

Although I'm making a case for a design agenda for privacy law, the concept of design and the blueprint I propose in Part II is not meant to cover every aspect of privacy law. The existing rules surrounding an individual or organization's gossip, data, and surveillance practices must still be nurtured for a sustainable society. Fines and liability for snooping, sharing, storing, and sorting are as important as ever. New efforts like Europe's new General Data Protection Regulation and increased enforcement by the U.S. FTC and state attorneys general largely compliment and reinforce the policy reforms I am proposing in this book. My critique of privacy rules in this book is largely limited to how they contribute to the design gap. For example, the laws that look to consent to justify data practices and the use of surveillance technologies allow design forces to frustrate the goals of these laws. By expanding the focus of privacy law, the entire system can better function.

Also, many of the policy reforms I suggest in this book must coexist alongside other, sometimes competing interests, such as national security and free speech. For example, the First Amendment to the United States Constitution has established a robust tradition of free speech. Other countries with strong privacy laws also recognize limits on speech encroachments. Many of these disputes, which often involve difficult questions involving the relationship between computer code and speech and longstanding debates about the extent of permissible interference, are beyond the scope of this book. However, I recognize the cost and limits of privacy law reform in a system that must balance multiple goals.

A History of Design Regulation in the Shadow
of the Electronic Frontier

On February 8, 1996, exactly twenty years ago to the day I typed these words, a founder of the EFF, John Perry Barlow, published his famous missive, "A Declaration of the Independence of Cyberspace." His address, which has inspired and captured the imagination of millions interested in a better, more just society, begins with the elegant introduction, "Governments of the Industrial World, you weary giants of flesh and steel, I come from Cyberspace, the new home of Mind. On behalf of the future, I ask you of the past to leave us alone. You are not welcome among us. You have no sovereignty where we gather."[71]

Perry's declaration was a response to the passage of the Telecommunications Act of 1996, which included the misguided and largely unconstitutional Communications Decency Act (CDA), which was designed to get rid of "obscene and indecent material" (e.g., nudity) from the Internet.[72] Let's just say the law was . . . overambitious. In a landmark First Amendment case, the Supreme Court struck down the CDA, except for one critical provision making intermediaries (like Facebook and YouTube) immune from liability for content posted by third parties. The Court's opinion in *Reno v. ACLU* ushered in a "hands-off" approach to the design of information technologies that has become entrenched.

The Supreme Court, and nearly every other governmental body, recognized the revolutionary nature of the Internet. With good reason, they sought to regulate the design of the Internet as little as possible to ensure that it was able to reach its potential. The fear was that when the Internet was new, it was far too fragile to regulate; if government meddled with it, it would break. This strategy mainly paid off, and the Internet is now an indispensable part of society.

But the Internet and most technologies that use it are no longer babies. Even genuinely new technologies are more resilient and robust than some give them credit for. Yet the notion that any kind of government intervention will break technologies persists. In many ways, it is good that laws do not monkey with the design of information technologies. But we should dispense with the idea that design-related laws are anathema to innovation and human flourishing. Design has been at the heart of many legal regimes for quite some time.

Since the 1960s the law of products liability has prohibited the manufacture and design of unreasonably dangerous goods. There have been scores of cases by manufacturers of cars, drugs, cigarettes, sports equipment, industrial machines, and dangerous materials like asbestos. Under contract, negligence, and strict liability theories, companies have been held liable for unreasonably dangerous design, inadequate instructions or warnings, breach of implied warranty of fitness for a particular purpose, and negligent enablement of harm.[73]

Regulatory agencies like the Food and Drug Administration and the Federal Aviation Administration have robust regimes that guide the design of medical devices and planes, respectively.[74] The National Highway Traffic Safety Administration ensures that our cars are designed safely.[75] Federal authorities have created many rules regarding the design of routers, signal boosters, antennas, phones, and many other kinds of communication equipment.[76] The design of voting machines is also regulated.[77] As I will note many times in this book, the Federal Trade Commission and European Data Protection Authorities have begun to wade into the design waters in the areas of notice and data security, setting boundaries on the design of user interfaces, the configuration of surveillance technologies, and requirements for protective systems that process and store personal information.

Specific, targeted statutes also regulate the design of structures and objects—even those associated with constitutional rights. For example, the Undetectable Firearms Act requires enough metal in a firearm to trigger metal detectors.[78] Each state has extensive building codes that dictate certain design requirements and restrictions.[79] These laws are just a fraction of the regulatory schemes that address design in some way.

Scholars have proposed how the law might embrace design to foster values and prevent harm.[80] For example, Neal Katyal has suggested using architecture as crime control. He argues that there are several ways to leverage the very design and structure of buildings to help minimize crime and suggests strengthening building codes and national fire prevention standards, requiring housing projects to promote security, and harmonizing neighborhoods by incorporating a focus on crime prevention. Katyal argues, "Building public housing that incorporates crime prevention principles will help the effort to reduce other social ills and can be done at costs equivalent to or less than those for existing projects."[81] My proposal in this book is in the same spirit as Katyal's proposal: the law should leverage design for individual and social good.

The case for Privacy's Blueprint is that our current approach relies too much upon how data is collected and used, a false idea of user control, and the search for tangible harms. Self-regulation of design is not working.

Because data is so valuable and easy to extract in the right context, the incentives for privacy-corrosive design put us too much at risk. While we do not need a complete overhaul of privacy law, we do need a more principled approach to better outline the boundaries of privacy-related design. Lawmakers could look to the extensive literature on sound privacy design for guidance. They can borrow approaches from existing regimes and rights that shape the design of objects and structures. We just need to put it all together. In Part II, I propose a theory of privacy law and design to help constitute a blueprint for policy makers, industry, and society.

PART TWO

A DESIGN AGENDA FOR PRIVACY LAW

3

Privacy Values in Design

THUS FAR I HAVE argued that design is critical for privacy and the law should take it more seriously. But lawmakers and courts should not confront privacy-relevant design without a plan. A haphazard approach to design would leave us all worse off. In this part of the book, I develop Privacy's Blueprint—a principled way for privacy law to approach design. The blueprint is designed to mitigate the vulnerabilities created by our reliance on technology.

We are all vulnerable. Spyware can catch our most intimate disclosures without our knowledge. The Internet of Things gives malicious actors many new paths to accessing sensitive information and surveilling us in our homes. Web pages and mobile applications can trick us and manufacture more personal disclosure than we realize or are comfortable with. Search engines and aggregation tools can expose previously hidden information without our knowledge. Privacy law should help ensure that our vulnerabilities and reliance are not exploited through technological design.

We also depend upon technology to protect our privacy. Encryption, privacy settings, authentication schemes, and even the aesthetics and layout of apps and websites all help us negotiate boundaries when interacting with people and assessing the risk of any particular disclosure of personal information or act that exposes us to others. But because of industry business models, companies often have little or no incentive to develop privacy-protective designs. To help counteract privacy-corrosive design, privacy law should articulate and support goals and boundaries for the design of privacy-sensitive technologies.

My proposal for Privacy's Blueprint proceeds in three steps: identifying the foundational privacy-related *values* affected by design, articulating basic *boundaries* to further those values, and plotting the specific legal *tools* to enforce those standards. In this chapter, I articulate the values that lawmakers and courts should focus on when shaping design through privacy law. A theory of privacy law and design is only as good as the values it seeks to preserve; otherwise we are just shooting blind. Through signals and constraints, design shapes our ability to develop relationships of trust and our ability to become or remain obscure to others. As a result, I argue that privacy law should nurture the values of trust, obscurity, and autonomy through design.

Before we begin, I must reiterate that, of course, there are some places technological design does not reach. Life is not always mediated. Design might only be a bit player in certain contexts, like doctor-patient confidentiality or wrongful discrimination based on personal information. Privacy's Blueprint should focus on the values directly impacted by design and leave the rest to the robust patchwork already in place to address other privacy issues. We can identify the most important values in design by looking at its function: channeling choice and function through signals and the invisible application of transaction costs.

Privacy implicates a wide array of related values that design could support. For example, privacy helps us determine our identity, preserve our dignity, and avoid wrongful discrimination based on personal information. Technologies, in turn, could be designed to help us shape who we are or to protect us from discrimination. Batya Friedman and Peter Kahn have suggested that other values implicated by design include property, freedom from bias, calmness, and environmental sustainability.[1]

But there are three privacy values in design worth focusing: trust, obscurity, and autonomy. These three values can best fill privacy law's design gap and make it sustainable in a digital world. Focusing on these three values will also keep Privacy's Blueprint from being unfocused and so broad as to be useless as a guide. These three values in tandem can also help correct privacy law's two biggest blunders: its overreliance on the

concepts of control and secrecy. Privacy's Blueprint is an opportunity appropriately enable control at scale and move beyond the misconceptual-
ization of privacy as secrecy.

Trust over Control, Obscurity over Secrecy, and Autonomy for It All

Privacy law's first critical mistake was to overleverage the notion of control.[2] By doing so, design is allowed to take functional control away from
people by overwhelming them with structured choices. In theory, when
people have control, they can decide for themselves how to weigh the costs
and benefits of such collection, use, and disclosure. Yet "control" regimes
too often end up as less meaningful "consent" regimes—weak ones at that,
because they almost never enable the revocation of consent. Daniel Solove
refers to this approach to privacy regulation as "privacy self-management."
He writes, "Privacy self-management takes refuge in consent. It attempts
to be neutral about substance—whether certain forms of collecting, using,
or disclosing personal data are good or bad—and instead focuses on
whether people consent to various privacy practices. Consent legitimizes
nearly any form of collection, use, or disclosure of personal data."[3]

As I argued in Chapter 2, we should resist the tendency to wager everything on our ability to control how *all* of our personal information is collected, used, and shared. Our ability to make decisions and to gauge the
impact those decisions will have is finite. While control can serve the value
of *autonomy,* the two concepts are not synonymous. If we care about being
free from the interference of others, then design should not burden users
with so many practical controls that it overwhelms them. The much better
option is for lawmakers to focus on how the signals and transaction costs
generated by design help us *trust* other people and reinforce that trust by
making sure those who invite the trust of others keep their promises.
The best design prioritizes control where it is most important and useful
without becoming a burden.

Privacy law's second critical mistake was to wed itself to a binary notion
of privacy that categorizes information as either public or private. This notion has been described as "the public / private dichotomy."[4] Others refer to
it more bluntly as the idea that there is "no privacy in public" or no privacy

in information shared with third parties.[5] Solove described this idea as the "secrecy paradigm," an understanding of privacy based on total concealment of information from all others.[6] Under this conception, disclosed information is no longer concealed and thus no longer private. The problem with the secrecy paradigm is that it does not accommodate our modern reality, which allows us to and in fact depends upon discreetly sharing information. It also fails to recognize our innate desire for some kind of privacy in so-called public spaces. For example, people probably consider their struggles with things like incontinence or depression private matters even though they could be seen purchasing adult diapers or books about how to cope with mental illness in businesses that are open to the public.

In fact, notions of privacy exist along a spectrum of *obscurity*. To maintain relative privacy—or obscurity—we rely on the designs of our online and offline environments to make certain personal information more difficult to access. Instead of relying on dubious private/public categorizations, lawmakers should focus on transaction costs that can protect us from unwanted exposure by making us and our personal information hard or unlikely to be found or understood. Transaction costs can protect our privacy even when we are in public spaces or when personal information has been shared with others.

The values of trust, autonomy, and obscurity are all implicated when our choices and expectations are modulated by signals and transaction costs. Deceptive and manipulative signals frustrate our ability to trust others and our ability choose for ourselves what kind of protections we need to flourish. We rely upon transaction costs to ensure that we are able to conduct our lives within zones of obscurity. This obscurity gives us the necessary space to engage in play and experimentation, speak freely, and develop as human beings.[7] These three fundamental privacy values are also instrumental in fostering other values like dignity, identity, freedom, equality, and free speech. In other words, trust and obscurity are enabling values; as a result, they should be the primary focus of privacy law's approach to design as well. Autonomy also helps us achieve other values like self-fulfillment and realization but it also is intrinsically valuable. For many, autonomy is the animating value for all privacy concerns. For the design of information technologies, I will link autonomy closely to the development of and reliance upon relationships of trust and zones of obscurity. These values are at the heart of Privacy's Blueprint.

Trust

The privacy self-management approach entrenched in the law is broken because it basically asks users to shoulder all of the risk of disclosure. If industry, users, and the government are to create a fair and just information economy, we must do it together. We must be able to trust each other. Trust is a necessary component of social relationships, commerce, expression, governance, and basically any activity that involves other people. Trust is arguably our most important privacy value in the digital age. We are lost without it.

Consider online merchants like Amazon. Amazon knows your browsing, listening, and viewing habits, your shopping history, your credit card information, how to get in touch with you, and where you live. It gives you recommendations about which products you might like and shows you reviews from other Amazon users to help you make your shopping decisions. It is one of the most popular and powerful companies in the world due to the fact that people trust it with all of their personal information.

Imagine we were to wake up one morning and read an exposé on Amazon's recently discovered data failures. The article reveals that Amazon recklessly sold its users' video viewing history, credit card data, and shopping habits to dubious businesses that in turn passed the information along to the black market. On top of that, we learn that Amazon ranked all our search results based on how wealthy it thought we were. If Amazon thought users were rich, it would show them nice, expensive stuff. If it thought users were poor, it would show them the cheaper stuff first. But it didn't tell its users what was going on, so we had no idea our experiences were so different from one another. Then we learn that a sizable chunk of people who write reviews for products are actually Amazon employees who get small bonuses and extra vacation time for doing so. To top it all off, we learn that Amazon had foolishly stored all of its users' passwords in plain text (as opposed to using encryption and other protective measures), and they were accessed by hackers and are now being sold on the dark web.

We would probably feel quite betrayed. By giving Amazon so much personal information, we were vulnerable to it, and it failed to protect our trust. What's worse, let's say we find out that we were given "notice" of Amazon's data practices in the dense, hidden terms of use that no one reads, and we probably don't have any private cause of action under existing

privacy laws. Not good. To be clear, this is an entirely hypothetical scenario involving Amazon. But my hypothetical disclosures, data uses, and
breaches were all modeled on real risk and things that have actually happened (though not at Amazon).[8] This is the failure of privacy self-
management: it punishes you for trusting others.

Neil Richards and I have argued that modern privacy law is incomplete
because from its inception it has failed to account for the importance of
trust.[9] Instead, privacy law and norms have embraced a pessimistic proceduralism focused only on harm avoidance. Trust in information relationships is necessary for the digital economy to not only function but to
flourish. Acting together, privacy and trust can do more than avoid harm—
it can create value.[10] Trust and the value it creates can be nurtured through
the design of information technologies.

Trust is necessary for any technology to be adopted. The Computer Science and Telecommunications Board used the terms *trust* and *trustworthy*
to describe systems that were predictably correct, secure, reliable, safe, and
capable of survival.[11] Trustworthy technologies are the only path forward.
But the trust that is most relevant to Privacy's Blueprint is trust in other
people and companies. Richards and I have adopted the definition of *trust*
as the willingness to make oneself vulnerable to the actions of others.[12] Ari
Waldman, Dennis Hirsch, Kristen Martin, Katherine Strandburg, and
other scholars have also explored the critical importance of trust with respect to privacy.[13]

Trust is an essential component of healthy relationships and healthy
societies. Although different disciplines define trust in various ways, at
bottom, "trust is a state of mind that enables its possessor to be willing to
make herself vulnerable to another—that is, to rely on another despite a
positive risk that the other will act in a way that can harm the truster."[14]
Trust allows cooperation with other people in spite of the fact that exposing
ourselves enables others to harm us. In the context of information relationships, trust means the willingness to become vulnerable to a person or
organization by disclosing personal information.

People entrust information to others all the time. Just this past week,
you probably trusted your bank, retailers like Target, and tech companies like Google with your financial data, information about what you
purchased, and search queries, respectively. Doing so made you vulnerable to these institutions. Bank employees could leave your account

numbers on a laptop in an airport. Target might suffer a massive data breach. Google might turn your queries over to the government. There are many different possibilities for disclosure or injury or manipulation in such cases. Once you've trusted others with your personal information, you've lost control. You are exposed and at the mercy of those you have trusted.

Every disclosure of personal information in the modern age leaves the discloser vulnerable in some way, if only incrementally. As a result, every information relationship involves some degree of trust or willingness to become vulnerable. This is true even if that trust is not a conscious one.

The design of technologies sends us signals that shape our expectations of trust and risk calculations. Companies design technologies that will convince people to trust them. Sometimes that trust is misplaced, as with spyware that presented users with the fake Microsoft Windows registration screen (see Chapter 1). Every aspect of that software was meant to convince people to share information that would make them more vulnerable.

So how can the law further the value of trust through design? Richards and I have argued that the notion of trust can actually rejuvenate, contour, and expand upon the ossified FIPs.[15] Recall that he FIPs give us foundational concepts of privacy law, such as confidentiality, transparency, and security. Trust can add nuance and force to these concepts by reimagining them as discretion, honesty, and protection. We have also argued that loyalty, which is not a traditional fair information practice, is a foundational concept in privacy law. Those we entrust with our data have a duty to avoid unreasonable and dangerous self-dealing.

These four concepts—discretion, honesty, protection, and loyalty—can all guide design to further trust. They are not new; they are foundations of one of the most established legal concepts involving trust in relationships: the law of fiduciaries. The central goal of fiduciary law is to protect against the exploitation of a vulnerability created by trust in another. Jack Balkin, like Daniel Solove, has argued that the notion of fiduciaries is a great fit for modern information privacy problems.[16]

Generally, fiduciaries owe a duty of care and loyalty to those who place their trust in them. For example, your attorney must protect your confidences, your doctor must be reasonably competent and informed before treating you (and must also not disclose your medical history publicly), and your accountant must refrain from encouraging you to invest in businesses in a way that will increase her own wealth. In arguing for greater legal responsibilities for information fiduciaries, Jack Balkin and Jonathan Zittrain argue that information fiduciaries should have a duty to "look out for the interests of the people whose data businesses regularly harvest and profit from. At the very least, digital businesses may not act like con men—inducing trust in end users and then actively working against their interests." As an example they assert that "Google Maps shouldn't recommend a drive past an IHOP as the "best route" on your way to a meeting from an airport simply because IHOP gave it $20. And if Mark Zuckerberg supports the Democrat in a particular election, Facebook shouldn't be able to use its data analysis to remind its Democratic users that it's election day—while neglecting to remind, or actively discouraging, people it thinks will vote for Republicans."[17] These kinds of obligations are critical for trust. Let's review how each of the trust principles might serve as an underlying value to guide the design of technologies.

Discretion

Perhaps the most basic assumption people make when disclosing personal information is that the recipient will be discreet. Discretion, defined as "the quality of behaving or speaking in such a way as to avoid causing offence or revealing private information," is an implicit part of most information relationships.[18] It is also a key aspect of design. Indiscreet technologies erode trust.

However, established privacy laws are too focused on the concept of secrecy to adequately facilitate discretion. One of most established notions of a privacy violation is the idea that someone is going to reveal your secrets. The entrenched law of confidentiality protects against this. But confidentiality can be a restrictive way of talking about privacy and the revelation of information. In the U.S., the law of confidentiality is not very broad. Most people in information relationships are not confidants. People often need or want to share the information they receive, whether they are businesses and intermediaries or friends and acquaintances, yet don't want their disclosures to be widely known. Consider social media. Most disclosures on social network sites like Facebook, Instagram, and Twitter are not *confidential* in the classic sense of the word. Yet there is an expectation that they are less than "public"; that they will not be read by most people, just our friends or, perhaps our Facebook friends.[19]

Privacy settings provide signals to other users regarding our desire for discretion. When I adjust my privacy settings so that my posts are visible to "friends only," this is a signal to my friends that I want to limit who can see my posts. When Twitter users protect their accounts (like I do), the software disables the Retweet button, simultaneously introducing a transaction cost for further disseminating my posts as well as signaling to my followers that I value a certain amount of obscurity. While I protect my account largely to stay off search engines and avoid automated bots, I know many people who view my protected account as a request for discretion. They often ask permission to manually retweet posts from a protected account. Privacy settings are discretion-friendly—except when they're not. Recall the outing of Bobbi Duncan I described in the Introduction to this book: Facebook's privacy settings for groups were not designed to automatically match the level of discretion requested or desired by individual users, and this created a problem.

Folded into many versions of the FIPs is a notion of protecting against improper disclosure. This notion is a little more flexible and is more closely related to discretion. One way privacy law can take design more seriously is to look for technologies that use signals and transaction costs to create and communicate expectations of discretion and reinforce those expectations. I call these signals *discretion indicators*. Consider a "closed" group or page on a social media platform. In the case of *Pietrylo v. Hillstone Restaurant Group*, a federal court was asked to determine the privacy interest in information contained on a "closed" Myspace page.[20] Brian Pietrylo, a waiter at Houston's, a New Jersey restaurant, created a group for himself and his fellow employees to vent about their employer "without any outside eyes spying" on them.[21] Pietrylo stated on the group's page, "This group is entirely private, and can only be joined by invitation."

Pietrylo effectively restricted the group to users in possession of an invitation and a password-protected Myspace profile. Under pressure at a party one night, a Houston's hostess disclosed her password to her managers. Pietrylo was then fired for creating the group, which resulted in a lawsuit alleging that the managers violated the group's privacy. The court found that "Plaintiffs created an invitation-only internet discussion space. In this space, they had an expectation that only invited users would be able to read the discussion."[22] Ultimately a jury found that Houston's managers had violated the Stored Communications Act and the New Jersey Wire Tapping and Electronic Surveillance Act but did not support Pietrylo's claim for invasion of privacy.

Suppose the fired employees brought a claim against the hostess for breach of an implied obligation of confidentiality, or against the managers for inducement to breach confidentiality. Would the discretion indicators have supported the plaintiff's cause of action? The design of the group's site indicated that disclosures were made for a specific purpose: to vent "without any outside eyes spying" on the members of the group. The group also provided that its icon, which was the restaurant's trademarked logo, "would appear only on the Myspace profiles of those who were invited into the group and accepted the invitation."[23] The fact that the privacy settings were used to restrict access to the group also served as a discretion indicator. The need for discretion to further the purpose of the group would likely have been evident to most participating members. Given such design, it is at least arguable that participants were obligated to be discreet.

Recognizing design as a request or promise is just one way privacy law might nurture trust through discretion. Other ways, which will be discussed in Chapter 5, include developing industry standards for the design of discreet technologies and mandating design processes that ensure that technologies are built to be discreet and to honor the disclosure expectations of the parties.

Honesty

Deceptive technologies erode trust. One of the bedrock notions of privacy law is that companies should be transparent about their data collection, use, and disclosure practices so that individuals will be on notice of any potentially worrisome practices and can tailor their disclosures accordingly. Transparency is enshrined in the FIP known as the "openness principle," which provides that data collectors should have a general policy of openness about personal data practices. They should have a process for validating the existence, nature, and use of personal data in addition to the identity and usual residence of the data controller.

But if trust is to be kept, it is not sufficient to be merely "open" or "transparent." Trust in information relationships requires an affirmative obligation of honesty to correct misinterpretations and to actively dispel notions of mistaken trust. We must do more than our current regime, which procedurally serves transparency through "notice and choice" self-management.

Consider the Snapchat user interface discussed at the beginning of Chapter 1. The interface invited people to trust the software with sensitive photos. The timer and ghost designs were built to give the impression that such disclosure was safe. This was not completely honest design; according to the Federal Trade Commission (FTC), the signals it gave users did not match the reality. In its complaint against Snapchat, the FTC noted that through its user interface and other representations, "Snapchat has represented, expressly or by implication, that when sending a message through its application, the message will disappear forever after the user-set time period expires." The commission found these representations false and misleading because "when sending a message through its application, the message may not disappear forever after the user-set time period expires."[24]

But that wasn't the only design the FTC found to be dishonest. Snapchat also gave its users a chance to find friends during the registration process with the following prompt[25]:

According to the FTC, Snapchat implied "through its user interface that the mobile phone number was the only information Snapchat collected to find the user's friends. . . ." The FTC found this user interface deceptive because "the mobile number that the user entered was not the only personal information that Snapchat collected. Snapchat also collected the names and phone numbers of all contacts in the user's mobile device address book" without informing the user.[26]

This complaint by the FTC is a good example of how regulators might help fill privacy law's design gap. By focusing on the signals given off by the user interface of the software and design of marketing materials, this complaint encourages more honest and trustworthy design.

Technologies should also be designed to accommodate requests for inspection. For example, Facebook has designed its software and storage in a way that would allow users to download their own data.[27] Tools like these can be used to comply with privacy law. For example, the European Union's Data Protection Directive 95/46/EC gives a person the "right of access to data relating to him" in order to verify the accuracy of that data and the lawfulness of how it is being used. While the directive does not directly mandate more open and honest design, it encourages honesty through the recognition of this individual right and data processor obligation. Obligations of transparency and honesty help ensure that the trustees are complying with their duty of care and duty of loyalty.

Protection

Insecure technologies erode trust. Our personal information has always been in need of protective design. Doors and filing cabinets have long had locks, and passwords have served as "digital locks" for almost as long as computer databases have existed.[28] Data troves have been traditionally maintained by "secretaries," a profession dating to medieval times conceived of as "one who is entrusted with private or secret matters; a confidant; one privy to a secret."[29] Secrets are literally in the name. Lawmakers can encourage trust by ensuring that technologies are designed to protect and secure our personal information.

The FIPs have always required data security, with language usually along the lines of "Personal data should be protected by reasonable security safeguards against such risks as loss or unauthorized access, destruction, use, modification or disclosure of data." Data security includes more than just the design of technologies. Policy makers have tended to interpret security requirements in terms of the process data holders must take to protect against attackers. This mainly consists of good design on the "back end" of the collection process, where the data is resting in storage as property of the collector. Such obligations include regularly auditing data assets and risk; minimizing data collection and retention; implementing technical, physical, and administrative safeguards; and creating and following a data breach response plan. Less legal attention is paid to user-facing data security issues, such as interfaces at collection points and the hardware and sensors that collect the data. As I'll address in Chapters 7 and 8, privacy law's design agenda should address security in both the back end and user-facing contexts.

In addition to mandating the creation of secure technologies, Privacy's Blueprint is designed to prevent design decisions made for reasons other than security that happen to make people's data insecure. Such decisions betray our trust. For example, computer company Lenovo surreptitiously installed malware on its new laptops. This code altered users' search results to show them ads different from those they would otherwise have seen. The secret deployment of the malware also weakened the laptops' security settings, exposing the computer's browsing history to hackers with the ability to use a particular exploit against the software. In addition to being dishonest and disloyal, this weakening of the computers' security settings violated the duty of protection.

Protection means more than just setting up technical safeguards like firewalls, user authentication requirements, and encryption. It requires that information technologies be designed according to updated threat models and with the objectives of minimizing data collection and storage, instituting procedural and physical safeguards, and preparing a response plan in case of a breach.

Loyalty

Technologies that enable betrayal erode trust. One of the most deep-seated concerns we all have about disclosing information is that people and companies will use our disclosures against us. The best way to protect against this is to require a duty of loyalty to users and data subjects in the design of information technologies. One of the foundational obligations of a fiduciary is loyalty, which is an obligation to avoid self-dealing at the expense of the entrustor. This generally means that fiduciaries cannot use information obtained in the course of their relationship in ways that harm, undermine, or create conflicts of interest with the entrustor. For example, when we entrust funds to a third party—a trustee—the trustee must manage the funds in the beneficiary's best interest. A trustee cannot lend entrusted funds to herself or buy a trust property unless explicitly authorized to do so.

The duty of loyalty is a bedrock principle of the law of fiduciaries. The rationale behind the obligation to avoid self-dealing is to cut off avenues for fraud. As one court has put it, "The rule is founded in the highest wisdom. It recognizes the infirmity of human nature, and interposes a barrier against the operation of selfishness and greed. It discourages fraud by taking away motive for its perpetration."[30] Formal trustees are bound to act in the interest of the beneficiary. In the same way we can entrust property to a trustee, we entrust our data to the entities that collect, hold, and use it.

Yet the concept of loyalty is missing from the privacy laws that regulate those who accept information in a fiduciary-like context. Richards and I have proposed that trust in information relationships can be promoted by establishing loyalty as a foundational concept in privacy law.[31] When companies build technologies to secretly extract far more value from their consumers than they made clear to them at the outset, they are being disloyal. Privacy law should guide companies to build technologies that serve the interests of their users ahead of the narrow, short-term profit motives. When companies build products to facilitate digital data strip mining without proper concern for how that information might be used against consumers later, they are eroding the trust necessary for commerce, intimacy, and expression.

Because our social interaction is now regularly mediated, companies can leverage your personal information against other people, too. You didn't know it at the time, but Facebook may have used some of your disclosures to manipulate your friends. The company tweaked its news feed based on emotional indicators, showing some people mostly negative posts and others mostly positive posts, to measure the effect it would have on mood.[32] But this study is not unique. Social media regularly manipulates how user posts appear. We are at the mercy of those who shape our mediated realities; we entrust companies with our data, but we receive no guarantee of loyalty in return. We need to limit the extent to which media can engage in self-dealing at our expense.

Critically, not all technologies that benefit their makers are disloyal. Of course, companies can build things to collect, use, and share personal information to their benefit (and the benefit of others) in many different ways. Data can be mined to offer and improve services, effectively deidentified for public research, and even shared with others who are also willing to preserve our trust. Online entertainment services like Netflix for movies and TV shows and Pandora for music mine personal preferences to suggest new shows and songs. One of Amazon's most valuable features is its recommendation system, which relies upon user data. Websites routinely share de-identified data with others for profit and to simply fine-tune their services without betraying the trust of their users. Public health research and initiatives can benefit everyone, including organizations that collect and process personal information.

The problem comes when these technologies are unreasonably costly to their users. Scammers look for disclosures that can be used to target the vulnerable. This kind of information is so valuable that violent gang fights have erupted over possession of so-called suckers lists (lists of those vulnerable to scams) in places like Jamaica.[33] The FTC has observed websites and online technologies designed to obtain "financial account data for inexpensive trial products and then deceptively enroll consumers into programs with recurring monthly charges, or malware scams that purport to alert consumers to alleged viruses on their computers that can be fixed for a fee."[34] The costs of disloyal technologies are not always financial. Sometimes technologies discriminate based on personal information that might result in opportunity costs. For example, Google's targeted ad delivery system showed an ad for high-paying jobs to users it thought were men much more often than it showed the ad to women.[35]

Consider the trove of data that Amazon holds on behalf of its users. It can use that information to suggest new movies they might want to rent or accessories for the products they already own. These kinds of offerings can be loyal and create value for both the company and its customers. Privacy's Blueprint would caution against Amazon building a system to find out the highest price each customer would want to pay for each such product. And it would be a betrayal of the duty of loyalty for Amazon to sell insights about its customers to those who might harm them, whether data brokers, insurance companies, employers, or others.

It will not be easy to draw a clean, bright line to determine when self-dealing becomes disloyal. Like with most privacy issues, it is context dependent. But there are clues to look for, including consumer expectations, the amount of data collected as surplus over what was necessary for the service; the existence of stand-alone fees for services, processes, and safeguards put in place to ensure fair dealing; and the available of reasonable alternatives to adversarial uses of information, among others. To find consensus on how this impacts design, policy makers, industry, advocates, and users should more regularly frame our dialogue about how information technologies are built in terms of loyalty.

Obscurity

Take a second and remember the last time you ate in a restaurant. Do you remember what the couple sitting right next to you looked like? Probably not. They probably don't remember you either. That's because we go about our day-to-day lives in zones of obscurity. Obscurity as a privacy value is the notion that when our activities or information is unlikely to be found, seen, or remembered it is, to some degree, safe. People calculate risk every day based on how obscure they are or are likely to be. For example, you probably feel comfortable discussing relatively sensitive topics (or perhaps just being a gossip) over dinner in a public restaurant because the likelihood of that disclosure being more publicly disseminated or coming back to harm you is pretty low: you're in a room full of strangers, and they are probably not eavesdropping.

In work with Evan Selinger and Fred Stutzman, I have explored the concept of obscurity as an essential component of modern notions of privacy. Every day we make decisions about where we go, what we do, and what we share based on how obscure we think we are. Most of our information online is obscure as well. Think of obscurity as the counterpart to trust. When we can reliably trust people, we have less of a need to be obscure. Yet in contexts where there is no one to trust, obscurity becomes invaluable.

Unlike trust, obscurity is not a widely established concept in law or policy. Therefore some explanation is in order to establish it as a foundational value of Privacy's Blueprint. The term *obscure* is defined as "[n]ot readily noticed or seen; inconspicuous; . . . [n]ot clearly understood or expressed; ambiguous or vague."[36] Obscurity is a simple concept that basically reflects a state of unknowing. It involves at least two parties: the individual and the observer. An individual is obscure to an observer if the observer does not possess or comprehend critical information needed to make sense of the individual. For example, does an observer know your personal identity, social connections, or the context in which you disclosed something about yourself? Without this information, an observer has a limited ability to make sense of what you do and what you say. Finding this information is often costly. In the language of privacy as obscurity, transaction costs are a good thing.

Obscurity is common and natural. As a result, people have come to expect it both online and off. Obscurity is also valuable. When we are obscure, we are protected by an observer's inability to comprehend our actions. We seek to be obscure in our everyday lives. We close doors, talk in hushed tones, take risks of very briefly exposing ourselves, comfortable that the odds of adverse results are low. For example, when in hotel rooms people often quickly walk by open windows in their underwear because the odds are low someone will be standing there watching. Without the notion of obscurity, we would be forced to assume that everything we do outside our bathrooms and bedrooms is going to be observed, stored, or used. There's no way we could consistently act on those assumptions without serious costs and regular slip-ups.

One of the reasons obscurity is natural is because our brains can only store and process limited amounts of information. Evolutionary psychologist Robin Dunbar's work on the social brain hypothesis has famously demonstrated that human cognitive groups—clusters of individuals that have shared communication, memories, and interpersonal relationships—are fairly small. One person's meaningful and active social network maxes out at around 150 people;[37] this cap on the number of people you can maintain an ongoing relationship with is called by some as your Dunbar number. These limitations create zones of obscurity.

Dunbar was careful to draw a distinction between simply identifying and truly knowing people. He pointed out that we can recognize about two thousand people, far more than the maximum number of people knowable at the individual level. To prevent the overburdening of memory, we necessarily limit our cognitive groups to a manageable size.[38] Accordingly, most interactions with those we are not maintaining active relationships with occur in states of obscurity. That's why you can't remember who sat next to you the last time you ate in a restaurant.

We depend upon cognitive limitations to protect us from exposing ourselves to the world, even though we can be observed by others. Indeed, the possibility of being identified breeds conformity to social norms. You will be familiar with this concept if you've ever been told to behave a certain way because "you never know who is watching." Therefore, people produce obscurity every day in several different ways to increase the odds that what they do and say and who they are cannot be fully comprehended (in some cases) or identified (in others). People use privacy settings, lock phones, close doors and curtains, and make phone calls to discuss sensitive topics rather than using email, which leaves a more persistent and findable trace.

It's why computer filter screens are popular. They darken on-screen information when viewed from the side, making screen data visible only to persons directly in front of the monitor without blurring or distortion. They create obscurity by making prying glances difficult. In this way, obscurity promotes and is essential to freedom.

Erving Goffman has argued that we give off a range of signals, both on purpose and by accident, that determine how we are identified and comprehended. Our dress and demeanor convey "front-stage" signals—those we intend our observers to draw upon as they make sense of our actions. Of course, we also give off subconscious or accidental signals. It is often these "backstage" signals that truly enable people to make sense of what they are observing. For example, as a child growing up in the American South, I developed a natural southern drawl when I spoke. As I left the Deep South and worked as an attorney in urban Washington, DC, I occasionally found myself using a more neutral, nonregional dialect. But the way I pronounce some words still reveals traces of a southern accent. When I do, I unintentionally reveal information about my background.

According to Goffman, our ability to "read" a scene and judge how we present ourselves is a critical component in social interaction. We use a range of cues and physical structures to figure out how we should present ourselves. For example, our understanding of the private nature of a conversation is moderated by the presence of walls and doors. These structures provide not only physical privacy but also signals that inform the overall structure and content of interpersonal interaction; we often say things behind a closed door that we would not say in public.

Obscurity is key to helping people "perform" an identity and draw upon cues from the audience of observers to construct an optimized zone of obscurity. I perform several different identities every day: husband, father, son, professor, friend, etc. It would be difficult to do my job if my karaoke singing with my friends, imagination games with my children, and really bad attempts at romantic poems with my wife were obvious to my students. Obscurity is thus both a context and a biological and social process—one that is culturally and cognitively embedded and reinforced through social interaction. We do the same thing online, such as with privacy settings. Though the spaces are different, transaction costs are a powerful force in both contexts.

Recall the central premise of obscurity as a privacy value—when our activities and information are hard to come by, the only people who will seize upon it are those with sufficient motivation to expend the necessary effort and resources. While the Internet has famously removed some information from obscurity—think mug shots and criminal records—much of the information on the web remains hidden. The original one-way broadcast nature of the web has given way to a virtually endless patchwork of private conversations, back alleys, hidden forums, and walled gardens. It has been estimated that 80–99 percent of the World Wide Web is completely hidden from general-purpose search engines and only accessible by those with the right search terms, uniform resource locator (URL), or insider knowledge.[39] Other pieces of online information are obfuscated by the use of pseudonyms, multiple profiles, and privacy settings. Practically speaking, is this functionally obscure information really less likely to be discovered than information that is protected by a weak password?

Even if obscure information is found, if it is contextually vague, then the only people who will grasp it when it is hard to understand are those with sufficient motivation to push past the layer of opacity protecting it. Those mining data for value, for example a law enforcement agency investigating a crime, a journalist investigating a story, nosy neighbors, and the like, must engage in a process of making sense of what they are told in order to understand it. If it is too hard to understand information, people can come to faulty conclusions. They might grow frustrated and give up the detective work. Effort becomes a deterrent, just as if the information were not readily available.

Internet users have come to rely upon obscurity for privacy protection online. The mere act of disclosing information online does not necessarily mean that the individual seeks wide publicity, even if the information disclosed is theoretically available to the Internet at large. Just as someone shouting from a street corner will only be heard by a few people (her audience is limited by architecture, social interaction, and pure physics), most of us have similar expectations with content shared online.[40] Your Instagram account might be popular, but don't flatter yourself; relatively speaking, hardly anyone on earth will ever see it.

The choice to disclose information online involves a highly contextual risk analysis. People control the information disclosed by limiting the audience of the disclosure, by limiting the meaning of the disclosure, choosing the forum for disclosure, and by adapting the disclosure to a particular website.[41] As will be discussed in Chapter 6, because anonymity would violate norms and limit benefits attained from many social network sites such as Facebook, individuals instead develop techniques that effectively produce obscurity in disclosure. Internet users routinely hide information by making it invisible to search engines through the use of pseudonyms and multiple profiles and by taking advantage of privacy settings. In short, signals and transaction costs produced by technological design help users produce and induce reliance upon obscurity online. Thus, obscurity is an ideal value to help define Privacy's Blueprint.

Selinger, Stutzman, and I have articulated a framework for understanding the factors that combine to create obscurity: information is obscure online if it exists in a context missing one or more key factors that are essential to discovery or comprehension. We have identified four of these factors: search visibility, unprotected access, identification, and clarity. These are all functions of transaction costs. The presence of these factors diminishes obscurity, and their absence enhances it. These factors are all moderated by design and can be key parts of Privacy's Blueprint.

Our disclosures and whereabouts can be plotted on a spectrum of obscurity that will allow regulators, designers, and organizational stakeholders to adopt guiding principles regarding the protection of online information through design. The spectrum ranges from completely obscure to completely obvious. The aim of this model of obscurity is to identify obscurity risk factors that are subject to design choices.

Search Visibility

Search visibility is the degree to which individuals and the content they produce are locatable and accessible through an online search. Search invisibility is one of the most significant factors in online obscurity because it is the primary method for discovering information online. Without a search, information can only be discovered in less efficient ways, such as a following a series of links via other websites, messages, or manual URL entry.

Most information on the web is actually invisible to search engines.[42] Search invisibility can be achieved by intentionally shielding websites from search engines using the robots.txt file as well as by using privacy settings or other access restrictions such as passwords, which are another factor in online obscurity. Because search is a primary and common vector for discovery of individual content, designers should consider offering users control over inclusion of their information in both internal and external search services. Some people may want their Facebook profile to appear in Google search results, while others would prefer to limit searchability even within Facebook—for example, by being searchable only by friends of friends. Designers may also consider offering various levels of search engine obfuscation, where only certain aspects of the profile are placed into a search or search placement is manipulated to raise or lower the placement of results.

Unprotected Access

Access protection covers a range of technologies and methods for controlling access to content. A common example of an access control is the password. Access controls can serve multiple functions apart from merely technologically restricting who can view information; they can also serve as normative signals indicating the private nature of the information. Conversely, unfettered access to information, particularly when technologies like privacy settings are available but unused, can have the opposite effect on obscurity, leaving the information exposed and subject to being scraped, indexed, and aggregated.

There are many different kinds of access controls, including biometrics, encryption, privacy settings, and passwords. These controls can provide for user control over several variables, including the content shared, the specifics of the potential audience, or both. Along with search visibility, access controls are one of the most important factors in creating online obscurity. Consequently, they should be considered bedrock tools for designers embracing the principals of obscurity.

Identification

Identification refers to the degree to which individuals are identified through personal and interpersonal disclosures in online settings. Identification can occur by any piece of information that links content online to the individual's person. Information that cannot be linked to a person offers a degree of anonymity and poses a reduced threat to that person's privacy. Pseudonyms and ID variants can be used to obscure identity. Like passwords, ID variants like initials and pseudonyms can somewhat protectively delink content and identity. For example, WH could, without more context, be referring to anybody from Woodrow Hartzog to Whitney Houston. Readily apparent ID variants and pseudonyms can also signal to the recipient of the information that the identity of the discloser is sensitive or private.

Social media present multiple challenges to identity management. For example, on social media your networked connections can reveal a great deal about you, including who you are. Users maintaining a pseudonymous profile may become publicly identifiable based on whom the person connects to or what a friend writes on that individual's wall. Therefore, designers should be aware that the individual's intention to protect her or his identity extends beyond self-disclosure to managing disclosures about the individual and selective crafting of the online persona.

Clarity

Finally, clarity covers the degree to which an outside observer can make sense of content shared by an individual. Often online information is easily discoverable, but important aspects of that information do not make sense to the reader or viewer. Have you ever seen a meme floating around online but had no idea what it meant? Sometimes unclear information is intentionally vague or incomplete, such as when a person shares something on social media that is crafted to be understood by close friends but not casual acquaintances. Information that is sufficiently lacking in clarity can be as privacy protective as information that is difficult to find.

Whereas identification depends upon the link between identity and information, clarity focuses on the link between content and some other contextual factor. Stripping context from information reduces its clarity and increases the obscurity of information by reducing the number of people who are likely to understand the meaning of the disclosure. This technique is common in our everyday social interactions. Groups that are familiar with each other can "presuppose" contexts in conversation instead of explicitly providing for it with each disclosure. Clarity can be thought of as the range of shared knowledge and social, cultural, and linguistic factors that enable presupposition.

For example, if I were to tell you right now, "The big day is here! I'll keep you updated," you would have no idea what I was referring to. However, if you were part of the limited Facebook group I created titled Waiting for the Hartzog Baby and I posted the message within that group, you would know that my wife just went into labor. That's because you had the presupposition information necessary for message clarity.

Designers and lawmakers can recognize and value the individual strategies people have for managing clarity (i.e., respecting this normative practice in both policy and technology), and by considering the degree to which outsiders can construct clarity using metadata, data stores, and data recombination. Such considerations are especially important given the risks to people that can emerge from inadvertent disclosures. For example, consider the information that is embedded in most digital pictures you take. Kate Murphy noted in a story about privacy and photographs that Adam Savage, host of the popular science program "MythBusters," revealed the GPS location of his home when he posted a picture on Twitter of his automobile parked in front of his house. Murphy wrote, "Embedded in the image was a geotag, a bit of data providing the longitude and latitude of where the photo was taken. Hence, he revealed exactly where he lived. And since the accompanying text was "Now it's off to work," potential thieves knew he would not be at home." Savage accidentally eroded the obscurity of his home address because of the hidden design of cameras and digital photographs.[43]

Taken together, search visibility, unlimited access, identification, and clarity determine how obscure you or your information are. The presence of these factors diminishes obscurity, and their absence enhances it. Thus, in determining whether information is obscure online, courts and lawmakers should consider these factors individually, then collectively.

Consider a family blog that is visible only to invited users and is not searchable via general search engines like Google. It is close to being completely obscure because it is missing two of the most important factors for finding and understanding information: search visibility and unprotected access. Compare that family blog to a Twitter account that is not protected and uses only the first name "Taylor" and a blurry photo to identify the poster.

While this account is more obvious than the family blog because it is freely searchable and accessible, it is still obscure because only certain Internet users would be able to identify the poster of the content or completely comprehend any idiosyncratic posts. Under traditional privacy law, the family blog would be seen as "private" and the Twitter account would be regarded as "public." If only it were so simple.

Obscurity can be easier to refine and implement than the broader concept of privacy. Whereas the pursuit of "privacy" in design often seems like a quest for near-perfect protection, the goal of designing for obscurity is to be good enough for most contexts or for a user's specific needs. Protection is achieved via obscurity, not necessarily through guarantees regarding the strength of the "armor" but through a significant reduction in the probability of finding or understanding information. That's because the cost of finding and understanding dissuades people and organizations. Designing for higher transaction costs will produce more obscurity. Obscurity is a more nuanced and accurate reflection of the expectations of users of social technologies than the broader, slippery concept of privacy.

Let's take a second to recap our two values of trust and obscurity and how they relate to each other. Trust is about relationships. Obscurity is about risk. Combined, these two traits form the foundation of Privacy's Blueprint. They are the two privacy-related values most directly affected by design signals and transaction costs. They are also both largely descriptive, enabling values. Obscurity and trust let us explore and create identity and be intimate with each other because they create zones of safety. They can be combined to give us holistic protection. Trust protects us when dealing with other people. Obscurity protects us when there are no people we can trust. Most important, they are both related to the larger moral value of autonomy. If Privacy's Blueprint explicitly embraces autonomy, it can help ensure that people are free to make decisions about whom they trust and how obscure they want to be.

Autonomy

Humans have an innate need for autonomy. In order to flourish, we must have a certain degree of freedom from external control or influence. This notion is at the heart of the "right to be let alone" developed so many years ago by Samuel Warren and Louis Brandeis. Alan Westin, one of privacy's most famous theorists, has written that the most significant threat to one's autonomy is "the possibility that someone may penetrate the inner zone and learn his ultimate secrets, either by physical or psychological means. This deliberate penetration of the individual's protective shell, his psychological armor, would leave him naked to ridicule and shame and would put him under the control of those who knew his secrets."[44]

Autonomy is at the core of a number of developed theories of privacy. As Julie Cohen argues, "A protected zone of informational autonomy is valuable, in short, precisely because it reminds us what we cannot measure."[45] Helen Nissenbaum observes that the relationship between privacy and autonomy can be thought of in three different ways: privacy as autonomy or control over the information itself, privacy as facilitating an environment where individual autonomy is likely to flourish, and privacy as creating space for the ability to actually follow through on autonomous decisions.[46]

But there is a problem with autonomy as the most important tenet of privacy: it is a near limitless concept. Consider Jeb Rubenfeld's critique:

> What, then, is the right to privacy? What does it protect? A number of commentators seem to think that they have it when they add the word "autonomy" to the privacy vocabulary. But to call an individual "autonomous" is simply another way of saying that he is morally free, and to say that the right to privacy protects freedom adds little to our understanding of the doctrine. To be sure, the privacy doctrine involves the "right to make choices and decisions," which, it is said, forms the "kernel" of autonomy. The question, however, is which choices and decisions are protected?[47]

To that end, the function of design can help cabin the meaning of autonomy in Privacy's Blueprint. Autonomy is furthered as a design value when privacy law guides technologies to use signals and transactions costs to reinforce trust and obscurity. In other words, technological design serves autonomy when it allows individuals to freely and reliably enter into trust relationships and create and maintain obscurity. Design is most corrosive to autonomy when it wrongfully manipulates or distorts trust in relationships and interferes with zones of obscurity.

Trust is most valuable within market economies when it is freely given. We are more likely to choose to trust others when we know that promises to keep a trust will be backed up by law. Once within reliable relationships of trust, we are freer to disclose personal information in useful ways. We can rely on recipients keeping the trust they were given.

Obscurity is most valuable when it enables us the freedom to make choices around an accurate and stable calculation of risk. I'm more free to post what I desire on social media when I can reliably anticipate that my disclosure will remain obscure. Thus, autonomous choices and spaces occur within zones of trust and obscurity. Trust and obscurity are the conceptual core of Privacy's Blueprint, and autonomy gives the blueprint its moral rationale.[48]

About That Rejection of Control

It might seem contradictory for me to advocate autonomy as a core value for Privacy's Blueprint after critiquing the overleveraging of "control" in both law and design. However, autonomy is about more than control. Design constraints can create the obscurity that enables free, autonomous choices. When people are in reliably trustworthy relationships, they have more freedom to disclose because doing so is less risky. Technology that does not work against or interfere with people's interests is the embodiment of autonomous values.

Even when autonomy is synonymous with control over how our information is collected, used, and shared, it is far too precious to be exhausted by a "notice and choice" regime that is not serious about notice or choice. Our desire for control over our personal information is largely rooted in our value of autonomy. To the extent that design truly enables freedom from external control, it services autonomy and should be encouraged.

However, when design overleverages control, it shifts the risk of loss onto the user of the technology. By collectively overwhelming people with control that manufactures a shallow "consent" to the collection, use, and disclosure of personal information, designers can simultaneously ditch the responsibility for harmful design while claiming to simply give users the "control" they want. Privacy law should discourage this sort of autonomy-corrosive design, perhaps simply by failing to give it legal effect. People want real and meaningful choices about how to protect themselves in the digital world. Privacy's Blueprint should prioritize and facilitate the fundamental choices about information access and storage technologies and unburden users from the tornado of choices, which are less about true autonomy and are more about furnishing the basis for mass data processing.

Companies should look to the values of trust, obscurity, and autonomy when making decisions about what they hope to accomplish. Good privacy design gives off signals and modulates transaction costs in ways that reflect these values. Lawmakers should commit to nurturing trust, obscurity, and autonomy in design because they are the most proximate to design's function—shaping expectations, making tasks easier or harder, and channeling user choice. Trust is the key to being able to safely share information within relationships. Outside of trustworthy relationships, obscurity is the key notion for assessing and responding to the risk of information collection, use, and disclosure. Both trust and obscurity require the autonomy that is needed to self-disclose, form relationships, and respond to risk. These three values enable other values. Nearly all of the other values that are associated with privacy—control, intimacy, dignity, fairness, self-realization—can be nurtured through trust, obscurity, and autonomy. This is the first part of Privacy's Blueprint. In the next chapter, I'll propose how lawmakers and courts might set standards to ensure that these values thrive in information technologies.

4

Setting Boundaries for Design

CREATING LAWS that govern the design of technology is hard. When the purpose of these laws is to nurture the notoriously slippery concept of privacy, it can be downright maddening. Should these laws be specific? For example, national electrical codes that require a power outlet to be spaced "so that no point along the wall space is more than 6 feet, measured horizontally along the floor line" from another outlet tell designers exactly what they need to do.[1] Or should they be flexible and technologically agnostic? Tort law often simply prohibits "unreasonably dangerous products," which captures a wide array of risky designs.[2] Should the Fair Information Practices (FIPs) serve as the model for design standards? After all, they are the template for virtually all data protection law. Or might other areas of the law be more useful and relevant?

If lawmakers fail to provide enough guidance for companies, they risk creating ineffective and confusing laws. But if the rules are too specific, lawmakers risk micromanaging new technologies. Rules then become simultaneously over- and underinclusive and leave little room for adaptation to context and competing needs. Companies must juggle many different considerations when creating a technology; designers and engineers must accommodate business, marketing, legal, and engineering concerns, to name a few. Above all, when companies create a product, they must manage risk. Designers must juggle risks that spring from compliance, security, poor market performance, negative press, and competition, among many others. The best product designs are useful, desirable, and also minimize risk.[3]

Any legal blueprint for privacy should be flexible enough to provide adequate breathing room for designers to manage all of this risk and create marketable products. To do so, privacy law should largely guide design at the margins by articulating goals and erecting boundaries designed to achieve those goals by preventing the types of harmful designs that contradict them. These rules should take the form of flexible standards rather than rigid requirements.

In this chapter, I propose design boundaries for privacy law. I begin by laying out the legal frameworks whose principles should inform the privacy design standards: product safety and consumer protection law. I argue that while the FIPs can be useful in setting privacy design goals, they should not be the dominant model for design boundaries. Lessons from product safety and consumer protection counsel prohibitions on unreasonably *deceptive, abusive,* and *dangerous* design. In the second half of this chapter, I use these lessons to build out a typology of bad privacy design. These three kinds of adversarial designs exploit trust, erode obscurity, and interfere with autonomous decision making.

A Standards-Based Framework for Privacy Design

Usually, lawmakers can most effectively fill privacy's design gap by articulating design boundaries in the form of flexible standards for companies. Companies should generally have the freedom to design technologies how they please, so long as they stay within particular thresholds, satisfy certain basic requirements like security and accuracy, and remain accountable for deceptive, abusive, and dangerous design decisions.

By being flexible and sensitive to context, privacy laws can act as guardrails for design. These laws should usually be articulated more as common standards than specific rules. Generally speaking, standards are less deterministic than rules—that is, there are fewer possible options for complying with rules. While a rule might prohibit drivers from exceeding fifty-five miles per hour, a standard would simply require drivers to "drive reasonably under the circumstances." Yet when standards would provide too much wiggle room to be effective or are too difficult to follow, design laws should be more specific and rule-like. The "rules versus standards" debate is a foundational legal inquiry, but it is particularly important for design.

There are costs to both the determinate and indeterminate approach. Rules are easy to follow because people know exactly what is expected of them. But they are rigid and hard to get right. Sometimes fifty-five miles per hour is too permissive because of road conditions or traffic. In other contexts, fifty-five miles per hour is a wildly inefficient restriction because there is no traffic. Cars could safely travel faster.

Meanwhile, standards are valuable because they are flexible and do not become obsolete upon the development of new technologies. In theory, standards can always get us the right outcome in any context.[4] But while standards are easy to make, they can be hard to enforce and follow. What exactly is a "reasonable speed?" Who makes that call, and from what vantage point? Need drivers only focus on traffic and weather, or do other variables affect this equation?

I argue that standards are generally appropriate to guide design because of the rapid pace of technological change, the contextual dependency of all privacy problems, and the wealth of common knowledge companies can draw from regarding sound privacy design.[5] This approach will enable companies and designers to harness industry engineering wisdom and balance competing interests. Well-chosen requirements will also incorporate the wisdom of technologists, researchers, and academics from relevant disciplines like computer science, engineering, psychology, sociology, information science, mass communication and media effects, and other cognate fields. They will enable privacy professionals like chief privacy officers and counsel to guide design in context of a particular company's goals, abilities, and limitations. Recall from Chapter 2 the plethora of principles, guides, approaches, disciplines, and standards companies can look to for specifics regarding the design of privacy-friendly technologies. Privacy law's design agenda can also draw from established, well-developed principles such as deception, defective design, and warnings.

By arguing for a preference for standards in setting boundaries, I do not mean to say that privacy law should address design in an entirely technologically neutral way. Technologically specific design rules will be preferable in many contexts. Paul Ohm has highlighted some of the many benefits of technologically specific privacy laws, including natural sunsets on laws that become irrelevant.[6] If it is true that new technologies create new problems, then these natural sunsets help ensure that lawmakers continually revisit privacy rules to make sure they are working in light of new technologies. Michael Birnhack has argued that true technological neutrality is probably impossible anyway because even the most technologically agnostic laws were based on some kind of technological mind-set shaped by the state of the art.[7]

Thus, privacy design boundaries should be articulated as technologically specific rules on occasion. For example, it might be necessary to specifically target malicious code like spyware. Rules prohibiting spyware are less risky because the technology is relatively easy to define in a way that will not become obsolete; spyware is also rarely justified. In other contexts, like user interfaces, more broad and flexible laws might be best. User interfaces are ubiquitous and foundational components for consumer-facing technologies. Specific rules for them are destined to be simultaneously over- and underinclusive. Thus, standards would likely be more appropriate so long as the harm to be avoided remains the same.[8] And, of course, there is a scale of technological neutrality. Laws could be totally agnostic, so that they could apply to any technology; they could also be totally specific to a particular technology. There's even room for a middle ground—that is, laws that apply to applications with particular functions such as geolocation or diagnostics "and their functional equivalents." It is for lawmakers to ensure that they have properly set boundaries to counteract the incentives companies have to merely technically comply with design rules while using the wiggle room they've been given to counteract the spirit of the restriction.

Consumer Protection for Boundaries, FIPs for Goals

In looking for a model to guide design, lawmakers almost instinctually look to FIPs.[9] Ann Cavoukian's Privacy by Design movement was built upon the FIPs. It's easy to see why. The FIPs are the world's common language of privacy. Structures and laws are already in place to implement the FIPs. Cavoukian's FIP-based Privacy by Design concept is an excellent starting point for companies seeking to incorporate privacy into every aspect of their data collection business, including organizational structure and better rules about how data is collected, accounted for, and used. At first, it might seem like the FIPs are an ideal foundation for privacy law's design agenda for consumer-facing technologies. But I disagree.

While the FIPs can be useful to articulate data-related design goals like transparency and data minimization, they are not ideal for setting design boundaries for information technologies for two main reasons: They are primarily concerned with how data is controlled and processed, and they too often serve to elevate formalistic notions of "choice" and "control" over meaningful privacy protections in a way that wrongfully transfers the risk of loss from data controllers to data subjects.

The FIPs articulate desirable endpoints: openness, security, data quality, accountability, and the like. But they are mainly concerned with data collection, processing, and storage, and not with the design that facilitates these actions. The FIPs do not always directly address the effect of design signals and transaction costs on trust, obscurity, and autonomy. The FIPs also fail to provide meaningful concrete guidance to lawmakers or companies regarding specific design choices like how to effectively disclaim or warn people regarding an important privacy-related practice or function.[10] When the FIPs first rose to prominence in 1980, James Rule and his colleagues criticized the FIPs for their failure to meaningfully limit surveillance systems. They categorized the FIPs as "efficiency" principles that endeavored to smooth the harsh edges of information systems to operate better for both data controllers and data subjects, instead of substantively limiting data collection against the interests of data controllers.[11]

Rule and his colleagues also criticized the efficiency mission of the FIPs because it opportunistically allowed those who were engaging in mass, corrosive data collection to get the benefit of the perception of "privacy protection" through formalistic compliance. They wrote that under the FIPs' criteria, "organisations can claim to protect the privacy of those with whom they deal, even as they demand more and more data from them, and accumulate ever more power over their lives."[12] Graham Greenleaf noted that this fundamental tension in the FIPs remains today, with questions still asked too infrequently, such as "to what extent do and should data privacy principles and laws go beyond attempting to ensure the 'efficiency' of personal information systems, and provide means to limit and control the expansion of surveillance systems?"[13] As I discussed in Chapter 2, companies often use design to circumvent the goals of the FIPs while retaining the optics of compliance.

James Grimmelmann, Deirdre Mulligan, and Jennifer King have critiqued the FIPs as ineffective to guide the design of information technologies because they ignore the privacy problems inherent in the social exchange of information like social media.[14] The FIPs are concerned with how powerful entities deal with aggregated personal information. But as Grimmelmann notes, even if social media companies were completely compliant with the FIPs, "users would still create false profiles, snoop on each other, and struggle over the bounds of the private. For this reason, while reports dealing with privacy and other platforms often propose strong restrictions on data collection and transfer, the focus of reports on social-network-site privacy is appropriately elsewhere."[15] Privacy design boundaries will only be effective if they address the full spectrum of risks from information technologies.

Sarah Spiekermann and Lorrie Cranor have drawn a clear distinction between the FIPs and privacy design principles for information technologies. They categorize FIP-based "notice and choice" strategies as "privacy-by-policy" and strategies based on privacy-friendly technical mechanisms and constraints as "privacy-by-architecture."[16] Again, the FIPs are largely perceived as a guide to data processing, not rules about how to build technologies that collect and use data. This distinction between FIPs and technical privacy solutions counsels that the FIPs are, perhaps surprisingly, not the natural place for lawmakers to look for guidance on privacy-friendly design boundaries for consumer technologies.

Instead of regimes built around the FIPs (save, perhaps, laws effectuating the data minimization principle), I propose that two areas of the law that have developed flexible, standards-based regimes should serve as the model for setting privacy design boundaries: product safety (also called product liability) and consumer protection. These two areas have taken design seriously in various ways for years and can guide privacy design in many other areas of the law. I do not mean that privacy law's design agenda should be limited to tort law and administrative regulations. Rather, lawmakers and industry seeking to take design seriously should borrow traits and established concepts from product safety and consumer protection law to build a design framework that nurtures the values of trust, obscurity, and autonomy.

Products safety law is structured to prevent and compensate for—among other things—defective design and defective warnings. It focuses on deterring the production and sale of unreasonably dangerous products and encouraging effective, truthful communication to properly set people's expectations about how a thing is to be used. Consumer protection law is structured to protect people as market participants. It focuses on deterring consumer harm and wrongful interference with consumers' ability to make market decisions. In the United States, the most prominent consumer protection agencies like the Federal Trade Commission (FTC), the Consumer Financial Protection Bureau (CFPB), and state attorneys general target deceptive, abusive, and unfair technologies. With respect to information technologies, both regimes look to signals and transaction costs from companies and the technology itself. Taken together, these regimes counsel Privacy's Blueprint to set boundaries to prevent *deceptive, dangerous,* and *abusive* design.

This means that lawmakers should discourage design that tricks us, lies to us, exploits us, or dangerously weakens or destroys practical hiding places for our personal information. Such technologies betray our trust and threaten the obscurity we rely upon to make autonomous choices.

The practical effect of this focus on deception, abuse, and danger will be to scrutinize specific design decisions and functions rather than technologies as a whole. It will also help differentiate between seemingly similar technologies. For example, cell phones with cameras do not quite threaten the values of trust, obscurity, or autonomy as much as spyware or particular features of a user interface that hide or omit important information. This is because cell phones generally do not give off false signals, they require enough effort to use that they are not "always on," and they are usually visible when in use.

Lessons from Product Safety Law

The most basic lesson to draw from product safety law is that companies that manufacture and design dangerous things should be liable for the harm those things cause.[17] This is true even when people misuse a product in foreseeable ways or are otherwise also at fault.[18] Product safety empowers people through private law. Instead of waiting on legislatures and administrative agencies to act, people who are harmed by design can (in theory) seek redress in the courtroom. As I'll discuss in Chapter 5, product safety law should be directly used as part of privacy law's design agenda. But its features can more broadly provide guidance for policy makers in setting boundaries as well as instructing companies on better privacy design.

Through product safety law, technologies can become less hazardous and more predictable. When people's mental models can accurately predict how technologies will work, people can better adjust their expectations and use of the technology. For example, if the risks in sending explicit Snaps via Snapchat were more apparent, people might be more discreet with what they share. The idea is to use product safety law to help close the gap between perceived and actual vulnerability when using a technology.[19]

Privacy law should emulate product safety law insofar as it draws from many different theories and sources of law. The law of product safety is a smorgasbord of legal concepts like "foreseeable use" and "reasonable alternative design." It is a mix of common law and statutory law, tort and contract, fault-based regimes and strict liability. No one approach is a panacea. Rather, lawmakers pick certain tools to address certain problems.

Several scholars have argued that product safety law can inform privacy law.[20] Grimmelmann notes that front-end consumer technologies, like user interfaces, are more like a "product" than an unseen data processing technique governed by the FIPs. User expectations regarding digital technologies are relatively predictable. So are their frustrations when the technologies do not meet those expectations. Grimmelmann argues that when websites and apps cause privacy harm that could have been prevented with better design and more careful programming, it is fair to ask whether and how to hold companies accountable for those harms.[21]

The most important lessons privacy law can borrow from product safety law are its risk-utility balancing requirements and its focus on the way an object's structure communicates information to users about the object's risk. Risk-utility balancing tests force companies to ask whether the benefit of a particular product's design is worth the risk that design will create for the product's user. For example, the cost of placing gas tanks in automobiles in locations where they will explode upon impact is not worth the marginal efficiency that might be gained through the design. Product safety law also looks to what kinds of mental models people have when using products. If a particular risk would be obvious, or could be minimized with a clear warning, then a design might be acceptable. For example, knives are dangerous, but sharp blades and pointy edges clearly communicate the risk of misuse because everyone has had experience with them.

Of course, the goods that are commonly affected by product safety laws—pharmaceuticals, industrial and medical machinery, children's toys, and automobiles—are different in important ways from information technologies. Modern information technologies now usually retain a link to their designers. The Internet of Things must be constantly patched through remote updates. The design and warnings for social media are constantly tweaked and updated. Product recalls are a huge, costly deal, but software updates to devices with Internet connections are common and often automatic. The ability to alter design remotely lowers the burden on companies to make such changes. In product safety law, this can change the potential liability of companies that create defective products.

Product safety law is concerned with making sure that products do not create unreasonable risks. As the Restatement of Torts, an influential summary of common law, provides, "Products are not generically defective merely because they are dangerous. Many product-related accident costs can be eliminated only by excessively sacrificing product features that make products useful and desirable. These trade-offs must be considered in determining whether accident costs are more fairly and efficiently borne by accident victims or by consumers generally through higher prices driven by liability costs imposed by courts on product sellers."[22] For example, chainsaws could be designed to be harmless to humans, but that would probably make them pretty terrible at cutting down trees.

Product safety law requires courts to perform a risk-utility or risk-benefit analysis regarding the design of technologies. The risk-utility test dictates that manufacturers adopt precautions proportionate to the magnitude of the expected risk; it states that a product is "defective in design when the foreseeable risks of harm posed by the product could have been reduced or avoided by the adoption of a *reasonable alternative design* . . . and the omission of the alternative design renders the product not reasonably safe."[23]

In other words, courts assess whether the burden of safer alternative designs is less than the seriousness of the harm risked and the probability of the harm occurring. If so, the design of the product is considered defective if the reasonable alternative design is not implemented. Because courts consider reasonable alternative designs in allocating liability, companies have incentive to make better, safer choices when creating technologies.

One of the main benefits of focusing on product safety and liability law is that it is concerned with how people actually use technologies. It looks to people's expectations, rather than the mere function of a product, to determine whether a design is adequate. This is consistent with Don Norman's demand that designers must plan for human error and help form an accurate mental model.

Grimmelmann notes, "If consumers were perfectly informed about exactly what a device would do in every case, there would be no accidents. They would not have bought the trampoline with the wobbly leg or they would not have done handstands on it or they would have stopped jumping a minute sooner. Every accident is an example of frustrated consumer expectations."[24]

One of the ways product safety law accounts for people's expectations is its treatment of instructions, warnings, and disclaimers. The Restatement of Torts provides that a product "is defective because of inadequate instructions or warnings when the foreseeable risks of harm posed by the product could have been reduced or avoided by the provision of reasonable instructions or warnings . . . and the omission of the instructions or warnings renders the product not reasonably safe."[25] The key here is the quality and quantity of the warnings.

Product safety law requires reasonable warnings, not just ineffective, confusing boilerplate tucked away where no one will find it. Here is where the contrast to notice and choice regimes becomes acute. Good warnings and disclosures are critical for consumers to make good decisions. Product safety law cares about the effectiveness of warnings. Notice and choice regimes and other privacy-relevant areas like contract law could be more attentive. While consent regimes like the European Union's General Data Protection Regulation are adapting to try and implement meaningful consent provisions, warnings and consent regimes are ultimately trying to accomplish two different things. Warnings are built around dissuading unsafe uses of products; getting consent means asking people for permission to engage in what is often risky behavior with their information.

Lawmakers and courts have been regularly content to validate even the most rote, procedural, and meaningless forms of "notice" so long as people could theoretically see and read impenetrable text. If they proceed with using a good or service after this notice, they have given "consent."[26] Thankfully, many lawmakers are coming around to the limitations of notice and consent. The Office of the Privacy Commissioner of Canada has released a discussion paper critical of consent as the lever by which privacy is protected. The paper notes that the modern digital economy has changed so much since Canada's FIPs-based Personal Information Protection and Electronic Documents Act was drafted that meaningful consent may no longer be possible. In a press release, the office noted that "it would take 244 hours—roughly equivalent to 33 work days—to read all of the privacy policies and related legalese that the average Internet user encounters online each year. Not surprisingly, many people simply click 'I accept' rather than read the full terms and conditions governing the use of a site."[27] Simply put, privacy law must move away from meaningless consent toward substantive, scalable warnings.

Of course, judging the merits of a warning is not easy. The calculus for what makes a warning reasonable is complex because users are so diverse. Sophisticated and experienced users might benefit from more information and the full panoply of possible risks. Novice and less sophisticated users might need more concise warnings. If companies list every risk, the truly important ones might be lost in the crowd among unlikely risks. Children might require more vivid and specific warnings than adults. Companies must anticipate foreseeable misuse when calculating warnings. Obvious risks do not have to be warned against.[28] Other risks are so severe that even the most effective warnings will not cure them.[29] Courts must balance all of these factors when determining whether a warning was adequate, which means companies must as well.[30] Privacy law should move beyond a formalist notice, choice, and consent model in favor of the kind of qualitative legal scrutiny required by product safety law that seeks to prevent dangerous uses of technology and not just shift the risk of loss onto users.

Lessons from Consumer Protection Law

The law of consumer protection, broadly speaking, is designed to facilitate accurate marketplace information, discourage fraud, and protect the vulnerabilities of market participants. Like product safety law, consumer protection law is a combination of federal and state statutes, administrative regulations, common law doctrines and, in some countries, constitutional rights. Consumer protection law is an ideal framework to help form privacy law's design agenda because it looks to power imbalances and the vulnerability of people who use technology, it cares about how people use the products they buy, and it has developed a means and instrumentalities theory to hold accountable some who build products that facilitate harm directly inflicted by third parties.

The hallmark of consumer protection law is its focus on human vulnerability and those who exploit it.[31] Entire consumer protection regimes in the United States, such as the Children's Online Privacy Protection Act, are designed to protect people when they are at their most vulnerable. All of us are vulnerable as consumers because we are not omniscient and because we cannot always be perfectly vigilant. Some populations are particularly vulnerable because of their age or mental awareness, such as with children and the elderly. Consumer protection law also aims to protect those who cannot fully protect themselves due to their economic situation, medical conditions, or simply those who are vulnerable because an investment of time, effort, or money makes leaving a commercial relationship difficult.[32] In other words, consumer protection law is, among other things, aimed at keeping companies from taking unreasonable advantage of consumers. It is acutely sensitive to the vulnerable position people are put in when they choose to trust others or rely upon zones of obscurity to go about their day-to day-lives.

When it comes to the adequacy of warnings and disclosures, the law of consumer protection usually rejects rote proceduralism. In the United States, the FTC's standard focuses on disclosures that are "clear and conspicuous." In determining what is clear and conspicuous, the FTC uses the useful mnemonic of "the 4Ps": prominence, presentation, placement, and proximity.[33] In other words, disclaimers should be presented in such a way that consumers are likely to see and understand them and their importance.

This approach recognizes human nature and cognitive and practical constraints in protecting against empty disclosure with little concern for effectiveness. Lawmakers might improve upon this approach by looking to the relevant academic research. For example, Florian Schaub, Rebecca Balebako, Adam L. Durity, and Lorrie Faith Cranor have developed a useful design space for privacy notices that works for online notices regarding a website, app, or Internet of Things device's information practices, as well as offline notices regarding surveillance such as closed-circuit TV cameras in public places. According to Schaub and colleagues, there are four basic dimensions to be considered when delivering privacy notice: timing (when it is provided), channel (how it is delivered), modality (what interaction modes are used), and control (how choices are provided).[34]

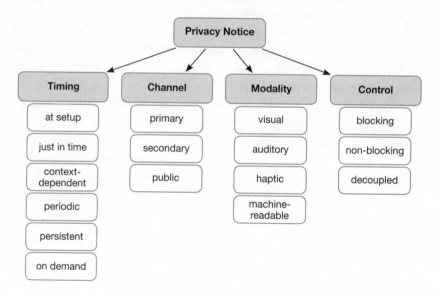

Consumer protection law is sensitive to these four dimensions because of its focus on the quality of a disclosure in context. This contextual sensitivity is key for privacy law's design agenda when design acts as a signal.

The FTC has also targeted those who provide the "means and instrumentalities" to harm and deceive consumers. This is a theory of culpability for design choices that indirectly harm consumers. Recall DesignerWare, the company that created the fake Windows 10 registration page (see Chapter 1). The FTC alleged in its complaint against the company that DesignerWare provided the means and instrumentalities for others to commit unfair acts and practices.[35] These "means and instrumentalities" theories have been alleged in other areas of FTC jurisprudence, such as in the commission's antifraud complaints against payment processors and purveyors of technologies designed to facilitate harmful pyramid schemes.[36]

The means and instrumentalities theories draw from a tradition of indirect liability. For example, tort law recognizes liability for negligent behavior that creates risk and leads to "harms caused by third-party intervening conduct."[37] Thus, people can be liable in negligence for giving their car keys to a visibly intoxicated person who goes on to injure someone with their vehicle.[38] Courts often justify recovery against "enablers" of harm in tort law to help fill a deterrence gap. It can be difficult to find or punish those who took advantage of an enabler's action to directly harm others.[39] Sometimes the harm can be prevented by deterring conduct that is one step removed. Dram Shop Acts impose liability on those providing alcohol to visibly intoxicated people in an attempt to regulate the means of impairment in addition to the impaired actors themselves. Means and instrumentalities theories can also deter harmful activity upstream by denying potential wrongdoers the "means or instruments" of harm. This provides more than one path for mitigating risk.

This focus on design as a facilitator of harm is consistent with the FTC's general strategy of looking beyond the most proximate and direct source of harm. Representatives from the commission have said that a top priority is to target gatekeepers and facilitators that enable others to defraud and deceive consumers. The FTC has specifically targeted "payment processors, lead generators, affiliate marketers, telemarketers, robocallers, billing aggregators, and others who make it easier for the fraudsters to mass market their harm."[40]

The lessons of product safety and consumer protection law can be summed up as focusing on the risk created by people's vulnerabilities, how people actually perceive and interact with things, and rules that reflect as reasonable balance between risk and utility.

Three Boundaries for Privacy Design

If we understand the design of consumer-facing technologies as an issue of product safety and consumer protection, then design boundaries should be easier to identify. People's expectations and mental models about how a technology works become paramount. When lawmakers, courts, industry and civil society confront design, they should start by considering our expectations in a manner similar to that of product safety and consumer protection law. This means a combination of warnings, protocols, and design choices meant to keep users safe and appropriately aware of the risks posed by a product.

Our expectations about technology are shaped by countless internal and contextual factors, but the factors that matter most with respect to the obligations of companies were covered in Chapter 1: the signals communicated by design and the extent to which technologies affect the transaction costs of particular tasks. When these factors work against consumers, they contribute to three different kinds of harmful design: those that materially deceive us, those that unfairly abuse us, and those that unreasonably endanger us.

In other words, I argue that the main boundaries for privacy law's design agenda should focus on deception, abuse, and danger. Such boundaries will help lawmakers and courts identify why particular designs are harmful, why certain protocols in the design process are deficient, and which legal responses or recognition might be appropriate. For example, it's a problem when people are lured into a false sense of security online and they disclose personal information because they think they are safe when they really are not. When courts and lawmakers focus on deception they can look beyond the words in a privacy policy to find blameworthy misrepresentations built into user interfaces, such as padlock icons and other symbols for unreasonably insecure and risky services. Regulators and courts would be compelled to ask how the signals given by these designs would be interpreted in light of people's commonly held assumptions and other relevant contextual cues. When courts and lawmakers focus on abusive design, they are compelled to look for the way systems are designed to exploit predictable biases to interfere with the decision-making process in an adversarial way. When companies unreasonably manipulate us, they abuse us. When courts and lawmakers focus on dangerous design, they should look to the ways in which products unreasonably expose people and their information to others, putting them at risk of harm and anxiety or chilling their behavior in undesirable ways.

Deceptive Design

People need cues to figure out how technologies work. We rely upon signals, like the silhouette of a house on our browser's Home button, to know what to click on or press. People rely upon what they perceive to make choices about how they interact, so design signals should be legitimate and true. When information technologies misrepresent or omit a fact that is material to our trust, obscurity, or autonomy, they are deceptive. Privacy law should do more to discourage deceptive design.

Deception is a useful standard for privacy law's design agenda because lawmakers and courts can look to established, developed theories of preventing deception. For example, fraud is a well-developed tort. As the Restatement of Torts notes, "One who fraudulently makes a material misrepresentation of fact, opinion, intention, or law, for the purpose of inducing another to act or refrain from acting, is subject to liability for economic loss caused by the other's justifiable reliance on the misrepresentation."[41]

More important, deception is the cornerstone of consumer protection law. Deception prevents consumers from being able to fully and freely participate in the market. The FTC's most effective and commonly used regulatory tool is its authority to protect against deceptive trade practices in section 5 of the Federal Trade Commission Act. A deceptive trade practice is any material "representation, omission or practice that is likely to mislead the consumer acting reasonably in the circumstances, to the consumer's detriment."[42] The FTC has found myriad practices to be deceptive, including "false oral or written representations, misleading price claims, sales of hazardous or systematically defective products or services without adequate disclosures, failure to disclose information regarding pyramid sales, use of bait and switch techniques, failure to perform promised services, and failure to meet warranty obligations."[43] The next step for the agency should be a framework for honest design.

Deceptive design prohibitions are probably one of the least controversial ways to plug privacy law's design gap. The FTC has already issued several important complaints about deceptive design. When technologies are designed to deceive us, the trust we place in others is broken and we have difficulty making decisions regarding our obscurity because our risk calculations are incorrect. When we assume we are safer than we really are, we risk disclosing too much. To discourage deceptive design, privacy law boundaries should focus on scams, deceptive representations, and deceptive omissions made by the labels, symbols, and other aspects of design that signal information to users.

Scams

Deceptive designs are everywhere, though they vary in degree. Some designs are simply outright scams. For example, software bots have infiltrated dating apps like Tinder to trick you into clicking on a link or disclosing personal information like your credit card number. Security company Symantec discovered that scam bots were attempting to lure users into downloading a messenger program and engaging in an explicit webcam session.[44]

This sort of scam technology is common,[45] and it runs afoul of fraud and consumer protection law when people are fleeced. But many of the companies that design and use these deceptive technologies are difficult to locate and punish. If this problem continues, lawmakers might consider requiring platforms like Tinder to incorporate warnings, policies, and procedures designed to minimize such deceptive design as part of the law of data security and data protection.

Means and instrumentalities theories could also be used to shut down scam facilitating technologies. Consider ransomware technologies; these malicious pieces of code are designed to allow hackers to encrypt all of your data and hold it hostage until you pay the hacker money via the difficult-to-trace digital currency Bitcoin. Once you pay the fee, they give you the encryption key to unlock your data. One of the reasons ransomware is growing is that "plug-and-play" software tools work—just about anyone can start a crime syndicate these days, and victims will pay.

Security researchers have discovered this kind of software on the black market. It makes scams remarkably easy. All scammers have to do is enter in a few pieces of information to get paid, and voilà![46]

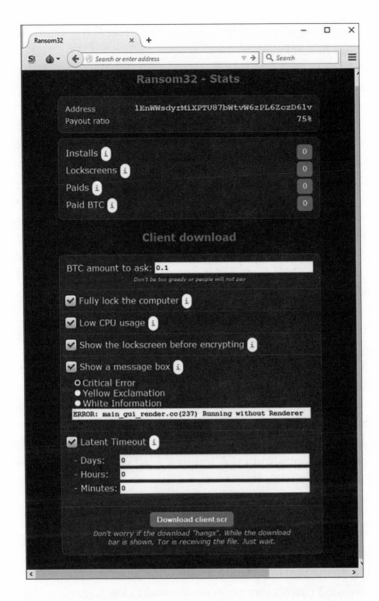

Privacy law can regulate scam technologies like these with little controversy (even if they are among the most difficult to reach);[47] they are unjustified and already prohibited. But lawmakers, courts, and regulators should remain vigilant, as scam and theft technologies are always evolving. A good example is the recent trend of soliciting or harvesting personal information from all over the web and using it to create an undesirable profile or web page that can be "removed" for a fee. These companies use tech design to scam people.

For example, the FTC filed a complaint against the operators of the website Jerk.com for harvesting personal information from Facebook to create profiles labeling people as "Jerk" or "not a Jerk." The operators built a deceptive website that falsely led consumers to believe they could revise their online profiles by paying thirty dollars. According to the FTC, operators at Jerk.com created profiles for more than seventy-three million people, including children.[48]

Jerk.com's design was deceptive because it made people think that the profiles had been created by other Jerk.com users. In reality, most of the profiles were harvested from Facebook. The design also tricked people into paying for a Jerk.com membership by falsely signaling "premium" features that would allow them to change their "Jerk" profile.[49] In Chapter 6, I will discuss how deceptive design involving nonconsensual pornography is being used to exploit and harm people (mostly women).

Scams are not exclusively online creatures. Sometimes technologies are designed to trick us offline as well. One day while walking, cybersecurity expert Matt Blaze noticed an SUV outfitted with a license plate reader that had Pennsylvania State Police placards and a Google Street View decal.[50] Yet the car did not belong to either the Pennsylvania State Police or Google. It's unclear who the vehicle belonged to, though it appeared to be some sort of government vehicle.[51] Was this an attempt to impersonate both Google and the police? Imprimaturs of "legitimate" surveillance designed to justify the use of obscurity-eviscerating license plate readers?

Design as Deceptive Representation

Many of the signals sent by design could be interpreted as representations by companies to users (or as promises between users). A growing body of literature in the field of human-computer interaction has focused on what are known as "privacy indicators"—designs such as logos, icons, settings, and seals used to intuitively convey a website's policy regarding collection and use of personal information.[52] The common padlock icons I mentioned in Chapter 1 are a great example of privacy indicators.

Privacy indicators are common. A number of websites employ "privacy seals" issued by companies like TRUSTe to assure users of the websites' responsible privacy practices. Amazon allows users to create a public profile and "private wish lists"; it reinforces the confidential-by-default nature of these lists by encouraging users to create a list that friends can see. Recall that Twitter places little padlock icons on the profiles of users who chose to "protect" their accounts. Is Twitter representing that it will not share these protected disclosures with any other parties? After all, it did not include "protected tweets" when it gave the Library of Congress every tweet from every public account for archival.[53]

These indicators are designed to improve consumer confidence and instill consumer trust in a website's privacy practices. When broken, they can cause just as much harm as explicit promises of privacy. Much of the FTC's privacy jurisprudence is based on a deception theory of broken promises. Common broken promises of privacy include:

> promises to maintain confidentiality or to refrain from disclosing
>   information to third parties
> promises to only collect data consistent with the company's privacy policy
> promises to provide adequate security for personal data
> promises to maintain anonymity
> promises not to disclose personal data to third parties by selling it in
>   bankruptcy proceedings

Most of the time, the broken privacy promises were made within a company's privacy policy, but design is just as capable of sending signals that constitute "representations" by companies. Consumer protection agencies have begun to recognize the communicative power of design. This is a critical step for Privacy's Blueprint. For example, in the United States the FTC has alleged that failure of a company to respect a user's previously established privacy settings such as "blocked" accounts and visibility settings constitutes a deceptive act based on an implicit promise that those settings would be respected.[54]The FTC has alleged that privacy seals are deceptive designs if the company issuing them has failed to review the privacy practices of those displaying the seals.[55]

The commission alleged a theory of deceptive design against the social media company Path; in its complaint, the FTC stated that Path "represented, expressly or by implication, that personal information from the user's mobile device contacts would only be collected if the user clicked on the 'Add Friends' feature and chose the 'Find friends from your contacts' option. In truth . . . [Path] automatically collected and stored personal information from the user's mobile device contacts each time the user launched the Path App and, if the user signed out, each time the user signed in again. This occurred even if the user never selected the 'Find friends from your contacts' option."[56]

The key to regulating deceptive design is to broaden the scope of what traditionally is considered a representation. The way something is built communicates information to people about how it works. Buttons in the right place are asking to be pressed. Symbols like locks and seals and labels like Privacy Settings are remarkably influential in affecting people's perceptions and behavior.[57] When the user interface is a lie, information spills can occur.

Design as Deceptive Omission

Sometimes design is deceptive because of what it omits. Recall the flashlight app that collected people's geolocation data even though such data was not related to the function of the app (see Chapter 1). The FTC has stated, "The nature, appearance, or intended use of a product may create an impression on the mind of the consumer . . . and if the impression is false, and if the seller does not take adequate steps to correct it, he is responsible for an unlawful deception."[58] Design is deceptive when it fails to include material information that will keep the overall representations made via technology to consumers from being misleading.[59]

Deceptive omissions in technology are especially important given the limited space of mobile apps and limits on our attention span. In its staff report on mobile disclosures, the FTC recommended using icons, a privacy dashboard, and "just-in-time" disclosures, among other things. The commission has stated, "Providing such a disclosure at the point in time when it matters to consumers, just prior to the collection of such information by apps, will allow users to make informed choices about whether to allow the collection of such information."[60] Just-in-time disclosures might be a good way to remedy deceptive design omissions, but they should be used sparingly. They must be balanced with usability concerns, the overall purpose of any application, and the information ecosystem within which most users exist.

Privacy law should shore up the boundaries around deceptive design omissions by requiring warnings that make indiscriminate data collection more burdensome for companies. In other words, if companies build their systems in a way that collects personal data in counterintuitive or hidden ways, companies should be required to effectively warn of, and not just disclose, this fact. This approach can encourage companies to design technologies that either minimize the collection and storage of data or in the least keep people from being surprised by requiring companies to wear the move adversarial aspects of personal data collection on their sleeves.

The concept of "insufficient notice" in consumer protection law deals with deceptive omissions. The FTC cried foul when Facebook failed to properly notify users of privacy-related changes at the website. Facebook used a multipage notice system called a Privacy Wizard to notify its users of the changes. The Privacy Wizard consisted of an introductory page, "privacy update pages, which required . . . users to choose, via a series of radio buttons, between new privacy settings that Facebook 'recommended' and the user's 'Old Settings,' for ten types of profile information," and "a confirmation page, which summarized the user's updated Privacy Settings."[61] According to the FTC, the Privacy Wizard failed to disclose the fact that users could no longer limit the visibility of certain parts of their profile to some third parties. The FTC deemed this to be a deceptive trade practice.

Users draw upon their previous experiences with technology to make assumptions about how the technology they are currently using will work. For example, most computer users probably assume that digital files in folders are discrete from one another and that in the absence of a clear indication otherwise, software they use will not expose files elsewhere on their hard drives. But that's what happened with the peer-to-peer file-sharing software created by Frostwire. The FTC alleged that Frostwire misrepresented its privacy practices in its user interface. In a separate count, the FTC found that Frostwire failed to notify consumers adequately regarding how its file-sharing software operated. This included the fact that downloaded files were shared publicly by default, as well as the fact that the software "would publicly share files that consumers previously downloaded from the Gnutella network and stored in 'unshared' folders even after consumers deselected the Share Finished Downloads setting in the Options-Sharing dialog box."[62]

Consumer protection has started to recognize the many ways in which design signals can deceive people. But as we will explore in Part III, many areas of privacy law can better incorporate design to prevent deception and honor trust.

Abusive Design

There is a ton of regret over sharing online. People commonly disclose something personal and then wish they hadn't. We trash bad dates, mean bosses, faithless friends, and poor customer service every chance we get. But we often think better of it after the deed is done. One research subject who vented on Facebook about how badly an interview went said, "I regretted the minute I pressed 'share.'"[63] This is a common view. People regularly disclose things online in ways that are against their own interests, even when they are not lied to. We also keep clicking and consuming on our phones and tablets long after we have found what we are looking for. We push buttons and keep scrolling in ways that expose us more than we likely would prefer without consciously thinking about it. Sometimes we even explicitly agree to be exposed! Why do people do this? It's not that we are idiots, though many things we do online are probably ill advised. Rather, our mediated environments are built to exploit us. It turns out we humans are pretty susceptible to manipulation because we have addictive tendencies and predictable biases. This means that those who control our environments can exploit our addictions and biases to get us to act in their own interests.

The idea that technology can be used to persuade people and change their behavior isn't a crackpot theory; it's an entire industry supported by established research on human vulnerability. There is a Persuasive Tech Lab at Stanford University whose purpose is to "to create insight into how computing products—from websites to mobile phone software—can be designed to change people's beliefs and behaviors."[64] Books with titles like *Hooked* demonstrate how to create "hook cycles," which enable products to "reach their ultimate goal of bringing users back again and again without depending on costly advertising or aggressive messaging."[65] Natasha Dow Schüll depicts in her book *Addiction by Design,* about machine gambling in Las Vegas, how the intentional design of casinos and slot machines can place people in "the machine zone," which keeps players in a trance as the world seems to dissolve around them and they are calmed by machine play.[66] Alexis Madrigal invokes the machine zone to describe what it feels like when you can't stop scrolling through photos on Facebook.[67]

It's no accident that we keep coming back for more and exposing more of ourselves every time.[68] Bottomless wells, pings, likes, badges, and loops are all designed to reduce the fiction of interaction and exploit our need for social approval and instant gratification. Much of this is business as usual. We have a word for communication meant to persuade us to use a product or service: *advertising.* But occasionally the design of information technologies crosses the line and becomes abusive. It unreasonably frustrates our ability to make autonomous decisions and puts us at greater risk of harm or makes us regret our decisions. I call this abusive design.

Abusive design is distinct from deceptive design, though the two can overlap. Deceptive design misrepresents reality and subverts expectations, interfering with our ability to trust others and remain obscure. But design need not be untrue to create problems. Sometimes design interferes with our ability to understand what we perceive or intentionally exploits our willpower to resist sharing and data extraction. Sometimes our confusion and misunderstanding of risk are predictable. Deceptive design lies to us; abusive design uses our own internal limitations against us.

Recall our exploration of the limitations of human cognition. The obvious notion that our brains have a limited ability to assess risk and benefits is called our "bounded rationality."[69] There is simply no way for users to weight all of the available pieces of information to get an accurate risk assessment for every personal disclosure they make. Such a quest could take hours or days for just one website. Life demands that we make split-second decisions regarding what to disclose, how, and to whom.

To compensate we use heuristics, which are mental shortcuts or rules of thumb, in predictable, consistent ways.[70] For example, researchers have found that people look to the popularity of a brand in determining whether to trust it with information. The mere fact that companies appear transparent about their data collection and use practices imbues them with credibility: "If a website makes its privacy policy transparent, then my information is safe." Users also look to the ephemeral nature of data to guide their disclosure decisions: "If the information is not stored, but disappears, it is safe to share."[71] People often think the longer a message is, the more credible it is (sometimes called the "length equals strength" heuristic).[72] Companies have great incentive to design systems that exploit our predictable misunderstanding of risks and benefits.[73]

The notion of abusive design can be found in consumer protection law, which aims to protect consumer choice. The most prominent prohibition on abusive practices in the United States comes from the relatively new Consumer Financial Protection Bureau (CFPB). The Dodd-Frank Wall Street Reform and Consumer Protection Act authorized the CFPB to prohibit any "abusive" act or practice that

(1) *materially interferes* with the ability of a consumer to understand a term or condition of a consumer financial product or service; or
(2) takes unreasonable advantage of—
    (A) a *lack of understanding* on the part of the consumer of the material risks, costs, or conditions of the product or service;
    (B) the *inability of the consumer to protect* the interests of the consumer in selecting or using a consumer financial product or service; or
    (C) the reasonable *reliance* by the consumer on a covered person to act in the interests of the consumer.[74]

I borrow from this notion of abusive acts to argue that privacy law should seek to recognize and limit abusive design. Lawmakers and judges should set standards to prohibit design that unreasonably exploits our cognitive limitations, biases, and predictable errors to undermine autonomous decision making.

The focus on abuse would shore up some of the limitations of regulating deceptive design, which relies upon untrue signals or broken promises. Abusive design overlaps with deceptive and dangerous design, but it is unique. Deception largely deals with problems of false or imperfect information, such as when the signals shaping users' expectations do not match reality. The focus of deceptive design is on outward-facing signals, like the padlock icon on the fake Windows 10 registration page.

Abusive design has a different focus. It looks to the problems people have in assessing risk and benefits even with accurate, truthful information. It begins with an internal inquiry into how we process information.[75] Confusing permission forms are a good example of abusive design. They use vague terms, jargon, and double negatives to confuse people and induce agreement while being technically accurate. Consider the following question regarding a child's directory information, which is common on forms sent home from school to be signed by parents:

4. Decline Release of Directory Information **(Note: most parents do _not_ choose this option)**
Decline Release of Directory Information
I **do not** want the District to release "directory information" (see Packet for examples) to qualified individuals or groups, such as official parent-teacher organizations, college recruiters, Oakland Education Fund, or employers.

Student's Name	
Parent/Guardian's Signature	

There are several elements in the design of this question that, taken together, might interfere with parents' ability to understand what is being asked of them. For example, the subhead contains a double negative—it informs parents that most other parents do *not* choose to *decline* the release of directory information. This is also a nudge for those susceptible to displays of consensus, i.e., those who tend to look for trends to guide their decision. The body of the text then notes that parents will be declining release to "qualified groups." Examples of qualified groups are given, but the term is not defined or meaningfully limited, making it seem more legitimate than it might be.

And these are common, not extreme, types of forms people must deal with every day to exercise their "control" over personal information. Each of these questions might be fine in isolation, but in the context of the daily barrage of privacy-related decisions we must make, they can be confusing, frustrating, and hard to square with our natural privacy inclinations.

Thus, an inquiry into whether design is abusive does not ask whether information is true. Rather, privacy law should be concerned about designs that *interfere* with people's ability to discern whom to trust and how to maintain obscurity or that *take unreasonable advantage* of people's *understanding, limited abilities,* or *reliance* on relationships and transaction costs. In other words, privacy law should ask whether a particular design interferes with our understanding of risks or exploits our vulnerabilities in unreasonable ways with respect to our personal information.

Sometimes abusive design will *leverage* our personal information against us. Companies have learned that targeted, personalized appeals are more persuasive than ads designed for a general audience. We all have our weak points, and my weak points are probably different from yours. Sure, there may be some categories where people are almost universally susceptible: "free" things, appeals to sex, and cat memes. But each of us has different passions and impulses and reacts to things in different ways. Digital advertisers collect and analyze our data—purchase and browsing history, location, demographic information—to find out what makes us tick so that they can deliver more persuasive messages.

With knowledge of our predilections and vulnerabilities, companies can design systems that unreasonably interfere with our ability to make decisions in the market. Compare a nonpersonalized banner ad for cigarettes on a web page to a system that identifies regular smokers who are trying to quit and targets them on their smartphones with digital coupons for cigarettes at their weakest moments, like right when they walk out of a bar. Ryan Calo's theory of "digital market manipulation" is helpful here. He writes, "A specific set of emerging technologies and techniques will empower corporations to discover and exploit the limits of each individual consumer's ability to pursue his or her own self-interest. Firms will increasingly be able to trigger irrationality or vulnerability in consumers— leading to actual and perceived harms that challenge the limits of consumer protection law, but which regulators can scarcely ignore."[76]

Calo notes that consumers respond to forms of persuasions in different ways. Some consumers are susceptible to displays of consensus; they consistently like to follow the herd. Other consumers value scarcity; they predictably are more likely to be persuaded by the feeling of exclusivity or missing out if they don't act soon. Calo cites research showing how companies might figure out what motivates a consumer and dynamically change an advertisement accordingly in real time: "Therefore, for the natural follower, the ad for toothpaste will refer to it as a 'best selling' item. Whereas, for the scarcity-phobic, the same ad will ominously read 'while supplies last.'" This technique is called persuasion profiling.[77]

While not every form of persuasion is abusive, at some point personalized persuasion becomes unreasonable. The literature surrounding behavioral economics and price discrimination—charging some groups or people a different price than others for the same good or service—might help pinpoint when abusive design goes further than it should. This is particularly true when it is used in contexts where people do not understand their mediated reality is different than others and the costs of such discrimination.[78] For example, Jeff Rachlinski has argued that exploiting the cognitive vulnerabilities of subgroups of consumers is different from general attempts at price discrimination. Price discrimination usually involves identifying people who value a product more than others (and thus would be willing to pay more for it). Meanwhile, identifying people's cognitive vulnerabilities involves finding people "who probably should not engage in the transaction and induc[ing] them to do so by exploiting cognitive errors that they are apt to make."[79] Designs that persuade by unreasonably exploiting cognitive vulnerabilities are abusive.

Of course, the act of identifying people who "probably should not engage in a transaction" is fraught with peril. When the law attempts to protect people from themselves it risks being overly paternalistic. But that doesn't mean the law should ignore this kind of abusive design. The key will be isolating acceptable persuasion from blameworthy manipulation. One way to do that would be to look for regret or substantially increased risk.[80] Another would be to look for instances where people's confusion as to how a product works is clearly exploited. The legal response to abusive design can also vary according to its severity or blameworthiness. As I'll argue in Chapter 5, there are many "soft" and "moderate" ways that the law could mitigate abusive design that leverages personal information to exploit the cognitive errors of people in adverse ways short of outright prohibitions.

Design doesn't have to leverage our personal information against us to be abusive. Sometimes technologies are simply designed to be adverse to our own goals. They are designed to *extract* our personal information when we otherwise might not share it or to *encourage* information disclosure that is adverse to our interests. Recall from Chapter 1 the many different ways "consent" to the collection, use, and disclosure of personal information is extracted online. Privacy's Blueprint targets all of these varieties of abusive design.

The world is littered with technologies that "aggressively divert users toward the goals of the designer and away from those of the user."[81] Gregory Conti and Edward Sobiesk, researchers on this form of computer abuse, define malicious interfaces simply as those that "deliberately violate usable design best practices in order to manipulate, exploit, or attack the user."[82] They have collected thousands of examples of adversarial interfaces, ranging from the classic pop-up ads designed to trick you into clicking

them to the layout and design of gas pumps meant to maximize the likelihood of selecting a premium-grade gasoline.

Common examples of malicious interfaces include "disabled back buttons, browsers with 'sponsored' default bookmarks, unexpected and unnecessary forms, blinking advertisements, and pop-ups covering desired
content." These malicious interfaces often coerce users into disclosing private information.[83] Conti and Sobiesk have identified eleven kinds of malicious interfaces:

> *Coercion*—Threatening or mandating the user's compliance.
>
> *Confusion*—Asking the user questions or providing information that they
> do not understand.
>
> *Distraction*—Attracting the user's attention away from their current task
> by exploiting perception, particularly preattentive processing.
>
> *Exploiting Errors*—Taking advantage of user errors to facilitate the
> interface designer's goals.
>
> *Forced Work*—Deliberately increasing work for the user.
>
> *Interruption*—Interrupting the user's task flow.
>
> *Manipulating Navigation*—Creating information architectures and
> navigation mechanisms that guide the user toward interface designer
> task accomplishment.
>
> *Obfuscation*—Hiding desired information and interface elements.
>
> *Restricting Functionality*—Limiting or omitting controls that would
> facilitate user task accomplishment.
>
> *Shock*—Presenting disturbing content to the user.
>
> *Trick*—Misleading the user or other attempts at deception.[84]

These design techniques are common. Often they are only mildly annoying,
if they are noticed at all. Yet in context and in combination with each
other, many should be seen as unreasonably abusive. Drawing the boundaries for abusive design will be very difficult because they need to be sensitive to context yet clear enough to follow. Researchers have only relatively
recently begun to empirically study malicious design. This research should
continue to be funded and supported so that it can, among other things,
help lawmakers and judges determine the limits of abusive design.[85]
Through an iterative process and attention to the state of the literature,
lawmakers, courts, and industry can better understand when companies
have gone too far in using our own limitations against us.

Dangerous Design

The final kind of bad privacy design puts us in a dangerous position by making us vulnerable to others; it exposes us through dramatic reductions in obscurity, hidden surveillance, and poor data security safeguards. For example, the adultery facilitation website Ashley Madison failed to construct its system to protect against snoops curious about the site's membership. A security researcher discovered that the website revealed slightly different "password retrieval" messages for members and nonmembers.[86] This allowed those who were curious as to whether their lovers and friends had registered with Ashley Madison to trick the website into revealing whether an email address was tied to a user's account. Because the interface was different for those who actually had an account than it was for those who did not, people could use the design to effectively out people who had an account with Ashley Madison.

Sometimes dangerous design is not "front-facing"—that is, technology users don't interact with it. It runs in the background, invisible to the people it adversely affects. For example, surveillance and aggregation technologies often affect people outside of interactions with others and interfaces. Facial recognition technologies and drones can be used to track and identify otherwise obscure people in ways that are not outright deceptive and do not interfere with their ability to understand the consequences of a particular disclosure.

In other words, honest and permissive technologies can still create trust, obscurity, and autonomy problems for people by exposing them in dangerous ways. Objects that are part of the Internet of Things can be designed in ways that facilitate unwanted and harmful surveillance or leave us vulnerable to hackers without tricking us or exploiting our cognitive biases. For these reasons, privacy law needs a broader, catchall standard that discourages dangerous design.

Legal approaches to mitigating dangerous design should incorporate aspects of "defective design" from tort law and "unfair acts or practices" from consumer protection law. When the design of a product is unreasonably dangerous, it is defective.[87] To determine what is unreasonably dangerous, companies, courts, and lawmakers must engage in the risk/utility analysis regarding reasonable alternative design mentioned earlier in this chapter. Reasonable alternative designs are those that are safer, of similar cost to the user, and practical enough to remain consistent with the product's primary purpose.

It is important to note that the law of defective design uses two variables to keep people safe: structure defects and information defects. The two work in tandem. *Structure defects* refer to the actual design of the product, while *information defects* refer to warnings about the product's risks. If danger created by the structure, layout, function, or composition of a product can be reasonably remedied by supplying product users with a warning about the risk, then the design of the product is not defective. Adequate warnings must be clear, prominent, and accessible to the full spectrum of anticipated users. But if the design risk is serious enough, no reasonable warning will cure the defect: asbestos simply cannot safely be used as a building material because it can cause cancer; fuel tanks are clearly unsafe when they are placed in cars in ways that cause them to be easily ruptured during collisions.[88]

The concepts of risk / utility balancing, reasonable avoidance, and the dual notions of structure and information defects are also incorporated into consumer protection's notion of "unfair design." In the United States, an "unfair" trade practice is one that "causes or is likely to cause substantial injury to consumers which is not reasonably avoidable by consumers themselves and not outweighed by countervailing benefits to consumers or to competition." This test, which has been codified in the Federal Trade Commission Act, has come to be known as the "three-part test."[89]

The unfairness standard is useful because it is flexible and changes over time to adapt to new technologies. According to the FTC, "The present understanding of the unfairness standard is the result of an evolutionary process. The statute was deliberately framed in general terms since Congress recognized the impossibility of drafting a complete list of unfair trade practices that would not quickly become outdated or leave loopholes for easy evasion."[90] Notably, the FTC can find a practice unfair even when it is otherwise legally permissible.

There are three specific kinds of dangerous design lawmakers should discourage: technologies that facilitate obscurity lurches, hidden surveillance technologies, and insecure design.

Obscurity Lurches

A common metaphor for privacy violations is an eyeball peering through a keyhole. It's everywhere; it wouldn't surprise me if there was an entire stock photography website dedicated to eyeballs looking through peepholes. This is a poor metaphor for many modern privacy problems. Key-holes and walls actually represent transaction costs. They are structural constraints that lower the likelihood of someone finding or understanding information. Walls and locks, practically speaking, block almost all prying eyes. Old-fashioned keyholes make snooping technically possible, but difficult. The difficulty of spying through a keyhole without being spotted by someone outside or in the hallway is so great that we don't usually worry about it. These structural constraints are so common we take them for granted. So too with other forms of obscurity.

We rely on limited searchability, accessibility, identification, and clarity of our information to maintain obscurity online. When we move about in public, we might assume that at some point our picture might be taken or that we might pop up every now and then on store surveillance cameras. But most of us don't assume that someone is constantly tracking us from place to place, piecing together a mosaic that tells a much more detailed story about us than "person shopping in aisle 7."

When technology dramatically reduces the cost of finding or under-standing information—when it "lurches"—people's reliance on these costs becomes detrimental. The rug is pulled out from under us, and we have no time to adjust to our new reality. In the case of information that has already been disclosed, our information is now less safe than it was when we disclosed it. In the case of prospective surveillance, our day-to-day activities now become much riskier because we can no longer rely upon the obscurity that we have become accustomed to.

A better metaphor than an eye peeping through a wall is that the *wall is suddenly gone*. When structural design constraints are quickly or dramatically removed, we become exposed, making it much easier—and thus more likely—that our information and activities will be seen and understood by others. Harry Surden has made the argument that the law should recognize a right to rely upon structural constraints as a way of protecting individual privacy, noting that "society shapes the conduct of individuals using, among other devices, norms, markets, and the real-world physical and technical limitations known collectively as structure. . . . [T]hese various mechanisms share the common attribute that they constrain behavior by regulating the costs of certain activities."[91] This is a way of articulating how transaction costs create zones of obscurity that we rely upon every day.

Consider the accessibility of public records. You might be shocked to realize that an incredible amount of your personal information is made available by the government to the public. State governments keep records of births, marriages, divorces, professional licenses, voter information, worker's compensation, personnel data, deeds, arrests, mug shots, the names of crime victims, transcripts of criminal and civil court proceedings, and much more. Public records include information about a person's physical appearance, race, nationality, and gender; family life, residence and contact information; political and financial information; employment, health, and criminal history; mother's maiden name; and social security number.[92] The list goes on, and all is ostensibly open for public inspection.

This is a dizzying amount of data. Any random Joe has the right to look at any of these records that are designated as "public." If this is surprising to you, it's probably because most public records are dispersed among many different government offices, tucked away, and difficult to find or understand. Inspecting any one of these records typically means spending hours in a government office or filing a request and waiting to receive copies in the mail. They are obscure.

So you can imagine the surprise of many California residents when they woke one morning to find that the California Public Employees' Retirement System (CalPERS) planned to post their names, pensions, the amount of their monthly retirement stipends, and other personal information online in an accessible, searchable way.[93] These records had always been classified as public, but until this planned obscurity lurch, few people noticed or seemed to mind. But when news spread, people became concerned this would be a target for scammers who wanted to prey on the elderly, or for anyone who was nosy.

As I will discuss in Chapter 5, privacy law's design agenda should not require the law to ban all obscurity lurches. Rather, lawmakers should ask whether transaction costs can be reduced in a safe way. Courts, lawmakers, and administrative agencies could better recognize the role of obscurity in shaping our notions of privacy. Obscurity lurches cannot be outright eradicated in the age of big data, but they can be mitigated. Some transaction costs can be retained while others are reduced. A requirement to consider people's reliance upon obscurity could mitigate the problem of lurches. For example, in Chapter 5, I argue that Privacy Impact Assessments should be an indispensable part of the design process. These risk assessments should include the degree to which designs will erode obscurity. Consider Facebook's news feed dustup, whereby everyone's status updates and profile changes were aggregated and made highly visible overnight.[94] A sort of "obscurity impact assessment" might have caught the dramatic erosion of transaction costs and cautioned a slower rollout with more fair warning to users. This would allow people to scrub their profiles of anything they had thought was practically safe because few would see it. (This is also a context where the right to demand deletion is an invaluable example of control over data.) There is precedent for mandating impact assessments for dangerous activities. The European Union already requires such impact assessments for things like high-risk data processing.[95]

Sometimes obscurity protects us from surveillance. Other times it protects us from harassment. It can foster autonomous decision making as well as freedom of thought. Institutions can make information accessible to the appropriate audiences, but they—and privacy law itself—should find more creative ways to maintain transaction costs that protect obscurity. In the case of the CalPERS database, perhaps the searchability could have been limited by the number of searches or search fields. Access could have been limited to an on-site terminal rather than online. The public records could be pseudonymized, if appropriate, to protect people's individual privacy while making the data available in bulk. Such imposed transaction costs could deter casual snooping and other unwelcome inquiries while preserving much of the accountability function of public records. Lawmakers should consider various soft and moderate approaches to temper the design of technologies that facilitate obscurity lurches like that of CalPERS' online database.

Hidden and Unexpected Surveillance

Surveillance is dangerous enough when we know we are being watched, but it's even worse when we don't. At least if we are aware of surveillance, we can alter our risk calculus to adjust to being watched. But if we don't, we wrongfully rely upon the freedom that not being watched provides. We show sides of ourselves we don't want certain others to see. We undress. We gossip. We take risks. We explore in ways that might be questioned by authority figures or misunderstood if taken out of context.

There are now more opportunities for hidden and unexpected surveillance than ever before. This means that the peephole metaphor, of course, is still incredibly relevant even if it's not universal. Technologies designed to engage in hidden or unexpected surveillance are dangerous. Privacy law should limit not just the act of surreptitious surveillance but also the technologies that facilitate it.

One of the most common and dangerous technologies that facilitate surreptitious surveillance is spyware. It is designed to be undetectable; it allows stalkers and domestic abusers to terrorize and physically abuse victims. Unfortunately, violence aided by spyware is increasingly common.[96] Spyware represents a profound threat to intellectual privacy and free expression.

Not to mention the harm caused when data collected by spyware is breached. Consider the hack of spyware app maker mSpy, which markets itself as the ideal technology for, among other things, helping husbands catch cheating wives.[97] The company failed to keep its data safe. After hackers broke in, they leaked hundreds of gigabytes of data to the dark web after mSpy failed to cooperate with the hackers' extortion demands. According to security journalist Brian Krebs, "Included in that huge archive is a 13 gigabyte (compressed) directory referencing countless screen shots taken from devices running mSpy's software—including screen shots taken secretly by users who installed the software on a friend or partner's device." This breach was compounded by poor data protection practices, which left millions of screenshots taken from surveilled devices "wide open and exposed to the Internet via [mSpy's] own Web site."[98]

Spyware data breaches give us much more to worry about than just identity thieves selling our credit cards, social security numbers, and insurance information in dark markets. The mSpy breach exposed information revealing everything people do with their phones—their precise geolocations, passwords, browsing histories, emails, texts, phone books, calendars, health histories, and far more. Want to know when someone is not home so you can break into his home? Leaked spyware information will let you know! Want to know if someone is seeing a psychiatrist so you can blackmail her? Spyware companies have got you covered. Spyware apps are engaged in an unjustifiable enterprise by surreptitiously providing access to others' cell phone data. They also are creating massive treasure chests for thieves.

The FTC has alleged that the sale of spyware, as well as providing the means and instrumentalities to install spyware and access consumers' personal information, constitute unfair and deceptive trade practices.[99] The commission has also concluded that installing spyware and gathering data without notice is an unfair practice. The agency has cited the substantial harm caused to consumers from such invasive surveillance and noticed that "[c]onsumers cannot reasonably avoid these injuries because [the surveillance] is invisible to them."[100] Again structure and information work together to determine whether the design of information technologies are beyond the pale.

Spyware is another area where privacy law has already started to fill its design gap. In the United States, federal and some state laws prohibit the manufacture, sale, or advertising of technologies whose principal use is likely to be for wiretapping or eavesdropping. Title 3 of the Wiretap Act actually makes such activities a crime.[101] But all of privacy law should better protect against such technologies. Danielle Citron has noted that such laws do not limit tools devoted to the secret collection of location data. And prosecution under these laws remains rare.[102] Consumer protection agencies can only do so much, and state attorneys general could use more of their own consumer protection authority consistently to fight spyware. As we will explore in Chapter 7, privacy law can be modified to better limit pernicious surveillance design.

Insecure Design

It seems like we just can't stop getting hacked. The Privacy Rights Clearinghouse has reported that as of September 2017 there had been 1,070,186,516 records breached from 7,674 data breaches made public since 2005.[103] That's bonkers. And those are just the breaches we know about. Yet we keep digitizing data and installing chips in every conceivable object—including, as we have seen, toothbrushes and refrigerators. While there are many benefits to doing so, the number of attack vectors for hackers is rapidly growing. Secure design is more important than ever before.

Like scam designs, the law of insecure design is one of the most important and established parts of Privacy's Blueprint. The law of insecure design includes what is commonly called data security law, which generally mandates that companies create procedures and systems to protect against and recover from the unauthorized access, use, and disclosure of personal data. Derek Bambauer describes one notion of data security as "the set of technological mechanisms (including, at times, physical ones) that mediates requests for access or control."[104]

Some kind of data security is (more or less) mandated at both the state and federal levels in the United States. The law typically imposes a standard-like requirement of "reasonable data security" consistent with my proposal that Privacy's Blueprint remains flexible. The FTC generally prohibits unreasonable data security practices "in light of the sensitivity and volume of consumer information it holds, the size and complexity of its business, and the cost of available tools to improve security and reduce vulnerabilities."[105]What constitutes reasonable data security is determined almost entirely by industry standard practices.[106]

The law of data security recognizes that technical design must be adapted to respond to context and threats, among other things. But there are four general components of a reasonable approach to data security: identification of assets and risk; data minimization; administrative, technical and physical safeguards; and data breach response plans. Various frameworks exist to provide further detail for those operating in certain contexts, such as with credit cards and banks.[107] All of these rules show how the law can take the design of information technologies more seriously. Privacy's Blueprint involves more than just top-down dictation of design to companies. In Chapter 5 we will explore tools like mandatory notice, mandatory process, data architecture, and others that guide the design of technology in moderate but important ways.

Data security law as currently established could be refined to better protect against insecure design. In Chapter 8 we will explore how to mitigate insecure design in the Internet of Things. Data security law might also be expanded to cover systems that need to be resilient to abuse and deception.

To review, I propose that law and policy makers move beyond the FIPs when setting boundaries for privacy-sensitive design. Rather, they should look to notions developed in product safety law and consumer protection that focus on people's vulnerabilities and expectations regarding how technologies work.[108] I propose three boundaries to discourage bad design and help lawmakers nurture trust, obscurity, and autonomy: deceptive design, abusive design, and dangerous design. These three boundaries draw from established concepts in the law and can serve as flexible and self-sustaining touchstones for courts and lawmakers. In Chapter 5, I will develop the legal tools that can be used to enforce these boundaries and implement goals for good design.

5

A Tool Kit for Privacy Design

WHEN I TELL people that I think the law should take design more seriously, they sometimes assume I mean that the law should jump straight to
banning technology or imposing strict liability upon all designers or
manufacturers for everything they build. It's as though they immediately
picture some angry bureaucrat banging on a desk and yelling, "Shut it down!
Shut it *all* down!" But that's not what I mean, as I hope you've seen thus far.

Half of my argument is simply that existing privacy laws should better
incorporate the role of design in shaping our expectations and choices. The
effects of design should inform disputes involving existing regimes, like
contracts, consumer protection rules, surveillance law, and the U.S. privacy
torts. Judges and regulators (and industry and the public, for that matter)
must ask more questions and be more critical. For example, consider the
fight over the legal significance of the Do Not Track (DNT) setting within
Internet browsers. Essentially, DNT allows consumers to enable a sort of
browser protocol that indicates that she does not wish her browsing history
to be tracked. Yet courts ignore this preference when contemplating the
parties' agreement over data usage.[1] For all the hullaballoo about effectuating control, lawmakers and courts have not been very imaginative about
ways to enable and respect it. By taking design-enabled preferences and
promises like this into account, contracts and other legal regimes could hew
more closely to the realities of using technology. Another example of law

enforcement taking note of deceptive or abusive design is the settlement reached by thirty-seven state attorneys general with Google in a lawsuit alleging that the tech company was deceptive in designing cookies to circumvent the Safari browser's privacy settings by tricking the browser into treating Google as a "first party"—that is, the service a consumer is explicitly targeting and interacting with.[2]

The other half of my argument is that privacy law should more actively guide the design of technologies. While this might include specific technological restrictions and designer liability in certain contexts, there are many legal and policy tools courts and lawmakers can use to proactively shape design. Some of them would act as carrots, providing financial resources and educational initiatives. Others would act as sticks, requiring better notice or security process.

In this chapter, I explore the tool kit that courts, lawmakers, and regulators can draw on to implement a design agenda in privacy law. I highlight the strengths and weaknesses of each approach and suggest that lawmakers should seek proportionality with competing interests, harmony with surveillance and data processing rules, and ensure that the tool chosen is a good fit for the problem being addressed. Sometimes many tools can be used to address the same problem. Consider the law's response to the use of Internet cookies, the little bits of data that websites send and store in visitors' web browsers; they are one of the main ways websites collect a user's personal information.

Cookies can be used by websites to identify a computer and track a user's Internet activity. A real privacy problem comes when cookies are leveraged to track Internet users across different websites. This data can be dumped into profiles, which advertisers use to infer a user's interests. As anyone who has used the Internet can imagine, this data can reveal health information, political beliefs, and sexual desires, among many other things. Even though cookies don't usually collect people's names, there are many popular ways to link pseudonymous cookie data with real people.[3] And that's just on desktops. Mobile devices provide many more ways to track and identify people, such as through apps that collect detailed location information.

The law surrounding cookies has taken many turns and involved many different legal tools like mandated disclosure, truthfulness requirements under consumer protection law, tort liability, and outright regulatory prohibition without consent. Initially the use of cookies was legally challenged (but ultimately cleared) under electronic surveillance and computer anti-hacking laws.[4] Multiple complaints have been filed against companies for wrongfully sidestepping blocking measures to deploy cookies.[5] The European Union's E-Privacy Directive requires websites to provide "clear and comprehensive information" to and obtain consent from users before cookies can be deployed.[6] The Federal Trade Commission (FTC) has tried to ensure that companies using cookies are being honest with people. In 2011, the agency alleged that a company that used Flash cookies, which browsers could not block, mislead users about their ability to opt out of targeted ads powered by cookies.[7] All of these strategies attempt to indirectly regulate the design and deployment of the same technology in different ways.

The tools available to lawmakers fall along a spectrum of soft, moderate, and robust responses. Soft responses, which shape design through education and incentives rather than penalties and prohibitions, should be used early and often. When those aren't enough, regulators and courts should look to moderate responses, which impose obligations upon designers but stop short of outright bans, formidable top-down control on design decisions, and other robust legal responses.

Some moderate responses, like mandated disclosures, have been criticized as weak or ineffective. In this chapter I'll attempt to rehabilitate the use of disclosures in privacy law. Disclosures should be a key part of privacy law's design agenda. When conceived of more as warnings to be balanced with safe design, disclosures can generate skepticism and increase transaction costs even when they fail at truly informing people. So while disclosures are rarely a cure-all, they can work in tandem with other design interventions to keep consumers safe while mitigating the cost to companies. The key is to ensure that privacy law treats disclosure regimes as necessary but not sufficient. Companies must still bear some responsibility for safe products and a reasonable design process.

Finally, moderate responses might not be enough for some technologies. Robust responses, such as tort liability for design or outright categorical prohibitions, might be necessary. While robust responses should be judiciously and sparingly deployed, privacy law has too often ignored them. Such robust responses will require confronting some hard questions about privacy harm, technological obsolescence, and necessary checks on governmental power. But it is time to answer those questions.

I end this chapter by noting that lawmakers aren't the only ones with the tools to cope with privacy-relevant design. Because all of us either use technology or have technology used upon us, we all have a part to play. To that end, I provide a sort of guide for the general public in doing our part to ensure that digital technologies are made and used in a safe and sustainable way.

We Can Do This the Easy Way or the Hard Way (or Somewhere In Between)

Most conversations between policy makers and other stakeholders about how law might better understand and shape privacy-related design is myopic. Too often policy makers focus largely on rules dictating what designers can and cannot do. People talk about tort liability for dangerous software, bans on certain technologies, and certification schemes to ensure safe devices. These are, of course, important conversations to have. But there are so many different ways for privacy law to take design more seriously: it could help set standards; it could mandate design processes instead of regulating the final product; it could modify the law of notice by leveraging the power of labels and symbols and the power of anthropomorphization— how humans respond to things that have human qualities.[8] Lawmakers and courts could create or recognize more individual remedies for victims in contract and equity; they could even simply educate themselves on design or exercise restraint in certain contexts. While many of these tools are established and even obvious, considering them as a group illustrates the great potential for law to leverage design to enable human flourishing.

Privacy law will need all of these tools in its design agenda to achieve the right balance and fit. Not all responses will further the values of trust, obscurity, or autonomy, and not all responses will equally discourage deceptive, abusive, or dangerous design. Additionally, lawmakers must think conceptually about the goal of any design intervention. Just as in building construction, the tool must match the target. A builder would not use a sledgehammer for small nails. Lawmakers should not use burdensome, restrictive laws if less onerous ones will do. Conversely, they should not be content to settle for an ineffective remedy when more dramatic responses are called for. Privacy design interventions should be proportional to the threat posed by certain designs. The tools discussed in this chapter proceed along a spectrum based on their degree of influence and control over technology companies and the severity of the penalty for bad design. When confronted with a privacy design problem, lawmakers, courts, and regulators can answer with soft, moderate, and robust responses.

Soft Responses

Taking design seriously doesn't require an act of Congress (literal or figurative). Privacy policy includes much more than just legal prohibitions. Some of the most effective ways privacy law can implement a design agenda are soft, meaning they do not impose a penalty on companies for exceeding the boundaries of privacy design. Rather, they are initiatives aimed at supporting and educating companies, users, and themselves about design.

Soft responses also include working with industry to encourage common standards and innovation in privacy design. Soft responses are attractive to companies because they are the least intrusive into the design processes. This makes them good candidates for some designs that do not result in significantly blameworthy, dramatic harms but instead detrimentally affect people in more subtle and ambiguous ways. For example, law makers might look to soft ways and moderate ways to steer companies toward safer, more sustainable user interfaces that do not seek to subtly manipulate people into disclosing personal information in a casual, reckless way.

Many designs are corrosive to trust, obscurity, or autonomy in understated ways. Harry Brignull refers to these designs as "dark patterns," meaning interfaces that have been "carefully crafted to trick users into doing things, such as buying insurance with their purchase or signing up for recurring bills."[9] Design ethicist Tristan Harris has studied the subtle but important ways technology is used to manipulate us, often in undesirable ways.[10] He has argued that menu choices presented in user interfaces can force us into a sort of myopia by blinding us to important choices that aren't included on the menu. When we uncritically accept menus, it's easy to lose track of the difference between "empowering choices" and "lots of choices." Open-ended questions like "Who would I like to interact with?" too easily become drop-down menus of people we've added as friends or connections for many different reasons. Social media are designed to prey upon our addictive tendencies and need for social approval through devices that work like slot machines—buttons that feed our need for instant gratification. Auto-replays and infinite "up nexts" nudge us into spending more of our finite attention in one place, and choices we might make that are adverse to companies (such as unsubscribing) are laden with transaction costs to get you to give up and accept what is in the companies' best interests.

Some of these dark patterns and other kinds of abusive designs might now warrant outright prohibitions (a robust response). But collectively these under-the-radar patterns have serious effects on our trust, obscurity, and autonomy.[11] Privacy law should embrace soft and moderate responses to discourage these kinds of design traps regularly and with gusto. Soft responses can act as carrots instead of sticks, educating government and the public and encouraging ethical designs.

Education

Perhaps the simplest, easiest, and most fundamental thing lawmakers, courts, regulators, and everyone involved with privacy policy should do to take design more seriously is educate themselves and others on design. First, the government must educate itself. This means hiring more staff that understand not just technology but also how users respond to technology. There should be a staff of technologists in every administrative agency that deals with technology—which these days is most of them. Courts should have access to technologists, social scientists, and other experts to better understand the role of technology in our everyday lives.

Government education also means providing law and policy makers an opportunity to learn by carving out space for learning, funding travel, and engaging with industry, civil society, and the academic community to stay on top of how design affects our privacy. The FTC has hosted a series of public workshops on topics like disclosures, facial recognition, and other topics relevant to privacy and design.[12] The more the better.

Government should also continue to educate people about design and privacy. Digital tools can be used to dramatically affect people's lives, and we should treat them accordingly with tips and training for safe, sustainable use. People can't be expected to be experts on privacy and design, but some basic perspective and rules of the road are necessary not only to minimize harm but also to give companies a baseline set of expectations to work with when creating consumer-facing technologies. This is particularly true for disadvantaged populations and communities that do not have the same resources or education as the affluent. It's easy for the elite class to argue in favor of regimes that prioritize individual preferences (and thus shift risk away from companies) because they are better equipped to assess potential harm and protect themselves. It's much harder to get a clear picture of what's going on without resources and support.

The key with soft responses like educational efforts is to make sure they are not used to water down privacy's design agenda. Education alone is not the answer. It should support, not replace, more robust responses. For example, while education of users, industry workers, and lawmakers is critical, information overload can actually be counterproductive. Recent experiments show that education about the reality of modern data practices is positively correlated with helplessness and resignation regarding the surrender of personal data.[13]

Funding

Sometimes what your privacy really needs is some cold, hard cash. It is amazing how much can be accomplished when governments fund research; this is, after all, more or less how we got the Internet. Privacy policy can take design more seriously by providing funding for design research and new privacy protective technologies. We need more initiatives like Brandeis, funded by the Defense Advanced Research Projects Agency to develop research and tools to protect online privacy. The funding is meant to help "explore how users can understand, interact with and control data in their systems and in cyberspace through the expression of simple intentions that reflect purpose, acceptable risk and intended benefits such as 'only share photos with approved family and friends.' "[14] The anonymizing tool Tor (The Onion Router) is a great example of a high-profile, widely used government-funded privacy project; it has received millions of dollars in funding—most of its annual budget—from the US government.[15]

Organizations within the European Union (EU) have advocated for funding privacy design as well. The European Union Agency for Network and Information Security (ENISA) published a white paper titled "Privacy and Data Protection by Design—From Policy to Engineering" recommending that agencies fund a multidisciplinary approach to privacy engineering research. ENISA's entire report strongly advocates for soft, collaborative responses to taking privacy design seriously.

Another strategy for funding better privacy design is through the "bug bounty" model. Facebook, Google, Yahoo, and many other tech companies offer financial rewards for those who detect critical security vulnerabilities and other "bugs" in a company's software.[16] Policy makers should look for creative ways to support industry and government bug bounty efforts; perhaps the bug hunting could extend to bad privacy design as well as security flaws. There are thousands of social scientists and user interface / user experience experts who would likely be motivated by bounty programs to help identify bad privacy design.

Facilitating Standards

Good privacy design requires eventually addressing some specific technical details, and you can't do that consistently without technical standards. Technical standards can either provide a defined way of doing something for the sake of interoperability or facilitate the most efficient engineering approach to accomplishing something.[17] If you want good privacy design at scale, you need an effective and sustainable set of standards that most within an industry can agree upon. (Though as we've seen with attempts to set standards for facial recognition technologies and Do Not Track, it's important to ensure that the standards setting process does not get co-opted solely to drive an industry's agenda.[18])

Standards play a critical role in regulating and implementing privacy and security. When organizations seek to demonstrate to regulators that they use responsible data and design practices, they affirm their compliance with rigorous and thorough industry standards, such as those promulgated by the Cloud Security Alliance and the National Institute of Standards and Technology (NIST). These standards regularly guide organizational compliance and give meaning to regulatory requirements to "act reasonably" and "follow industry standards."[19]

Standards come in many different flavors, ranging from high-level goals to technically specific requirements. For example, specification standards provide specific details about how a thing must be implemented to comply with a standard. A common example is computer programing languages like C and Ruby. Standardized test methods leave the details of design open to interpretation and achieve standardization through tests. Any design that fails the test is not standard. Guidelines and procedures are sometimes developed simply to provide higher-level goals to be applied during the engineering process. For example, Representational State Transfer is a common guideline used to make application programming interfaces predictable, interoperable, and stable.[20] And sometimes standards evolve, like the Hypertext Markup Language (HTML) for web pages.

Standards are a useful regulatory tool because of their broad applicability and potential to evolve. Evolving standards are particularly important for technology design, which is constantly changing. Governing boards that set standards can meet regularly to ensure that standards are up to date. Standards can also span jurisdictions in ways that regulations cannot. Companies around the world follow ISO 27001 for information security management, set by the International Organization for Standardization.[21] Standards can be quite technologically specific, which gives industry a degree of certainty. And industry input helps ensure that standards are feasible to implement and generally agreed upon.

Technical standards are a promising way for privacy policy to take design more seriously. Lawmakers and regulators can bring parties together and provide the impetus to facilitate new standards. Standards can be used to compliment policy initiatives that seem intractable on their own. Importantly, these standards should ideally be free and accessible. In the wake of the discovery of a significant flaw in the popular WPA2 WiFi security protocol, computer scientists observed that the IEEE standards that dictate the protocol were expensive and hard to find through a general search engine. This meant the standards were not as useful as they could be for finding and fixing flaws.[22]

Design standards can also be a way to improve implementation of certain laws or policies. Consider the European Union's "right to be forgotten," which requires search engines to delist "inadequate, irrelevant or no longer relevant" data from its results when a member of the public requests it.[23] There are a number of issues regarding the implementation of this right, but the largest so far has been the uncertainty around the decision making and actual takedown process for links. Search engines like Google have been saddled with the obligation, which raises fairness, due process, and transparency issues for Google, its users, and those requesting a delisting.

Rigo Wenning, legal counsel for the international standards organization World Wide Web Consortium, has suggested that the standardization of a web protocol known as robots.txt could help.[24] A robots.txt file is a simple text file that, when inserted into a website's file structure, signals to a search engine a wish to avoid being indexed and searchable. Every major search engine like Bing, DuckDuckGo, and Google respects the robots.txt protocol. Wenning has suggested standardizing the protocol to include a tagging function that will only ignore websites for certain search tagged queries—for example, someone's name. In other words, a web page would be included in search results unless you searched for a specifically tagged term like a person's name and its variants (like "Bill" and "Will" for "William"). A governing and adjudicatory structure could be created to make relevance determinations and require that the website hosting the content insert the proper text file into its hierarchy. This sort of standardization would remove search engines like Google from the decision-making process, so long as they respected the robots.txt protocol. This solution has its own issues, of course. A list of folders obscured by robots.txt is easy to locate for each website. A basic hacking technique is to pull the robots.txt and then start exploring the "disallowed" folders, for example. So tinkering would be necessary to fortify the protocol. But this solution shows how technological standardization might be leveraged in existing privacy conflicts. Jonathan Zittrain has also written about the promise of robots.txt and other standards to protect privacy, which can create "code-backed norms."[25]

The downside of standards is that they can become entrenched, which causes problems if they become outdated or do not reflect the values they were designed to serve. For example, industry standards for data security, such as NIST 800-53, have yet not evolved to incorporate new information about recovering from data breaches as outlined in the NIST Cybersecurity Framework.[26] Another limitation of technical standards is that they are a bad fit for problems that are fundamentally nontechnical, such as people's general unease about receiving targeted advertisements.[27] So technical standards are an important part of privacy design, but they cannot be the only or even the main approach. They should be used to help find a common approach to privacy problems that require technically detailed solutions.

Affirmative Voluntary Restraint

Sometimes the best way to make sure privacy design is on the right track will be for the government to keep its hands off it. Design interventions will be necessary in some contexts, but not always. Some design interventions will actually mess things up and endanger your privacy. Consider the controversial ongoing battle over whether encryption technologies should be weakened or have a mandated "back door" to facilitate law enforcement, sometimes called the Crypto Wars. One of the most recent battles in this war was the legal dispute that arose when the Federal Bureau of Investigation asked Apple to create a weakened version of its iOS operating system. The FBI needed this "FBiOS" or "GovOS" to help it bypass the security protocols on an iPhone owned by the man who committed a mass shooting in San Bernardino, California.

Ultimately, the White House cooled on legislation to force privacy-corrosive encryption back doors, though there are perennial introductions of legislation to do just that.[28] Computer scientists have found consensus on the point that there is simply no way to build a back door that guarantees only the "good guys" can use it.[29] Forcing a security system to provide third-party access, by definition, weakens the technology. Politically, such a path would also likely fail. Encryption is a vital protection for U.S. infrastructure and the privacy of its citizens; proposals to weaken it would face stiff resistance.

Thus, the administration of President Barack Obama's restraint in debilitating privacy-protective technologies can be seen as a critical strategy in the tool kit for Privacy's Blueprint. The president made this decision after several years of research into the viability, costs, and benefits of the options.[30] This is a good strategy for any lawmaker or regulator considering affecting the design of information technologies. Of course, there are also costs to this decision. Encryption makes the job of law enforcement officials more difficult. These costs are serious and deserve full consideration by lawmakers. Values like safety exist awkwardly with privacy and security here, particularly given that encryption is a vital resource that also protects information important for national security. But at least by recognizing the value that restraint has for privacy law's design agenda, more fruitful conversations can be had about encryption. Courts and lawmakers can better value the tradeoffs and consequences of action and inaction.

Another key restraint strategy should be to protect independent security and privacy researchers who tinker with the design of technologies. If we want good design for our consumer technologies, we should support the work of experts who can identify and help fix bad tech design. Currently, laws like the US Computer Fraud and Abuse Act (CFAA) and the anticircumvention provisions of the Digital Millennium Copyright Act (DMCA) threaten to impose liability on legitimate security research.[31] The Library of Congress has temporarily provided for an exemption to the DMCA for security research done in good faith. This is a start, but the exemption should be bolstered and made permanent. Digital rights management technologies are far too protected by copyright law, which keeps people from figuring out how these technologies might be flawed in terms of privacy and security.[32] Additionally, the CFAA, a notoriously vague law with astonishing theoretical reach, has no such exemption.[33] One of the first orders of business for lawmakers seeking better privacy and security design should be to change that. While not sufficient, in the very least, prosecutorial discretion should exercise much more judiciously in favor of those making good faith efforts to find a technology's vulnerabilities for the purpose of improving security. The government simply has to give researchers room to breathe and tinker if we are to find and fix bad privacy and security design.

Moderate Responses

While soft responses should be a favorite of lawmakers, regulators, and courts, sometimes technology design needs a little more of a push or critical eye. There are several more moderate or "middle ground" responses in the design policy tool kit. I define moderate responses as those that have some kind of penalty or cost for exceeding design boundaries, but only moderately interfere in the design of technologies. Moderate responses should be used for the clearer, more significant privacy design problems capable of being resolved without exercising direct control over design.

Promissory Design

Above maybe every other recommendation in this book, lawmakers, regulators, and judges simply must do a better job of recognizing the implicit (and sometimes even explicit) promises embedded in and expressed through design. Companies are accountable to users for promises using words. Why are companies less accountable for promises conveyed to users via design?

The user interfaces of information technologies are ubiquitous, yet regularly overlooked by courts and lawmakers. Interfaces are powerful because they completely dictate a user's options regarding how a technology can be used. Users cannot negotiate contractual terms with companies through an interface.[34] A user cannot limit the visibility of social media posts in a nuanced way if the only options that are provided are buttons marked Private and Public. Posts to social media will persist unless a Delete or Expiration button is offered to users. Because user attention and available visual space are scarce, notifying users of particular practices or consequences of their decisions via a user interface is tricky.

Online, virtually all contracts come in the form of dense, unreadable terms of use agreements, sometimes called boilerplate for their nonnegotiability. These contracts set the rights and obligations regarding the relationship between website and user. They are uniformly unread and yet uniformly enforced. It is a stretch to even call them contracts in the classical sense, which embodied a "meeting of the minds." Yet companies use these agreements to manage risk by "informing" users about the various permissions they must give websites in exchange for service. One of the most important parts of these contracts involves user privacy and the collection and use of personal information.

When courts seek to determine a website user's privacy expectations and the website's promises to that user, they look to the terms of use agreement or to the privacy policy. Courts rarely look to the privacy settings or other elements of a website where users specify their privacy preferences. (Though given the rise of binding arbitration clauses in consumer contracts, courts barely consider any consumer contractual disputes anymore). The settings and elements of the interface are typically not considered to be part of any contract or promise to the user. But, of course, virtually no one reads terms of service or privacy policies they agree to;[35] it would be crazy to even try. In contrast, users regularly take advantage of and rely upon design features like privacy settings.[36]

Consider Facebook. It has a terms of use agreement with a section titled "Privacy." The agreement references Facebook's privacy policy, a separate document.[37] This document is largely unread.[38] But when a user sets up a Facebook profile, the user can set a series of privacy settings that allow her to control how widely accessible her profile is. The user can set it to be viewed by friends only—those people explicitly invited to see the profile— or to friends of friends, which expands the exposure much further to anyone who is linked to the user's friends. If the user wants to expose personal information to all Facebook users, the profile can be set to be public. The visibility of each individual post can be changed by the privacy settings. The user can also specify whether the profile appears in Internet search results.

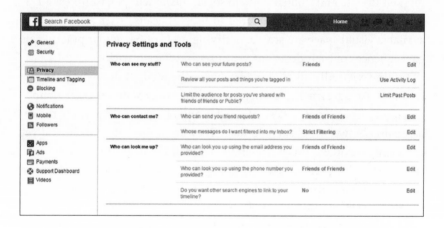

People use these settings, and they continue to tweak them over time. And, notably, they rely on them to be effective when disclosing information.[39] These settings, more than confusing and rightfully ignored terms of service and privacy policies, are what help determine a user's privacy expectations when using Facebook. Without the ability to restrict a profile's visibility to friends, a user might not sign up to use Facebook at all, or might reveal far less intimate information in the online profile. Why are privacy settings not considered part of the agreement between the user and Facebook? In an age when website interactivity is the hallmark of many sites, courts must rethink what constitutes an online agreement, and designers must continue to respect the fact that design communicates messages to users. It is also capable of empowering users to give messages to companies. Design can be a promise and expression of assent.[40]

A promise does not have to be in words to be legally binding. A promise can be any "manifestation of intention to act or refrain from acting in a specified way, so made as to justify a promisee in understanding that a commitment has been made."[41] Valid promises can be legally enforced if they are part of a contract or are detrimentally relied upon.

It is puzzling that courts have focused almost entirely on the language in terms of use and privacy policies when analyzing online agreements. This is especially true since the contracting parties' course of performance and dealing, and external evidence like trade usage, are regularly considered in most consumer contracts. Terms in privacy policies are not the only reasonably perceived promises at a website. In some contexts, website code—page design, icons, or features—can reasonably be perceived as an offer or promise by the website to protect certain pieces of information.

The modern web has provided individuals with a greater ability to negotiate terms regarding their own privacy by accepting offers to delete personal information, remove identifying tags, and use privacy settings—online activities that clearly indicate a user's desire to control the flow of her personal information. Yet courts often fail to recognize these code-based promises, instead considering them little more than luxuries offered by websites. This is the case even though these features are often couched in a contractual setting by being referenced in terms of use.

Privacy settings can be considered a form of code-based negotiations for confidentiality, which can form implied-in-fact contracts. Privacy settings and other features of website design can also give rise to a claim for promissory estoppel, a legal doctrine that allows for the enforcement of promises that were detrimentally relied upon even in the absence of a binding contract.

Doctors, lawyers, financial professionals, priests, and even intimate partners regularly make implicit promises to respect the privacy of others based on the context of their relationship. Yet on the web, courts seem to recognize only boilerplate terms of use when analyzing contractual agreements. By primarily relying on standard-form terms to analyze online agreements, courts risk ignoring the full agreement between the parties. This approach has inhibited the use of promises and contracts to protect the flow of personal information. The ubiquity of apps and the interactive web compels a reexamination of the contractual relationship between websites and their users.

As I will explore in Chapter 6, there are a few ways the law should evolve to consider the user interface design. To the extent website design is incorporated into, or is consistent with, a website's terms of use, or to the extent website design induces reliance, courts should consider these design features enforceable promises. Courts should also expand their analysis of the doctrine of unconscionability, a concept used to render certain terms unenforceable, to include consideration of malicious interfaces that manipulate, exploit, or attack users in areas of a website beyond the terms of use. While online agreements can threaten an individual's privacy, the extension of contract doctrine to website design represents an opportunity for users to regain at least some autonomy over the flow of personal information.

Because users are constrained by code (they generally cannot effectively negotiate with a website using words), the online interaction takes on additional significance. Instead of simply meaning "I wish to delete this information," user activity could mean "I wish to protect this information, so I am accepting your offer to take it down and keep it confidential."

By failing to recognize code-based promises, courts risk ignoring the many ways in which contracts can be formed digitally. Recognition of code-based acceptances, such as use of privacy settings, could also fulfill the desired "modicum of bilaterality" or mutual participation capable of defeating some claims of unconscionability. This more nuanced analysis of contract formation could recognize a privacy policy or terms of use as one layer of the agreement and code-based promises as additional layers.

This objective expression of intent for website design to be part of a contract can sometimes be found in a website's terms of use and privacy policy, which often explicitly address ways a user can affect a website's collection and use of personal information. For example, Facebook's terms of use agreement limits the scope of the license granted to the website according to the user's privacy and application settings.[42] By incorporating references to the ability to alter personal information in an online agreement, these websites invite acceptance of offers of discretion. An offer to keep deleted or protected information confidential need not be explicit to form a contract so long as such a manifestation of intent was otherwise conveyed.

Many privacy policies, such as the one once provided by the *New York Times,* are given contractual effect through incorporation into the website's terms of use. The *New York Times* privacy policy, which is part of the website's terms of use agreement, promises not to "share personal information about you as an individual to third parties without your consent." Following that clause, under the heading "Your Privacy Choices," the agreement informs users, "To view and edit your personal information, please visit the appropriate part of any of our Web sites."[43] By offering "privacy choices" and promising to disclose only that information consented to by the user, the *New York Times* effectively promises to protect information designated as private by the user.

Promises can come in many forms on a website, but there's a material difference between the perception of privacy policies and privacy settings. Users who read or even scan privacy policies are more judicious regarding the disclosure of information, while people who use privacy settings tend to disclose *more* information than users who did not. Researchers Fred Stutzman, Robert Capra, and Jamila Thompson have found that both privacy policy consumption and privacy behaviors, such as the utilization of privacy settings, were significant factors affecting disclosure on a social media site.[44] Because privacy policies and code-based features such as privacy settings are so intertwined, courts should not ignore these code-based features in their contractual analysis.

Some terms of use explicitly offer to protect the privacy of deleted or protected information. In its terms of use, former social networking giant Myspace once offered protection to users who took advantage of privacy protection features, providing, "After you remove your Content from the Myspace Services we will cease distribution as soon as practicable, and at such time when distribution ceases, the license will terminate. If after we have distributed your Content outside of the Myspace Services, you change the Content's privacy setting to 'private,' we will cease distribution of such 'private' Content outside of the Myspace Services as soon as practicable after you make the change."[45] Facebook has also given contractual authority to a user's privacy settings in its statement of rights and responsibilities, stating in its terms of use, "You own all of the content and information you post on Facebook, and you can control how it is shared through your privacy and application settings" and "We require applications to respect your privacy."[46] This language could be interpreted to create a contractual obligation to respect a user's privacy preference because it has become a significant aspect of the contract between the user and the website.

I'm proposing a solution that can be distilled to a simple proposition: if a website promises to respect a user's personal information and her privacy preferences, then a user's expression of privacy preferences through website features like privacy settings should serve to make the website's promise binding. Or, even simpler: if a website offers privacy settings, they should work. If they do not work, the provider has breached its promise to the user.

This proposal would require support to work. Increased website transparency would be required for the user to realize that an agreement with the website had been broken. Damages for these kinds of privacy harms are notoriously difficult to recover. Yet a website's failure to adhere to these agreements could be punished by the FTC in the same manner that the agency pursues those who fail to abide by their own privacy policies. Additionally, the mere threat of a private cause of action could help deter reckless practices regarding a website's disclosure of user information.

Mandatory Disclosure and Transparency

One of the most popular tools lawmakers and regulators could use to take design more seriously is mandatory disclosure and related transparency mechanisms. Deceptive, abusive, and dangerous designs feed off information imbalances. When people don't know the truth, don't realize they are being manipulated, or don't know when they are at risk, they are acutely vulnerable.

One way to make sure people know enough to avoid danger and use technologies safely is to mandate disclosures. This works by requiring the party with the information advantage (the discloser) to give the disclosee the right information to help make better decisions and keep the discloser from abusing its superior position.

People get information through mandatory disclosure regimes everywhere, though not all of them are effective. Data breach notification laws require that companies who have suffered a breach of your personal data must let you know about it. Truth-in-lending laws ensure the relevant credit terms are highlighted for the borrower. The law of informed consent ensures doctors must adequately detail the risks and benefits of recommended procedures like surgery so that patients may indeed give informed consent. Contract law requires vendors to articulate terms like warranties. And if you are arrested, the law requires that police officers inform you of your right to remain silent among other due process rights—the famous Miranda warnings.[47]

In theory, mandated disclosure regimes ensure that people are informed well enough to make smart decisions about their health, relationships, self-expression, personal data, and purchases. People are not naturally in the best position to be well informed about most of the decisions we must make in life, and more information is always better than less, right? Mandated disclosures enhance our autonomy by fortifying the decision-making process for us, thus giving us more control.

In practice, less so. Mandated disclosure regimes have recently come under scrutiny. Some are ineffective. Others serve as poor substitutes to more meaningful regulation. Still others are just flat out bad. Omri Ben-Shahar and Carl E. Schneider have prominently argued that mandated disclosure regimes are chronic failures; disclosure regimes regularly fail to actually achieve their purpose, and even when they do, the "costs in money, effort, and time generally swamp its benefits." They argue that too often mandated disclosure regimes make false assumptions about how people live, think, and make decisions, rest on false assumptions about the decisions they intend to improve, and expect too much from lawmakers, disclosers, and disclosees. In other words, "the prerequisites of successful mandated disclosure are so numerous and so onerous that they are rarely met."[48]

Fair enough. We've all been bothered by, buried in, and bored over disclosures. For example, did you know that Q-tips have warnings all over the box not to put them in your ear?

Admit it. This is the first time you've read this. Do you remember what that data breach notice you got from Target or the Office of Personnel Management even said? I didn't even fully read all the important disclosures in my mortgage agreement. My *mortgage!*

So, yes, we should admit that mandatory disclosure has important limitations; it will only work in certain situations and only when they are implemented in the right way. Yet I'm going to stick up for mandatory disclosure as one of many useful tools to implement privacy's design agenda. Clearly some warnings and directions work. People regularly obey stop signs and heed warnings about the safe temperature for cooking oils, for example. There are two reasons mandatory disclosure is an important privacy design approach. First, a disclosure can be effective even if most people don't notice it. It can serve as a jurisdictional hook for regulators. Mandatory disclosure must be truthful; if it is not, companies are subject to liability under the law of fraud and deception. Additionally, mandatory disclosure can force companies to get organized and make better internal decisions about what data they are collecting and how they use that data.[49]

Second, when making privacy-relevant decisions, you often don't need to be fully informed. You just need to be skeptical. Warnings can be really useful in making people generally skeptical. When the goal isn't to transmit information but rather to discourage behavior or simply facilitate a mind-set, the full panoply of notice techniques is available to regulators. This includes notice through design in the form of symbols, interface aesthetics, feedback mechanisms, sound, haptics, and any other notice that might not convey

substance but will affect you on a deep, intuitive level. This is how warnings interact with requirements for reasonable safe design in product liability law to help ensure products that don't hurt. A good example of intuitive warning in a user interface is the flashing blue bar at the top of some
mobile phones that indicates an app is using location information.[50] Instead of a dense block of text, imagine a siren, flashing light, universal
prohibition symbol, series of vibrations, or even a distinct smell warning
you about what kinds of information will be collected. Ryan Calo calls this
leveraging a "visceral notice."[51]

Much of disclosure regimes' failure is due to the fact they are all trying
to get us to notice and internalize specific and different pieces of information. The success of the Miranda warnings depends upon arrestees understanding a simple fact: that they don't have to answer questions. The success
of data breach notifications, on the other hand, depends upon whether you
understand the extent to which your personal information was compromised, how much you are at risk, and what the proper remedial steps are.
There is so much mental processing necessary for mandatory disclosure
regimes that it's no wonder they fail when we can't keep up.

There are countless obstacles to ever fully "informing" individuals about
a certain practice or risk.[52] The relevant information is often too vast or
complex to convey, and audiences vary in technological sophistication and
ability to understand the information conveyed. When we create mandatory
disclosure regimes to inform people, we are often chasing the wrong goal.

Instead we should think of privacy notices as warnings. Regarding privacy law's design agenda, we should use mandatory disclosure regimes to
generate *skepticism* about the trustworthiness of information recipients
and the obscurity of our personal information. In other words, notice can
play a key role in nourishing the critical thinking necessary for us to assess
risk and develop sustainable relationships of trust and zones of obscurity.
In a "notice as warning" model, emphasis is placed on highlighting risk
factors to accommodate people's mental models and heuristics rather than
simply targeting "truths" like what information is collected or the strength
of encryption used by a website.

With the right indicators, privacy law can help us figure out whom to
trust and with what, and it can keep us from detrimentally relying on false
or misleading expectations of trust and obscurity. Consider Google's new
initiative to "name and shame" the "nearly half of the world's websites that

don't use strong encryption, putting a clear 'Not secure' warning next to thousands of popular online destinations that use unencrypted HTTP connections rather than encrypted HTTPS connections."[53] Instead of bogging users down with information about specific encryption levels and other security practices, such warnings would give users a quick and easy way to gauge how much to trust a particular website or technology with their personal information.

One of the biggest barriers to informing people is attention scarcity. There is only so much information people can read and internalize. Notices as warnings should prioritize skepticism; hesitation caused by skepticism provides an ordering principle for notices and helps users avoiding detrimental reliance on assumptions of trust or obscurity. Skepticism about disclosing information would better allow the disclosee to tailor her activity and avoid detrimental reliance—a hallmark of contract and consumer protection law.

A focus on trust and skepticism might mitigate some of the problems with privacy policies as a tool for consumers. While it is one thing for a company to be forced to list in the fine print the ways in which it collects and shares people's information, it is something else entirely for a company to be forced to admit through design that it is not trustworthy. In other words, companies should keep users' trust or be blunt about the risks of disclosure and the protections that will not be taken. Indications of trust are more intuitive and useful to consumers than dry recitations of what types of information are collected and vague assurances that personal information will only be disclosed to "third-party affiliates."

My defense of mandatory disclosure comes with a few strong caveats: disclosure should not usually be the sole legal response, unaccompanied by some other protections. Without some sort of supportive, concurrent effort, disclosure risks becoming a sort of cop-out, an easier alternative instead of harder but ultimately more effective rules. Companies should not have free reign to build harmful, abusive, or invasive technologies so long as they provide notice. Sure, disclosure might be useful, but if it is permitted to crowd out other approaches it will hurt more than help. There is also ample evidence that mandated disclosure regimes can have unintended consequences and be counterproductive. For example, Daniel Ho has argued that the restaurant sanitation grading regimes in New York and San Diego were seriously flawed. In theory, a simple letter grade (A, B, or C) enabled consumer choice and encouraged restaurants to reduce the risk of foodborne illnesses. But Ho found that grade inflation was rampant (nearly all restaurants in San Diego got A's), there was no real decrease in foodborne illnesses, and precious resources were spent resolving grade disputes.[54]

What's worse, even skepticism-based regimes must still grapple with people's limited bandwidth to process information. Skepticism regimes might still overburden people with the risk of loss and to block other fixes because they don't scale well. The number of decision points the average person faces each day still might be prohibitively high. The best approach is to deploy warnings as a supplement rather than to rely entirely upon "notice and choice" to protect users.

Mandatory Process

Another promising moderate response to design is to mandate process. This approach to privacy law would not require specific design elements or demand certain safety thresholds but would instead require certain procedures designed to produce privacy-friendly design. For example, privacy law might require companies to conduct threat modeling, appoint privacy and security officers, or test their technologies in order to assess privacy risks.

Mandatory process is a moderate response because even certain risky designs can be tolerated so long as companies take the right steps to mitigate potential harm and ensure that debatable design decisions were justified. In other words, process-based design rules are tolerant of risk. They are designed with the goal that most technologies will be privacy-friendly most of the time.

When companies and lawmakers talk about privacy by design they are often referring to procedures meant to ensure that privacy is a priority in organizational structure, organizational decision making, and the design of technologies. For example, Ann Cavoukian's highly influential Privacy by Design (PbD) movement is "an approach to protecting privacy by embedding it into the design specifications of technologies, business practices, and physical infrastructures. That means building in privacy up front—right into the design specifications and architecture of new systems and processes."[55]

Cavoukian has been a leader in thinking about how to make sure privacy is built into the structure and operation of companies and the technologies they make and use. In thinking about what PbD could look like in terms of mandatory process, Cavoukian has advocated for legal regimes that require organizations to train employees on privacy and security, implement a system for tracking what information is collected and how it is stored and used, require regular reporting from departments dealing with personal information on the privacy impact of their products, and conduct regular audits.[56]

Most regulators are already equating privacy by design with this kind of mandatory process. The 32nd International Conference of Data Protection and Privacy Commissioners included a resolution to encourage Cavoukian's conceptualization of privacy by design as an international standard.[57] Privacy by design as mandatory process has shown up in state smart grid legislation, proposed legislation for a commercial privacy bill of rights, and interpretations of how to best implement Canada's omnibus Personal Information Protection and Electronic Documents Act.[58] Privacy by design makes up the basic framework for the Asia-Pacific Economic Cooperation's Cross-Border Privacy Rules.[59]

The FTC has also prominently embraced privacy by design as mandatory process. It is one of the three major tenets of the commission's approach to privacy outlined in its 2012 report.[60] FTC chairwoman Edith Ramirez has said, "The FTC advocates an organizational or process component; we call on companies to maintain data management personnel, procedures, and controls to help ensure that substantive privacy by design principles are respected at all stages of the design and development of products and services. Companies should have personnel with responsibility for privacy. The company must also assess and mitigate privacy risks before a product launches and afterwards to address any privacy risks. The size of the program depends on the size of the company and the consumer data it uses."[61]

The FTC has also imposed privacy by design as mandatory process on companies that have committed unfair or deceptive trade practices. For example, the consent order between Google and the FTC regarding the alleged unfair design of Google's Buzz software, which shared user information with other users without permission, required that Google establish and maintain a "comprehensive privacy program." This program required procedures to designate a point person for privacy within the company, identify informational assets and risk, implement privacy controls, verify privacy efforts by third-party vendors, and regularly reassess the company's privacy protocol.[62]

The EU has enshrined the progressive procedural notion of "privacy by default" into its new General Data Protection Regulation (GDPR). Specifically, article 25 of the new GDPR states that data controllers "shall implement appropriate technical and organisational measures for ensuring that, by default, only personal data which are necessary for each specific purpose of the processing are processed." It goes on to state, "That obligation applies to the amount of personal data collected, the extent of their processing, the period of their storage and their accessibility. In particular, such measures shall ensure that by default personal data are not made accessible without the individual's intervention to an indefinite number of natural persons."[63] What does this obligation actually mean in practice? It's not entirely clear. It seems like a requirement for a mandatory check on the design process. It could also be more strictly interpreted as a design requirement whereby the most protective privacy settings must be offered and activated by default. It's likely both.[64]

One of the most popular forms of mandatory process aimed at achieving privacy-sensitive design is known as the Privacy Impact Assessment (PIA),[65] which is a structured inquiry into how personally identifiable information is collected, used, shared, and maintained within an organization.[66] For example, the Office of Management and Budget's guidance mandates that the PIAs required of government agencies include a risk assessment that specifically identifies and evaluates potential threats to individual privacy, discusses alternatives, identifies appropriate risk mitigation measures, and articulates the rationale for the final design choice.[67]

Michael Froomkin has advocated for regulation mandating a kind of Privacy Impact Notice (PIN), based on the PIA, as a way of encouraging good privacy design. By requiring that companies be publicly accountable for their data collection efforts and giving data subjects a right of action where public notice was inadequate, a PIN requirement could help set the right incentives for companies to build in privacy protections to potentially dangerous technologies or look for alternate designs or strategies. Froomkin argues that a private right of action is necessary to give the PIN framework teeth.[68] Note that Froomkin's framework has both mandatory process and mandatory notice elements; combining the two requirements helps ensure that formalistic compliance is not elevated over substantive protection.

But mere mandatory process and notice alone is likely not enough. As Kenneth Bamberger and Deirdre Mulligan have noted, the effectiveness of PIA regimes is contingent upon agency personnel and political commitment to prioritizing privacy.[69] And it's not just executives, privacy professionals such as Chief Privacy Officers, Chief Information Officers, and the like, who must be part of the corporate commitment to privacy. The designers in charge of instantiating privacy goals into steel, silicon, and code must be committed and structurally supported to do their job.[70] This means that administrative structure is key to ensuring that mandatory process can be an effective tool for good privacy design. Another problem with mandatory process is that it requires a delicate balance between establishing methodologies that can be used consistently across contexts while taking care to avoid the rote formalism trap that has engulfed the regimes based on the Fair Information Practices (FIPs). Seda Gürses, Carmela Troncoso, and Claudia Diaz have cautioned "against reducing such methodologies to 'privacy by design check lists' that can easily be ticked away for compliance reasons while not mitigating some of the risks that privacy by design is meant to address."[71]

While mandatory process is promising, it is not the only way for privacy law to take design more seriously. Rather, it should be one of many different ways to ensure privacy-friendly design.

Design as a Regulatory Airbag

Another moderate response to design problems is for privacy law to recognize sound privacy design as a mitigating factor or safe harbor for otherwise prohibited activity. For example, companies in some jurisdictions can avoid data breach notification obligations by using encryption.[72] Using the right notifications and the right administrative, technical, and physical safeguards can weigh heavily in favor of companies seeking to show that they have met their burden to reasonably protect information. In other words, lawmakers could use design as a kind of airbag. Good design would blunt the legal sanction for otherwise dangerous and harmful prohibited activity.

So far, lawmakers have failed to use their imagination regarding design here. Current privacy law is ailing in two important ways. First, it is very "bumpy" in the sense that lots of questionable conduct is completely tolerated up to a certain point, then everything after that one (sometimes arbitrary) point is equally prohibited with the same punishment. Contrast this with "smooth" laws, as articulated by Adam Kolber, where gradually more culpable conduct leads to gradually more punitive or robust responses.[73] In other words, privacy law should make the punishment and wrongful conduct more proportional to each other.

Second, privacy law is also ossified.[74] The four privacy torts have barely changed at all since Dean Prosser first enshrined them in the Restatement of Torts, and the torts of negligence and fraud have been surprisingly staid in privacy-related contexts even though stable evolution is the hallmark of the common law. Even our regulatory regimes are stuck in a rut. The EU and U.S. governments have been loudly kicking around PbD for almost ten years now, yet when it comes time to put design into regulatory action, we seem to fall back to "just do the FIPs earlier instead of later." As important as they are, the FIPs continue to constrain the imagination of regulators and the potential of design in privacy law.

Design could be leveraged to accomplish more proportional laws, acting as burden-shifting devices or even safe harbors. For example, damages and fines could be reduced for companies that implement prominent skepticism-generating notices or privacy-enhancing design such as data minimization, encryption, and more secure localized (instead of cloud) storage of personal information. Safe harbors have worked moderately well in creating information exchange regimes in copyright law and health privacy law.[75] Consider section 512 of the Digital Millennium Copyright Act, which shielded online platforms from secondary liability for hosting copyrighted content so long as they followed proper protocol when put on notice of infringing content. Section 512 caused websites to take rights holders seriously. Perhaps the same could be true of consumers and their data. A notice-and-takedown regime providing safe harbor status for site providers might actually generate some significant consumer-corporate dialogue and privacy rights.

Robust Responses

Finally, some privacy and design problems require robust responses from lawmakers, regulators, and judges. A robust response is one that directly and significantly punishes bad design or dictates design specifics. For example, tort law imposes liability on unreasonably dangerous designs. Criminal law currently prohibits manufacturing, selling, or advertising a device designed as primarily useful for the covert interception of electronic, wire, or oral communications.[76] Robust responses can be quite effective because they are direct and can provide nuanced control or powerful incentives. Lawmakers can punish specific design failures to compensate victims and deter future bad design. When there is little room for error, such as with Internet-connected health devices like pacemakers that, if hacked, could kill someone, robust responses ensure technical specificity by removing any guesswork and wiggle room.[77]

Yet the virtues of robust responses are also their vices. That's because all design, all software code and the best engineering plans, are full of bugs and flaws.[78] It would be crazy for us to expect designers to get everything exactly right all the time. Plus, design goals change over time; the process of good design requires constant trial and error. For example, in 2016 Apple announced that it would be using a privacy-protective technique known as differential privacy when analyzing user data.[79] This technique basically uses "noise" to allow Apple to gain insight from data with personal information without being able to tell whether the data is about you specifically. Will it work? Maybe. There's much more that we need to know from Apple. But almost certainly it won't be an ideal protection when it is first used. There is only so much testing that can be done while a technology is in quarantine. If we want good design, we must build a system that tolerates reasonable failure.

Directly punishing bad design might cause us to be overly cautious, which might prevent experimentation with new designs than are better matched with the risks of use. Micromanaging with an iron fist limits evolution though experimentation and failure. Privacy law should embrace robust design solutions judiciously—and chiefly when soft and moderate responses would be insufficient. Think of robust responses as setting the outer boundaries of acceptable design.

But the ultimate goal of robust responses is to place the onus of safety on the designer and the company, not the user. Companies are the cheapest cost avoider with respect to unreasonably dangerous technologies, and users are operating on the bad end of information asymmetries. The term *user* implies some form of dominance over a technology, as though it is subservient to our will. But that's not entirely accurate. Those who make technologies, not those who use them, are in control. When companies create unreasonably dangerous products, they should bear the risk of loss.

Liability for Defective or Dangerous Design

The most basic principle justifying a robust response is that when a company designs a technology in a defective way, it should be liable for the harm caused by the defect. The Restatement of Torts provides a similar expression: "One engaged in the business of selling or otherwise distributing products who sells or distributes a defective product is subject to liability for harm to persons or property caused by the defect."[80] Perhaps the most obvious way to hold companies liable for dangerous and defective design is through tort law—most notably the law of products liability, a creature of the torts of negligence and strict liability.

A tort is a civil wrong. It's a way of allocating the risk of loss in society. When someone is unjustly harmed, torts serve to shift the risk of loss onto the parties that caused the harm by giving the injured party a cause of action against culpable parties. One of the most common torts is negligence, which provides injured parties a cause of action against those who create unreasonable risks of harm that caused an injury. Another common tort cause of action is known as strict liability—that is, liability regardless of fault. Strict liability is most commonly imposed on people who engage in inherently dangerous and ultrahazardous activity and injure others in the process.

Incorporating at least some aspects of products liability into privacy law would have significant advantages. Design is key in the law of products liability; courts weight the costs and benefits of alternative designs to figure out how reasonable it was to rely upon the allegedly defective one. Good product design minimizes or outright prevents dangerous uses of a product. It makes consequences predictable by providing people with mental models of how a thing is supposed to work and matching that model. Product safety law is almost entirely about the relationship between design and user expectations. These expectations are shaped by the design of the product itself, people's past experiences and knowledge, and any accompanying warnings and disclaimers. Tort law recognizes that people don't need to be warned of every potential danger presented by a technology, only the ones that are significant and not obvious.

Several scholars have suggested a tort-based, products liability approach to privacy and data security, noting the inability of people to successfully protect themselves in a digital world.[81] Danielle Citron has argued in favor of imposing strict liability on those who fail to process and store data securely and confidentiality.[82] She describes large data sets as akin to large reservoirs of water, both of which can be incredibly destructive if their contents escape.

Yet as James Grimmelmann has argued, it probably won't work to simply port over products from liability law into online privacy. Products liability tort suits typically do not compensate plaintiffs for the economic loss and other nonphysical injuries that are typical of privacy violations. There is also much debate about whether the kinds of design targeted in this book are embodied in the "products" that are the subject of products liability torts. These limitations are important to keep products liability law focused and efficient.[83]

Tort law was built to respond to new challenges, however. The balancing assessment built into tort law helps avoid the stagnation that can occur when statutes are enacted and specific technological standards are created. There are doctrines that support holding companies liable for privacy harms caused by design or those that should have been reasonably foreseeable to companies. Consider the "crashworthiness" doctrine in tort law, which requires manufacturers to evaluate the safety of their products and to take reasonable steps to eliminate, or mitigate the seriousness of, injuries resulting from accidents or collisions.[84] We humans are a reckless bunch. Might companies also be required to assess the "crashworthiness" of technologies? In other words, courts might consider requiring companies to build technologies that anticipate foreseeable privacy accidents and incidents and protect against them.

Tort law could also evolve to recognize privacy and data breach harms that have traditionally been seen as too dispersed or incremental to be recognized. Daniel Solove and Daniel Citron have argued that with respect to companies that negligently cause data breaches, "there are foundations in the law for a coherent recognition of harm based upon increased risk and anxiety."[85] While not all increases in risk should be actionable, there are some that are significant enough to make one quite meaningfully worse off. People are forced to change their behavior in constraining and harmful ways to account for the risk of harm. Their autonomy is infringed, their time and opportunities in life are drained and depleted, and the well-being of people that tort law seeks to protect is threatened. While courts must be careful to avoid creating a general right to be free from risk—life is risk, after all—they could provide a framework to consistently determine when the creation of risk is unreasonable and harmful. If courts are concerned about runaway tort claims alleging increased risk from data breaches, they could require that only truly reckless conduct (not just negligent conduct) will give rise to a recovery or limit the kinds of recovery available to tortfeasors. But to deny the elasticity of the common law to confront these problems is to ignore the critical functions of tort law to compensate and deter.

Alternatively, tort law could hold companies liable for failing to adopt cheap known preventative solutions to privacy and security harms. Specifically, I argue that regulators should consider how design might serve as the "means and instrumentalities" of privacy and security harms or be used to induce a breach of confidentiality.

Design as the Means and Instrumentalities of Privacy Violations

Products liability and consumer protection theories can guide lawmakers in holding companies directly liable for their designs. For example, the FTC has developed a "means and instrumentalities" theory of liability for design choices that harm consumers. For example, in *DesignerWare*—the FTC complaint involving the fake Windows 10 registration screen (see Chapter 1)—the agency alleged that by providing such adversarial spyware, the company DesignerWare "provided the means and instrumentalities for the commission of unfair acts and practices and thus have caused or are likely to cause substantial injury to consumers that cannot be reasonably avoided and is not outweighed by countervailing benefits to consumers or competition."[86]

In *FTC v. Neovi*, also known as the Qchex dispute, the FTC asserted a theory of indirect liability against a company that created a check creation and delivery website that, by design, facilitated the creation of fraudulent checks drawn upon people's bank accounts.[87] The FTC has also stated that providing the means and instrumentalities to install spyware and access customers' personal information was an unfair trade practice.[88]

Means and instrumentalities theories must be carefully deployed so as not to unfairly punish general-purpose technologies that have mostly legitimate uses. For example, the iPhone can be used to secretly record people, but it would seem extreme to punish Apple for providing the means and instrumentalities for surreptitious surveillance. "Open" platforms that can be adapted for any purpose—like, say, a robot you could run apps on—would also be less culpable under a means and instrumentalities theory because its design choices were not articulable as pernicious.[89] Instead, under this theory regulators should look to specific design decisions that nudge people toward unjustified behavior.

The Tort of Inducement to Breach Confidentiality (through Design)

While the law of negligence and strict liability primarily protects against physical and emotional harm, other parts of tort and contract law might be relevant in holding companies directly liable for deceptive, abusive, or dangerous design. In particular, the law of confidentiality holds great promise.[90] Confidentiality directly serves the value of trust. Compared to the amorphous concept of privacy, confidentiality is relatively straightforward. *Black's Law Dictionary* defines confidentiality as "the state of having the dissemination of certain information restricted."[91] Ethicist Sissela Bok has defined confidentiality as "the boundaries surrounding shared secrets and . . . the process of guarding these boundaries. While confidentiality protects much that is not in fact secret, personal secrets lie at its core."[92]

The law will impose an obligation of confidentiality on recipients of information when they have agreed not to share the information with third parties or when they receive information within the context of a confidential relationship.[93] Obligations or privileges of confidentiality are found in multiple areas of the law in the United States, including express and implied contracts for confidentiality,[94] the still-developing tort of breach of confidence,[95] evidentiary privileges regarding confidentiality, procedural protections like protective orders to prevent the disclosure of embarrassing personal information in court records,[96] and statutes explicitly creating confidential relationships.[97]

Typically, obligations of confidentiality arise through voluntary promises or agreements to respect designated information. They are also created through consensual confidential relationships as well as cooperative relationships marked by power and information asymmetry, such as the employer / employee relationship.[98] Confidentiality agreements are legally binding agreements that are commonly used to prohibit the disclosure of information.[99] Such contracts are used to protect anonymity, arbitration proceedings,[100] settlement agreements,[101] and trade secrets.[102] Additionally, these contracts may protect sensitive information such as health information, sexual orientation, intimate feelings, and other pieces of similarly personal information.[103] Even quasi-contractual promises of confidentiality are enforceable if disclosers of information rely on them to their detriment.[104]

In addition to confidentiality agreements, an obligation of confidentiality may be created by entering into a confidential or fiduciary relationship. The law of equity has traditionally designated certain relations, such as principal / agent and trustee / beneficiary, as fiduciary.[105] Breach of these confidential relationships can, in some instances, give rise to liability under the breach of confidence tort. This tort, while well-developed in England, is limited in the United States.[106] The tort is deceptively simple: "Courts impose liability under the tort when a person discloses information that he received in confidence." While the tort has been most successful with regard to professional relationships, liability can also occur "in an informal setting if the party receiving the information either explicitly or implicitly agrees to keep the information confidential."[107]

From a doctrinal perspective, the law of confidentiality offers many benefits over the common law privacy torts and current privacy statutes. Under the law of confidentiality, courts can largely avoid the difficult question of whether information was private, newsworthy, or offensive and focus instead on whether a trust was breached.[108] Information can typically be protected by a duty of confidentiality without regard to the extent that it has been disclosed to others.[109] Additionally, the law of confidentiality is less constitutionally suspect than the disclosure tort, which has significant First Amendment limitations.[110] The Supreme Court ruled in *Cohen v. Cowles Media Co.* that the First Amendment does not bar an action for breach of a promise of confidentiality.[111]

One key overlooked feature of the law of confidentiality is that those who *induce* a breach of confidence, even if they are not a direct party in a confidential relationship, can be liable. For example, under American and English law, in some contexts, third-party recipients who induce confidants to breach their obligation can be liable in tort to the original discloser or subject of the information.[112] Under some theories of the breach of confidentiality tort in the United States and England, a claim for inducement of breach of confidentiality could be successful.[113]

There is no reason the law of confidentiality should be limited to words. As we've seen thus far, design is equally capable of forming expectations and shaping behavior. Consider technologies specifically designed to solicit nonconsensual pornography, often called "revenge porn." Intimate partners often share explicit materials with each other within the confines and understandings of a confidential relationship. This was the buzz surrounding the initial basic conceit of Snapchat, though the app is used for many different purposes.[114]

Sharing entrusted explicit images with third parties is a brazen and legally actionable breach of confidence. Yet companies like My Ex have created websites specifically designed to induce confidants to violate the trust they have been given. They have marketing slogans like "Get the dirt before you get hurt or submit your ex gf or bf." The submission page of My Ex is designed to collect the name, nickname, country, and state of residence, all of which serve exclusively to violate the privacy of victims. There's even an open text box where betrayers can give "some details or tell your story."

The website does nearly everything imaginable to make it trivially easy to upload nude photos in a way that will wreck the victim. It is marketed explicitly to those who obtained photos within an intimate and confidential relationship. This website is designed to induce breaches of confidentiality, pure and simple. Tort law can and should evolve to hold such companies liable for the harm they cause.

Certification and Authorization Schemes

Holding companies accountable for the harm their technologies cause may be effective in compensating victims and encouraging better design and warnings, but it still leaves most of the design specifics up to companies. While the design freedom offered by tort law is largely a virtue, sometimes the risks are so high that design must be precise and completely according to plan. In situations like this, lawmakers can institute certification and authorization regimes. These regimes would require companies to seek preapproval from a regulatory agency before they are allowed to market and sell their technologies. The approval by the agency could be contingent upon a review of design practices, the amount of research and development that went into the device, demonstrations of efficacy and output thresholds, or compliance with articulated design specifications.

This is how the Food and Drug Administration (FDA) regulates medical devices; all companies that want to sell a medical device in the United States must register their product with the FDA.[115] The level of precaution required by companies varies according to the risk and complexity of the device. Given that the Internet of Things (IoT) is inching closer and closer to critical infrastructures and collecting increasingly sensitive information at the heart of our most intimate and fundamental traits, lawmakers might consider requiring some form of registration and certification from new IoT devices. Doing so could help ensure basic privacy and security design. Instead of generally prohibiting deceptive design or abusive design, regulatory regimes could come right out and say "all defaults for options should be privacy friendly" (like the GDPR's "privacy by default" requirement) or "all IoT devices should certify compliance with ISO 27001," the international data security standard.

Certification schemes can be costly, in terms of both opportunities lost and resources required. They act as default prohibition on technologies until permission is granted.[116] In some circumstances, they can stymie experimentation and risk, which are necessary in moderate and sustainable doses to understand good design in any given context. However, they can also keep out many disruptive, reckless companies that might poison the well of consumer goodwill built up by more established and prudent companies.

Lawmakers will need to tread cautiously with authorization and certification schemes to avoid being ineffective or even counterproductive. Consider the work of Lauren Willis, whose research shows that even the most well-intentioned schemes, such as privacy by default, seem destined to be thwarted by other design choices that confuse consumers or play to their biases. Companies have great incentive to ensure people consent to being tracked, and privacy by default schemes are a great way for lawmakers to avoid asking the hard questions about whether companies are out to surveil people. Privacy by default saddles people with the decision about whether to be tracked and keeps lawmakers from having to balance incommensurable values and substantive judgment calls that are sure to draw heat. Willis writes, "If all policymakers are aiming for with a notice-and-choice regime of information privacy defaults is to avoid political heat, they may succeed. But if they seek to use tracking defaults as a way to set norms, guide consumers to individually or socially desired positions, or inform consumers through the opt-out decision process, they are likely to fail."[117]

Willis also cautions that nudges may not be an effective way to help people make better choices about information privacy: "Nudges can be powerful when no one is pushing back. But a push can easily overwhelm a nudge. Existing research supporting such nudges is performed in artificial conditions where firms do not have an opportunity to intervene." If there's a singular worry in this book, it's that companies can rather easily co-opt nudging techniques to their own end. Design is powerful, and currently it is badly misused to make a mockery of the consent-based framework. Willis argues that the only way to really approach design is to anticipate and account for the way companies will respond to design requirements.

Furthermore, perhaps some expressed consumer preferences should be suspect given the environment in which they are produced. Hyperbolic discounting—the tendency of people to choose smaller rewards sooner rather than larger rewards later—is easily leveraged by companies to generate data. People have a difficult time assessing the risk of exposure or accurately valuing their own data. It is difficult for anyone to fight the internal and external forces encouraging exposure.[118]

So while the options for certification or outright bans might ensure that design goes according to plan, lawmakers should reserve such rules for exceptional circumstances. Instead, lawmakers, regulators, and courts should weave together many different approaches as consistently as possible to further the values of trust, obscurity, and autonomy and discourage deceptive, abusive, and dangerous design.

Behold, then, Privacy's Blueprint—a design agenda for privacy law and policy. To review, the agenda has three components: values, boundaries, and tools. Privacy law should focus on furthering the values of trust within relationships, obscurity when there is no one to trust, and the autonomy to negotiate relationships of trust and zones of obscurity. A framework of standards for privacy law should look to the law of consumer protection and product safety as a way of moving beyond the Fair Information Practices. Lawmakers, regulators, and courts should target deceptive, abusive, and dangerous design through a combination of soft, moderate, and robust responses. Regulators should seek co-regulatory approaches that result in sound rules created by an ongoing dialogue between companies and governments.[119] However, it may be that if companies consistently flout design rules, then private actions, fines, and equitable remedies should be available to compensate those harmed and deter bad design in the future.

This agenda isn't perfect. It's not even complete. Some might argue for different, roomier values as priorities for design, such as dignity or intimacy. Important concerns about low enforcement, free speech, and intermediary liability must be addressed. Others might think I'm being too hard on the Fair Information Principles or be suspicious of an approach to privacy design based in consumer protection and product safety, preferring an explicit and more traditional data protection regime. Because I'm focusing mainly on consumer-facing technologies, there is certainly much more to be done in developing a design agenda for back end technologies and through concepts like network security and data architecture. Organizational structure and procedures remain critical to good design as well. Data collection and use ethics and rules remain critical even if design is improved. Good design will not obviate the need for privacy-protective surveillance laws. And there are many ways to mix and match the possible legal responses identified in this chapter.

But Privacy's Blueprint is a start. I offer it up as a way for all of us to move past an increasingly ossified data-centric approach to privacy. It can bring coherence and a plan to elevate design in privacy law and policy. We can fairly quibble with many of the details of this agenda, but the law cannot continue to marginalize design or approach it in a haphazard manner. Agendas are always subject to change, but they are necessary to effectively move forward.

PART THREE

APPLYING PRIVACY'S BLUEPRINT

6

Social Media

IT IS *so* easy to post things on social media. Anyone who wants to use services like Facebook, Snapchat, or Twitter can create an account and start sharing photos within seconds. Virtually every design element of social media technologies is made with one goal in mind—to get you to share, baby, share. That's because if you don't, the service will fail. Just ask the people who used to work for Friendster or Myspace. Designers are tasked with reducing sources of "friction"—the transaction costs of finding and sharing on a social technology.[1] Every little required expenditure of effort is seen as a barrier between you and the Post button. For example, the menu bar for the mobile Facebook app wasn't moved to the bottom of the screen just for aesthetics. It was to get those buttons closer to your thumbs.[2]

Sometime in 2015, social media giant Facebook started getting concerned because there was a big drop in people sharing "original content"—meaning personal information like status updates, photos, and videos.[3] For companies like Facebook this can be seen as an existential threat. Design to the rescue. New features like the "On This Day" feature were built to nudge users to repost previously submitted photos and updates. Reminders about special occasions like Mother's Day were engineered to nudge you to stay in contact with other users. The Facebook app has even started going through the new photos and other content on your phones and asking if you'd like to post them.[4]

Technologies that mediate social interaction almost always use design to create, capture, and sustain personal disclosure. Apps like SwiftKey and Bitmoji request "full access" to your smartphone's keyboard, which enables these apps to capture and transmit everything you type.[5] Professional social networking site LinkedIn tethers its inbox of connection invitations with a feature nudging you to send out invitations of your own to create a perpetual linking machine.[6]

Other times social media fail to leverage design to protect against foreseeable privacy threats posed by other users. Social media like Snapchat allowed users to share ephemeral content but originally failed to protect against the foreseeable risk that others will use third-party services to store otherwise hidden photos.[7] Social media services where online harassment is common, like Twitter, have struggled to give users the right technological tools to mitigate the onslaught of hate and protect their privacy.

In this chapter, I explore how the design of social media has failed us with respect to privacy and how the agenda proposed in this book might help reverse the trend. First, I show how the design of social media presents two distinct yet related sets of privacy problems—platforms and people. Platforms like Facebook are often at the forefront of the privacy discussion because of concerns about big data and things like facial recognition technologies. But often we are just as vulnerable to the other users of a social medium. And the design of social media can make us more vulnerable to both.

Then this chapter examines social media design in five different contexts: manufacturing disclosure, extracting consent, overexposure, faithless "friends," and online harassment. Risks in these contexts come from both platforms and other people using the service. Good design would protect against these risks by creating or preserving obscurity, signaling fidelity from platforms, and encouraging trust between users. Above all, good social media design should give users accurate mental maps for safe and sustainable use through signals, constraints, and affordances regarding how the technology works, who they are sharing information with, and the rules and risks of disclosure.

The Twin Risks of Social Media: Platforms and People

Before figuring out what constitutes good and bad social media design, we first need to define the concept. Obvious examples of social media include popular social networking sites and apps like Facebook, Instagram, Snapchat, and Twitter.[8] But this book takes a much more holistic view of social media, which I define broadly here to be any digital communication technology using the Internet to connect people for social reasons. This includes texting and messaging apps, blogging software, any utility with a social networking feature, and even good ol' email.

And to reiterate, I use the concept of *design* here to mean the actual function, structure, and appearance of consumer-facing technologies. For social media, this largely means the way user interfaces work and how they look, as opposed to back-end data-centric concepts like data architecture and data de-identification techniques. Back-end design choices, while critical, are relevant to this chapter only to the extent they are reflected in consumer-facing technologies.

The design of social media is particularly critical because social media are unique among digital technologies. Unlike, say, your banking app, social media have two distinct audiences for your information: platforms and people. These two audiences present overlapping but distinguishable privacy issues. Platforms, meaning the companies that provide the social media software, have robust concentrations of electronic information aggregated into colossal databases.[9] They are risky because of how much data they can obtain from you and the fact that they control the terms of your mediated experience. After all, it is the company that designs the software.

People on social media are risky because there are so many of them and it is difficult to keep our boundaries straight among so many relationships. In other words, the harm from platforms usually is enabled by the aggregation of lots of data by one entity. But the harm from people is often that one piece of information is exposed to the *wrong* audience. And these two distinct audiences present different challenges. Platforms are dangerous because of the power imbalance between platforms and users. People are dangerous because social interaction is messy and contextual with a vengeance. So in order to get good privacy design for social media, the challenges presented by both of these audiences must be understood.

Platforms Use Interfaces as Data Spigots

Social media companies would like to know everything about you. The more data they have on you, the more profitable and useful you become for them. These platforms don't often come right out and say that, of course, but they don't need to. The actual design of the software will reveal the motives of social media. For example, Facebook has toyed with the idea of using "cursor tracking" technology to figure out not just what you click on but how long you let your cursor *hover over* certain links on a page.[10] Platforms don't just want to know your expressed desires. Now they want your hesitations and internal decision-making process.

Design is key for platforms because social media user interfaces are essentially data spigots. They are designed to help social media platforms like Facebook collect more and richer personal data. Privacy and security expert Bruce Schneier has developed a very useful taxonomy of Social Networking Data:

> Service data is the data you give to a social networking site in order to use it. Such data might include your legal name, your age, and your credit-card number.
>
> Disclosed data is what you post on your own pages: blog entries, photographs, messages, comments, and so on.
>
> Entrusted data is what you post on other people's pages. It's basically the same stuff as disclosed data, but the difference is that you don't have control over the data once you post it—another user does.
>
> Incidental data is what other people post about you: a paragraph about you that someone else writes, a picture of you that someone else takes. . . . Again, it's basically the same stuff as disclosed data, but the difference is that you don't have control over it, and you didn't create it in the first place.
>
> Behavioral data is data the site collects about your habits by recording what you do and who you do it with. It might include games you play, topics you write about, news articles you access (and what that says about your political leanings), and so on.
>
> Derived data is data about you that is derived from all the other data. For example, if 80 percent of your friends self-identify as gay, you're likely gay yourself.[11]

This data is incredibly valuable to social media companies, which use it in many different ways. For example, the photos posted on Facebook make up what is probably the largest and most powerful commercial facial recognition database in the world. Facebook uses the information you post to create profiles for advertisers. (Though the interface Facebook provides to advertisers was at one point somewhat privacy protective, which we'll get to later). Facebook also uses the data collected from your posts and browsing habits to continually refine its software and algorithms, sometimes in controversial ways. For example, Facebook triggered outrage when it tweaked its news feed to study whether uses would act differently if they were shown more negative posts.[12]

In short, much of the concern about privacy on social media is the same as the concern over all forms of corporate surveillance and "big data"[13]: that companies will collect, sell, and use our information in ways adverse to us or in ways we don't expect. In this sense, social media is not exceptional. It brings up many of the same concerns as wearables and health apps like Fitbit, online banking services, e-commerce websites like Amazon, and data brokers. Social media just serve as a better spigot for your data, because through them we're more inclined to give it up regularly. We spend more time on social media than any other online service, and network effects will keep us from leaving. It's harder to leave Facebook than, say, a bank, because much of the reason we value Facebook is because everyone else is on it. This makes the design of social media user interfaces for advertisers and users incredibly important.

While I will discuss some problem areas for social media design below, it's worth noting that certain kinds of privacy-protective design were at one point being deployed for the world's best data spigot. When I talk to people about social media and privacy, one of the most common responses I hear goes something like "Facebook is sharing my information with everybody. Who knows who has my personal information now?" But this particular fear that Facebook will share its entire trove of personal data is unfounded. The data Facebook has on its users is far too valuable in house to sell in bulk to third parties.

Instead, Facebook acts as an intermediary—a sort of filter—between its users and advertisers. In this way, early versions of its ad interface were somewhat privacy protective. Here is how Facebook described its ad interface in a previous version of its data policy:

> When an advertiser creates an ad on Facebook, they are given the
> opportunity to choose their audience by location, demographics, likes,

keywords, and any other information we receive or can tell about you and other users. . . . [W]e serve the ad to people who meet the criteria the advertiser selected, but we do not tell the advertiser who any of those people are. So, for example, if a person clicks on the ad, the advertiser might infer that the person is an 18-to-35-year-old woman who lives in the US and likes basketball. But we would not tell the advertiser who that person is.[14]

Of course, even anonymized ad targeting can still be harmful and discriminatory.[15] Precision advertising can be used to exploit biases and perpetuate falsehoods in significantly corrosive ways, as the controversy in 2017 over systematized "fake news" revealed.[16] But while there are many privacy challenges presented by platforms and design, better privacy filters should be encouraged.

Social Media Hell Is Other People

The common narrative about harms caused when we share something we regret on social media is that it's our own damn fault. The promise of social media is that not only do we get to choose our audience but we also get to choose what we disclose online. We aren't compelled to share anything if we don't want to. So social media is all about audience and message control, right?

Not so fast. This misguided narrative of personal failure is usually premised on a faulty assumption that either the information we share with others is no longer private, or we are consistently capable of assessing risk and managing boundaries when we disclose using social media. The values of trust and obscurity show how the first assumption is glaringly wrong. Information entrusted to others is routinely considered private. Even when there is no trust, people rely upon the obscurity of their social exchanges every single day. Think of how you might bristle if a stranger leaned in to listen to a conversation you're having with someone else in the hallway of a public building (You might say "This is an A/B conversation, so you need to C your way out of it"). It seems instinctual that a disclosure to some is almost never meant as a disclosure to all, yet this point is consistently lost on those who dismiss privacy concerns on social media.

The second faulty assumption, that we are capable of adequately assessing the risk of social media disclosure, arises when other people fail to

recognize user's cognitive limitations, which are magnified at scale. The privacy design problems associated with disclosing to other people on social media can be divided into two major categories: forced errors and context collapse. Forced errors happen when design facilitates or co-opts sharing in ways the user did not intend or anticipate. A good example is the story of Bobbi Duncan, whose experience with being outed as a lesbian to her father on Facebook was detailed in the Introduction to this book. Or the story of Nick Bergus, whose humorous post questioning whether anyone would actually need a fifty-five-gallon vat of sexual lubricant turned him into an apparent user of and pitchman for the product to all his friends through Facebook's "Sponsored Stories."[17]

"Context collapse" occurs when discrete audiences bleed together in awkward and harmful ways.[18] Harms that come from this sort of exposure are almost routine. Many employees have lost their jobs when employers accessed social data.[19] Sometimes social media posts cause others to make bad judgments based on decontextualized or misinterpreted social data. For example, when Natalie Blanchard's insurance company saw on Facebook photos of her looking happy in social locations like at a bar or on the beach, it denied her benefits for the treatment of depression because she looked happy. Blanchard said that her insurance agent described several pictures Blanchard posted on Facebook as evidence that she is no longer depressed. "In the moment I'm happy, but before and after I have the same problems," she said.[20] Like everything we post online, our disclosures only show small and decontextualized parts of our lives.

This risk of context collapse is grounded not just in a usage error but also in the inevitabilities of exposure. In other words, disclosure on social media is risky because it becomes more searchable and persistent and it's easy to lose track of our audience and misperceive the risk of sharing. The more often design nudges you to share your personal information, the more likely it is that one of those disclosures will come back to haunt you. As I'll cover later, faithless "friends" abound on social media.

Exactly what kinds of audiences are a problem for social media users?[21] Maritza Johnson, Serge Egelman, and Steven Bellovin have identified the most unwanted audiences viewing social media disclosures as "future employers, supervisors, family members, peers and subordinates," and general "social threats" in addition to "organizational threats" related to the collection and use of data from social network sites.[22] So, basically, at some point everybody you know and a ton of people you don't will be an unwanted audience on social media.

But these relationships are different in important ways from users' relationships with platforms. The relationship between social media users and platforms is ostensibly governed by, among other things, the website's privacy policy and consumer protection rules.[23] But the relationship between users and their peers is governed by a much more complex and unstable set of norms, shared assumptions, informal terms, and a host of other signals and cultural contexts, all of which are malleable and affected by design. Consider the two major kinds of parties who are relevant to the privacy of social media users: *insiders* and *outsiders*.

The most proximate privacy risks to social media users (besides the platform itself) are from *insiders*—those people who are selected to be recipients of, or at least have authorized access to, online disclosures. Our friends, followers, and other networked connections are all in positions to misuse social data immediately upon disclosure. Design has been used in several different ways to facilitate insiders' disclosure of users' personal information in adverse and harmful ways.[24] In one instance, Facebook asked its users to report whether their friends were using their real names, a requirement under the website's terms of use.[25]

Often, people we have authorized to be in our networks are not the desired recipients of certain disclosures. Users forget or do not always realize the true extent of their potential audience when they post.[26] Similar concerns are raised by the automatic, accidental, or forced sharing of browsing and reading habits through "frictionless sharing."[27] When design makes our discourses leaky or encourages us to be reckless, it is a privacy problem.

Outsiders are people not explicitly authorized to have access to people's social media information. A great example would be your boss who is not your friend on Facebook. Outsiders can serve as threats by both seeking access to your profile and sharing your information elsewhere on social media. There have been numerous instances of employers asking for employees' social media passwords or otherwise trying to access their profile.[28] School administrators are often tempted to monitor social media usage.[29] Police officers and other law enforcement and national security officials have an interest in accessing social data.[30] In short, social media users have a legitimate interest in keeping their profile and posts discreet. Design must respect this interest.

In the remainder of this chapter I'll examine five different contexts where privacy design is an issue in social media: design that manufactures disclosure; design that extracts consent and makes people vulnerable to platforms; design that overexposes us, leaving us vulnerable to both people and platforms; design that aids faithless friends; and design that facilitates or fails to mitigate online harassment. Privacy law should take them all more seriously.

Manufacturing Disclosure

The only way social media can stay in business is if their users continue sharing personal information. Personal information ("original content" like selfies and "likes") is far more valuable and important to companies than links you post to the news (though even sharing links reveals something about you). Facebook values your own personal sharing so much that it's actually downgrading the prominence of news media in your news feed to favor content posted by friends and family.[31] And the pressure is always on to get you to share more. This simple motivation is the impetus behind so many new design features in social media. Facebook's streaming service Live, Instagram's "stories" feature, Snapchat's new filters, and Twitter's now shuttered video service Vine are all attempts to up the disclosure ante with designs that allow you to share in new ways.

And with every disclosure we reveal just a little more about ourselves. The effect is similar to traditional notions of surveillance—revelations through the close observation of people. But this modern surveillance has less to do with watching people to learn something about them and more about getting them to *tell* you the thing you want to know on their own.[32] Surveillance theorist Gary Marx describes this new, soft form of surveillance as "scrutiny through the use of technical means to extract or create personal or group data, whether from individuals or contexts."[33]

Some of these design upgrades pack a twofer punch: they make people share more while providing more granulated data for platforms. For example, in early 2016, Facebook introduced a series of new ways to interact with someone else's posts beyond the Like button.[34] Now users could react with buttons that signify Like, Love, Haha, Wow, Sad, and Angry. Facebook made this change partly in response to user demand. No one felt comfortable "liking" a status post that disclosed bad news, for example. But this new design feature is also a way for Facebook to coax even more nuance and granularity out of what we share and how we interact with others online. Social media companies see designs like this as key to their operation. This data can be used to make ads, content, and features more personal and responsive to your desires so that you never get bored. Bored people switch to different apps or log off altogether. Interested people keep producing data that, in turn, can be used to keep you interested.

Applying Privacy's Blueprint to Manufactured Disclosure

Most social media interfaces are designed to encourage people to share information and interact with the service and other users. The hard part is figuring out where to draw the line between acceptable nudging and unreasonable persuasion. The worst among these designs can be outright deceptive, such as when the adultery facilitation service Ashley Madison used fake profiles to flirt with users and get them to pay for additional features.[35] But those are the easy cases.

Less obvious troubling examples of manufactured sharing are everywhere.[36] For example, Facebook decided to set the default sharing setting for teen users to "public."[37] It also uses facial recognition technologies to make tagging people in photos effortless. Mobile apps like Candy Crush Saga have used difficult-to-understand, preselected checkboxes that often fool users into blasting out invitations to their Facebook friends.[38] LinkedIn uses our built-in instinct for social reciprocity to nudge us into adding friends and endorsing their skills. For example, when I say "thank you," the person I'm talking to likely feels compelled to say "you're welcome." LinkedIn is leveraging this tendency when it tells you so-and-so's invitation has been "waiting for you" for six days or when it recommends that you return the favor when someone endorses you on the website.[39] Using design to coax disclosures and information out of people can jeopardize the trust between people and platforms.

Designs that manufacture disclosure might be disloyal to users if they benefit companies at the unreasonable expense of those who trust them. These sorts of designs can be abusive. If the design tries to get you to disclose in a way that is contrary to your interests and leaves you worse off in a meaningful and articulable way, it is a form of adversarial design.

Robust legal responses to adversarial design are difficult, because it is hard to identify exactly when design becomes *too* persuasive or the benefits that people receive from disclosing on social media. Soft responses like encouraging adherence to ethical user interface and user experience (UX) standards could be useful here. Lawmakers might also consider moderate responses like greater scrutiny of when explicit disclosures are required by the Federal Trade Commission (FTC) and Consumer Financial Protection Bureau (CFPB) under their authority to regulate deceptive, unfair, and, in the case of the CFPB, abusive behavior. In egregious cases, tort liability could follow when technologies of persuasion become unreasonably dangerous and harm people. Additionally, moderate responses like mandatory process could be quite useful. For example, a requirement to assess the "crashworthiness" of interfaces before and after the deployment of potentially overly persuasive features could be required to measure the level of regret people have about disclosure. Regret is a key metric for scientists studying privacy and disclosure.[40] While it is not the only way to judge when manufacturing disclosures goes too far, it could be a factor. And while regretful social disclosures are bad enough, there's another piece of information social media seek from its users—consent.

Extracting Consent

The "it's your own damn fault" ethos regarding privacy and social media is most visible when it comes to the concept of consent—that little "I Agree" button or checkbox that every single social media user clicks as part of the registration and setup process. We agree to lots of privacy-invasive practices in the dense, unreadable boilerplate called terms of use. We also routinely agree to specific kinds of data collection by clicking the Agree button when apps ask for access to our phone's cameras, our location, and our address book. And if that decision ever comes back to haunt us, we can't complain because we "agreed," right?

Many of us feel some sort of injustice is being done when these boilerplates are foisted upon us. Marx calls this a form of "mandatory volunteerism": "disingenuous communications that seek to create the impression that one is volunteering when that really isn't the case."[41] People are made to feel as though giving up a host of rights, including privacy rights, was a knowing and just exchange for online services, even though it's doubtful that dense, boilerplate agreements can ever support truly meaningful consent at scale.[42]

We can feel so overwhelmed by the thousands of requests for access, permission, and consent to use our data that we say yes just because we are so worn down. Other times, design leads us to click Agree even though we didn't realize what we were doing. Buttons, signals, and designs can be manipulated for us to gloss over, accidentally click on, or significantly underestimate in importance.

For example, Apple's iOS 6 included a feature called the Identifier for Advertisers (IDFA). This feature assigned each device a unique identifier used to track browsing activity, which is used by information advertisers to target ads. The IDFA makes reidentification very difficult, but many people who care about their privacy would still like to have it turned off just to avoid another source of data collection and reduce as many risk vectors as possible, even if that risk is remote. The good news is that Apple included a way to disable the feature; the bad news is that it nested this option at the bottom of a series of vague, unintuitive, and confusing menu options like General, About, and the only slightly more helpful Advertising. First-time users are unlikely to have much of a clue as to where these menu options lead or what they do. If you are lucky enough to find the option to disable the IDFA ad tracking, you'd find that the toggle button labeled Limit Ad Tracking is probably preset to *off*. Simple enough, or so it would seem. Harry Brignull, a UX designer and founder of the website Dark Patterns, notes that this button is not what it seems: "It doesn't say "Ad Tracking—Off" it says "Limit Ad Tracking—Off." So it's a double negative. It's not being limited, so when this switch is off, ad tracking is actually on. Off means on!"[43]

Confusing wording, nested menus, and other tricks to confuse and obfuscate are commonplace for consent mechanisms. Before we can tackle the best legal response to design that extracts consent, let's first explore why consent to terms of use is so central to people's privacy on social media.

Consent and the Tyranny of Terms of Use

Boilerplate. Ugh. It has become a truism that virtually no one reads standard-form online agreements. A recent study found that less than one in a thousand e-commerce website users read the terms of use.[44] Even Supreme Court Chief Justice John Roberts has admitted he does not read the fine print on websites.[45] Yet these agreements are routinely enforced.

The law of online contracts is largely counterintuitive and a bit of a historical accident. Online standard-form contracts are typically categorized as "clickwrap" or "browsewrap" agreements, although that distinction can be blurred at times. Both of these concepts derive from the days when our software used to come shrink-wrapped in a box. You would open the shrink-wrap, and inside were the terms of use. Just how we add *-gate* to scandals, hailing from the Watergate scandal, the *-wrap* label indicates a kind of contract for software services.[46]

A clickwrap agreement requires some kind of affirmative act, like the click of a mouse on a button, indicating an assent prior to accessing a website. Browsewrap agreements dictate that additional browsing past the homepage constitutes acceptance of the contract.

Terms of use agreements, which often incorporate privacy policies, are types of clickwrap and browsewrap agreements. These agreements contain many standard terms, such as arbitration clauses, damage limitations, and warranty disclaimers. Increasingly, terms of use also include consent to spyware, vague behavioral restrictions, and severe limitations on the use of content from the website.

You might be tempted to think that you can't be bound by a contract you've never read, but you'd be wrong. Accepting an offer to enter into a contract, called assent in contract law, is demonstrated by an outward manifestation of intent to be bound. By manifesting intent to be bound by a contract, adherents assume the duty to read. The practical result of this duty is that individuals who objectively agreed to be bound by contract will be deemed to have agreed to all terms contained in the writing, regardless of whether they read the terms or understood them. In other words, it doesn't matter what you meant to convey when you clicked Agree without reading the terms; it only matters what a reasonable person would have thought you were conveying.

The parties' state of mind during the formation of these agreements is irrelevant. Rather, courts consider what the parties objectively conveyed to each other in what is known as the objective theory of contract. Only external acts and manifestations—not subjective, internal intentions—determine mutual assent to a contract. For example, when a website contains the phrase, "We respect your privacy," it does not matter what the site intends. The question is what a reasonable person in the user's position will understand from that communication. Thus, in principle, courts should consider the entire online user experience to adequately understand the average user. Unfortunately, it hasn't worked out quite like that in practice.

Courts appear to have reached a loose consensus in applying standard-form doctrine to online agreements. Courts tend to enforce clickwrap agreements that require an action on the part of the user, but they tend to shy away from enforcing browsewrap agreements that require no outward manifestation of assent. Courts oscillate on "notice sentence browsewraps," which provide users with a link to terms of use but do not require them to acknowledge that they have seen them.[47]

Thus, standard-form contract doctrine on the web, while controversial, is relatively stable. Courts relying on this doctrine give great weight to the specific language of the terms, often with little regard to other understandings and representations that arise within relationships.[48] These terms have great significance for user privacy, but they do not always reflect the complete understanding between the parties, which is significantly shaped by the design of technologies.

Facebook's Data Use Policy, the more accurate name for what most call a privacy policy, contains a laundry list of information the site collects:

Things you do and information you provide.
Things others do and information they provide.
Your networks and connections.
Information about payments.
Device information.
Attributes such as the operating system, hardware version, device
    settings, file and software names and types, battery and signal
    strength, and device identifiers.
Device locations, including specific geographic locations, such as
    through GPS, Bluetooth, or WiFi signals.
Connection information such as the name of your mobile operator or
    ISP, browser type, language and time zone, mobile phone number
    and IP [Internet protocol] address.
Information from websites and apps that use our services.
Information from third-party partners.
Facebook companies.[49]

To some this might be a shock. Because this policy is incorporated into the terms of service, the user is granting Facebook a broad license to collect, use, and share her personal information. Yet the most shocking aspect is that Facebook's terms are not unusual. While there is little that is exciting about online contracts, the most boring thing about them is that they are pretty similar to each other. These contracts collectively form a significant threat to user privacy because "consent" to them is largely meaningless to users. Yet courts seem unfazed.

Standard-form contracts are common in intellectual property, alternative dispute resolution, and limitations on liability. Those areas of law typically have a standard "default" position in the absence of contractual provisions. In the intellectual property context, if a website's terms of use fail to grant the appropriate licenses, then implied licenses will exist to govern the use of intellectual property and the parties will retain their rights. If a contract fails to include an arbitration clause, then courts are the default arbiter of disputes. Similarly, the Uniform Commercial Code fills in gaps where no specific terms exist. Yet the law regarding the default status of self-disclosed information online is inconsistent and unpredictable. Thus, for good or ill, contracts that address privacy issues provide a degree of clarity.

But privacy policies in fact usually end up being *antiprivacy* policies. In effect, they usually provide a liability shield for companies looking to take advantage of users' failure to actually read the policy they agree to. The policies often enable companies to track, exploit, sell, or share user information. They are drafted to protect the company, not the user. Most privacy disputes involving online agreements look to the "consensual" aspect of the agreement when validating a company's data practices. Judges are reluctant to provide a legal remedy to those who have consented to surveillance, collection, or use of their information.

Applying Privacy's Blueprint to the Problem of Extracted Consent

Design that extracts consent to boilerplate terms can be disloyal and corrosive to people's autonomy. Contracts are instruments of trust, yet designs that force them upon people corrode trust. Specific, unambiguous requests for consent to particular things like the collection of location data are preferable, though these can also overwhelm and confuse people, rendering consent equally meaningless.

Like manufacturing disclosures, manufacturing consent can be an abuse of persuasive tactics. A good approach is for courts embrace the more holistic view of promissory design proposed in Chapter 5. The law of contracts, as a creature of the common law, is supposed to evolve. Courts should not ignore the contractual significance of user interfaces and the user experience. Standing alone, interactive features of a user interface might be little more than bells and whistles. Yet many websites, apps, and platforms make user privacy and, by extension, user privacy settings, a central feature of the user's experience and a prominent part of the terms of use. Because companies that employ these features are in a contractual relationship with their users, user interface design should be part of an online agreement when it is incorporated into or consistent with the terms of use.

Predigital contracts were largely formed in the commercial or transactional contexts—not in the contexts of social interaction and media consumption. After all, when one turns on the television, listens to the radio, or reads a newspaper, contractual relationships are not formed. Thankfully, every time someone picks up the phone, writes a letter, or gossips in the hallway, they are not presented with a long and confusing list of terms dictating their communication. Yet virtually every time individuals access a website, app, or platform, they are asked to agree to a cadre of terms against which their only recourse has been simply to close their screen or go use a different service.

As our experience online grows richer, our relationships with tech companies and other tech users become more nuanced. Elements of contract law manifest themselves throughout the user experience. Promises like "We respect your privacy" are made on splash pages. Padlock icons inform users that their accounts are "protected." Checkboxes allow you to choose whether applications will have access to your phone's address book. Recognition of these elements—code-based promises and malicious interfaces that corrupt the integrity of contract formation—could reduce the schism between contracts as a source of, and solution for, privacy problems online. In other words, courts should look to design and peoples' actual experiences in a mediated environment to augment boilerplate agreements.

Courts could also render adversarial and malicious design that wrongfully extracts consent unenforceable. Interfaces that obscure information or manipulate navigation have already been considered significant, or even dispositive, by some courts in invalidating electronic agreements. In one of the most prominent browsewrap cases, *Specht v. Netscape Communications Corp.*,[50] the Second Circuit refused to enforce terms of use where "[t]he sole reference to [the terms] was located in text that would have become visible to plaintiffs only if they had scrolled down to the next screen."[51] Thus, if links to terms of use are buried at the bottom of a screen or anywhere where they are unlikely to be seen, courts have refused to find notice of terms sufficient to form a contract. The *Specht* decision was an excellent example of judicial recognition of a malicious interface, but it should be seen as just the beginning of exploration regarding how user interfaces can affect contract formation.

Hidden links are not the only type of malicious interface elements that can invalidate notice of terms. Distraction and interruption techniques could also negate the notice required for contract formation. Distracting video, animation, blinking, color, and motion could attract the user's attention away from inconspicuous terms by exploiting perception, particularly preattentive processing and our susceptibility to subliminal information.[52] Overly large ads and other rollover design elements could interrupt the contract formation process or obstruct the presented terms.

Malicious interfaces must be considered in context to determine their contractual significance. Malicious interfaces should not automatically invalidate a contract. Rather, they should be balanced with other evidence of contract formation. Clear, nonmalicious interfaces could be entitled to a rebuttable presumption of valid consent in light of an otherwise clear manifestation. The presence of a number of malicious interfaces (or a single significantly malicious interface) should, however, receive a strong presumption of invalidity with regard to the disputed terms.

Overexposure

The "Move fast and break things" corporate philosophy in Silicon Valley, with its evangelist "Give people the power to share and make the world more open and connected," inevitably creates leaky and pushy interfaces that expose users to far more than they bargained for. Social media companies often overexpose their users by design.

Social media are constantly introducing new features that make our information more visible, more searchable, and more complete to others. For example, Facebook has had a series of high-profile design changes that dramatically reduced the obscurity of its users. When it rolled out its news feeds, users were shocked when all of their information was aggregated in one place, lowering the transaction costs for other users to seek out posts and profile changes.[53] When Facebook introduced its Graph function, which let users search others' profiles and posts in very specific and nuanced ways, additional transaction costs to finding information disappeared.[54]

Information unrestricted by privacy settings and protected accounts can be easily aggregated and indexed by platforms, and found with ease by other users. The phrase "publicly available" is often used as a marker for acceptable snooping. It is more difficult for government and law enforcement officials to access information protected privacy settings and protected accounts than to access "publicly available" information, because they must request the information from the platform or the users themselves rather than just accessing it via the Internet without anyone's help. For example, in 2016 U.S. Customs and Border Protection proposed asking visitors to reveal their social media accounts.[55] Under the proposal, the government would review public social media information but would not ask for applicants' passwords in order to read private messages and posts. In 2010 Twitter turned all of its unprotected posts over to the Library of Congress for archival, but it withheld tweets from protected accounts.[56] This act further reflected the growing misperception that equates "accessibility" with "public" or "not private" information.

Weakened access controls also erode obscurity on social media by making more information more accessible by default. Facebook has gradually been chipping away at the obscurity of user profiles for years through subtle tweaks to things like default settings. Consider its decision to remove the option to keep your account hidden to everyone except "friends of friends."[57] In 2013 Facebook reversed its restriction on public posts by teenagers. Under its former policy, younger users could communicate only within their extended network; their biggest nonplatform privacy concern was whether one of their friends or a friend of friend would release their information to an unintended audience.

Facebook's slow creep to expose your personal information to the world via default settings is startling when you compare how protective its default settings were when it was first launched with how exposed they leave users five years later. In short, you're a lot more accessible and a lot less obscure than you used to be.

This sort of overexposure can be harmful to people who are relying on access protections like privacy settings and protected accounts when deciding whether to disclose. When social media design exposes people, it changes the rules and realities that people use to assess risk. When we cannot accurately gauge risk, our ability to create relationships of trust and maintain zones of obscurity is diminished.

Applying Privacy's Blueprint to Overexposure

Social media design that overexposes a company's users is indiscreet and untrustworthy. It erodes the obscurity users rely upon in deciding what and how to disclose. Leaky designs and obscurity lurches are dangerous. Yet deciding what constitutes unreasonable exposure can be difficult. One approach might be to focus on user expectations, since much of the harm comes from people's incorrect or frustrated risk assessments due to shifting transaction costs of finding information. This could lead lawmakers to adopt a robust approach of liability for obscurity lurches in extreme situations, either through consumer protection laws such as the FTC's deception and unfairness jurisprudence or product safety laws, both of which look to people's expectations about how a product will work. The FTC's complaint against Snapchat was a great example of how people who expected the photos they sent to "disappear" felt overexposed when the photos were revealed to be merely hidden but accessible or persistent.[58]

Sometimes social media design leaves people overexposed and vulnerable to malicious third parties. For example, security researchers noticed a bug in Facebook's Messenger software that lets anyone with a small amount of know-how see the web links shared by others in private messages.[59] Here, impact assessments could be used to help mitigate the harms. Governments could require companies creating user interfaces for social media to engage in a form of mandatory process. Under some data security laws, companies must assess the data they collect and the risk associated with its storage and use. They must design systems that minimize the storage of data and implement reasonable technical, physical, and administrative safeguards. Perhaps the law should treat designing user interfaces similar to collecting and processing personal data. The law should require companies to engage in regular obscurity impact assessments to limit overexposure.

Faithless Friends

Sometimes *friends* is the wrong word to describe the people we interact with on social media. On October 3, 2005, Cynthia Moreno vented her frustrations online. As a self-described "nerdy girl" and student at the University of California–Berkeley, Moreno was happy to be free of high school classmates in Coalinga, California, who had shot spit wads in her hair, taunted her for being chubby, and pulled chairs out from under her.[60] When she returned for a high school football game in the fall of 2005, she was reminded of her former misery and dislike for her hometown.

In an attempt to share her frustration with a close group of friends, Moreno published a missive about her hometown, titled "Ode to Coalinga," on the journal section of her personal profile on the social network site Myspace. The principal of Coalinga High School read the ode before it was removed and forwarded it to the local newspaper, the *Coalinga Record*, which published it in the newspaper's "Letters to the Editor" section. The Coalinga community reacted violently to the publication of the ode, threatening Moreno and her family and ultimately causing the Moreno family to close its twenty-year-old family business. Predictably, Moreno lost on her claims of invasion of privacy and intentional infliction of emotional distress against the principal, because modern privacy law incredulously yet consistently rejects the notion that information can remain private once it is shared with others.[61]

Stories of faithless "friends" are quite common on social media, yet the law rarely provides a useful remedy for those who were betrayed. Recall the story of Brian Pietrylo,[62] who created a "closed" Myspace group for him and his fellow employees to vent about their employer "without any outside eyes spying in on [them]." (see Chapter 3).[63] Although the group was private, and protected by the fact that each member needed to access it via his or her password-protected profile, one of Pietrylo's coworkers disclosed her password to her managers under pressure.

Stories of untrustworthy social media audiences are so common, in fact, that they are entirely foreseeable. Snapchat explicitly acknowledged that it knew about the fact that users were saving people's Snaps, which were supposed to become inaccessible. When hackers posted thirteen gigabytes of saved Snaps online, the company said "Snapchatters were allegedly victimized by their use of third-party apps to send and receive Snaps, a practice that we expressly prohibit in our Terms of Use precisely because they compromise our users' security."[64] But instead of keeping its users safe with a fortified application programming interface (API) that would prevent Snap-saving software from using the service, it buried its prohibition against using third-party software in the dense, unreadable terms of use it knew no one reads. Foreseeability is legally significant for companies providing the medium for these kinds of betrayals. Companies must design products that reasonably protect against foreseeable misuse. This should include the risk of faithless friends.

At this point, you might be thinking, "if faithless friends are so common and foreseeable, aren't the trusting social media users to blame for being so foolish in sharing online?" If social media disclosures were unsolicited by platforms and no indications of trust or obscurity were given, it might be justifiable to lay more of the blame on users who share online. But that's rarely the case with social media.

Instead social media and its users regularly solicit people's disclosures under the auspices of trust and obscurity. Recall the many different trust indicators described in Chapter 4. Features like Snapchat's ephemerality and Facebook's privacy settings embody these promises in design. Still other platforms just come right out and say it in marketing. The founder and CEO of the secrets sharing social app Whisper said that it is the "safest place on the Internet" to share.[65] Platforms set the ground rules for privacy online through design and language, transaction costs and signals, architecture and contract.

In order for online social interaction to be effective, there must be trust and obscurity. This is true for most social media save possibly those meant for speaking to as broad and public an audience as possible, but it is particularly true for social media that serve as support groups, such as the online communities for alcoholics struggling with dependency and veterans struggling with post-traumatic stress disorder.[66] Faithless friends on social media cannot be seen by platforms as simply a user problem. They are a foreseeable hazard that springs from the use of these technologies. The risk of betrayal can be increased or decreased by design. Platforms have power over their uses to help mitigate the risk of faithless friends, and privacy law should take this power seriously.

Applying Privacy's Blueprint to Faithless Friends

Faithless friends on social media often act, in the language of the blueprint, in disloyal and indiscreet ways. When design and context make it evident that one social media user is promising to keep the confidence of another and then fails to follow through, they are betraying a trust and acting faithlessly. When companies fail to mitigate the risk of faithless friends, they are failing to protect their users. All of this threatens the trust that is fundamental to meaningful sharing, a healthy online ecosystem, and human flourishing.

Failing to protect against the foreseeable risk of faithless friends on social media is a kind of dangerous design. Lawmakers should take steps to better ensure that people are more discreet and platforms are more protective against faithless friends.

The Privacy Box

There are several soft responses lawmakers could take to leverage design in mitigating the harm of faithless friends. Policy makers could fund technologies that gives people the ability to enter into contracts to preserve the trust between themselves and other social media users. For example, imagine a sort of "privacy box" for social media—an interface that requested an explicit promise of confidentiality from other social media users before a particular piece of information was revealed.[67] This interface would act to help people disclose information within a binding confidentiality agreement. People wanting to share something confidentially would enter that information (let's say a relatively serious medical diagnosis they wished to keep private) into a text box. A notification would then be sent to social media connections.

The potential promisor might be presented with a box that said merely, "The information contained within this box is considered private. In order to view it, the user has requested a promise of confidentiality from you." The user, upon clicking on the "proceed" link would then be required to accept a prewritten promise of confidentiality or some other form of protection. The language of the promise might read, "By clicking Agree, the user promises to keep the private information contained within confidential. [Privacy Box User name] is relying on user's promise of confidentiality as the condition for disclosure." Perhaps the discloser only wants recipients to keep the information obscure by not posting it in a searchable format elsewhere online. Obscurity exists on a spectrum, and this agreement can be customized. Documentation of the completed agreement could be sent to both the promisor and promisee for archival.

This technology would allow people to create obligations and clarify the mutual expectations of the parties regarding sharing on social media. It might gradually reinforce privacy norms merely by making confidentiality values salient and putting trust ethics into practice. Even in the absence of a binding contract, such notifications could make the importance of confidentiality more salient in their minds and impose a small transaction cost in accessing information. Of course, use of this technology would be overkill for trivial information and probably not enough for gravely sensitive personal information, which is probably best disclosed through more secure channels or in person to emphasize the personal nature of the disclosure.

Overuse of this technology would also be bad for our privacy. If people are not judicious in requesting discretion, we might end up with the same kind of fatigue and fatalism that surrounds boilerplate privacy policies. Confidentiality should be sparingly requested and enforced. The design of the privacy box would also require extra clicks that might seem burdensome to casual users, though they might also serve as a built-in protection against overuse. While it might be a cumbersome and impractical service for most kinds of common disclosures, it could be a useful privacy-enhancing service in some limited contexts.

Contracts and Confidentiality Indicators

Judges and regulators must pay better attention to context and trust indicators in online environments. Specifically, the law of implied confidentiality should evolve to accommodate the ways in which design shapes people's expectations. Online relationships involve a horde of implicit signals, cultural practices, power differentials, and shared assumptions that can reflect an unspoken confidence between the parties. Yet when these digitally implied confidences are breached, privacy law provides surprisingly little guidance for the betrayed.

At best, the concept of implied confidentiality plays a negligible role in the developing doctrine surrounding modern privacy disputes.[68] Despite over twenty years of social media,[69] there are not many opinions that directly address the concept of implied confidentiality created via the

Internet.[70] So what accounts for the disappearance of implied confidentiality in the digital era? Empirical evidence and logic do not support the contention that the only understandings of confidentiality between parties in online relationships are explicit.[71] Rather, implied confidentiality law has not been refined enough to be a workable concept in many kinds of common social interactions, including online relationships. It has not evolved to accommodate how design shapes people's expectations.

This developmental failure has resulted in the practical death of implied confidentiality online. Offline confidentiality has the advantage of traditional notions of readily perceptible context. Those seeking to disclose in confidence in face-to-face relationships can close doors, speak in hushed tones, and rely on other signals to convey a trust in the recipient that has not been explicitly articulated. Yet online relationships between people are frequently perceived by courts as missing the same implicit cues of confidentiality that are present in face-to-face relationships.

A better accounting for design could right this ship. The history of implied confidentiality disputes shows that courts mainly rely upon context and confidentiality indicators in determining the presence of an implied agreement of confidentiality. Both context and confidentiality indicators are abundant on social media. But it takes scrutiny to get a handle on them.

Let's revisit Cynthia Moreno, Brian Pietrylo, and their faithless friends within the context of a possible implied obligation of confidentiality. What was the context of disclosure in these cases? Did Moreno use privacy settings? Privacy settings, in isolation, are not dispositive, of course. But they aren't irrelevant, either. The group page created by Brian Pietrylo explicitly stated, "This group is entirely private, and can only be joined by invitation." The website indicated that the icon for the group, which was the restaurant's trademarked logo, would appear only on the Myspace profiles of those who were invited into the group and accepted the invitation. These are confidentiality indicators. Under some circumstances, particularly within small, established, intimate groups of people exchanging sensitive information, courts would be justified in finding implied obligations of confidentiality on social media.

Protective Design

Courts and lawmakers should recognize an obligation on the part of social media companies to reasonably protect their users against faithless friends.

This does not mean that companies should be asked to protect against all indiscretions—gossip is a way of life, and there is only so much intermediaries can do to limit the conduct of information recipients. Rather, companies should be restrained from unreasonably exacerbating the threat of faithless friends and should design their technologies to protect against foreseeable extraordinary threats. Like nearly all product safety issues, this will involve a combination of warnings and design.

Rather than prescribing requirements for sharing functions, secure-design regimes could be process based. Companies could be required to conduct PIAs and risk analysis and develop a plan for implementing and updating safeguards. Here companies would not be responsible for preventing faithless friends but would instead be required to account for the risk of faithless friends in a reasonable way. For example, certain foreseeable risks might require changing designs to make them more protective of people by implementing more rigorous authentication protocols or limiting users' visibility, searchability, or storage. Companies might respond to other risks by providing delete buttons, accessibility settings, de-tagging options, pseudonymity allowances, and harassment reporting buttons.

The law could also require that any nonobvious, extraordinary risk of faithless friends is presented clearly, prominently, and regularly. This would relieve companies from the obligation of warning and protecting against run-of-the-mill betrayals that would be obvious to social media users. For example, you might know good and well that Jim from accounting is going to tell everyone in the office about that drunk selfie you posted on Instagram. But neither he nor Instagram really promised otherwise. But what about dating apps, support group apps, and "exploding" media services? The context of social networks that connect people struggling with mental health issues is different from that of the Words with Friends social gaming app. There is likely a higher expectation of trust and more extraordinary risk of faithless friends, depending upon design and purpose. Good notice in this context means not burying warnings about and disclaimers of liability for faithless friends in the boilerplate terms of use. Boilerplate terms do not generate skepticism. They're not even read.

Let's put this in the context of Snapchat's failure to protect against "The Snappening." As we explored in Chapter 1, Snapchat implicitly offered safe, "disappearing" disclosure through explicit promises and design. One common kind of disclosure that resulted from this assurance was the nude photo. But Snapchat failed to secure its technology well enough to resist the inevitable motivation of people who wanted those photos.

The photos leaked in "The Snappening" were seemingly obtained by unauthorized third-party applications that used Snapchat's application programming interface.[72] While API security is challenging for all social media, it is paramount for a company that markets "disappearing" messages, inspires many third-party apps that reverse-engineer its API, and has already been subjected to a complaint by the FTC that specifically faulted the company for an insecure API.

Perhaps it would be unreasonable to expect most modern software applications to take extraordinary steps to secure their APIs. But ephemeral media companies are extraordinary; they invite sensitive sharing and unusual amounts of trust. There is more that these companies can and should do to protect the trust their users place in them because of the elevated risk of faithless friends and attacks. While it is difficult, there are ways to ensure that only authorized software can interact with an API, like rigorous client authentication in addition to standard user authentication. It should be a warning sign when hundreds of different users access an API from the same Internet protocol address. This was dangerous, insecure design.

Sometimes companies can render dangerous products safe through warnings, like Google's warning that pops up every time people open its Chrome Internet browser in "incognito" mode. The warning says, "Pages you view in incognito tabs won't stick around in your browser's history, cookie store, or search history after you've closed all of your incognito tabs. Any files you download or bookmarks you create will be kept. However, you aren't invisible. Going incognito doesn't hide your browsing from your employer, your internet service provider, or the websites you visit."[73] Descriptive, efficient, and persistent.

Most people were probably unaware of the security risk posed by third-party Snapchat applications. Third-party applications for social media are quite common. The application marketplaces for Apple and Google regularly feature third-party applications for Facebook, Twitter, and even Snapchat. Snapchat claims to have been diligent in patrolling these applications, but the average user would likely have no idea such popular technologies were so risky and prohibited by Snapchat. Shifting risk onto users through contracts that no consumer should be expected to read cannot be the way companies approach privacy risks in the modern age.

Dangerous design is opaque to most of us. It is almost impossible to tell which companies have reasonable data security practices. Companies have so much more information about the risk of their technologies than their users do. Information asymmetries are one of the defining characteristics of our relationship with companies that make digital technologies. People are just very poorly equipped to monitor the complex and rapidly changing threats to our privacy posed by each technology we use. If a common practice like using third-party applications is forbidden, notice should be much clearer. Companies should, at the very least, notify us through the user interface, not the fine print. And if meaningful notice is unfeasible or undesirable because of usability concerns, then companies must find a different way to make their products safer or be legally responsible for the harm that comes from insecure design.

Online Harassment

Harassment is the scourge of the Internet. Social media is teeming with petty hate mobs and vicious, callous, and usually anonymous individuals who regularly make life hell for anyone unfortunate enough to be caught in their crosshairs. This harassment comes in the form of repeated insults and bullying, threats of violence, stalking, posting people's private or identifying information online with malicious intent (called doxing), and the distribution of nonconsensual pornography, often called revenge porn. The victims of online harassment are overwhelmingly women, with common targets being people of color, and members of the LGBTQ community.[74]

Harassment on social media can be devastating. Victims can lose their jobs, have their reputations tarnished, and suffer from extreme emotional anguish. Harassers often betray others' trust, as when romantic partners who received intimate photos or videos in confidence share them with third parties. This erodes victims' autonomy and makes them reluctant to express themselves or trust others in the future. The chilling effect of online harassment is palpable. Harassment like doxing also eviscerates people's cherished obscurity, turning their identity and contact information into weapons for mobs and stalkers.

The very structure and design of the Internet and social media technology play key roles in facilitating this harassment. In her book *Hate Crimes in Cyberspace,* Danielle Citron extensively documents how the

Internet, specifically communication technologies like social media, have dramatically exacerbated the presence and harm from harassment. "The Internet extends the life of destructive posts," Citron writes. "Harassing letters are eventually thrown away, and memories fade in time. The web, however, can make it impossible to forget about malicious posts. Search engines index content on the web and produce it instantaneously. Indexed posts have no built-in expiration date; neither does the suffering they cause. Search engines produce results with links to destructive posts created years earlier. Strangers can put abusive posts to malicious use five days or five years after they first appear. Now and far into the future, victims' social security numbers may be used to steal their identity and their home address used to stalk them in person."[75] In short, the ability of social technologies to dramatically erode obscurity by lowering transaction costs exacerbates the harm of harassment.

Transaction costs are a key function for mob-like behavior as well. Communicating almost effortlessly at distance can heighten emotional detachment and blunt moral sensitivity. When it is easy to harass people, it happens more often. Citron writes,

> Networked technologies exponentially expand the audience for cyber harassment. Why would perpetrators spend the time and money to send letters by mail when the online audience for a given post is limitless and free? Posts that go viral attract hundreds of thousands of readers. The Internet's ability to forge connections enables stalking by proxy, whereby perpetrators recruit strangers to help them stalk victims, and group cyber stalking, whereby more than one person is involved in the online abuse. Online harassment can quickly become a team sport, with posters trying to outdo each other. Posters compete to be the most offensive, the most abusive.[76]

In short, harassment is nothing new, but the ease of it is. This is largely a function of transaction costs.[77] With a few notable exceptions, the design choices that facilitate harassment are not malicious or even blameworthy. The Internet and social media make *all* communication easier, not just harmful communication. And technologies that allow people to be anonymous have many virtuous uses, such as protecting political dissidents, but at the same time they shield harassers from accountability.

Since the structure and design of social technologies can fuel harassment, designing online spaces to make harassment difficult—in economic
terms, costly—should diminish it. One key is to moderate the signal and
transaction costs through design. There are three major areas where design
can help mitigate harassment by adjusting transaction costs: speech, access,
and self-defense.

The Cost of Speech

Online harassment usually requires communication, so the most direct
way to limit harassment is to make harmful speech costly to conduct. For
example, social media messaging systems can be restricted to designated
users. Twitter users can limit private messages to their "followers" and
Facebook users can do the same with their "friends." Additionally, nearly
every social platform allows users to block others. Blocking restrictions
impact behavior by forcing those who are blocked to comply with or else
expend the effort required to work around (e.g., deception) or override
(e.g., hacking) the constraints.

More modest interventions can effectively nudge civility, too. Before it
shut down, content filters on the anonymous social media app Yik Yak were
used to prevent users from posting someone's full name. Gossip on Yik Yak
about "John" was more obscurity-friendly than gossip about "John Smith."
While hardly airtight, this intervention tried to make it at least somewhat
harder for abusers to locate and learn about potential targets.

Yik Yak also targeted potentially problematic content by prompting
users (under triggering circumstances) with the following message: "Pump
the brakes, this Yak may contain threatening language. Now it's probably
nothing and you're probably an awesome person but just know that Yik Yak
and law enforcement take threats seriously. So you tell us, is this Yak cool
to post?"[78] This notification imposed additional time and effort for of-
fenders to process and respond to what had been conveyed, and thus increased the cost of speaking. It also signaled to users that their behavior
was possibly harmful and reinforced norms against threats. Was it a foolproof plan? Of course not. But it just might, in some cases, have let cooler
heads prevail over temporarily heated emotional reactions.

A number of social media companies are investing in technologies and
design strategies that seek to emulate the slight sense of social inhibition

people feel in face-to-face conversations and speeches in front of an audience. Civil Comments is a start-up based on a very simple concept: "[B]efore posting a comment in a forum or below an article, users must rate two randomly selected comments from others for quality of argument and civility (defined as an absence of personal attacks or abuse). Ratings are crunched to build up a picture of what users of any given site will tolerate, which is then useful for flagging potentially offensive material."[79] While a balance must be struck between awarding users a heckler's veto to others' speech through design, technology companies and governments have room to think more creatively about ways to increase the cost of harmful speech.

The Cost of Access

Blocking features can make it harder for abusers to access their intended victims' information. Users can be blocked at various levels, ranging from being unable to share, tag, and "upvote" others' posts to being fully unable to access any aspect of content associated with another user's profile.

The efficacy of and desire for strong blocking controls was made explicit in 2013 when Twitter briefly altered its blocking policy. For a limited time, blocked users could follow, retweet, and "favorite" public users who had blocked them, and blockees stopped being notified when users blocked them.[80] Harassment victims responded swiftly and loudly because they felt as though the blocking feature accomplished very little. As a result, Twitter reversed course. Harassment can even be deterred by raising transaction costs and making information unsearchable, a key factor for keeping information obscure. Harassment and abuse victims worry when Facebook makes all profiles searchable regardless of privacy settings.[81] Obscurity is all about the cost of finding people and interacting with them. Those seeking protection from abuse and harassment should be given better tools to raise the cost of access to try and dissuade bad actors.

The Cost of Defending

Transaction costs are also important for defending against harassment. Unlike the previous two examples, however, the goal here is to reduce transaction costs to facilitate action. For example, it should be easy to report abuse to social media administrators. Recognizing this, most popular social media have a report button in close proximity to users' posts. Yik Yak even implemented a voting system that immediately removed any post that received five "downvotes." Crucially, all users easily could downvote a post without jumping through bureaucratic hoops (like satisfying registration requirements) or engaging in additional clicks.

By contrast, systems designed to make abuse difficult to report show little respect for users. Mary Anne Franks has criticized Twitter's previous abuse reporting system, alleging that it "set up a game that targets of abuse can never win."[82] Under Twitter's old policy, parties conveyed harassment complaints on forms that took more time to complete than reporting spam, which required only a click on a readily available button.

Franks notes that when opening the form to report harassment on Twitter, "a user [was] confronted with a series of questions about their involvement with the abuse and what kind of abuse is being reported, the answers to which generate further options (a bit like one of those old 'Choose Your Own Adventure' books), followed by the aforementioned required links, description of the problem, a strangely cheery request to 'Tell us about yourself,' and an electronic signature."[83]

She observes that, compared to its then-existing system for reporting harassment, "Twitter is oddly unconcerned about false or unauthorized reports of spam: There are no questions about the user's involvement with the alleged spam, no requirement to provide links or explain how the content qualifies as spam, no requirement of a signature, no need to fear retaliation from the reported spammer."[84] This particular design of social media failed its victims because of the transaction cost it placed on them. It was a design that prioritized disclosure and ease of use over the well-being of its users. Twitter has responded to this design failure by better streamlining the process for reporting abuse. This is evidence that market pressure and an open dialogue with companies play an important role alongside privacy law's design agenda.

Of course, these categories of speech, access, and self-defense are fluid and imprecise. And design strategies aren't magical technofixes. For example, increasing the transaction costs for communicating online can lead to unpopular opinions being censored and strongly worded convictions being watered down.[85] Automated takedown filters are still clumsy and don't work great. But companies cannot ignore transaction costs related to harassment when creating social technologies.

Applying Privacy's Blueprint to Online Harassment

Online harassment is corrosive to the values of trust, obscurity, and autonomy. Spurned confidants often betray trust in order to shame ex-lovers. Doxing can destroy the obscurity of something only known to some, like a home or email address, making it more broadly accessible. Threats of violence and bullying, particularly in the aggregate, can deprive people of their autonomy to establish meaningful reputations and take advantage of life's opportunities.

Harassment is facilitated by efficient technologies more than any particularly malicious kinds of design. For example, general social media platforms like Facebook and Twitter are largely not deceptive or uniquely abusive regarding harassment. However, social media that fails to reasonably account for foreseeable harassment is dangerous to users, who must rely upon the tools and constraints of the medium.

Thus, to right the ship for online harassment, it is just as important to encourage protective design as it is to discourage bad design. Many of the same design-based responses to faithless friends would mitigate online harassment as well. Faithless friends are often the source of nonconsensual pornography, for example. There are also several responses outside of trust-based contexts that can be used to improve design.

Policy makers could work with industry to settle on some basic design principles to mitigate online harassment. The FIPs cover data protection. Standards like the International Organization for Standardization's ISO 270001 and the National Institute of Standards and Technology's NIST 800-53 cover data security, but there has been no significant, successful, and sustained coregulatory attempt to articulate design standards, features, or requirements for technologies to protect against harassment. We are seeing some loose themes arise already. This chapter has described the feedback techniques, access restrictions, and streamlined takedown systems that social media use to combat harassment. Standardization attempts could popularize new techniques, help refine promising approaches, and pool collective wisdom to understand what is and isn't working.

Like with the responses proposed in this chapter to mitigate the problem of faithless friends, lawmakers and regulators might require processes designed to assess the risk users face of being harassed while using a service and determine optimum transaction cost levels and signals to mitigate that risk through design. It is hard work to construct and assess a transaction cost framework for fighting abuse. But the finished product will be a useful tool for helping companies and policy makers focus their design efforts on effective and wise options. A mature version can give us a sense of how committed companies really are to preventing harassment and fostering civility.

And, of course, as with the entire design agenda proposed in this book, these approaches are only one piece of the puzzle. While the thesis of this book is that privacy law should take design more seriously, it should be followed with the caveat "there's only so much design can do." Other laws, policies, education, and self-regulatory efforts will also be necessary to solve this problem. The work of advocacy groups like the Cyber Civil Rights Initiative, Without My Consent, consumer protection agencies, state attorneys general, and companies like Microsoft and Google—who, as I will discuss in Chapter 7, have agreed to de-index nonconsensual pornography—is critical in mitigating harassment in social media.

7

Hide and Seek Technologies

ON APRIL 9, 2016, users of the Russian imageboard Dvach (2chan) launched a campaign that took the practice of "doxing"—searching for and publishing private information with malicious intent—to an ominous new level. Users leveraged the facial recognition technology FindFace, which matches random photographs to people's social media profiles, to identify and de-anonymize photographs of Russian pornography actresses. They then used the photographs to harass the actresses and their friends and families.[1]

Facial recognition technologies frustrate our ability to blend into a crowd. While we expect that people we encounter in public might occasionally recognize us, for the most part we go about our day in relative obscurity. Facial recognition technologies change the calculus by dramatically lowering the cost of finding and recognizing people. With the right database of faceprints linked to names (a "name-face" database) any stranger with a smartphone, surveillance camera, and drone can easily identify you. Search engines have also made it harder for us to hide. Every request to a search engine is an opportunity for anyone online to quickly and easily consult billions of sources and pinpoint what the rest of the world knows about you.

I call inventions designed to find, recognize, surveil, or hide people's activities *hide and seek technologies*. This category includes, among other things, cameras, Internet browsers, facial recognition technologies, license plate readers, drones, tracking beacons, and spyware. Some of these technologies are indispensable in the modern world. Search engines and surveillance cameras are now necessities for education, commerce, security, human resources, and basically every other activity that requires knowledge and accountability.

But they can also be incredibly destructive.[2] Hide and seek technologies are capable of facilitating both dramatic and visceral privacy harms, such as revealing deeply sensitive, secret information like nude photos, sexual preferences, health struggles, and political activities. Abusive partners regularly use the surveillance capabilities of smartphones to locate, control, and harm their victims.[3]

Hide and seek technologies are also deceptively inconspicuous. They are capable of eroding our valued obscurity so slowly and steadily over time that we don't notice the process.[4] Most people probably don't regularly think about the fact that nearly everywhere we go, hundreds of surveillance devices are either always on or ready to record at a moment's notice. Surveillance has become so normalized that we as a society rarely protest when surveillance cameras go up at every other corner and in every public building. Facial recognition used to be rare, but now it's getting built into our smartphones for authentication. Before we wake up and ask how we got to a state of perpetual surveillance, we should create some rules for when surveillance technologies go too far.

Of course, we have many complex rules that regulate surveillance by the government, private entities, and private citizens. Governments around the world regulate, to some extent, *when* and *how* hide and seek technologies may be used. In the United States, there are laws that regulate electronic surveillance, government search and seizure, the use of obfuscation technologies like masks to thwart facial recognition, and intrusion upon seclusion. But with only a few notable exceptions, privacy law around the world is largely agnostic about the design of hide and seek technologies. By ignoring design, lawmakers and judges implicitly subscribe to the myth of neutral technologies.

The law's blind spot for design is often justified. Most of the uses for technologies like Internet search engines and smartphones with cameras are legitimate, but some design decisions warrant scrutiny. In certain contexts, the harm caused by "seeking" technologies, which dramatically reduce the transaction costs of finding and understanding people's identities and activities, is not outweighed by their benefits. Policy makers should approach the design of these technologies with a similar balancing calculus or at least look for some proof of significant legitimate uses.

Policymakers often underemploy and too often try to hinder "hiding" technologies, like encryption and privacy settings. These privacy- and security-preserving technologies should be generally supported within regulatory structures. Lawmakers should consider not only the specific problems posed by design choices but also the cumulative effect these designs will have on people individually and on society as a whole. While many problems posed by hide and seek technologies can be mitigated by rules surrounding their use, a design agenda remains critical. Design rules can shore up lingering holes in a regulatory framework, make technologies more trustworthy for consumers, and stop entire categories of problems before they occur.

The key will be to adequately identify the values implicated by design decisions shaping hide and seek technologies and the specific problems these designs cause. In Chapter 6, I argued that social media was largely about trust and relationships. In this chapter, I argue that surveillance is largely about obscurity and transaction costs. First, I make the case that the best way to frame the problems presented by technological surveillance is as a loss of obscurity. This frame should give stakeholders a common language for articulating the diaspora of dangers flowing from surveillance and information retrieval. Next, I review critical design features from technologies designed to seek, recognize, spy, and hide. It is often difficult to determine when certain design features for hide and seek technologies go too far and do more harm than good. But to focus solely on use of these technologies ignores how their design to an extent determines their function. This is why modern debates surrounding technologies like biometrics, drones, and encryption could be improved with an increased focus on design.

I conclude this chapter with a call to action for lawmakers and policy makers. To help remedy privacy law's design gap, lawmakers should better scrutinize designs that dramatically reduce the cost of finding, recognizing, or watching people. These designs should be reasonably safe. At the least, the design of surveillance technologies must be justified by their overriding benefits to society, with special care to those made vulnerable through surveillance. Conversely, law and policy makers should foster "hiding" technologies, those that allow people to preserve or increase the transaction costs of finding or understanding people and data. This includes embracing—not crippling—technologies like encryption, anti-surveillance masks, ad blockers, and other obscurity-preserving technologies.

Surveillance as Loss of Obscurity

Troubling new surveillance disclosures are becoming too common. Since the 2013 revelations of Edward Snowden's leaks of classified National Security Agency documents, the public has learned about not only sweeping intelligence surveillance programs but also widespread domestic use of surveillance technologies. These technologies include drones, Stingray cell phone trackers, and other cell-tower-mimicking technologies that allow police to intercept phone conversations;[5] facial recognition technologies;[6] and license plate readers that allow both police and private parties to keep tabs on vehicles' whereabouts.[7] These technologies enable more persistent and elusive public- and private-sector surveillance than ever before.[8] Stories of misuse of these technologies feed the anxiety about a surveillance nation.

One of the major problems with these hide and seek technologies is that people seem concerned about their use, yet we have a hard time agreeing on when and why they are a problem and what we should do about it. For example, when is surveillance by drones in public unjustified? Does widespread collection of metadata raise privacy concerns? Should encrypted devices have a back door for law enforcement officials? Despite increased attention on surveillance, the public discourse, jurisprudence, and theory surrounding it still struggle for coherence.

The threats arising from different kinds of surveillance are often framed as distinct from each other, not grouped as part of the same problem. People worry about facial recognition technologies because it is impractical to hide your face when in public or change it to frustrate surveillance. Biometric databases including things like fingerprints and faceprints create a new class of "searchable" information. Discussions surrounding license plate readers focus on the aggregation of information. Then there are drones. In addition to persistent surveillance, drones also present a "peeping tom" problem.[9] Small drones can effortlessly surveil things that are hard to see by the naked eye. Related debates surround cleavage, "upskirt," and "creeper" photos in public.

Thus, depending upon the tools and methods of surveillance, the harms can involve the disclosure of secrets, fleeting public exposure, aggregation of formerly hard-to-find information, unavoidable biological identifiers, and the interception or requisition of communications and stored information. Scholars have grounded surveillance theory in such diverse notions as anonymity, contextual integrity, structural constraints, information asymmetries, boundary regulation, and dignity.[10]

So it's no surprise that a common thread for understanding and dealing with modern surveillance problems has been difficult to find. This lack of common ground has sometimes resulted in inconsistent and confusing policy, as well as discrete and diverse reform attempts. Proposed remedies vary according to who is the watcher, what is being watched, and the tools used to accomplish the surveillance. A common ground for the modern surveillance debate would be useful. But first we must find a different language for talking about privacy—one that unites the mixed bag of concerns caused by overreaching surveillance. One thing is certain: when surveillance and information retrieval become too easy, people start to worry. When people talk about modern surveillance problems, they usually say something like, "There is more data than ever before, and it is increasingly easier for the government to access this data and understand what it means."

That's actually a great starting point. When it is difficult to surveil or retrieve information, our obscurity is strengthened. When it is easy, our obscurity is jeopardized. Obscurity is the key to understanding and uniting modern debates about hide and seek technologies. As I have discussed in Chapter 3, it is also key to Privacy's Blueprint. The concept of obscurity should inform regulatory responses regarding the design of technologies. The best way to do this is to moderate the transaction costs of surveillance by leveraging designs that create friction and inefficiency.

I have identified obscurity as one of the three primary enabling values for Privacy's Blueprint, along with trust and autonomy. Obscurity is defined here as the state of information or people being hard or unlikely to be found or understood. It can serve as a theoretical common ground and regulatory focal point for the problems posed by the design of hide and seek technologies.

U.S. law has long treated issues of data collection and aggregation implicitly as an issue of obscurity. Sometimes the law explicitly embraces obscurity as a concept. For example, "practical obscurity" first became an issue in the American judicial system is the 1989 ruling of *U.S. Department of Justice v. Reporters Committee for Freedom of the Press*.[11] There the Supreme Court recognized a privacy interest in information that is publicly available but nevertheless difficult to obtain.[12]

Specifically, the Court determined that the Freedom of Information Act requirements do not compel the federal government to use its criminal records database to expedite access to rap sheets so that inquirers are spared effort and expense. Justice is not violated if they have to seek out the information from inconveniently located places, such as courthouses' files.[13] In delivering the Court's opinion, Justice John Paul Stevens wrote, "In sum, the fact that 'an event is not wholly 'private' does not mean that an individual has no interests in limiting disclosure or dissemination of the information' . . . the substantial character of that interest is affected by the fact that in today's society the computer can accumulate and store information that would otherwise have surely been forgotten long before a person attains age 80, when the FBI's rap sheets are discarded."[14] In other words, in order to protect the obscurity of personal information, we should focus on preserving the effort and expense required to find or understand that information. We should focus on how transaction costs create and preserve obscurity. Unfortunately, *Reporters Committee* has turned out to be, thus far, the legal apex of the case for obscurity.[15] In subsequent years, there has been precious little case law acknowledging that the logic underlying the decision is valid and has broader applicability.[16]

Transaction costs make a difference. Evan Selinger and I have argued that people are routinely deterred from pursuing goals that require expending effort or assets when they lack the requisite motivation or resources.[17] This means that when information is difficult to find or understand, the only people who will be inclined to do the detective work are those who are willing to invest the resources required for said work.

Of course, obscurity protections do not guarantee safety. They are probabilistic. Creating restraints by adding transaction costs can never provide the peace of mind offered by more absolute safeguards like encryption that will frustrate even competent and determined parties—including busybodies, enemies, aggrieved members of a community, hackers, and government agencies. But then again, it is doubtful that foolproof safe-guards actually exist. As Paul Ohm rightly notes, "No technology is perfect, and advocates who comment on privacy and technology in truth almost never advocate for perfect privacy."[18]

Obscurity is a unifying and enabling value on which to center the debate over the design of hide and seek technologies. Obscurity can be the key to unifying the scattered modern surveillance theories and policies. Because obscurity is fundamentally reliant on transaction costs and probabilities, it is broadly applicable. Nearly all theories about surveillance dangers and how to best regulate surveillance can be reduced to the valence and utility of making surveillance costly. Obscurity enables other values. To increase autonomy, make technological surveillance more challenging and reduce interference from external parties. To protect dignity, make surveillance more challenging and reduce the actual number of personal intrusions out of respect for individuals. To protect intellectual privacy, intimacy, and room for play, make surveillance more challenging and help people feel safe when they engage in intellectual, social, and introspective exploration that they might not want revealed to others.[19] To accomplish all of these things, raise the transaction costs of finding information.

Hide and Seek Technologies

Before we jump into how to best create privacy rules for the design of hide and seek technologies, we must understand the extent to which such technologies permeate our lives. It's more than just cameras and encryp-tion. Regulators, companies, and people should also care about leaky technologies—those that fail to hide our personal information even though they are supposed to. Technologies that make seeking *easier* also deserve scrutiny. The different designs of hide, seek, and leak technologies affect our privacy in unique ways. And as you will see, it's not going so well.

Technologies Designed to Hide

In the Internet's infancy, there weren't many tools people could easily use to hide personal information. If you didn't want someone to see your in-formation, the most common thing to do was (and to some degree still is) to lock it up behind a password or other authentication protocol. Encryption was the gold standard then, of course, and remains so now. But it and most other robust hiding technologies were not available to the masses. The best protection most of us had for information exchanged online was the practical obscurity gained by the fact that pre-Google search engines were only moderately effective and most people and companies didn't have the time or resources to dig that hard. In the information security realm, this was called security through obscurity.[20] Although security through obscurity is seen as a weak primary security strategy, it is useful as one of several methods of protecting data.

Times have changed. Today there is a wide variety of technologies that can be used to hide things along the obscurity spectrum from "hidden in plain sight" to "virtually impossible to find." These technologies are often called privacy-enhancing technologies, or PETs. Ira Rubinstein has argued that there are really two different kinds of PETs: substitute and complimentary. Substitute PETs are designed to allow zero collection of personal data. If successful, they can mitigate the necessity of some legal privacy protections (or even make them redundant). Complementary PETs, however, have the slightly different goal of being either privacy-friendly or privacy-preserving. Rubinstein defines privacy-friendly PETs as those that facilitate "individual control over personal data, mainly through enhanced notice, choice, and access."[21] He defines privacy-preserving PETs as those "offering provable guarantees of privacy, mainly through cryptographic protocols or other sophisticated measures."

In this way, not all PETS are "hiding technologies" that directly contribute to obscurity and resist surveillance. Some privacy-friendly PETs further other of the Fair Information Practices (FIPs) like transparency or notice. Here are a few examples of obscurity-enabling "hiding" technologies and possible uses that policy makers could foster.

Smart Hyperlinks and Access Walls

Sometimes people want to share information in a limited way without using passwords or social media platforms. Designers could use cookies and other background authentication technologies to create a "paywall"-like technology that would only recognize requests to access links containing personal information if they came from certain trusted sources.[22] For example, a link might not lead to the correct page unless the user clicked it while within a protected online community or if certain cookies existed on the user's computer authorizing the disclosure.[23] Anyone who has tried to access a university's digital repository off campus might be familiar with how this technology works. Alternatively, the link might work only when the web server can confirm that the link is embedded within a certain web page.

These "smart hyperlinks" could help ensure that only members of the protected community or other verified users could access the information. Additionally, these links would help maintain the obscurity of information by frustrating the ease of dissemination online. Most links can be easily shared by pasting them into emails, texts, or social media postings. Smart links would require the extra step of manually disseminating the information itself rather than the hyperlink. Such a technique might not adequately protect confidential or secret information, but it would likely help obscure information by reducing the number of people likely to disseminate it.[24] While not perfect, this flexible approach could meaningfully help enable selective disclosure.

Privacy Settings

As was discussed in Chapter 6, some of the most common tools to help users produce obscurity are privacy settings.[25] These settings, which generally allow Internet users to control the potential audience of their disclosures on a website, are often criticized as poorly protecting privacy since hundreds, if not thousands, of people can still have access to "protected" disclosures.[26] This critique highlights the problems with relying upon conceptualizations of privacy as secrecy to guide design.

These technologies are likely better understood as "obscurity settings." They help users hide from search engines and control who accesses their personal information. These are two of the most important factors of my conceptualization of online obscurity in this book. The empirical research I conducted with Fred Stutzman supports the assertion that Internet users take advantage of privacy settings for numerous reasons such as propriety, audience management, and obscurity.[27] These settings can serve as bedrock technologies to enable obscurity by design for social technologies.

Search Blockers

Search invisibility is a primary way to achieve obscurity. Technologies that prohibit websites from being indexed by search engines are highly effective ways to design for obscurity. Technologies such as password systems, privacy settings, and paywall-like technologies serve the dual purposes of restricting access while also keeping certain pieces of information from being cataloged by search engines.

Other technologies can also provide this function, however. The robot.txt file is a simple and effective way for websites to indicate nonparticipation in search engines.[28] Search invisibility can be woven into the design of social technologies. For example, the popular blogging platform Tumblr allows users to hide their blogs from search engines. On the settings page for any particular blog, users can reverse this result by checking a box to indicate the user's desire to "allow search engines to index your blog."[29]

Some software design offers various levels of search engine obfuscation, where only certain aspects of a profile or website are placed into search. These designs can make information searchable only at the site level, but remain invisible to general search engines. Search engine optimization techniques can be inverted to lower the placement of certain results, a sort of search engine diminishment. If you can push a particular search result to the tenth or eleventh page of results, it's practically invisible for most purposes.[30]

De-identifying Tools

Every day your odds of being identified through technological means increase. Facial recognition technology is evolving rapidly.[31] According to a study by the Georgetown Law Center on Privacy and Technology, one in two American adults is in a law enforcement face recognition network. It is only a matter of time before individuals in photographs and videos online can be automatically identified.[32] "Augmented reality"—that is, "a live, direct or indirect, view of a physical, real-world environment whose elements are augmented by computer-generated sensory input such as sound, video, graphics or GPS data," will continue to find its way into social technologies.[33]

The identities of people in photos and videos online are often obscure. For example, people in YouTube videos are obscure if their name is not tagged or otherwise typed out on a video's homepage or in the video itself. Post hoc identification of these individuals would destroy the obscurity they enjoyed with regard to these videos and images. Thus, any technology that frustrates facial recognition and other identification tools can create obscurity by design.

For example, Google has developed a technology that allows users to blur the faces of those appearing in videos before posting them to YouTube. The tool was envisioned as another option for dealing with privacy complaints submitted by people depicted in another user's videos. Instead of having to delete videos due to privacy complaints, video creators will also have the option to blur the complainant's face, allowing the videos to remain on YouTube.[34]

While face blurring might still leave individuals subject to identification in some contexts, this technique could have two positive outcomes for obscurity: only those with external knowledge of individuals with blurred faces would likely be able to identify them, effectively protecting the individual from recognition by most strangers, and blurred faces will frustrate facial recognition technologies.

Applying Privacy's Blueprint to Hiding Technologies

With respect to hiding technologies, Privacy's Blueprint is simple: lawmakers should support them or do their best to leave them alone. Policy makers should use soft responses like funding and educational efforts to improve PETs to get better and more appropriate usage. A cognate to a general "live and let live" approach to fostering hiding and access-control technologies would be regulators easing up on rules that hinder good privacy and data security research. As was mentioned in Chapter 5, lawmakers should work to ensure that third parties like independent security researchers are not unduly hamstrung by rules that arguably impose liability for discovering bad privacy design. For example, the protections for digital rights management technologies in the Digital Millennium Copyright Act prohibit circumventing a technological measure that controls access to a copyrighted work. These rules make it difficult to research security vulnerabilities, which require poking around to see which technologies too easily facilitate unauthorized access.[35] These anticircumvention rules should be modified to encourage external security and privacy audits of consumer technology. It also means the broad U.S. antihacking statute, the Computer Fraud and Abuse Act, should be narrowed in a way that protects good faith security research. In this way, lawmakers can protect against dangerous, insecure design of consumer technologies.

Don't Compromise Hiding Technologies

Of all the long-standing battles between advocates of hiding technologies and governments, none are more visible or important than the fight over encryption. For the uninitiated, encryption through cryptography is "the art of creating and using methods of disguising messages, using codes, ciphers, and other methods, so that only certain people can see the real message."[36] Thanks to fancy math, encrypted messages appear as unreadable gobbledygook unless you have the decryption key, which renders the message readable again. Encryption enables secrets, which is a power that cannot be taken lightly.[37]

Encryption can make it difficult, and in some cases impossible, for the government to obtain information from people. This creates a problem for law enforcement. Encryption can make information unavailable even when the government has a lawful basis to seek the information and a legitimate need for it.[38] From the perspective of encryption advocates, the ability to ensure secrets is a critical tool for assuring privacy in the face of increasingly effective surveillance technologies and techniques.

These tensions came to a head in the 1990s in what is commonly known as the Crypto Wars.[39] The government sought a compromise by seeking rules that forced companies to use encryption that was breakable by the government on demand. Often these proposals included government holding encryption keys in an "escrow" or otherwise building in "back doors" for the government. The idea was that such schemes would keep everyone out except the government, thereby maintaining the value of security.

The problem, however, is that it appears impossible to build a system that only keeps the parties with bad intentions out. The consensus from computer scientists and security experts seems to be that escrow schemes create problematic new targets and there is no settled method for securely designing a system for third-party access to cryptography.[40] In other words, even if we wanted to correctly build encryption back doors and key escrows, we probably couldn't. Much ink has been spilled over the importance of encryption and the folly of compromising it.[41] Our crucial information infrastructure and privacy depends upon it. Yet the costs of good encryption to law enforcement and intelligence should not be casually dismissed. Our safety depends upon effective law enforcement. A balance can be struck, but for the purposes of the blueprint, lawmakers should resist the temptation to ban or cripple encryption. Other "hard but possible" options to access information in the tradition of surveillance due process might, upon scrutiny, prove to be an effective compromise.[42] But given their importance to safe and secure communication around the world, the integrity of encrypted technologies should remain a priority for lawmakers.

Don't Co-opt Ephemeral Technologies, Either

The fight over weakening hiding technologies is not going away and the need for government prudence extends beyond just encryption technologies. There have been several well-documented battles in the Crypto Wars; the most recent iteration involved a monthlong standoff between the U.S. Justice Department and Apple over access to an iPhone belonging to an alleged shooter in San Bernardino, California. In early 2016, at the government's request, "a federal court ordered Apple to create a software tool that would bypass security mechanisms in Apple's software so that the government could perform what's known as a brute force password attack to guess the password on the phone."[43] While the Justice Department eventually dropped its request because it found an alternate method to access the information on the phone, the case generated an enormous amount of controversy and public discourse about the importance of both encryption and law enforcement access to information.

In the debate, the term *warrant-proof phones* was thrown about in an ominous way. In his testimony before the House Judiciary Committee on March 1, 2016, FBI director James Comey said, "We're moving to a place where there are warrant-proof places in our life. . . . That's a world we've never lived in before in the United States."[44] In its response to a court filing Apple made in California, the government claimed that the "modest burden" Apple faces in complying with the FBI's request is "largely a result of Apple's own decision to design and market a nearly warrant-proof phone."[45]

This is a curious argument. For most of humankind's history, the overwhelming majority of our communications were warrant-proof in the sense that they simply disappeared. They were ephemeral conversations.

Even wiretapping was limited to intercepting phone transmissions, not re-trieving past conversations. For law enforcement purposes, encrypted phones are equally inaccessible: no one can recover information from them. But Comey's description of warrant-proof technologies is vague enough to apply to many different things. We should use a different term if we care about preserving the ephemerality and obscurity of some communications. Lawmakers should avoid compromising obscurity-friendly technologies—particularly those designed to delete information or otherwise make it inaccessible. Otherwise we might end up with a requirement to store everything.

Right now there are essentially three categories of information technol-ogies that matter to law enforcement:

1. Those that make data accessible to the government when it has a warrant or has complied with some other form of due process.
2. Those that make data inaccessible to both government and manufac-turers. Think of these as lockout technologies.
3. Those that fail to store information as data or that systematically and completely erase data after a brief period. These are ephemeral technologies.

Most modern information technologies fall into category 1. This is why Peter Swire and Kenesa Ahmad have critiqued the government's fears of "going dark," arguing that we actually live in the "golden age of surveil-lance."[46] The Internet of Things adds an additional layer of surveillance to our lives. The competing force is that the threat of harm from modern tech-nology has never been great. Previous ages have never had to endure dis-tributed access to destructive technologies, and the ability to communicate anonymously, cheaply, and across distances only puts us further at risk. But surveillance boundaries must be drawn somewhere, or else any amount of surveillance can be justified for our safety. One good place to start drawing boundaries is around technologies that do not store or make in-formation accessible.

The iPhone was in category 1—accessible—before 2014, when Apple strengthened its encryption practices. Now the company is trying to get the devices into category 2: lockouts. Apple could have helped the government unlock San Bernardino shooter Syed Farook's phone. But is Apple going to be allowed to design a phone that it truly could not break into even if it wanted to? Will legislatures deem data too valuable to be forever imprisoned on a hard drive?

If so, a new problem will arise, given that both lockout and ephemeral technologies are "warrant-proof." Unless there is some kind of clarity from legislatures, the only realistic way to ensure legal compliance could be to design technologies that record and store everything. Consider digital assistance technologies like the Amazon Echo, which are designed to "always listen" for words like "Hello, Alexa" but do not fully process, store, or transmit what they hear until they are activated.[47] For law enforcement purposes, most of the information the devices listen to is functionally impossible to recover. Does this mean legal authorities should consider Echo a warrant-proof technology? The emergence of the Internet of Things is shrinking the number of "dumb" objects by the day. Governments have requested laws that mandate data retention for over ten years.[48] Must all technologies be built to ensure that what they hear is retained and made available for law enforcement's inspection?

Warrant-proof technologies are not inherently bad. Both ephemeral and inaccessible technologies free us to explore, inquire, and play in ways that have always been necessary for human development. If we care about the freedoms that being warrant-proof gives us, we should find a more measured way to talk about facilitating law enforcement's access to information. Otherwise we might find ourselves wondering how we wound up saddled with the concept of permanent data retention.

We should also consider more robust efforts to mandate certain types of design in contexts where it is feasible and would impose minimal burden on other values or utility. For example, hypertext transfer protocol secure (HTTPS), the standard for encrypting web traffic, should be deployed everywhere.[49] If any protocol were to justify either a hard or soft mandate, it should be HTTPS, given the relatively low cost of implementation and the high benefits from plugging the leak that is standard HTTP. In fact, we're already seeing a de facto mandate of HTTPS around the web. The White House has mandated HTTPS for federal websites.[50] Apple has publicly discussed requiring HTTPS for its iOS apps.[51] If these kinds of soft (or partial) mandates still leave holes in the Internet ecosystem, it might be time for the law to more directly encourage this protocol.

Technologies Designed to Seek

Some technologies are designed to facilitate the discovery and collection of information. They are *seeking* technologies, and they are everywhere. Some of them, like Internet browsers, are so commonplace that people don't think of them in terms of privacy. Others, like facial recognition technologies and license plate readers, are so new that we are still searching for the right vocabulary to describe the problems they present. But by far, the most common and entrenched seeking technologies are everyday consumer devices like our smartphones. Below is a short review of the different kinds of seeking technologies that implicate our privacy.

Consumer Devices and Data Collection

Our daily lives are awash in surveillance devices. Our homes sometimes have nanny cams, teddy cams, and every manner of surveillance device meant to keep tabs on those we allow into our house. Our personal computers are also data-sucking machines. Computer maker Lenovo has been accused more than once of inserting hidden data collection software in its laptops.[52] Your computer's video camera and microphone can be turned on remotely and without your permission or knowledge.[53] Even Facebook creator and CEO Mark Zuckerberg covers his camera and laptop microphone with tape to protect against unauthorized surveillance and data collection.[54] And your smartphone is just a small computer that has the additional capacity to report on where you've been and who you are talking to.

Mobile phones are now top targets for law enforcement and industry surveillance. In 2015 the Federal Trade Commission brought a complaint against retail tracking company Nomi, alleging that the company failed to provide adequate notice that it "tracked consumers both inside and outside their clients' stores, tracking the MAC [media access control] address, device type, date and time the device was observed, and signal strength of consumers' devices. In reports to clients, Nomi provided aggregated information on how many consumers passed by the store instead of entering, how long consumers stayed in the store, the types of devices used by consumers, how many repeat customers entered a store in a given period and how many customers had visited another location in a particular chain of stores."[55]

The software that runs on our consumer devices is also designed to extract incredible amounts of personal information. Supercookies respawn even if you delete them.[56] Facebook's Like button is basically a ubiquitous tracker of your preferences and reading habits.[57] "What They Know," an award-winning *Wall Street Journal* series about online tracking of personal information, detailed the thousands of different ways digital technologies are engineered to extract our personal information.[58] One of the most pernicious and sadly common kinds of "seeking" technology is the kind of spyware covered earlier in this book—software that is secretly deployed on someone's computer or mobile device and covertly transmits data to the deploying party about the user's activities. Spyware is a scourge of the modern digital landscape, and it has been difficult to combat.[59] It seems that when all of that data is ripe for the taking, sometimes people and organizations just can't help themselves. If you build a surveillance infrastructure, then that's exactly what will happen.

Biometric Tools

Biometric surveillance is slowly but surely creeping into our everyday lives. We should be much more critical about how these technologies are built and used. A biometric is any method by which your identity or personal information can be revealed through evaluation of one or more of your distinguishing biological traits; the most common examples are fingerprints and facial recognition technologies. But you might be shocked that many of your biological traits can out you, including your eyes, hands, handwriting, voice, veins, and even the way you walk.[60] These technologies are used everywhere. Law enforcement seems to have gone all in on facial recognition technologies, creating a "next generation identification" system billed as "the world's largest and most efficient electronic repository of biometric and criminal history information" for the criminal justice community.[61] So has social media like Facebook, which can spot you in a photo through object, gait, and posture recognition even when your face is hidden.[62]

License Plate Readers

License plate readers (LPRs) are also becoming popular with law enforcement, lenders, and even hobbyists.[63] These cameras, which are often mounted on cars or signs are designed to track the movements of every passing driver. The American Civil Liberties Union has investigated the use of LPRs, stating, "The information captured by the readers—including the license plate number, and the date, time, and location of every scan—is being collected and sometimes pooled into regional sharing systems. As a result, enormous databases of innocent motorists' location information are growing rapidly. This information is often retained for years or even indefinitely, with few or no restrictions to protect privacy rights."[64] As with many forms of surveillance, it is the poor and marginalized populations that feel the largest impact of this surveillance.[65]

What's worse, these readers are being implemented in insecure ways. As Ars Technica, which has featured some of the most probing stories on LPRs, detailed in 2015, the Electronic Frontier Foundation learned that "more than a hundred ALPR [automatic license plate registration] cameras were exposed online, often with totally open Web pages accessible by anyone with a browser. In five cases, we were able to track the cameras to their sources: St. Tammany Parish Sheriff's Office, Jefferson Parish Sheriff's Office, and the Kenner Police in Louisiana; Hialeah Police Department in Florida; and the University of Southern California's public safety department. These cases are very similar, but unrelated to, major vulnerabilities in Boston's ALPR network uncovered . . . by DigBoston and the Boston Institute for Nonprofit Journalism."[66] In short, LPRs are coming, and they are particularly attractive to municipalities. Like politics, all design is local.

Drones

Few modern technologies feed our anxiety like drones. These new robotic "eyes in the sky" are getting smaller, more powerful, and able to stay in the sky longer. They're being designed to follow you wherever you go.[67] Amazon already has a patent for a voice-activated miniature shoulder law enforcement drone meant to provide backup to police officers.[68] They're getting shot out of the sky as an antisurveillance measure.[69] When I talk to people about drones, inevitably the first fear they mention is that they are basically robotic, automated Peeping Toms.

Certainly, that's one concern about drones. But there are many others.[70] Margot Kaminski has argued that we shouldn't let the Peeping Tom narrative drive the debate about drones and privacy. According to Kaminski, when people worry about drones because they can be used to illicitly surveil young sunbathers in their own backyards, "it provides a woefully incomplete account of the kinds of privacy concerns that drones raise." Kaminski notes that there is little to govern the kinds of data that drones share with other devices or each other. Retailers and insurance companies are bound to try and use drones to create intimate portraits of people. Kaminski writes, "We are already profiled online by data brokers; companies have every incentive to try to extend that profiling to physical space. And they don't want to have to ask for permission to get it."[71]

I agree with Kaminski that the Peeping Tom narrative is woefully inadequate. For example, it doesn't cover how drones with facial recognition technologies can obliterate our practical obscurity. You can't be lost in a crowd if drones will always recognize your face. Drone owners could easily follow and profile people. Even so-called "public" surveillance presents privacy problems. The Peeping Tom narrative also fails to address the facts that drones will be gathering information we don't even think about being collected and cannot hide from, like thermal imaging. Finally, drones collecting personal data are just another data security problem. As Kaminski notes, "If you think drones are disruptive now, just wait until they're hacked."[72]

Ambient Surveillance for Microphone Enabled Devices

One of the seemingly fastest-growing types of surveillance is the ambient sort that occurs with "always on" technologies that have virtual assistants ready to respond to voice commands. Technologies like Apple's Siri in iPhones and Amazon's Alexa in Echos, are designed to be always listening in the background for a "wake word" or phrase, such as "OK, Google," or "Alexa." Samsung smart TVs even give you a warning (of course, buried in a privacy policy), "Please be aware that if your spoken words include personal or other sensitive information, that information will be among the data captured and transmitted to a third party through your use of Voice Recognition."[73] These sensor-enabled devices are everywhere, and they're listening.

In fact, these devices might catch more than most of us realize. An Arkansas prosecutor recently demanded that Amazon turn over information collected by one of its Echo devices that was in the house of a murder victim, in the hopes that its ambient data might help solve the crime.[74] The Echo was deemed relevant to the murder investigation because someone present on the night of the victim died allegedly recalled hearing music streaming through the device that evening. Amazon resisted the request, but if such information is available and relevant, most likely it can be re-purposed to help solve a crime.

But Stacey Gray at the Future of Privacy Forum has argued that the term "always on" for microphone enabled devices could be misleading, noting instead that the surveillance issues from these sorts of technologies continued along a spectrum of three major categories:

(1) manually activated (requiring a press of a button, a flip of a switch, or other intentional physical action);

(2) speech activated (requiring a spoken "wake phrase"); and

(3) always on devices (devices, such as home security cameras, that are designed to constantly transmit data, including devices that "buffer" to allow the user to capture only the most recent period of time).

Here is where design matters. According to Gray,

> Each category presents different privacy implications, influenced in part by whether data is stored locally (an increasingly rare practice) or whether it is transmitted from the device to a third party or external cloud storage. Local storage keeps control over the data in the hands of whoever has the device. Cloud storage is riskier because it is easier for law enforcement to obtain and provides more opportunities for hackers. Another key issue is whether the device is used for voice recognition, the biometric identification of an individual by the characteristics of her voice, or for speech recognition, the mere translation of voice into text.[75]

Sensor-enabled devices illustrate the importance of privacy-friendly defaults and structural protections that practically minimize the data that is collected. Design that serves other values, such as convenience, often has risky or annoying privacy side effects.[76] For example, one of the latest models of the iPhone "will be set by default to automatically record a constant stream of sound and video whenever the camera app is in use, without the user pressing the shutter button and even if the camera isn't set to take video."[77] We're being nudged to collect more and more by default, in small but increasingly troubling ways.

Body Cameras

In an effort to increase police officer accountability, some jurisdictions are allowing or mandating the use of body-worn cameras on police officers.[78] These cameras can provide transparency, but they also act as persistent surveillance and data collection devices. In addition to capturing video of witnesses, suspects, and bystanders sometimes at their most vulnerable and stressful moments, these cameras produce an incredible amount of data.[79]

Many of the inherent privacy issues presented by these cameras are related to the design of the technologies that are part of a body camera system. For example, are the cameras designed to be "always on," or will there be an on / off button? Will that button be remote or located on the camera itself so that the officers wearing them have discretion as to when they are turned on or off? Here there are conflicting values at play. For example, an officer might want to turn a camera off to protect victims of sexual assault. Yet such discretion also might undercut the accountability function of the camera. Will the camera give an indication when it is recording, like a red light? How will the data be stored, where will it be stored, and for how long? Will it be made searchable and accessible to the general public? Will it be shared with the industries working with governments to provide this technology?[80] Will these technologies be combined with facial recognition technologies? Good privacy design will address these issues in a way that preserves the accountability value of the technology while ensuring that the people captured by the cameras maintain their obscurity.

Applying Privacy's Blueprint to Seeking Technologies

The future of responsible surveillance and data retrieval is in reasonable friction, judicious retention, and liberal deletion. In essence, speed bumps and ephemera. In order to create rules for obscurity-friendly seeking technologies, lawmakers should embrace minimization and reasonably render seeking technologies less efficient in order to protect against harmful obscurity lurches.

Embrace Data Minimization

At this point in the book, I have to eat a few of my words criticizing the FIPs and laud the virtues of one of the most important of the practices: data minimization. Although most of the FIPs do not provide much guidance for design, data minimization is key for design. Data minimization is a version of the "collection limitation" principle and it dictates that technologies should be designed to only collect and keep personal information that is directly relevant and necessary to accomplish a specified purpose. Once that purpose has been fulfilled, the data minimization principle dictates that the personal information is no longer necessary and should be deleted.

This is a key protection in the digital age. Advocates of big data often argue that the data minimization principle is an outdated FIP, but this position can be overly optimistic about the current strength of rules limiting how data can be used and shared. Given the flimsiness of "consent" and the lack of information relationships for many kinds of surveillance, data minimization represents one of the great tools to build out Privacy's Blueprint. One easy way to channel data minimization into design is a better Delete button. Although I've argued that "control" over information is too overleveraged in law and policy, the Delete button is magnificent. It's simple and direct; people intuitively know what it means. If it's easy to find it's easy to use, and it can be one of the best ways to meaningfully exert control over user information. If you want something gone, just delete it. Delete buttons will not work for everything, of course. Sometimes information cannot be disentangled from other data or even located because it is anonymized. If there are too many, people get overwhelmed, and delete options become little better that meaningless consent formalities. But legislation like California's SB 568, known as the "Online Eraser" law and the erasure rights embedded in the European Union's General Data Protection Regulation provide a foundation for more regulatory attention to mandated Delete buttons. The key will be making sure that people aren't overwhelmed, that their expectations about deletion match reality, that the right information is deleted, and that companies retain the ability to collect the information they need for their services to function properly. The mere option to delete data or accounts should not unreasonably burden users with all of the risk of data collection.

Add Friction to Technologies That Facilitate Obscurity Lurches

The problem with some obscurity-eroding technologies is that they are *just* benign enough to escape legal scrutiny but worrisome in the aggregate. Consider lip-reading technology, which in isolation seems like it might be not so bad. Researchers at Oxford University have created lip-reading technology that leverages artificial intelligence and, under structured conditions, "was able to identify 93.4 percent of words correctly. Human lip-reading volunteers asked to perform the same tasks identified just 52.3 percent of words correctly." Even in random video clips where words are more difficult to decipher, some lip-reading technologies can accurately read almost half of the words spoken.[81]

At first blush, the privacy issues with lip-reading technology might not seem severe. Speaking is a revealing act by its nature. When I speak in social places like a restaurant, any eavesdropper might hear what I'm saying. How is lip-reading any different from literally hearing the words that are spoken? The answer is that lip-reading technology facilitates obscurity lurches in ways that eavesdropping does not. In order to understand what people are saying, you usually need to be nearby or engage in electronic surveillance. Practical considerations keep the risk of people nearby from eavesdropping to a minimum. And the law regulates electronic surveillance. Equally, the law should take lip-reading technologies, even when used in public, seriously.

Some of the damage of obscurity-eroding technologies should be mitigated through traditional use restrictions found in electronic surveillance law and other protections in U.S. Fourth Amendment law. But media and video recording platforms also have an important role to play in allowing these technologies to be used in connection with their platforms. Google wisely prohibited the use of facial recognition technologies in its eyewear technology Glass. Smartphone makers like Apple could regulate lip-reading technologies by excluding them from the app marketplace or directly prohibiting their use on the phones themselves. In 2016, Twitter announced plans to deny application programming interface access (the data "fire hose") to those who use the social media for surveillance or other activities that violate its terms of use.[82] Productive regulation of third-party design and activity is critical to making sure new technologies are safe.

Mug shot aggregation websites represent a related kind of technological obscurity lurch. It might surprise many to learn that a person's mug shot—which is taken at the time of arrest, before guilt is determined—is generally considered a public record. The reason this might be surprising is that these records used to be practically obscure. Unless someone went actively searching for them, they usually stayed hidden from sight. This obscurity is critical for those hoping to make a fresh start. Mug shots are a visceral, incendiary symbol that one has been accused of breaking the law. But they do not tell the whole story. Most of the public's exposure to mug shot photos is with the hardened criminals in wanted posters or celebrities behaving badly. Thus, these photos carry incredibly negative connotations regardless of the actual offense or whether one was ultimately convicted or not. Potential employers, friends, and partners might never give a chance to someone if they see their mug shot before actually getting to know them. Mug shots have a particularly negative effect on African Americans, who are unjustly targeted and incarcerated at significantly higher rates than their white counterparts for the same crimes.[83]

Unfortunately, an industry has sprung up around the idea that people will pay to keep their mug shots obscure.[84] Websites with names like Mugshots, JustMugshots, and BustedMugshots were in the business of collecting mug shots through public records searches, aggregating them, tagging them with people's names, and then making the database searchable and highly visible through search engines like Google. For a while, those who were unfortunate enough to have their mug shots appear when someone searched their name had only one real option for regaining their obscurity—pay the website to take the photo down. It was a process some websites sadly made quite easy. While public records and open government are vital to democracy and a community's well-being, this cottage industry was essentially an extortion operation. In an age of overcriminalization, it is a mistake to treat all alleged crimes as worthy of a digital scarlet letter.

Then came the "friction," the idea that transaction costs can be used as a lever to make information more or less accessible, according to how open or private you want it to be.[85] Google struck the first blow against the mug shot industry by tweaking its algorithm to downgrade the prominence of mug shot websites in its search results.[86] MasterCard, PayPal, and other payment systems stopped processing payments to these websites, cutting off a major stream of revenue. These efforts did not completely stop the aggregation or tagging, but it did blunt their effect by obscuring them. It is now harder, but not impossible, to find people's mug shots online. Combined with rules preventing outright extortion, this friction represents a better balance between people's valued obscurity and the public's ability to learn.

Some judges have begun to recognize the role of design in lowering transaction costs. Although the term *obscurity* is not used in the Supreme Court of New York case *Bursac v. Suozzi*,[87] the ruling does cite the privacy interests acknowledged in *Reporters Committee*.[88] Here the court determined that although driving while intoxicated (DWI) arrests are a matter of public record, Nassau County, New York, executive Thomas Suozzi went too far in creating an online Wall of Shame containing mug shots and names of people who were arrested in his county for the offense.[89] According to Judge William R. LaMarca, "It is the scope and permanency of public disclosure on the Internet by a governmental agency that distinguishes the County's 'Wall of Shame' from traditional and regular forms of reporting and publication such as print media. The County Executive's campaign of publicizing DWI arrests serves a legitimate purpose but the use of specific identifying information on the Internet, with its endless implications, is of concern to the court."[90] Because publishing DWI arrests online can lead to "limitless and eternal notoriety, without any controls," the court moved to mitigate the harms that will come to those listed on the digital wall.[91] The ease of potential jury members accessing the DWI arrests presented due process concerns. In addition, the Wall of Shame could too easily induce bias and tempt potential employers and landlords to abuse their power in perpetuity.[92]

Policy makers, judges, and industry should continue to explore ways to frustrate harmful technological obscurity lurches. Think of this as the "speed bumps" theory of regulating design. When roads are designed in such a way as to allow dangerously fast driving, civil engineers often install speed bumps as a structural protection. The bumps introduce friction by physically slowing vehicles as well as encouraging drivers to go slower lest they damage their cars. Yet speed bumps still allow cars to arrive at their destinations. Technological friction works in a similar way: the increased difficulty of finding information means that only more determined searchers will succeed. If the level of friction is right, most people will be practically protected from needless voyeurism, gossip, and discrimination, while those who need the full picture about a person can find what they need.

Finally, policymakers should consider robust approaches to both friction and data minimization for biometrics. Technologies like face recognition are designed to facilitate dramatic obscurity lurches. They complete tasks in mere seconds that previously would have taken hours, weeks, or even years. While there are legitimate uses for facial recognition technologies, their power can easily be abused. They can be used to harass people, chill their expression and free movement, discriminate against them, and out any number of their secrets revealed by their physical presence in the world. Once these technologies are built and normalized, their effects will be difficult to reverse.

This is why I worry about face recognition and other biometrics being used as authentication tools for things like mobile phones. It normalizes robust uses of power and lays the infrastructure for an obscurity-eviscerating surveillance system. While biometric laws that require consent recognize the dangerous nature of face recognition technologies, we've already covered the limitations of consent regimes. Perhaps a more effective alternative would be to create rules that increase the cost of implementing face recognition technology by creating presumptions of invalid use of facial recognition technologies, rules regarding in what context and manner face recognition technologies can be used, and non-delegable fiduciary obligations regarding the storage, use, disclosure, and deletion of biometric data. Once face recognition ceases to be exceptional, our obscurity will be difficult to recover.

Leaky Technologies

Some technologies make surveilling and collecting data about others far too easy by leaking personal information. I use the term *leaky* to describe technologies that, through design, reveal people's personal information in unnecessarily risky ways. Leaky technologies are related to, but distinct from, the more recognized concept of data breaches, which typically involve unauthorized access on the part of third parties. Think of leaky technologies as unforced errors on the part of companies.

For example, most of the estimated thirty million Americans who regularly watch pornography online likely assume they are doing so with some semblance of privacy. One's sexual preferences are highly personal and could be damaging and prejudicial if made public. But online porn websites are quietly leaky. In a story titled "Your Porn Is Watching You," journalist Brian Merchant writes that "most of the top porn sites made explicit the exact nature of the film being viewed right in the URL—XVideos,

XHamster, and XXNX are all sending URL strings like http://www.pornsite .com/view/embarrassing-form-of-exotic-pornography-here.htm. . . . Only Pornhub and Redtube masked the nature of the video viewed with numerical strings, such as www.pornsite.com/watch_viewkey=19212."[93] A recent study on privacy on adult websites found that although third-party tracking is not nearly as prevalent on adult websites as on comparably popular websites, "Google trackers (Google Analytics and / or DoubleClick) were present on almost all the sites, and that search terms were often leaked in plaintext to third parties and sometimes encoded in cookies."[94]

Data leaks like this are common and often unintentional. An old version of the song-spotting app Shazam kept the microphone on Macintosh computers turned on, even when it had been turned off by users.[95] This sounds bad, but it's important to note the nuance of what was happening. The audio that was being picked up was not processed unless the user actively turned the microphone on. The design choice was made to improve the functionality of the app, though it did carry some risk of misuse. When the leak was discovered, it was patched. This is common for designers. Law and policy makers should keep in mind that bugs will still exist in code even when designers take reasonable efforts to eliminate them. Thus, soft and moderate responses should be used to lower the risk of harm from leaky technologies to acceptable levels before more robust responses are embraced.

Applying Privacy's Blueprint to Leaky Technologies

Data minimization is just as important for leaky technologies and seeking ones. But another critical factor involves making sure that the code is sound and double-checked for surprises.

Resist Design That Creates Data Reservoirs

One of the best ways to stop leaks is to make sure there's nothing to spill. Danielle Citron has compared the utility and danger of massive databases full of personal information to large reservoirs holding water that is incredibly useful when stored but can cause catastrophic harm when it escapes. She argues that "contemporary tort theory supports strict liability for bursting cyber-reservoirs of personal data instead of a negligence regime overmatched by fast-changing technology." A strict liability regime, which would hold companies liable for any damages caused by leakages of data in their control regardless of fault, would encourage technology designed only to store what is necessary, since the mere storage of information would come with a significant risk of liability.[96]

Even if lawmakers and courts were not inclined to hold companies strictly liable for data losses, they should encourage technological design that either deletes or obscures information or does not store or surveil information at all. Paul Ohm has repeatedly cautioned against the creation of a "database of ruin." He argues that at our current rate, "databases will grow to connect every individual to at least one closely guarded secret. This might be a secret about a medical condition, family history, or personal preference. It is a secret that, if revealed, would cause more than embarrassment or shame; it would lead to serious, concrete, devastating harm. And these companies are combining their data stores, which will give rise to a single, massive database. . . . Once we have created this database, it is unlikely we will ever be able to tear it apart."[97]

As mentioned above, design that minimizes data collection will be key to mitigating the harm from data reservoirs and "databases of ruin." Judges could give heavier scrutiny to the role of design when analyzing claims against companies for negligent data collection and management. Data is risk as well as utility and should be treated as such. But perhaps the most critical legal response to mitigating the harm of data collection is to resist data retention laws.

Data retention laws are those that require Internet service providers and other data holders to collect and store data that track the Internet activity of their customers.[98] The battle over data retention requirements has been going on for decades. In 2014 the European Court of Justice struck down the European Union's Data Retention Directive as a violation of the fundamental right to privacy. The court held that the directive imposed "a wide-ranging and particularly serious interference with the fundamental rights to respect for private life and to the protection of personal data, without that interference being limited to what is strictly necessary."[99]

Data retention is the antithesis of privacy-friendly design. Technologies that cannot be designed to delete information that is no longer relevant evoke many of the same risks posed by general, dragnet government surveillance. Joel Reidenberg has written critically of data retention mandates, arguing that requiring data to be collected and retained for subsequent government access without any individualized cause or suspicion is contrary to the presumption of innocence inherent in the constitutional philosophies of the European Union and the United States. Reidenberg writes, "If law generally requires collection and retention, the rationale is that all individuals in the data set are suspect. Similarly, if broad access is afforded to data sets that were created for commercial purposes, the core philosophy is that all individuals in the data set are suspect. These practices transform the presumption of innocence into a presumption of suspicion counter to the core constitutional philosophies."[100]

While there are certainly good reasons why governments want to preserve the data collected through consumer technologies, these claims should be tempered by people's need for privacy. Reidenberg advocates strict retention limitations and clear, firm access controls: "Red line boundaries should include (1) retention limits that, without a compelling justification specific to a target, do not go beyond a duration required for billing; (2) a ban on access without independent, public judicial oversight; and (3) no cross sharing between intelligence and law enforcement or between law enforcement and economic rights enforcement."[101] Scrutiny and reluctance for data retention should be built into privacy law's design agenda.

Check for Leaks

In addition to courses in privacy law, I teach torts. I often see certain problems in terms of reasonable precautions against risks of harm to others—the essence of the tort of negligence. Lawmakers and policy makers could effectively mitigate leaky technologies by requiring that companies that create consumer technologies and data collection systems routinely check for leaks. "Data leakage" is even a common aspect of data security protocols and privacy impact assessments.[102] Under such systems, the problem is not necessarily the leak itself but the failure to properly inspect and repair. Data breach notification laws can also motivate companies to check for leaks before a technology is deployed to avoid the reputational and financial costs of reporting after a leak is discovered, although notification is more reactive than affirmative rules or duties regarding safety checks.[103]

Warn People of Hidden Information Flows

A consistent theme in this book is that the reality of how consumer technology works should match the user's mental model. This includes assumptions about which, when, and how technologies are collecting information. Industry and lawmakers should pay close attention to the standard signals technologies send to users and others affected by those technologies. These signals might be legally significant because they can shape a person's expectations regarding mental models, affordances, and constraints. Lawmakers should, however, be careful not to overinvest in these signals as a mechanism for giving blanket consent for surveillance practices.

What's more, we as users must learn to better recognize clear, low-effort technological surveillance signals. For example, research has shown that many people fail to notice when their webcam light is on or understand that the light indicates the webcam is actively recording.[104] This is a basic, easy signal. If lights and other simple surveillance warnings were more broadly noticed and understood, they could effectively warn people of hidden information flows. These designs could be incorporated into disclosure regimes for consumer technologies. But better educational efforts by companies and users will be required to bridge the gap between signal transmission and user comprehension. And rules will need to be created to prioritize certain warnings and discourage others so as to avoid notice fatigue.

In the end, privacy law's design agenda for hide and seek technologies is relatively simple. Support design that protects, deletes, and increases the transaction costs of finding information. Make sure companies watch out for obscurity lurches and data leaks. Ensure that users have accurate expectations about how a technology works and that the expectation is respected in law. Hide and seek technologies can be an incredible force for good, but only if they do not undermine our trust, obscurity, and autonomy.

8

The Internet of Things

IF YOU'VE EVER wondered what it would be like to plug your delicates into the digital grid, I've got some good news for you. Vibrundies are here and they are exactly what they sound like: Internet-connected, vibrating underwear. The website for this wearable tech states, "Using vibrations from our special undies power pack, Vibrundies monitors Twitter for brand mentions and shoutouts—giving you a very special feeling each time one hits. . . . [W]hen you can't look at your phone, there's a better way to feel the buzz of your social activity."[1] So, now, not even your underwear is safe from the digital revolution.

This is just one of the many kinds of things you might be surprised to learn is part of the flourishing movement often called the Internet of Things (IoT). Cars, houses, clothing, fitness monitors, pregnancy test kits, health support devices like pacemakers, refrigerators, things in your refrigerators like wine bottles, and basically every other useful object in your day-to-day life is a target for Internet conversion.

A chip-centric mentality has taken over, one that is guided by an overly simplistic principle: "Internet connectivity makes good objects great." Guided by this upgrade mentality, we seem to be in a rush to connect everything. Meanwhile, seemingly none of us, including policy makers and regulators, has fully appreciated the significance of companies transforming from artifact and device "makers" to "service providers."

Objects are not necessarily better simply because they are connected to the Internet. Often, the Internet can make objects worse and users worse off. The IoT is notoriously buggy because it relies upon hardware and software. The more moving parts a device has, the more can go wrong. For example, a smart TV that was connected to the Internet at a crematorium in the United Kingdom malfunctioned and broadcast hardcore pornography during a funeral service for a father and his young son.[2]

Software that works today can crash tomorrow, leaving us with inoperable or dysfunctional objects.[3] Software needs regular upgrades to fix problems and patch vulnerabilities. Internet connectivity can make upgrades possible. But it also provides an attack vector for hackers, and it allows companies to render your IoT object inoperable whenever it likes; consider how Google Nest plans to shut down its Revolv hub, designed to control lights, alarms, and doors.[4] Though, as I'll cover in this chapter, leaving an unsecure IoT device operable is arguably worse than killing it before it becomes a neglected security liability.

In addition to adding instability and unreliability to networks, IoT objects also multiply the effects of Internet connectivity. Think of all the digital devices you have in your house, apartment, or dorm room. You might have a laptop, a phone, and possibly a tablet or gaming system. Others that live with you might have the same. In 2013, the Organisation for Economic Co-operation and Development (OECD) estimated that in member countries, an average family of four had about ten Internet-connected devices in their home.[5] By 2020, the OECD estimates, you'll have at least fifty such devices, including your cars, energy consumption displays, weight scales, home automation sensors, smart plugs, and more. *On average!* Just think how many connections the technophiles, the affluent, and early adopters will have. This growth will exacerbate design flaws and add complexity that will be increasingly difficult to manage. Not only will these devices create problems in talking with each other, but they will also create a bigger haystack for needles like data leaks, surreptitious surveillance, and critical vulnerabilities to hide in.

In this chapter I'll argue that the design of IoT objects, most notably the decision to "wire up" an object in the first place, should be a prominent concern for privacy and security law. Specifically, the very decision to add Internet connectivity to an object should be more legally consequential. This could be done through prerequisites and rules for connectivity or obligations that flow from connectivity. IoT technologies can be dangerous, meaning if designed poorly they will be insecure and facilitate unexpected or chilling surveillance. Like with social media and hide and seek technologies, a consumer protection and product safety approach to IoT design should focus on people's mental maps for how an object works, the affordances offered by the object, and the constraints imposed by design. Understanding how an IoT object will be used is the key to understanding which problems were foreseeable, which problems could be mitigated by the IoT's limited canvas for warnings, and which designs are structurally unsafe.

Of course, many of the problems with the IoT are indistinguishable from problems that come from using basic computers and databases. If it's a data-driven technology, it can and will be hacked. Like closed-circuit TV cameras and drones, IoT products have sensors and access. The IoT is in many ways just another outlet for data collection, use, and sharing. In other words, the IoT presents similar data security and data protection issues to those presented with your laptop, tablet, or smartphone.

But the difference between standard computer problems and the IoT is that the risks can be hidden or dispersed, objects are used differently than standard computers, and the benefit of wiring up things often isn't worth the hassle. The expansion of the Internet into everyday artifacts is gradually eroding people's autonomy for minimal gain, whereas the risk is often worthwhile for connecting standard computers. Maria Farrell has written, "With its insecure devices with multiple points of data access, user applications that routinely exfiltrate our sensor data, activity logs and personal contacts, and a Sisyphean uphill struggle required to exert any control over who knows what about us, the internet of things does more than create whole new cyber-security attack surfaces. It is so riddled with metastasizing points of vulnerability that you begin to sense that these are not bugs, but features. As we walk around our increasingly 'smart cities,' we are hemorrhaging data; but we will not be the ones to primarily benefit from mopping it up."[6] Industry is evangelizing connectivity, but it's not always clear whether the benefits of connectively are primarily for the user or industry.

What's worse is that the IoT raises the possibility that connectivity no longer even offers the pretense of choice for an offline life. Industry's zealous embrace of the IoT is driving companies to replace dumb products with smart ones. It gives them more data under the guise of bells and whistles for consumers. If we don't watch out, we will be reliant upon connectivity to use a host of "things" with no obvious upgrade. That's not true for every IoT device, of course. The case for connected automobiles offers the clear and powerful advantage of a car that can drive itself. But what about hair dryers and toothbrushes? Government agencies can compel information from connected devices in your home, like smart meters and digital assistants. Schools that buy into the data craze would likely be interested in making students own connected devices to track their progress in a more granulated way. If you build it, they will come (for the data).

It's time to start addressing this issue at the source: the design of IoT devices. While this chapter will explore many of these standard data protection and data security issues, what I'm really interested in are unique aspects of the IoT that should make design the primary concern of privacy law in this area—the objects that are being wired up and the way we use them.

Privacy, Security, and the Internet of Things

Hello Barbie is the iconic IoT device. This version of the famous doll has Wi-Fi capability and is programmed to respond to voice commands. Hello Barbie records a child's voice at the push of a button. As the doll "listens," the audio data is transmitted to a server, where the speech is recognized and processed. That data is then used to help the doll respond to the child.[7] Hello Barbie has sparked some of the most vocal fears about the IoT, and for good reason. It is in the position to collect sensitive data from children and provides a worrisome additional attack vector for home networks because dolls have tendency to linger long after other outdated technologies are thrown out. Children do not need Hello Barbie's connectivity to play with it. When Mattel eventually stops updating the device with security patches, it will become a weak link in a home network and parents and children will likely have no idea. This is where design matters. We should be particularly skeptical of IoT design with respect to our privacy and security.[8]

Regarding privacy, Scott Peppet has argued that sensor data are particularly hard to de-identify.[9] In addition, the IoT can produce incredibly granular personal data, such as what you eat and when you eat it, when you're home, what temperature you like your house to be, when you're in your bedroom, and even when you're having sex.[10] What's more, certain IoT devices will elicit our disclosures with little promise of keeping our secrets. Take Hello Barbie. Meg Leta Jones and Kevin Meurer have examined the architecture and workings of the toy to see if it was capable of keeping the secrets that children often entrust to their toys. The authors concluded that Hello Barbie's technology is advanced enough to indicate to the user whether she is capable of keeping a secret. But the toy "tends to share a child's private conversations with parents, third parties, and potentially entire networks of Twitter followers. This tendency to share data amongst so many parties has the potential to negatively impact children's ability to trust and simultaneously undermine parental authority in managing their child's data."[11] Consent to collecting and using information also is a true quagmire for the IoT, which is another reason regimes built around notice and control are failing us.[12] Where exactly do you put the privacy policy for IoT underwear and toilets? IoT devices have been granted more regular access to our intimate moments than computers or smartphones ever have, yet their mechanism for privacy permissions has never been more dysfunctional.

And the full version of the IoT is just getting warmed up. The "innovation at all costs" mantra of Silicon Valley has repelled many meaningful privacy laws over the last twenty years, allowing the Internet surveillance economy to flourish. In the United States, the default presumption is that you're allowed to collect any information until you're not. (As opposed to the reverse presumption in the European Union and some Asian countries that prohibit processing personal data without a legitimate basis for doing so.)

Consider, for example, the problem of cross-device tracking.[13] SilverPush is an Indian start-up company invested in identifying all of your computing devices. SilverPush uses inaudible sounds it embeds in web pages and television commercials to transmit that personal information back to SilverPush through the use of cookies.[14] This technique allows the company to track you across all your various devices. According to Bruce Schneier, SilverPush can associate the television commercials you watch with your web searches. It can correlate your tablet activities with what you do on your computer. As Schneier puts it, "Your computerized things are talking about you behind your back, and for the most part you can't stop them—or even learn what they're saying."[15] The Federal Trade Commission (FTC) has already stated that consumers should be told about such technologies and practices.[16]

Then there's the billion-dollar IoT problem mentioned above: data security. Successful hacks on IoT devices are legion. VTech and Fisher-Price have been hacked.[17] Researchers discovered that an IoT doorbell was revealing users' Wi-Fi keys.[18] Security flaws have been demonstrated in IoT dolls, Samsung refrigerators, Jeep Cherokees, and the Wi-Fi enabled TrackingPoint sniper rifle (allowing for hackers to choose their own targets).[19] A GPS child tracker had a flaw that would let hackers act as a child's parents.[20]

Andy Greenberg and Kim Zetter dubbed 2015 "[t]he year of insecure internet things."[21] According to Cisco, as early as 2008 there were already more objects connected to the Internet than people.[22] Every new IoT device provides more attack surface for hackers.[23] HP recently estimated that 70 percent of IoT devices have serious security vulnerabilities.[24] Simply put, we have yet to figure out a way to keep the security of the IoT up to speed with the demand for IoT products.

Government intelligence and law enforcement services are also quite excited about the Internet of Things, because it gives them another path to surveillance. And they are not shy about their intentions to exploit that sensor in your underwear or doll. For example, as former director of national intelligence James Clapper told a Senate panel as part of his annual "assessment of threats" against the United States, "In the future, intelligence services might use the [Internet of things] for identification, surveillance, monitoring, location tracking, and targeting for recruitment, or to gain access to networks or user credentials." Trevor Timm, a columnist for the *Guardian* and executive director of the Freedom of the Press Foundation, notes that Clapper's testimony actually undermines the FBI's recent claims that they are "going dark," or losing the ability to surveil suspects because of encryption. There are more avenues for surveillance now than ever before.[25]

The Internet of Heirlooms and Disposable Things

Regulators and industry are not taking the decision to wire up an artifact to the Internet seriously enough. Some IoT companies have become reckless with the ease and allure of wiring up objects. But when things are "easy come" to create, they can lead to "easy go" mentalities that fail to appreciate the risks companies create. Some IoT companies like VTech are washing their hands of responsibility. The company's IoT kids toys were hacked, leading to a massive data spill on Shodan (the search engine for the Internet of Things).[26] VTech's embarrassing data breach exposed personal data on six million children.[27]

In its terms and conditions for its software, VTech now includes the following ominous language in all-caps: "YOU ACKNOWLEDGE AND AGREE THAT ANY INFORMATION YOU SEND OR RECEIVE DURING YOUR USE OF THE SITE MAY NOT BE SECURE AND MAY BE INTERCEPTED OR LATER ACQUIRED BY UNAUTHORIZED PARTIES."[28] This reads more like fodder for a *Saturday Night Live* sketch than a reasonable terms of use agreement.

Even when companies intend to keep their products safe and secure over the course of their use, the fact remains that those companies might not be around to see their commitments through.[29] "Here today, gone tomorrow" might as well be the epigram of Silicon Valley, where the spirit of disruption drives innovation more than the ethos of sustainability.

There is very little to stop a whole bunch of well-intentioned companies from producing IoT products that sell moderately or poorly but fail to be sufficiently profitable to prevent them from going out of business shortly after their goods hit the shelves. If that happens, they likely will not have the resources to provide further security work. And yet, if the products remain functional past the point of being serviced, consumers either must stop using them or take personal responsibility for security breaches via the "buyer beware" mentality. This makes many IoT objects more costly and risky than their "dumb" counterparts.

Things are Different from Computers

The IoT is rife with privacy and security problems.[30] But our debate has, up to this point, been focused more on the "Internet" part of the IoT rather than the "Things" part. Our laws and rhetoric have failed to scrutinize the differing nature of "things," as if they all pose the same risks as computers and standard information technologies. But this is not true. Artifacts differ from computers and from each other. The nature of an artifact and its design will influence a range of outcomes, including how we use it, where we put it, how much attention we pay to it, how we tend to it, and how long we will keep it. In turn, these variables impact the extent to which vulnerabilities are created and persist.

Wiring a computer up to the Internet is not the same as wiring up an object that has nonprocessing uses like a doll or refrigerator. Computers that cannot connect to the Internet are of limited value in the age of cloud computing. The same cannot be said for the IoT, where Internet connectivity is often not essential to an object's core function. Even without Wi-Fi, dolls can be played with, clothes and diapers can be worn, coffee makers can still heat, and refrigerators can cool—at least ideally.

Some of these objects, like Hello Barbie, are likely to be used long after the vendor stops servicing them with critical security updates, known as "patches."[31] By contrast, objects like IoT diapers and shampoo bottles are meant to be quickly used and disposed of. These small, disposable objects are hard to service because of their limited bandwidth and storage capacities.[32] It is often too costly to invest in security for these disposable objects. The return on investment isn't high enough. Yet they remain persistent risks in our home networks.[33] Security researcher Brian Krebs notes that poorly configured default settings for IoT devices are a security nightmare.[34] This is particularly true for devices that are too costly to upgrade after they are deployed, like many disposable and cheap IoT devices.

Some companies are even developing products like thin, adhesive films that will turn *any* object into an IoT artifact.[35] This might be the quickest way to scale the IoT in our homes. But every new IoT connection brings new risks. For example, it might take people a while to treat everyday objects with the same care they give their computers. Until we change our mind-sets, our daily routines will not include updating our coffee maker's operating system.

Krebs asserts that "[b]efore purchasing an 'Internet of things' (IoT) device . . . consider whether you can realistically care for and feed the security needs of yet another IoT thing." He adds that "there is a good chance your newly adopted IoT puppy will be chewing holes in your network defenses; gnawing open new critical security weaknesses; bred by a vendor that seldom and belatedly patches; [and] tough to wrangle down and patch."[36] Krebs quotes Craig Williams, the security outreach manager at Cisco, who has said, "Compromising IoT devices allow unfettered access through the network to any other devices on the network. . . . To make matters worse almost no one has access to [an IoT's operating system] to notice that it has been compromised. No one wakes up and thinks, 'Hey, it's time to update my thermostats [*sic*] firmware.'"[37] This means that the Internet of Heirlooms and Disposable Things will likely stay compromised, giving hackers an ideal opening to laterally move through our networks.[38] Left vulnerable, the IoT could bring havoc upon the Internet. Krebs himself was subjected to a debilitating distributed denial of service (DDoS) attack powered by zombie-compromised IoT devices that resisted the best efforts of the top DDoS protection services.[39] In addition to the threat to critical infrastructure, when the IoT can be used to censor websites at will by hackers, it becomes a threat to free expression.

Bad defaults on IoT devices are common, and it is often a complex process for users to change them.[40] What's worse is that the software updating process for the IoT does not scale well. The typical lifetime of software (the length of time that a company actively patches and updates any bugs or problems with the software) is around two years. But the estimated lifetime of some objects now connected to the Internet is around ten years.[41] Just think about how long coffee makers and refrigerators last. The Internet of Things We Keep a Long Time is a security nightmare; in some cases it's even a physical and financial threat. As implantable technologies like pacemakers and contact lenses and payment systems like credit cards are Wi-Fi enabled, industry and lawmakers must ensure that the neglected code in these devices (and they will all be neglected eventually) does no harm.[42]

There's evidence that hackers are actually counting on companies to stop caring about IoT objects. Security professional James Maude has commented, "The dangers of unsupported software are often further reaching than people realize . . . The obvious dangers are running software that will no longer receive security updates so if an exploit appears tomorrow there is no easy way for you to stop it."[43] Maude notes that hackers often save up exploits until a vendor ends support for a product so they can use them more effectively.

Yet with few important exceptions,[44] the law has been largely agnostic regarding the decision to wire up an artifact. Most privacy laws are all about data rules. This abstracts away too many of the significant features of materiality—the very tangibility of things.[45] Companies are generally required to provide reasonable privacy and data security for the information they collect. But there is very little regulatory compliance cost for merely connecting artifacts to the Internet. The cost should be higher.

A more measured approach to the IoT would help ensure the development and sale of safer technologies. It would alleviate some of the risk of harm faced by IoT users—users who generally aren't in the best position to understand and respond to the risks posed by the Internet of Heirlooms and Disposable Things.

Applying Privacy's Blueprint to the Internet of Things

The first step in privacy law's design agenda is for lawmakers, regulators, and courts to better recognize the nature of "things" in the IoT. The good news is that the law recognizes that privacy and data security are context dependent.[46] Most data security rules require a broad, "reasonable" approach.[47] This makes most data security law nimble and adaptive to problems like those presented by the IoT. Courts and lawmakers can start there and dig deeper.

Stop Consent on the IoT Before It Becomes a Scourge

Let's get this one out of the way at the start: consent regimes are largely incompatible with the Internet of Things. First, many IoT devices have small screens or no screens at all and clunky user feedback mechanisms. Using apps to control devices only pushes us back into the failure of consent in the mobile space. It's not good when your car is directly asking for you to agree to the recently downloaded software's terms of use before it will allow you to start your commute, and it's even worse if it asks you while you're driving.

Peppet has argued that current IoT devices fail to meaningfully notify users of a company's privacy policies. He has also noted that, once found, such policies are often confusing, incomplete, and misleading. In reviewing IoT privacy policies, Peppet has found that they "rarely clarify who owns sensor data, exactly what biometric or other sensor data a device collects, how such data are protected, and how such information can be sold or used. Both state and federal consumer protection law has not yet addressed these problems or the general issues that the Internet of Things creates for consumer consent."[48]

Obtaining consent via IoT devices is a strange game for users. The only winning move is not to play. One possible solution for lawmakers is to treat the IoT as a bridge to far for valid consent. In other words, in consent-based regimes like contracts and data protection, lawmakers and judges should refuse to validate the consent given by agreeing to terms via miniature screens and multipurpose buttons that stretch the already thin concept of a "meeting of the minds" into oblivion. Instead, privacy law should provide baseline protections and warnings that can mitigate but not abdicate a company's responsibility to protect the users of its product.

Focus on Standardizing IoT Security

Standardization of IoT design and processes might also be useful. As was mentioned in Chapter 5, standardization of design has numerous benefits, and the government's involvement in facilitating standards is a preferable "soft" response rather than a top-down assertion of control over design. In addition to established standards-making bodies like the International Organization for Standardization and the National Institute of Standards and Technology, policy makers might leverage ground-up efforts by organizations like I Am the Cavalry to implement best practices among companies and provide notice to users of the strength of privacy and data security design for the IoT.[49] I Am The Cavalry is a group of concerned security researchers focused on critical infrastructure; the group has contemplated a five-star rating system for consumer-facing IoT devices that would enable consumers to more easily assess the security of an IoT device.[50] I Am The Cavalry has tentatively developed a set of criteria by which it will evaluate IoT products, which includes categories like *secure by default, secure by design, self-contained security,* and *privacy.*

Quit Hindering IoT Security Research and Start Supporting It

Law and policy makers should also help facilitate the identification and reporting of security vulnerabilities and bugs. This might include backing away from the support of digital rights management (DRM),[51] which presents security problems for the Internet of Things. DRM itself can be insecure, and laws that protect DRM can hinder sound security research. DRM limits your ability to protect your own devices.[52] Consider the Electronic

Frontier Foundation's proposal to have the World Wide Web Consortium—the nonprofit body that maintains the web's core standards and adopts rules that would minimize the risk of security—protect researchers who report bugs on DRM-protected software.[53]

Mandate Reasonable Data Security for IoT across the Board

Perhaps one of the least controversial and most fundamental way lawmakers could improve the design of the IoT is to mandate reasonable data security practices. They've already started down this path. In its *Strategic Principles for Securing the Internet of Things* the U.S. Department of Homeland Security (DHS) recommends, among other things, "Incorporating Security at the Design Phase." The report states that "in too many cases economic drivers or lack of awareness of the risks cause businesses to push devices to market with little regard for their security. Building security in at the design phase reduces potential disruptions and avoids the much more difficult and expensive endeavor of attempting to add security to products after they have been developed and deployed."[54] Among the DHS's suggested design practices is to enable security by default through unique, hard-to-crack default user names and passwords,[55] build the device using the most recent operating system that is technically viable and economically feasible,[56] use hardware that incorporates security features to strengthen the protection and integrity of the device,[57] and design with system and operational disruption in mind.[58] Other solutions would be to better utilize options for local (not connected / remote) processing and taking advantage of some of the incredible advances in homomorphic encryption.[59]

Designing for IoT security should be a firm legal mandate. Lawmakers should condition the nature of the legal obligation upon the nature of the object connected to the Internet. Dolls are different from diapers and cars, with different expected usages and life cycles. Instead of prescribing a rigid one-size-fits-all checklist for data security in IoT devices, lawmakers should continue the general trend of context-relative protection obligations.

The template for this has already been set. Generally speaking, most data security laws in the United States require "reasonable data security." For example, the FTC generally prohibits unreasonable data security practices "in light of the sensitivity and volume of consumer information it holds, the size and complexity of its business, and the cost of available tools to improve security and reduce vulnerabilities."[60] Many state and federal laws require reasonable data security practices rather than a specific list of prohibited or mandatory actions.[61]

The reasonableness standard is not perfect, but it is flexible and can account for new problems like those presented by the IoT. Lawmakers and courts might interpret "reasonable security" to include some minimum expectation for servicing IoT devices and a floor of data security for even disposable items. Imagine a system in which companies tell users how long they think a wired object will last and how long the company will commit to providing security patches. In the event that a company goes bankrupt before then, companies would work quickly to either notify users of the impending shutdown or delegate the responsibility for security patches to a third party. This would help us avoid the problem of zombie IoT devices.

Explore Kill Switches for Some IoT Devices

Many IoT devices become dangerous over time simply because they are neglected pathways hackers can exploit to gain access to a network. One way to protect against this is to build devices that have controls or a switch that will easily "kill" an object's connectivity. Paul Ohm has referred to such controls as "lobotomy switches" because they render the devices "dumb" but technically still operable. For example, Hello Barbie would function just fine as a doll without being connected to Wi-Fi; coffee makers could be built to function in a "nonconnected" mode.

In its guidelines for security for the Internet of Things, the DHS recommends looking into connectivity switches, saying industry should "[b]uild in controls to allow manufacturers, service providers, and consumers to disable network connections or specific ports when needed or desired to enable selective connectivity. Depending on the purpose of the IoT device, providing the consumers with guidance and control over the end implementation can be a sound practice."[62]

Lawmakers could encourage these kill switches as a factor to be considered when evaluating a company's "reasonable data security" efforts. They could even be mandated for certain devices where it would make sense to simply cut off connectivity after the software is no longer being serviced. Even devices that are not otherwise functional without Internet access might need to come with kill switches (or be remotely bricked) to keep them off the grid. Such options would need to be explicitly communicated to users, however; consumers would need to be told that they are leasing, not buying a technology. This means regulatory authorities must better scrutinize the claims of "buy now" that are common with software-based services and products. Aaron Perzanowski and Chris Hoofnagle argue that "buy now" in the digital era does not communicate that what consumers are actually getting is a license, with limited rights.[63]

But here's the rub. Kill switches might work well for some limited categories of closed-system IoT technologies, but they are much more difficult for open technologies that rely upon multiple interfaces and layers to function. Bruce Schneier has written that using kill switches in complex systems "involves building a nearly flawless hierarchical system of authority. That's a difficult security problem even in its simplest form. Distributing that system among a variety of different devices—computers, phones, PDAs, cameras, recorders—with different firmware and manufacturers, is even more difficult. Not to mention delegating different levels of authority to various agencies, enterprises, industries and individuals, and then enforcing the necessary safeguards."[64]

Thus, for certain devices, particularly those that have authority over other devices, kill switches create a host of problems. Schneier asks, "Who has the authority to limit functionality of my devices, and how do they get that authority? What prevents them from abusing that power? Do I get the ability to override their limitations? In what circumstances, and how? Can they override my override? . . . Do the police get 'superuser' devices that cannot be limited, and do they get 'supercontroller' devices that can limit anything? How do we ensure that only they get them, and what do we do when the devices inevitably fall into the wrong hands?"[65] Thus local, hardwired connectivity switches (for example, not remote touchscreen kill switches on apps) might work for some devices, but we should be very careful about embracing the option of kill switches across the board. Doing so could create more problems than it solves.

Finally, a Plea for Unplugging and IoT Exceptionalism

If lawmakers do nothing else, they should recognize that the IoT presents unique issues for general computing and for mobile devices like phones and tablets. As such, connectivity should be made judiciously. The DHS is coming around to this view, advising industry to "[c]onnect carefully and deliberately." In its guidelines on the IoT, the DHS notes,

> IoT consumers, particularly in the industrial context, should deliberately consider whether continuous connectivity is needed given the use of the IoT device and the risks associated with its disruption. IoT consumers can also help contain the potential threats posed by network connectivity by connecting carefully and deliberately, and weighing the risks of a potential breach or failure of an IoT device against the costs of limiting connectivity to the Internet. In the current networked environment, it is likely that any given IoT device may be disrupted during its lifecycle. IoT developers, manufacturers, and consumers should consider how a disruption will impact the IoT device's primary function and business operations following the disruption.[66]

I recommend taking this concept of care regarding the IoT one step further. Privacy law should treat the IoT as exceptional in the legal sense. In other words, it should not treat IoT devices as if they are just another computer or mobile phone. Rather, even greater care should be required of industry in their creation and deployment; they carry with them greater risk of abuse because they are more diffuse and their problems are less apparent to consumers. This could take the form of demanding more resources and planning from companies to provide "reasonable" security as required by law, minimum patching periods and a financial commitment to sustainable IoT maintenance, more effective warnings and transparency to users or, as discussed above, mitigation of problems through some sort of kill switch. If these do not work, then perhaps lawmakers should look into some form of a certification requirement for IoT devices to ensure safe devices and ease the collective strain on and risk to networks. These are all strategies to make it costlier to connect a device because of the resources legally required for its maintenance. And society can change the framing of connectivity. Right now connectivity is viewed as a superior feature. Why buy a normal Barbie when you can have a Hello Barbie that listens to you and responds? But unplugging has benefits that should be made more prominent in our daily conversations. I'm running out of ways to say that

the collective risk of connecting people's basketballs to the Internet probably isn't worth the benefit. Though that won't stop me from trying.

Merely connecting something to the Internet does not automatically make
it a better product. The calculus for whether it is a good idea to wire up an
object is much more complicated. Sometimes Internet connectivity makes
us more vulnerable in exchange for only minimal gain. Lawmakers and
industry should be more conscientious about the nature of the object that
is being connected and how easy it is to create a networked object. The Internet of Things can be revolutionary, but it needs nuanced boundaries to
be safe and sustainable. It's enough to make us really appreciate our old,
nonconnected underwear.

AS THIS BOOK was being completed in 2017, a sea change was underfoot in the world of privacy. Around the world there was an increasing appetite for government surveillance.[1] Computer and software giants like Google and Microsoft are evolving into analytics, automotive, and robotics companies. People are being tracked with more Internet-connected sensors than ever before. The Internet is no longer a baby, and our teenage romance with digital technologies is over. As our digital world matures, the stakes for getting design right have never been higher.

Privacy law has become more than just the law of media intrusion, government surveillance, and consumer protection. Technologies that collect and use personal information now fundamentally implicate diverse issues like data security, free speech, fair competition, public health, employee rights, social justice, and critical infrastructure. In 2016, zombie Internet of Things devices were harnessed by hackers to bring down parts of the Internet's critical infrastructure as well as silence the speech of security researchers though massive DDoS attacks.[2] Facial recognition technologies and predictive policing algorithms are used in disproportionally harmful ways against racial and religious minorities and the poor.[3] Platforms can leverage personal data to disrupt democracies by creating tools designed to influence people about social issues and candidates for political office with a tailored nudge at just the right time.[4]

And all of these issues begin with a device or software that collects or displays personal information. The personal data rules that were created when the Internet was a child—the Fair Information Practices—are still necessary, but they are no longer sufficient. A design agenda is needed because our lives are increasingly exposed by and subject to consumer technologies, but the design of these technologies faces little scrutiny. At the time this book went to press, there were few targeted rules about how social media interfaces, biometric surveillance technologies, or IoT devices should be built.

Design is not always the answer. But it is the right place to start. This is what I mean when I say design is everything. Because technologies are involved in nearly every act of modern information collection, use, and disclosure, the architecture of those technologies is relevant to every aspect of information privacy. Consumers must be able to trust the technologies they use. Without a way to ensure good, sustainable design for consumer technologies, every system that uses them will become dangerous and untrustworthy. Regulators risk putting too much strain on downstream actors that collect, use, or disclose information. Data collectors and processors are not the only actors that affect our privacy. Lawmakers and judges should not allow design to be used to skirt the intent of laws or take advantage of our weaknesses. They should support good design though all reasonable means.

I do not mean for the agenda I propose in this book to solve all our design problems. Instead, I offer Privacy's Blueprint as a way to identify a common set of goals, boundaries, and tools to help get us where we need to be. Not everyone will agree with the values and boundaries I have identified as paramount. Lawmakers can use the framework to substitute other public values and boundaries built around how people actually use technologies and the wisdom of consumer safety and surveillance jurisprudence.

Let's put this all together. I have argued in this book that privacy law should take the design of consumer technologies more seriously. I have proposed a design agenda for privacy law based on notions of values, mental models, and proportionality. If you were to glean nothing else from this book, I hope to have made three arguments clear: the design agenda should reflect and support human values, revolve around signals and transaction costs, and include a diverse set of soft, moderate, and robust responses.

The Design Agenda Should Reflect and Support Human Values

Although this book has focused mainly on trust, obscurity, and autonomy in consumer protection and surveillance, I offer Privacy's Blueprint as a way to help understand and respond to a larger set of diverse and universal issues. Trust, obscurity, and autonomy are enabling values. They can be leveraged to further other goals or values by providing safe areas for things like intimacy, exploration, and play. Being obscure helps people avoid unequal treatment. Rules of trust within relationships can reinforce how humans should treat each other. Autonomy ensures that people have the freedom to determine their own path and create their own spaces for development. But autonomy must be prioritized over control and consent, which can be counterproductive if overleveraged. We should stop treating control as the cosmos of privacy and start treating it like a precious finite resource.

The Design Agenda Should Revolve around Signals and Transaction Costs

Perhaps the most fundamental deficiency of modern privacy law and policy is that it doesn't focus enough on how people actually use consumer technologies. Good design ensures that a technology's affordances and constraints are appropriately set and communicated. Good design means that a user's mental map of how a technology works matches reality. To get design right, lawmakers should look to the signals given off by technologies and the transaction costs imposed or reduced by those technologies. Signals that are deceptive or abusively leverage people's own limitations against them should be mitigated or prohibited. Lawmakers should also seek to mitigate or prohibit dangerous reductions in the cost of others finding or understanding information. When lawmakers fail to take signals and transaction costs into account, they elevate form over function. Doing so facilitates cut corners and abuse.

The Design Agenda Should Include a Diverse Set of Soft, Moderate, and Robust Responses

Beyond creating direct design restrictions, law and policy makers should support design standards, provide resources for industry and consumers, require sound development processes and safe user experiences, explicitly avoid policies that weaken good privacy design, and better scrutinize the role of design in all areas of privacy law. Good design can be just as jeopardized by ham-fisted regulatory micromanaging as it can be by no design regulation at all. Only a proportional, diverse, and collaborative approach will provide the appropriate incentives for good design as well as flexibility for designers to adapt design to context.

Following the blueprint will not be easy. There is no way to provide a complete and clear checklist for companies who want to follow the rules. It will take a financial investment. Companies will not be able to do everything they want to do. But the alternative is worse. As we've seen in certain industries, like those of automobiles, infrastructure, medical devices, pharmaceuticals, and toys, taking design seriously can pave the road for tremendous mutual gain. We should look to these examples with optimism.

I, for one, am full of hope. I have been since the moment my parents brought home a Commodore 128 and I saw that green, blinking cursor. The void of that black screen with the flashing green placeholder signaled a world of endless possibilities to me. It still does. The Internet may not be a baby anymore, but its entire adulthood is still ahead. We can ensure that the Internet and digital technologies live up to their promise. But we must recognize that how information technologies are built is inextricably linked to how they are used.

Design is everywhere. Design is power. Design is political. It can protect our vulnerabilities or it can exploit them. We must all work for rules, guides, resources, and behaviors that will ensure our technologies are safe and sustainable for everyone. Tomorrow's privacy depends on what we build today.

Notes

Introduction: Designing Our Privacy Away

1. Geoffrey A. Fowler, "When the Most Personal Secrets Get Outed on Facebook," *Wall Street Journal,* October 13, 2012.

2. Jonathan Keane, "Hacked in 2014: The Year of the Data Breach," *Paste,* December 18, 2014, https://www.pastemagazine.com/articles/2014/12/hacked-in -2014-the-year-of-the-data-breach.html; Tara Seals, "2014 So Far: The Year of the Data Breach," https://www.infosecurity-magazine.com/news/2014-the-year-of -the-data-breach.

3. Karl Bode, "Ding-Dong—Your Easily Hacked 'Smart' Doorbell Just Gave Up Your WiFi Credentials," Techdirt, January 21, 2016, https://www.techdirt.com /articles/20160112/11405333312/ding-dong-your-easily-hacked-smart-doorbell -just-gave-up-your-wifi-credentials.shtml.

4. J. M. Porup, "'Internet of Things' Security Is Hilariously Broken and Getting Worse," Ars Technica, January 23, 2016, https://arstechnica.com /information-technology/2016/01/how-to-search-the-internet-of-things-for -photos-of-sleeping-babies/.

5. "Internet of Shit," http://www.twitter.com/internetofshit; Moikit Team, "Seed: A Smart Bottle that Never Forgets You," Indiegogo, https://www .indiegogo.com/projects/seed-a-smart-vacuum-bottle-that-never-forgets-you -fitness-health; Cory Doctorow, "The Internet of Things in Your Butt: Smart Rectal Thermometer," Boing Boing, January 14, 2016, https://boingboing.net/2016 /01/14/the-internet-of-things-in-your.html; Arielle Duhaime-Ross, "This

Headband Analyzes Your Sweat to Improve Your Workout," The Verge, January 27, 2016, https://www.theverge.com/2016/1/27/10840680/sweat-wearable -analysis-real-time-berkeley.

6. Jasper Hamill, "Hackers Take Control of a TOILET Using Bog-Standard Computer Skills," Mirror, February 10, 2016, http://www.mirror.co.uk/tech /hackers-take-control-toilet-using-7342662; Giles Crouch, "The Toilet and Its Role in the Internet of Things," Wired, April 2012, https://www.wired.com /insights/2014/04/toilet-role-internet-things/.

7. Abby Phillip, "Why the Wife of a Pastor Exposed in Ashley Madison Hack Spoke Out after His Suicide," Washington Post, September 9, 2015.

8. "Microsoft Stores Windows 10 Encryption Keys in the Cloud," Security Week, December 30, 2015, http://www.securityweek.com/microsoft-stores -windows-10-encryption-keys-cloud.

9. Kenneth A. Bamberger and Deirdre K. Mulligan, Privacy on the Ground: Driving Corporate Behavior in the United States and Europe (Cambridge, MA: MIT Press, 2015).

10. Ross Andersen and Tyler Moore, "The Economics of Information Security," Science 314 (2006): 610–613.

11. The seminal source for McLuhan's quote is up for debate, however. As the McLuhan Galaxy blog notes, "The quote was actually written by Father John Culkin, SJ, a Professor of Communication at Fordham University in New York and friend of McLuhan. But though the quote is Culkin's, I would argue that the idea is McLuhan's, as it comes up in an article by Culkin about McLuhan." McLuhan Galaxy, April 1, 2013, https://mcluhangalaxy.wordpress.com/2013/04 /01/we-shape-our-tools-and-thereafter-our-tools-shape-us/.

12. Neil M. Richards, "Four Privacy Myths," in A World without Privacy: What Law Can and Should Do?, ed. Austin Sarat (New York: Cambridge University Press, 2015), 33–82.

13. Julie E. Cohen, "What Privacy Is For," Harvard Law Review 126 (2013): 1904–1933; Julie E. Cohen, Configuring the Networked Self (New Haven CT: Yale University Press, 2012).

14. "Design," Merriam-Webster, https://www.merriam-webster.com /dictionary/design.

15. Value Sensitive Design Research Lab, http://www.vsdesign.org. Pioneered by Batya Friedman, Peter Kahn, and others in the 1990s, value sensitive design focuses on the method of creating information and computer systems to account for human values in a principled and comprehensive manner throughout the design process; "What Is Values in Design?," Values in Design, https://valuesindesign.net/about-2/. Helen Nissenbaum developed the values in design theory and method as "a way of considering human life that explores how the values we think of as societal may be expressed in techno-

logical designs, and how these designs in turn shape our social values"; "What is Values in Design?," Values in Design, http://www.nyu.edu/projects/nissenbaum /vid/about.html. I also draw from the larger notion of architectural design values, which looks to the values that influence all architects and designers. See Ivar Holm, *Ideas and Beliefs in Architecture and Industrial Design: How Attitudes, Orientations, and Underlying Assumptions Shape the Built Environment*, Con-text. Thesis 22 (Oslo: Arkitektur- og designhøgskolen i Oslo, 2006).

16. Don Norman, *The Design of Everyday Things* (New York: Basic Books, 1988).

17. For an important perspective on the critical role of algorithms and data in our lives, see Frank Pasquale, *The Black Box Society: The Secret Algorithms That Control Money and Information* (Cambridge, MA: Harvard University Press, 2015).

1. Why Design Is Everything

1. This particular interface was scrutinized by the FTC in its complaint against Snapchat for unfair and deceptive trade practices. Fed. Trade Comm'n., Complaint, In re Snapchat, File No. 132-3078, Docket No. C-4501 (Washington, DC: FTC, December 23, 2014), https://www.ftc.gov/system/files/documents/cases /140508snapchatcmpt.pdf.

2. Jon May, "Law Student Jailed for Snapchat Blackmail," *National Student,* October 22, 2015, http://www.thenationalstudent.com/Student/2015-10-22/Law _student_jailed_for_Snapchat_blackmail.html; James Dunn, "Law Student, 19, Convinced Teenage Girl to Send Him an X-Rated Picture Then Used it to Blackmail Her for More Photos and Money," *Daily Mail,* October 17, 2015, http://www.dailymail.co.uk/news/article-3277297/Law-student-19-convinced -teenage-girl-send-X-rated-picture-used-blackmail-photos-money.html.

3. Signals can also modulate transaction costs themselves. Weak signals burden users with the cost of finding more information. Strong signals reduce the burden of retrieving information. For example, buttons with labels send signals to users that make the decision as to when to press the button easier.

4. See, e.g., Omer Tene and Jules Polonetsky, "Big Data for All: Privacy and User Control in the Age of Analytics," *Northwestern Journal of Technology and Intellectual Property* 11 (2013): 242.

5. See, e.g., Sheldon Gilbert, "FTC, Stop Punishing Hacking Victims," Free Enterprise, October 5, 2012, http://archive.freeenterprise.com/regulations/ftc -stop-punishing-hacking-victims.

6. See Danielle Keats Citron, *Hate Crimes in Cyberspace* (Cambridge, MA: Harvard University Press, 2014); Danielle Citron, "The Importance of Section 230 Immunity for Most," Concurring Opinions, January 25, 2013,

https://concurringopinions.com/archives/2013/01/the-importance-of-section-230-immunity-for-most.html; and Jeff Roberts, "Don't Shoot the Messenger over User Content, Courts Confirm," GigaOM Media, February 21, 2012, https://gigaom.com/2012/02/21/419-dont-shoot-the-messenger-over-user-content-courts-confirm/.

7. See Fair Housing Council of San Fernando Valley v. Roommates.com, LLC, 521 F.3d 1157 (9th Cir. 2008) ("[P]roviding neutral tools to carry out what may be unlawful or illicit searches does not amount to 'development' for purposes of the immunity exception. . . . Providing neutral tools for navigating websites is fully protected by CDA immunity, absent substantial affirmative conduct on the part of the website creator promoting the use of such tools for unlawful purposes."); and Eric Schmidt and Jared Cohen, *The New Digital Age: Reshaping the Future of People, Nations, and Business* (New York: Knopf, 2013).

8. David Lyon, *The Electronic Eye: The Rise of Surveillance Society* (Minneapolis: University of Minnesota Press, 1994), 62–67.

9. Michael Foucault, *Discipline and Punish,* 2nd ed., trans. Alan Sheridan (New York: Vintage, 1995), 200.

10. Federal Trade Commission, "Android Flashlight App Developer Settles FTC Charges It Deceived Consumers," December 5, 2013, https://www.ftc.gov/news-events/press-releases/2013/12/android-flashlight-app-developer-settles-ftc-charges-it-deceived.

11. Annalee Newitz, "And This Is Why Gizmodo Doesn't Collect IP Address Data," Gizmodo, June 10, 2015, https://gizmodo.com/and-this-is-why-gizmodo-doesnt-collect-ip-address-data-1710446008.

12. Unless, of course, the user updates her phone and backs her data up to the cloud. Design is consequential in any event. Alex Hern, "Apple's Encryption Means It Can't Comply with US Court Order," *Guardian,* September 8, 2015, http://www.theguardian.com/technology/2015/sep/08/apple-encryption-comply-us-court-order-iphone-imessage-justice; see also Stuart Dredge, "Apple Boss Tim Cook Clashes with US Government over Encryption," *Guardian,* January 13, 2016, http://www.theguardian.com/technology/2016/jan/13/apple-tim-cook-us-government-encryption.

13. Specifically, Apple refused to comply with a request from law enforcement officials via a judge to "provide 'reasonable technical assistance' to the U.S. authorities, which would require the technology giant to overhaul the system that disables the phone after 10 unsuccessful password attempts. Once this feature kicks in, all the data on the phone is inaccessible." Arjun Kharpal, "Apple vs. FBI: All You Need to Know," *CNBC,* March 29, 2016, https://www.cnbc.com/2016/03/29/apple-vs-fbi-all-you-need-to-know.html.

14. Reproduced from Fed. Trade Comm'n., Complaint, In re DesignerWare, LLC, https://www.ftc.gov/sites/default/files/documents/cases/2013/04/130415designerwarecmpt.pdf.

15. Fed. Trade Comm'n., Complaint, In re DesignerWare, LLC, File No. 112-3151, Docket No. C-4390 (Washington, DC: FTC, April 15, 2013), https://www.ftc.gov/sites/default/files/documents/cases/2013/04/130415designerwarecmpt.pdf.

16. Ibid.

17. Paul Ford, "It's Kind of Cheesy Being Green," The Message, February 11, 2015, https://medium.com/message/its-kind-of-cheesy-being-green-2c72cc9e5eda#.vvjsknzlv.

18. "Introduction to HTTPS, The HTTPS-Only Standard," https://https.cio.gov/faq/; "HTTPS Everywhere," Electronic Frontier Foundation, https://www.eff.org/https-everywhere.

19. See, e.g., Eduardo González Fidalgo, "Transaction Cost Economics," http://intobusiness.weebly.com/transaction-cost-economics.html; Douglas Allen, "What Are Transaction Costs?," Research in Law and Economics 14 (1991): 1–18; The Elgar Companion to Transaction Cost Economics, ed. Peter G. Klein and Michael E. Sykuta (Cheltenham, UK: Edward Elgar Publishing, 2010).

20. "This 'Mutant Font' Is Designed to Protect Your Internet Privacy," Creativity Online, April 2, 2015, http://creativity-online.com/work/amnesty-international-mutant-font/40368; Megan Haynes, "Amnesty International's 'Mutant Font' Promises to Protect Your Privacy Online," Fast Company, April 1, 2015, https://www.fastcompany.com/3044569/amnesty-internationals-mutant-font-promises-to-protect-your-privacy-online.

21. Mohit Arora, "How Secure Is AES against Brute Force Attacks?," EE Times, May 7, 2012, http://www.eetimes.com/document.asp?doc_id=1279619.

22. See James Grimmelmann, "Privacy as Product Safety," Widener Law Journal 19 (2010): 820.

23. Don Norman, The Design of Everyday Things (New York: Basic Books, 1988), 2.

24. Ibid., 13.

25. Ibid., 9.

26. James J. Gibson, "The Theory of Affordances," in Perceiving, Acting, and Knowing: Toward an Ecological Psychology, ed. Robert Shaw and John Bransford, (Hoboken, NJ: John Wiley & Sons Inc., 1977), 127–143.

27. Norman, The Design of Everyday Things, 23.

28. Ibid., 55.

29. Ibid, 188–189.

30. Ben McGrath, "Oops," New Yorker, June 30, 2003, https://www.newyorker.com/magazine/2003/06/30/oops-4.

31. Michelle Madejski, Maritza Johnson, and Steven M. Bellovin, "A Study of Privacy Settings Errors in an Online Social Network," in *SESOC '12: Proceedings of the 4th IEEE International Workshop on Security and Social Networking* (Budapest: IEEE, 2012), http://maritzajohnson.com/publications /2012-sesoc.pdf.

32. See, generally, the literature reviewed in Alessandro Acquisti, Laura Brandimarte, and George Loewenstein, "Privacy and Human Behavior in the Age of Information," *Science* 347 (2015): 509–514.

33. "Power," Oxford Living Dictionaries, https://en.oxforddictionaries.com /definition/power.

34. Merritt R. Smith and Leo Marx, *Does Technology Drive History? The Dilemma of Technological Determinism* (Cambridge, MA: MIT Press, 1994); Langdon Winner, *Autonomous Technology: Technics-out-of-Control as a Theme in Political Thought* (Cambridge, MA: MIT Press, 1978); Langdon Winner, *The Whale and the Reactor: A Search for Limits in an Age of High Technology* (Chicago: University of Chicago Press, 1989); Langdon Winner, "Technology as Forms of Life," in *Readings in the Philosophy of Technology,* ed. David M. Kaplan (Lanham, MD: Rowman and Littlefield, 2004), 103–113.

35. Frank Lloyd Wright, quoted in Daniel J. Solove, *The Digital Person: Technology and Privacy in the Information Age* (New York: New York University Press, 2006), 98.

36. See, e.g., Beth Coleman, *Hello Avatar: Rise of the Networked Generation* (Cambridge, MA: MIT Press, 2011); and Jenifer Stromer-Galley and Rosa Mikeal Martey, "Visual Spaces, Norm Governed Placed: The Influence of Spatial Context Online," *New Media and Society* 11 (2009): 1041–1060.

37. Christopher Bergland, "Exposure to Natural Light Improves Workplace Performance," *Psychology Today,* June 5, 2013, https://www.psychologytoday.com /blog/the-athletes-way/201306/exposure-natural-light-improves-workplace -performance.

38. Alex Stone, "Why Waiting Is Torture," *New York Times,* August 18, 2012.

39. Christopher Mele, "Pushing That Crosswalk Button May Make You Feel Better, But . . . ," *New York Times,* October 27, 2016; Karen Levy and Tim Hwang, "Backstage at the Machine Theater," Reform, April 10, 2015, https:// medium.com/re-form/back-stage-at-the-machine-theater-530f973db8d2# .shiupfd02.

40. Richard H. Thaler and Cass R. Sunstein, *Nudge: Improving Decisions about Health, Wealth, and Happiness* (New York: Penguin, 2009), 3, 6.

41. Daniel Kahneman, *Thinking Fast and Slow* (New York: Farrar, Straus and Giroux, 2011); Dan Ariely, *Predictably Irrational: The Hidden Forces That Shape Our Decisions* (New York: HarperCollins, 2008); Daniel Gilbert, *Stumbling upon Happiness* (New York: Vintage, 2006).

42. Jeremy Smith, "Six Advantages of Hyperbolic Discounting . . . And What The Heck Is It Anyway?," Kissmetrics Blog, https://blog.kissmetrics.com /hyperbolic-discounting/.

43. Raymond S. Nickerson, "Confirmation Bias: A Ubiquitous Phenomenon in Many Guises," *Review of General Psychology* 2 (1998): 175–220; Kahneman, *Thinking Fast and Slow.*

44. Acquisti, Brandimarte, and Loewenstein, "Privacy and Human Behavior in the Age of Information," 509.

45. Ibid.

46. Ibid.

47. See, e.g., Erving Goffman, *Frame Analysis: An Essay on the Organization of Experience* (Cambridge, MA: Harvard University Press, 1974); Robert D. Benford and David A. Snow, "Framing Processes and Social Movements: An Overview and Assessment," *Annual Review of Sociology* 26 (2000): 614; Dennis Chong and James N. Druckman, "Framing Theory," *Annual Review of Political Science* 10 (2007): 104; Laura E. Drake and William A. Donohue, "Communicative Framing Theory in Conflict Resolution," *Communication Research* 23 (1996): 300; Daniel Kahneman and Amos Tversky, "Choices, Values, and Frames," *American Psychologist* 39 (1984): 341–350; and Amos Tversky and Daniel Kahneman, "The Framing of Decisions and the Psychology of Choice," *Science* 211 (1981): 453–458.

48. See, e.g., Thomas E. Nelson, Zoe M. Oxley, and Rosalee A. Clawson, "Toward a Psychology of Framing Effects," *Political Behavior* 19 (1997): 24, which notes, "Frames can be meaningful and important determinants of public opinion."

49. Thomas E. Nelson, Rosalee A. Clawson, and Zoe M. Oxley, "Media Framing of a Civil Liberties Conflict and Its Effect on Tolerance," *American Political Science Review* 91 (1997): 567–583. Richard L. Hasen, "Efficiency under Informational Asymmetry: The Effect of Framing on Legal Rules," *UCLA Law Review* 38 (1990): 393, provides this example: "[A]n 80 percent chance to survive a medical operation may mean something different to a consumer than a 20 percent chance to die on the operating table, even though these two 'frames' convey mathematically equivalent information."

50. Joseph Turow, Lauren Feldman, and Kimberley Meltzer, *Open to Exploitation: American Shoppers Online and Offline* (Philadelphia: University of Pennsylvania Annenberg Public Policy Center, 2005), http://repository.upenn .edu/cgi/viewcontent.cgi?article=1035&context=asc_papers.

51. See, e.g., Judith D. Fischer, "Got Issues? An Empirical Study about Framing Them," *Journal of the Association of Legal Writing Directors* 6 (2009): 3, which notes, "Researchers have applied framing theory to show that frames affect how people see issues. This analysis has helped politician's influence public

opinion by skillfully framing ideas. Similarly, a skillfully framed issue statement can help shape a court's perceptions of an appellate case." See also Chris Guthrie, "Prospect Theory, Risk Preference, and the Law," *Northwestern University Law Review* 97 (2003): 1128, which notes that "framing can negatively influence judicial intervention in settlement talks"; Jonathan Remy Nash and Stephanie M. Stern, "Property Frames," *Washington University Law Review* 87 (2010): 449–504; Cass R. Sunstein, "Moral Heuristics and Moral Framing," *Minnesota Law Review* 88 (2004): 1559; and Daniel M. Isaacs, "Baseline Framing in Sentencing," Yale Law Journal 121 (2011): 426–458.

52. Robert M. Entman, "Framing: Toward Clarification of a Fractured Paradigm," *Journal of Communication* 43 (1993): 52, 58, 53; italics in the original.

53. Ibid., 53–54: "The notion of framing thus implies that the frame has a common effect on large portions of the receiving audience, though it is not likely to have a universal effect on all."

54. Kahneman and Tversky, "Choices, Values, and Frames," 343. Conversely, 78 percent of respondents chose Program D, even though previously 28 percent had chosen Program D's clone, Program B. Kahneman and Tversky gave members of both experimental groups only two treatment options from which to choose.

55. Entman, "Framing," 54.

56. As Murray Edelman, "Contestable Categories and Public Opinion," *Political Communication* 10 (1993): 232, notes, "The character, causes, and consequences of any phenomenon become radically different as changes are made in what is prominently displayed, what is repressed and especially in how observations are classified. . . . the social world is . . . a kaleidoscope of potential realities, any of which can be readily evoked by altering the ways in which observations are framed and categorized."

57. Leslie K. John, Alessandro Acquisti, and George Loewenstein, "Strangers on a Plane: Context-Dependent Willingness to Divulge Sensitive Information," *Journal of Consumer Research* 37 (2011): 858–873.

58. Leslie K. John, Alessandro Acquisti, and George Loewenstein, "The Best of Strangers: Context Dependent Willingness to Divulge Personal Information" (unpublished manuscript, July 6, 2009), https://papers.ssrn.com/sol3/papers.cfm?abstract_id=1430482.

59. Ibid.

60. Idris Adjerid, Alessandro Acquisti, and George Loewenstein, "Framing and the Malleability of Privacy Choices," paper presented at the 2014 Workshop on the Economics of Information Security, Pennsylvania State University, June 23–24, 2014, http://www.econinfosec.org/archive/weis2014/papers/AdjeridAcquistiLoewenstein-WEIS2014.pdf.

61. Ibid., 32–33.

62. Acquisti, Brandimarte, and Loewenstein, "Privacy and Human Behavior in the Age of Information," 509.

63. Ibid.

64. With apologies to the great Kurt Vonnegut. See Kurt Vonnegut, *Mother Night* (New York: Delta, 1966, 1999), vi: "We are what we pretend to be, so we must be careful about what we pretend to be."

65. Academic literature also supports the idea that when users adopt and create workarounds, technologies also come to embody the values of its users. See Wiebe E. Bijker, *Of Bicycles, Bakelites, and Bulbs, Toward a Theory of Sociotechnical Change* (Cambridge, MA: MIT Press, 1995).

66. Winner, *The Whale and The Reactor*, 24.

67. Ibid.

68. Ibid; emphasis in the original. This account of Moses and the overpass has been contested by scholars, but even as apocrypha it demonstrates how design might further and frustrate human values.

69. Rebecca Greenfield, "The Rise of the Term 'Glasshole,' Explained by Linguists," *Atlantic*, April 22, 2013, https://www.theatlantic.com/technology /archive/2013/04/rise-term-glasshole-explained-linguists/316015/.

70. Ibid.

71. Dan Farber, "Hey Google Glass, Are You Recording Me?," CNET, May 1, 2013, https://www.cnet.com/news/hey-google-glass-are-you-recording-me/; Charles Arthur, "Google 'Bans' Facial Recognition on Google Glass—But Developers Persist," *Guardian*, June 3, 2013.

72. Winner, *The Whale and the Reactor*, 125.

73. Sony Corp. of America v. Universal City Studios, Inc., 464 U.S. 417 (1984); MGM Studios, Inc. v. Grokster, Ltd., 545 U.S. 913 (2005).

74. Clifford D. May, "Guns Don't Kill People," *National Review*, May 19, 2011, http://www.nationalreview.com/article/267549/guns-dont-kill-people-clifford-d -may.

75. Evan Selinger, "The Philosophy of the Technology of the Gun," *Atlantic*, July 23, 2012, https://www.theatlantic.com/technology/archive/2012/07/the -philosophy-of-the-technology-of-the-gun/260220/.

76. "Pinhole Spy Toothbrush Hidden Camera DVR 8GB," Omejo, http://shop .omejo.com/productsshow.php?id=118.

77. Winner, *The Whale and the Reactor*, 21.

78. Ibid, 21, 22; emphasis in the original. Another theory that addresses the role of objects in social associations is actor-network theory. See Bruno Latour, *Reassembling the Social—An Introduction to Actor-Network-Theory* (Oxford: Oxford University Press, 2005).

79. Winner, *The Whale and the Reactor*, 25; emphasis in the original.

80. Norman, *The Design of Everyday Things*, 34–36.

81. Julie Beck, "Study: People Who Overshare on Facebook Just Want to Belong," *Atlantic*, June 16, 2014, https://www.theatlantic.com/health/archive/2014 /06/study-people-who-overshare-on-facebook-just-want-to-belong/372834/.

82. Jessica Misener, "The 30 Absolute Worst Facebook Overshares," BuzzFeed, May 27, 2013, https://www.buzzfeed.com/jessicamisener/the-30 -absolute-worst-facebook-overshares; Britney Fitzgerald, "Facebook Overshare: 7 Things You Might Not Realize You're Telling the World," *Huffington Post*, August 17, 2012, http://www.huffingtonpost.com/2012/09/17/facebook-overshare _n_1844606.html.

83. Yang Wang, Gregory Norcie, Saranga Komanduri, Alessandro Acquisti, Pedro Giovanni Leon, and Lorrie Faith Cranor, "'I Regretted the Minute I Pressed Share': A Qualitative Study of Regrets on Facebook," in *Proceedings of the Seventh Symposium on Usable Privacy and Security* (New York: Association for Computing Machinery, 2011), https://www.andrew.cmu.edu/user/pgl/FB -Regrets.pdf.

84. As Farhad Manjoo, "It's Not All Facebook's Fault," *Slate*, November 30, 2011, http://www.slate.com/articles/technology/technocracy/2011/11/facebook _privacy_you_re_as_much_to_blame_for_the_site_s_privacy_woes_as_mark _zuckerberg_.html, writes, "If you follow this simple rule, you'll never be blindsided. . . . Facebook is a powerful tool, and the reason that so many people slip up on the site is that we fail to appreciate its power. It's time we all started taking it a bit more seriously. Sharing is fun. But if you don't plan on sharing with everyone, don't bother."

85. Farhad Manjoo, "How to Stay Private on Facebook in One Easy Step," *Slate*, February 7, 2013, http://www.slate.com/blogs/future_tense/2013/02/07/how _to_stay_private_on_facebook_in_one_easy_step.html.

86. Citron, *Hate Crimes in Cyberspace*, 77.

87. Michael Scott, "Tort Liability for Vendors of Insecure Software: Has the Time Finally Come?," *Maryland Law Review* 62 (2008): 425–484.

88. Even organizations that created the password standards are now revising them because they are not working. Robert McMillan, "The Man Who Wrote Those Password Rules Has a New Tip: N3v$r M1^d!," *Wall Street Journal*, August 7, 2017, https://www.wsj.com/articles/the-man-who-wrote-those -password-rules-has-a-new-tip-n3v-r-m1-d-1502124118.

89. Winner, *The Whale and the Reactor*, 25–26.

90. Danielle Citron & Frank Pasquale, "The Scored Society: Due Process For Automated Predictions," 89 Washington Law Review 1 (2014).

91. Winner, *The Whale and the Reactor*, 26. Consider, for example, how design is used to prey on the vulnerable, such as gambling addicts; see John Rosengren, "How Casinos Enable Gambling Addicts," *Atlantic*, December 2016, https://www .theatlantic.com/magazine/archive/2016/12/losing-it-all/505814/; and Natasha Dow

Schüll, *Addiction by Design: Machine Gambling in Las Vegas* (Princeton, NJ: Princeton University Press, 2012).

92. Cass R. Sunstein, "The Ethics of Nudging," Yale Journal on Regulation 32 (2015): 417.

93. Ibid., 421.

94. Andy Cush, "Here's the Number One Reason to Set Your Venmo Account to Private," Gawker, February 23, 2015, http://internet.gawker.com/heres-the-number-one-reason-to-set-your-venmo-account-t-1687461730.

95. Aran Khanna, "Your Venmo Transactions Leave a Publicly Accessible Money Trail," *Huffington Post,* October 30, 2016, http://www.huffingtonpost.com/aran-khanna/venmo-money_b_8418130.html.

96. Kate Kochetkova, "Users Are Still Too Careless in Social Networks," Kaspersky, February 3, 2016, https://www.kaspersky.co.in/blog/users-are-still-too-careless-in-social-networks/5633/; Evan Selinger and Woodrow Hartzog, "Why Is Facebook Putting Teens at Risk?," Bloomberg, October 24, 2013, http://www.bloomberg.com/news/2013-10-24/why-is-facebook-putting-teens-at-risk-.html.

97. Regulation (EU) 2016/679 on the protection of natural persons with regard to the processing of personal data and on the free movement of such data, and repealing Directive 95/46/EC (General Data Protection Regulation), 2016, OJ L 119/1. See also Lee A. Bygrave, "Data Protection by Design and by Default: Deciphering the EU's Legislative Requirements," Oslo Law Review 4 (2017): 105–120.

98. Sunstein, "The Ethics of Nudging," 421, 422.

99. Peter-Paul Verbeek, *Moralizing Technology* (Chicago: University of Chicago Press, 2011), 1, 2.

2. Privacy Law's Design Gap

1. Samuel D. Warren and Louis D. Brandeis, "The Right to Privacy," *Harvard Law Review* 4 (1890): 193–220.

2. Robert Gellman, "Fair Information Practices: A Basic History," June 17, 2016, http://bobgellman.com/rg-docs/rg-FIPShistory.pdf.

3. Paula Bruening, "Rethink Privacy 2.0 and Fair Information Practice Principles: A Common Language for Privacy," Policy@Intel, October 19, 2014, http://blogs.intel.com/policy/2014/10/19/rethink-privacy-2-0-fair-information-practice-principles-common-language-privacy/.

4. European Union General Data Protection Regulation, 2016/679, http://ec.europa.eu/justice/data-protection/reform/files/regulation_oj_en.pdf; Personal Information Protection and Electronic Documents Act, S.C. 2000, c. 5. A related version of the FIPs was incorporated into the Asia-Pacific Economic Cooperation

Privacy Framework. See Graham Greenleaf, *Asian Data Privacy Laws: Trade and Human Rights Perspectives* (Oxford: Oxford University Press, 2014).

5. Organisation for Economic Co-operation and Development, "OECD Guidelines on the Protection of Privacy and Transborder Flows of Personal Data," http://www.oecd.org/sti/ieconomy/oecdguidelinesontheprotectionofpriva cyandtransborderflowsofpersonaldata.htm.

6. Don Norman, *The Design of Everyday Things* (New York: Basic Books, 1988), 12.

7. The White House, "Consumer Data Privacy in a Networked World," https://www.whitehouse.gov/sites/default/files/privacy-final.pdf.

8. Federal Trade Commission, *Protecting Consumer Privacy in an Era of Rapid Change: Recommendations for Businesses and Policymakers,* https://www .ftc.gov/sites/default/files/documents/reports/federal-trade-commission-report -protecting-consumer-privacy-era-rapid-change-recommendations /120326privacyreport.pdf.

9. See European Union General Data Protection Regulation 2016/679, http://ec.europa.eu/justice/data-protection/reform/files/regulation_oj_en.pdf, which notes, "In order for processing to be lawful, personal data should be processed on the basis of the consent of the data subject concerned or some other legitimate basis."

10. Alan Westin, *Privacy and Freedom* (New York: Atheneum, 1967), 31–32.

11. Daniel Solove, *Understanding Privacy* (Cambridge, MA: Harvard University Press, 2010), 24–25.

12. See, e.g., Joe Kissell, *Take Control of Your Online Privacy* (n.p.: Take Control Books, 2015); Privacy Rights Clearinghouse, "Privacy Survival Guide: Take Control of Your Personal Information," https://www.privacyrights.org /privacy-survival-take-control-your-personal-information; Anick Jesdanun, "5 Ways to Control your Privacy on Google," *USA Today,* March 16, 2012; and Erick Griffith, "Take Control of Your Google Privacy," *PC Magazine,* June 25, 2015, https://www.pcmag.com/article2/0,2817,2486726,00.asp.

13. Kathy Chan, "On Facebook, People Own and Control Their Information," Facebook, February 16, 2009, https://www.facebook.com/notes/facebook/on -facebook-people-own-and-control-their-information/54434097130/.

14. Michael Zimmer, "Mark Zuckerberg's Theory of Privacy," *Washington Post,* February 3, 2014.

15. "Data Privacy Day 2015—Putting People in Control," Microsoft, January 28, 2015, http://blogs.microsoft.com/on-the-issues/2015/01/28/data-privacy -day-2015-putting-people-control/.

16. Guemmy Kim, "Keeping Your Personal Information Private and Safe and Putting You in Control," Google Official Blog, June 1, 2015, https://googleblog .blogspot.com/2015/06/privacy-security-tools-improvements.html.

17. Neil Richards and Woodrow Hartzog, "Taking Trust Seriously in Privacy Law," *Stanford Technology Law Review* 19 (2016): 431–472.

18. Alex C. Madrigal, "Reading the Privacy Policies You Encounter in a Year Would Take 76 Work Days," *Atlantic,* March 1, 2012, https://www.theatlantic.com/technology/archive/2012/03/reading-the-privacy-policies-you-encounter-in-a-year-would-take-76-work-days/253851/; Aleecia M. McDonald and Lorrie Faith Cranor, "The Cost of Reading Privacy Policies," *I/S: A Journal of Law and Policy for the Information Society* 4 (2008–2009): 540–561.

19. Julia Angwin, *Dragnet Nation* (New York: Times Books, 2014).

20. White House Civil Liberties and Oversight Board, *Report on the Telephone Records Program Conducted under Section 215 of the USA PATRIOT Act and on the Operations of the Foreign Intelligence Surveillance Court,* January 23, 2014, https://www.scribd.com/document/201740642/Final-Report-1-23-14.

21. President's Council of Advisors on Science and Technology Report to the President, "Big Data and Privacy: A Technological Perspective," May 2014, http://mddb.apec.org/Documents/2014/ECSG/DPS2/14_ecsg_dps2_007.pdf.

22. See Julie Brill, "Remarks by Commissioner Julie Brill, United States Federal Trade Commission: Keynote Address, Proskauer on Privacy," October 19, 2010, https://www.ftc.gov/sites/default/files/documents/public_statements/remarks-commissioner-julie-brill/101019proskauerspeech.pdf, which notes that "the Notice and Choice model, as it is often deployed today, places too great a burden on consumers"; and Jon Leibowitz, FTC, "Introductory Remarks, Chairman Jon Leibowitz, FTC Privacy Roundtable," December 7, 2009, http://www.ftc.gov/sites/default/files/documents/public_statements/introductory-remarks-ftc-privacy-roundtable/091207privacyremarks.pdf, which notes, "We do feel that the approaches we've tried so far—both the notice and choice regime, and later the harm-based approach—haven't worked quite as well as we would like."

23. Mary Madden and Lee Rainie, "Americans' Attitudes about Privacy, Security and Surveillance," Pew Research Center, May 20, 2015, http://www.pewinternet.org/2015/05/20/americans-attitudes-about-privacy-security-and-surveillance/.

24. Barry Schwartz, *The Paradox of Choice* (New York: Harper Collins, 2005).

25. Maurice Godelier, *The Mental and the Material,* trans. Martin Thom (London: Verso, 2012), 13.

26. Idris Adjerid, Alessandro Acquisti, George Loewenstein, "Framing and the Malleability of Privacy Choices," Workshop on the Economics of Information Security, July 2014, http://www.econinfosec.org/archive/weis2014/papers/AdjeridAcquistiLoewenstein-WEIS2014.pdf.

27. Kenneth Olmstead and Michelle Atkinson, "Apps Permissions in Google Play Store," Pew Research Center November 10, 2015, http://www.pewinternet.org/2015/11/10/apps-permissions-in-the-google-play-store/.

28. See Federal Trade Commission, "Retail Tracking Firm Settles FTC Charges it Misled Consumers About Opt Out Choices," April 23, 2015, https://www.ftc.gov/news-events/press-releases/2015/04/retail-tracking-firm-settles-ftc-charges-it-misled-consumers.

29. "FTC Statement on Deception," letter from James C. Miller III, chairman, Federal Trade Commission, to John D. Dingell, chairman, House Committee on Energy and Commerce, October 14, 1983, reprinted in In re Cliffdale Assocs., Inc., 103 F.T.C. 110, app. at 175–184 (1984) (decision and order), https://www.ftc.gov/system/files/documents/public_statements/410531/831014deceptionstmt.pdf.

30. Paula J. Bruening and Mary J. Culnan, "Through a Glass Darkly: From Privacy Notices to Effective Transparency," *North Carolina Journal of Law and Technology* 17 (2016): 515–579.

31. M. Ryan Calo, "Against Notice Skepticism in Privacy (and Elsewhere)," *Notre Dame Law Review* 87 (2012): 1028.

32. Ari Ezra Waldman, "Privacy, Notice, and Design" (unpublished manuscript, March 16, 2016), https://papers.ssrn.com/sol3/papers.cfm?abstract_id=2780305.

33. See, e.g., G. Susanne Bahr and Richard A. Ford, "How and Why Pop-Ups Don't Work: Pop-Up Prompted Eye Movements, User Affect and Decision Making," *Computers in Human Behavior* 27 (2011): 776–783; Paul Bernal, "Annoyed by Those Cookie Warnings?," Paul Bernall's blog, July 2, 2012, https://paulbernal.wordpress.com/2012/07/02/annoyed-by-those-cookie-warnings/; and Ronald Leenes and Eleni Kosta, "Taming the Cookie Monster with Dutch Law—A Tale of Regulatory Failure," *Computer Law and Security Review* 31 (2015): 317–335.

34. Peter P. Swire, "The Surprising Virtues of the New Financial Privacy Law," *Minnesota Law Review* 86 (2002): 1263–1323.

35. Mike Hintze, "In Defense of the Long Privacy Statement," *Maryland Law Review* 76 (forthcoming, 2017), notes that "efforts to make privacy statements significantly shorter and simpler are optimizing for the one audience least likely to read them—consumers—rather than the audiences in the best position to police privacy statements and the practices they describe.").

36. Federal Trade Commission Act, 15 U.S.C. § 45 (2016).

37. Spokeo v. Robins, 136 S. Ct. 1540 (2016).

38. European Union General Data Protection Regulation 2016/679, http://ec.europa.eu/justice/data-protection/reform/files/regulation_oj_en.pdf.

39. See, e.g., Forbes v. Wells Fargo Bank, 420 F. Supp. 2d 1018 (D. Minn. 2008); Guin v. Higher Educ. Serv. Corp., Inc., 2006 WL 288483 (D. Minn. 2006); In re Barnes & Noble Pin Pad Litig., 2013 WL 4759588 (N.D. Ill. Sept. 3, 2013); Hammer v. Sam's East, Inc., 2013 WL 3746573 (D. Kan. July 16, 2013) (explaining, "No court has found that a mere increased risk of ID theft or fraud constitutes an injury in fact for standing purposes without some alleged theft of personal data or security breach"); Reilly v. Ceridian Corp., 664 F.3d 38 (3d Cir. 2011); Hammond v. Bank of New York, 2010 WL 2643307 (S.D.N.Y. June 25, 2010); and Bell v. Acxiom Corp., 2006 WL 2850042 (E.D. Ark. Oct. 3, 2006).

40. Clapper v. Amnesty International, 133 S. Ct. 1138, 1152 (2013).

41. Daniel J. Solove and Danielle Keats Citron, "Risk and Anxiety: A Theory of Data Breach Harms," *Texas Law Review* 96 (forthcoming, 2017).

42. Ibid.

43. See, e.g., Omer Tene and Jules Polonetsky, "A Theory of Creepy: Technology, Privacy, and Shifting Social Norms," *Yale Journal of Law and Technology* 16 (2013): 59–102.

44. Restatement (Second) of Torts § 652C.

45. Restatement (Second) of Torts § 652D.

46. Neil Richards, *Intellectual Privacy: Rethinking Civil Liberties in the Digital Age* (New York: Oxford University Press, 2015).

47. Ann Cavoukian, the executive director of the Privacy and Big Data Institute and former information and privacy commissioner for Ontario, has developed an extensive body of resources for practicing Privacy by Design. See Ryerson University, "Resources," http://www.ryerson.ca/pbdi/privacy-by -design/resources/; and UK Information Commissioner's Office, "Privacy by Design," https://ico.org.uk/for-organisations/guide-to-data-protection /privacy-by-design/. Other resources are also available to those seeking to implement privacy by design principles; see Jonathan Fox and Michelle Finneran Dennedy, *The Privacy Engineer's Manifesto: Getting from Policy to Code to QA to Value* (New York: Apress, 2014); and Courtney Bowman, Ari Gesher, John K. Grant, and Daniel Slate, *The Architecture of Privacy: On Engineering Technologies That Can Deliver Trustworthy Safeguards* (Sebastopol, CA: O'Reilly, 2015).

48. Chris Jay Hoofnagle, *Federal Trade Commission Privacy Law and Policy* (New York: Cambridge University Press, 2016), 170.

49. Ibid.

50. Ibid., 170–171.

51. Umika Pidarthy, "What You Should Know about iTunes' 56-Page Legal Terms," CNN, May 6, 2011, http://www.cnn.com/2011/TECH/web/05/06/itunes .terms/index.html.

52. Alex Horn, "Apple Pulls 250 Privacy-Infringing Apps from Store," *Guardian,* October 20, 2015.

53. Kim Komando, "These 7 Apps Are among the Worst at Protecting Privacy," *USA Today,* September 23, 2015; PrivacyGrade, http://privacygrade .org/.

54. Peter Bright, "How to Remove the Superfish Malware: What Lenovo Doesn't Tell You," Ars Technica, February 19, 2015, https://arstechnica.com /information-technology/2015/02/how-to-remove-the-superfish-malware-what -lenovo-doesnt-tell-you/; Michael Horowitz, "Lenovo Collects Usage Data on ThinkPad, ThinkCentre and ThinkStation PCs," *Computerworld,* September 22, 2015, https://www.computerworld.com/article/2984889/windows-pcs/lenovo -collects-usage-data-on-thinkpad-thinkcentre-and-thinkstation-pcs.html; Michael Horowitz, "Trusting Lenovo," *Computerworld,* October 20, 2015, https://www.computerworld.com/article/2995012/windows-pcs/trusting-lenovo .html; Thomas Fox-Brewster, "How Lenovo's Superfish 'Malware' Works and What You Can Do to Kill It," *Forbes,* February 19, 2015, https://www.forbes.com /sites/thomasbrewster/2015/02/19/superfish-need-to-know/.

55. Mathew Lynley, "Google to Pay Out One Thousandth of its Quarterly Revenue for Its Biggest Privacy Snafu," VentureBeat, September 2, 2010, https://venturebeat.com/2010/11/02/google-buzz-payou/; Paul Boutin, "Google Admits Buzz Mistakes, Tries Again at SXSW," VentureBeat, March 14, 2010, https://venturebeat.com/2010/03/14/google-admits-buzz-mistakes-tries-again-at -sxsw/.

56. Jaron Lanier, *You Are Not a Gadget* (New York: Vintage, 2010), 6, 8.

57. Ethan Zuckerman, "The Internet's Original Sin," *Atlantic,* August 14, 2014, https://www.theatlantic.com/technology/archive/2014/08/advertising-is-the -internets-original-sin/376041/.

58. John Horgan, "Dave Farber, Internet's 'Grandfather,' Seeks to Cut Through Fog of Cyberwar," *Scientific American,* June 6, 2013, https://blogs .scientificamerican.com/cross-check/dave-farber-internets-grandfather-seeks-to -cut-through-fog-of-cyberwar/.

59. Claire Cain Miller, "Technology's Man Problem," *New York Times,* April 5, 2014; Kate Crawford, "Artificial Intelligence's White Guy Problem," *New York Times,* June 5, 2016; Grace Dobush, "White Men Dominate Silicon Valley Not by Accident, but by Design," Quartz, March 16, 2016, https://qz.com/641070 /white-men-dominate-silicon-valley-not-by-accident-but-by-design/.

60. "New Zealand Passport Robot Tells Applicant of Asian Descent to Open His Eyes," *South China Morning Post,* December 7, 2016.

61. Kathleen Miles, "Teens Get Online 'Eraser Button' with New California Law," *Huffington Post,* September 24, 2013, http://www.huffingtonpost.com/2013 /09/24/teens-online-eraser-button-california_n_3976808.html; Somini Sen-

gupta, "Sharing, with a Safety Net," *New York Times,* September 19, 2013, http://www.nytimes.com/2013/09/20/technology/bill-provides-reset-button-for-youngsters-online-posts.html.

62. Julie Cohen, *Configuring the Networked Self: Law, Code, and the Play of Everyday Practice* (New Haven, Yale University Press, 2012); Julie E. Cohen, "What Privacy Is For," *Harvard Law Review* 126 (2013): 1906, 19271931; Julie Cohen, "Privacy, Visibility, Transparency, and Exposure," University of Chicago Law Review 75 (2008):181201.

63. Mireille Hildebrandt, *Smart Technologies and the End(s) of Law: Novel Entanglements of Law and Technology* (Cheltenham: Edward Elgar, 2016).

64. Joel R. Reidenberg, "Lex Informatica: The Formulation of Information Policy Rules through Technology," *Texas Law Review* 76 (1998): 554–555. See also Joel R. Reidenberg, "Rules of the Road for Global Electronic Highways: Merging the Trade and Technical Paradigms," *Harvard Journal of Law and Technology* 6 (1993): 301–304, which argues that technical considerations establish normative standards which, in turn, impact system practice; and Joel R. Reidenberg, "Setting Standards for Fair Information Practice in the U.S. Private Sector," *Iowa Law Review* 80 (1995): 508–509, which argues that legal rules may be supplemented by technical considerations as well as business practices.

65. Reidenberg, "Lex Informatica," 555.

66. Larry Lessig, *Code and Other Laws of Cyberspace* (New York: Basic Books, 1999); Larry Lessig, "Reading the Constitution in Cyberspace," *Emory Law Journal* 45 (1996): 896–897; Larry Lessig, "Law of the Horse: What Cyberlaw Might Teach," *Harvard Law Review* 113 (1999): 501–546.

67. Lessig, *Code,* 6; emphasis in the original.

68. Neil Richards, "The Limits of Tort Privacy," *Journal of Telecommunications and High Technology Law* 9 (2011): 357–384; Diane L. Zimmerman, "Requiem for a Heavyweight: A Farewell to Warren and Brandeis's Privacy Tort," *Cornell Law Review* 68 (1983): 291–367.

69. Adam Thierer, *Permissionless Innovation: The Continuing Case for Comprehensive Technological Freedom* (Fairfax, VA: Mercatus Center, George Mason University, 2016), 1.

70. See David Golumbia, " 'Permissionless Innovation': Using Technology to Dismantle the Republic," Uncomputing, June 11, 2014, http://www.uncomputing .org/?p=1383, which asserts, " 'Permissionless innovation' is a license to harm; it is a demand that government not intrude in exactly the area that government is meant for—to protect the general welfare of citizens."

71. John Perry Barlow, "A Declaration of the Independence of Cyberspace," Electronic Frontier Foundation, February 8, 1996, https://www.eff.org /cyberspace-independence.

72. Telecommunications Act of 1996, title 3, section 301; 47 U.S.C. § 230.

73. Torts: Liability for Physical and Emotional Harm, Restatement (Third) of the Law (2012); Torts: Products Liability, Restatement (Third) of the Law (1998).

74. U.S. Food and Drug Administration, "Medical Devices," http://www.fda.gov/MedicalDevices/; Federal Aviation Administration, "FAA Regulations," https://www.faa.gov/regulations_policies/faa_regulations/.

75. National Highway Traffic and Safety Administration, "Federal Motor Vehicle Safety Standards and Regulations," http://www.nhtsa.gov/cars/rules/import/FMVSS/.

76. See generally 47 C.F.R. §§ 0–199.

77. See, e.g., 8 Colo. Code Regs. § 1505-1:21; Colo. Rev. Stat. Ann. § 1-5-618.

78. 18 U.S.C. § 922(p).

79. Construction Market Data, "Building Codes," http://www.cmdgroup.com/building-codes/.

80. Lessig, *Code*; Reidenberg, *Lex Informatica*.

81. Neal Katyal, "Architecture as Crime Control," *Yale Law Journal* 111 (2002): 1092.

3. Privacy Values in Design

1. Batya Friedman and Peter Kahn Jr., "Human Values, Ethics, and Design," in *The Human-Computer Interaction Handbook*, 2nd ed., ed. Andrew Sears and Julie Jacko (New York: CRC, 2008), 1177–1201.

2. See Fred H. Cate, "The Failure of Fair Information Practice Principles," in *Consumer Protection in the Age of the "Information Economy,"* ed. Jane K. Winn (Abingdon, England: Routledge, 2006), 341, 342; Omer Tene, "Privacy Law's Midlife Crisis: A Critical Assessment of the Second Wave of Global Privacy Laws," *Ohio State Law Journal* 74 (2013): 1218–1219; Daniel J. Weitzner, Harold Abelson, Tim Berners-Lee, Joan Feigenbaum, James Hendler, and Gerald Jay Sussman, *Information Accountability*, Computer Science and Artificial Intelligence Laboratory Technical Report MIT-CSAIL-TR-2007034 (Cambridge, MA: Massachusetts Institute of Technology, 2007); and Lisa M. Austin, "Enough about Me: Why Privacy Is about Power, Not Consent (or Harm)," in *A World without Privacy: What Law Can and Should Do?*, ed. Austin Sarat (New York: Cambridge University Press, 2015), 131–133.

3. Daniel J. Solove, "Introduction: Privacy Self-Management and the Consent Dilemma," *Harvard Law Review* 126 (2013): 1880.

4. Helen Nissenbaum, *Privacy in Context: Technology, Policy, and the Integrity of Social Life* (Stanford, CA: Stanford University Press, 2009), 113, 119.

5. See Gill v. Hearst Pub. Co., 40 Cal. 2d 224, 230, 253 P.2d 441, 444 (1953); Moreno v. Hanford Sentinel, Inc., 172 Cal. App. 4th 1125, 1130, 91 Cal. Rptr. 3d 858, 862 (2009), as modified (Apr. 30, 2009); Guest v. Leis, 255 F.3d 325, 333

(6th Cir. 2001); Brian Resnick, "Researchers Just Released Profile Data on 70,000 OkCupid Users without Permission," Vox, May 12, 2016, https://www.vox.com /2016/5/12/11666116/70000-okcupid-users-data-release; and Joseph Cox, "70,000 OkCupid Users Just Had Their Data Published," Motherboard, May 12, 2016, which quotes a researcher who analyzed personal information form a dating website as saying, "If you don't want other people to see things, don't post them publicly on the Internet. . . . Public is public."

6. Daniel J. Solove, *Understanding Privacy* (Cambridge, MA: Harvard University Press, 2010), 43–44.

7. Here I draw from the theories of Julie Cohen and Neil Richards on the value of privacy. See Julie Cohen, "What Privacy Is For," *Harvard Law Review* 126 (2012): 1904–1933; Julie Cohen, *Configuring the Networked Self: Law, Code, and the Play of Everyday Practice* (New Haven, CT: Yale University Press, 2012); Neil Richards, *Intellectual Privacy: Rethinking Civil Liberties in the Digital Age* (Oxford: Oxford University Press, 2015).

8. Andrea Peterson, "These Data Brokers Cost Consumers Millions by Illegally Selling Off Their Financial Information," *Washington Post,* August 12, 2015; Dan Goodin, "Hack of Cupid Media Dating Website Exposes 42 Million Plaintext Passwords," Ars Technica, November 20, 2013, https://arstechnica.com /information-technology/2013/11/hack-of-cupid-media-dating-website-exposes -42-million-plaintext-passwords/.

9. Neil Richards and Woodrow Hartzog, "Taking Trust Seriously in Privacy Law," *Stanford Technology Law Review* 19 (2016): 431–472.

10. See Joshua A. T. Fairfield and Christoph Engel, "Privacy as a Public Good," *Duke Law Journal* 65 (2015): 385–457.

11. Computer Science and Telecommunications Board, National Research Council, *Trust in Cyberspace,* ed. Fred Schneider (Washington, DC: National Academies Press, 1999).

12. Richards and Hartzog, "Taking Trust Seriously in Privacy Law"; Friedman and Kahn, "Human Values."

13. See, e.g., Ari Waldman, *Privacy as Trust: Information Privacy for an Information Age* (New York: Cambridge University Press, forthcoming 2018); and Ari Waldman, "Privacy as Trust: Sharing Personal Information in a Networked World," *University of Miami Law Review* 69 (2015): 559–630; Dennis D. Hirsch, "Privacy, Public Goods, and the Tragedy of the Trust Commons: A Response to Professors Fairfield and Engel," *Duke Law Journal Online* 65 (2016), https://dlj.law.duke.edu/2016/02/privacy-public-goods-and-the-tragedy -of-the-trust-commons/; Kirsten Martin, "Transaction Costs, Privacy, and Trust: The Laudable Goals and Ultimate Failure of Notice and Choice to Respect Privacy Online," *First Monday* 18 (2013): http://firstmonday.org/ojs/index.php/fm /article/view/4838/3802; Katherine J. Strandburg, "Freedom of Association in a

Networked World: First Amendment Regulation of Relational Surveillance,"
Boston College Law Review 49 (2008): 741–821.

14. Claire A. Hill and Erin Ann O'Hara, "A Cognitive Theory of Trust,"
Washington University Law Review 84 (2006): 1724, citing Denise M. Rousseau,
Sim B. Sitkin; Ronald S. Burt, and Colin Camerer, "Not So Different After All: A
Cross-Discipline View of Trust," *Academy of Management Review* 23 (1998): 394.

15. Richards and Hartzog, "Taking Trust Seriously in Privacy Law."

16. Jack M. Balkin, "Information Fiduciaries and the First Amendment," *UC
Davis Law Review* 49 (2016): 1183–1234.

17. Jack M. Balkin and Jonathan Zittrain, "A Grand Bargain to Make Tech
Companies Trustworthy," *Atlantic,* October 3, 2016, https://www.theatlantic.com
/technology/archive/2016/10/information-fiduciary/502346/.

18. "Discretion," Oxford Living Dictionaries, https://en.oxforddictionaries
.com/definition/discretion; Lee Rainie, Sara Kiesler, Ruogu Kang, and Mary
Madden, "Anonymity, Privacy, and Security Online," Pew Research Center,
September 5, 2013, http://www.pewinternet.org/2013/09/05/anonymity-privacy
-and-security-online/(which details the importance of control over information
and importance of authorization of recipients); Susannah Fox, "Trust and
Privacy Online," Pew Research Center, August 20, 2000, http://www.pewinternet
.org/2000/08/20/trust-and-privacy-online/.

19. Lauren Gellman, "Privacy, Free Speech, and 'Blurry-Edged' Social
Networks," *Boston College Law Review* 50 (2009): 1315–1344; Lior Jacob Strahilevitz, "A Social Networks Theory of Privacy," *University of Chicago Law Review*
72 (2005): 919–920.

20. Pietrylo v. Hillstone Restaurant Group, No. 06-5754 (F.S.H.), 2008 WL
6085437 (D.N.J. July 25, 2008).

21. Ibid., at *1.

22. Ibid at *6.

23. Ibid., at *1.

24. Complaint for Permanent Injunction and Other Equitable Relief, FTC v.
Snapchat Inc., No. C-4501 (filed Dec. 23, 2014).

25. Photograph reproduced from In re Snapchat, File No. 132-3078, Docket
No. C-4501 (Washington, DC: FTC, December 23, 2014), https://www.ftc.gov
/system/files/documents/cases/140508snapchatcmpt.pdf.

26. Complaint for Permanent Injunction and Other Equitable Relief, FTC v.
Snapchat Inc., No. C-4501 (filed Dec. 23, 2014).

27. Facebook, "Downloading Your Info," https://www.facebook.com/help
/131112897028467/.

28. Robert McMillan, "The World's First Computer Password? It Was Useless
Too," *Wired,* January 27, 2012, https://www.wired.com/2012/01/computer
-password/.

29. Kate Hilpern, "Why "Secret" Is Part of Secretary," *Guardian*, November 24, 2003.

30. In re Ryan's Will, 52 N.E.2d 909, 923–24 (N.Y. 1943) (quoting Justice Kent in Bergen v. Bennett, 1 Caines, Cas., 19); see also Charles Bryan Baron, "Self-Dealing Trustees and the Exoneration Clause: Can Trustees Ever Profit from Transactions Involving Trust Property?," *St. John's Law Review* 72 (2012): 43–80.

31. Richards and Hartzog, "Taking Trust Seriously in Privacy Law."

32. Robinson Meyer, "Everything We Know about Facebook's Secret Mood Manipulation Experiment," *Atlantic*, September 8, 2014, https://www.theatlantic .com/technology/archive/2014/06/everything-we-know-about-facebooks-secret -mood-manipulation-experiment/373648/.

33. E. S. Browning, "Financial Scammers Increasingly Target Elderly Americans," *Wall Street Journal*, December 23, 2013.

34. Federal Trade Commission, "Prepared Statement of the Federal Trade Commission before the Subcommittee on Commerce, Manufacturing, and Trade of the House Energy and Commerce Committee on Elder Fraud and Consumer Protection Issues," May 16, 2013, https://www.ftc.gov/sites/default/files /documents/public_statements/prepared-statement-federal-trade-commission -elder-fraud-and-consumer-protection-issues/130516elderfraudhouse.pdf.

35. Claire Cain Miller, "When Algorithms Discriminate," *New York Times*, July 9, 2015; Amit Datta, Michael Carl Tschantz, and Anupam Datta, "Automated Experiments on Ad Privacy Settings," *Proceedings on Privacy Enhancing Technologies* 2015 (2015): 92–112.

36. "Obscure," *American Heritage Dictionary of the English Language*, https://ahdictionary.com/word/search.html?q=obscure.

37. See, e.g., Robin I. M. Dunbar, "Coevolution of Neocortical Size, Group Size, and Language in Humans," *Behavior and Brain Science* 16 (1993): 681–735; R. I. M. Dunbar and M. Spoors, "Social Networks, Support Cliques, and Kinship," *Human Nature* 6 (1995): 273–290; and Robin I. M. Dunbar, "The Social Brain Hypothesis," *Evolutionary Anthropology* 6 (1998): 184.

38. Viktor Mayer-Schönberger has extended this logic, highlighting work that demonstrates that forgetting is a cognitive advantage. Our memories are purposefully selective to prevent cognitive overburdening. This realistically means that most of the individuals with whom we interact in passing, or share common space in transit, are obscure to us and we to them—they are strangers. See Viktor Mayer-Schönberger, *Delete: The Virtue of Forgetting in the Digital Age* (Princeton, NJ: Princeton University Press, 2009), 16–49, which explains why remembering is more resource intensive than forgetting.

39. See Network Working Group, "Uniform Resource Locators (URL)" (memorandum), December 1994, http://www.ietf.org/rfc/rfc1738.txt, which notes that URL describes "the syntax and semantics of formalized information for

location and access of resources via the Internet." For example, the web address http://yahoo.com is a URL that takes one to the Yahoo website.

40. For example, numerous papers have documented the characteristics of the "attention economy" online, where a multitude of information producers compete furiously for limited attention. To attain large-scale attention requires the expense of significant resources; individuals who do not seek—or seek limited—publicity have very good reason to expect obscurity. See, e.g., Mark Newman, Albert-László Barabási, and Duncan J. Watts, *The Structure and Dynamics of Networks* (Princeton, NJ: Princeton University Press, 2006); and Jon M. Kleinberg, "Authoritative Sources in a Hyperlinked Environment," *Journal of the Association for Computing Machinery* 46 (1999): 604–632.

41. See, e.g., Amanda Lenhart, "Adults and Social Network Websites," Pew Research Center, January 14, 2009, http://www.pewinternet.org/2009/01/14 /adults-and-social-network-websites/; Amanda Lenhart and Mary Madden, "Teens, Privacy and Online Social Networks," Pew Research Center, April 18, 2007, http://www.pewinternet.org/2007/04/18/teens-privacy-and-online-social-networks /; Amanda Lenhart, Kristen Purcell, Aaron Smith, and Kathryn Zickuhr, *Social Media and Young Adults,* Pew Research Center, February 3, 2010, http://www .pewinternet.org/files/old-media/Files/Reports/2010/PIP_Social_Media_and _Young_Adults_Report_Final_with_toplines.pdf; Frederic Stutzman and Woodrow Hartzog, "The Case for Online Obscurity," *California Law Review* 101 (2013): 1–49; and Martin Tanis and Tom Postmes, "Social Cues and Impression Formation in CMC," *Journal of Communication* 53 (2003): 676–693.

42. See, e.g., Michael K. Bergman, "White Paper: The Deep Web: Surfacing Hidden Value," Journal of Electric Publishing 7 (2001), https://quod.lib.umich .edu/j/jep/3336451.0007.104?view=text;rgn=main, which notes, "Since they are missing the deep Web when they use such search engines, Internet searchers are therefore searching only 0.03%—or one in 3,000—of the pages available to them today"; Norm Medeiros, "Reap What You Sow: Harvesting the Deep Web," *OCLC Systems and Services* 18 (2002): 18–20; Yanbo Ru and Ellis Horowitz, "Indexing the Invisible Web: A Survey," *Online Information Review* 29 (2005): 249–265; and Russell Kay, "Quickstudy: Deep Web," *Computerworld*, December 19, 2005, which notes that "more than 500 times as much information as traditional search engines 'know about' is available in the deep Web." See also Paul Pedley, *The Invisible Web: Searching the Hidden Parts of the Internet* (Abingdon: Taylor and Francis, 2004).

43. Kate Murphy, "Web Photos That Reveal Secrets Like Where You Live," *New York Times,* August 11, 2010.

44. Alan Westin, *Privacy and Freedom* (New York: Atheneum, 1967), 33.

45. Julie E. Cohen, "Examined Lives: Informational Privacy and the Subject as Object," *Stanford Law Review* 52 (2000): 1423–1425; Hyman Gross, "Privacy

and Autonomy," in *Nomos XIII: Privacy,* ed. J. Roland Pennock and John W. Chapman (New York: Atherton, 1971), 169, 173–174, 181.

46. Helen Nissenbaum, *Privacy in Context: Technology, Policy, and the Integrity of Social Life* (Stanford, CA: Stanford University Press, 2009), 81–82.

47. Jed Rubenfeld, "The Right of Privacy," *Harvard Law Review* 102 (1989): 750–752.

48. This notion is built off arguments made in Elizabeth L. Beardsley, "Privacy: Autonomy and Selective Disclosure," in *Nomos XIII: Privacy,* ed. J. Roland Pennock and John W. Chapman (New York: Atherton, 1971), 56.

4. Setting Boundaries for Design

1. Mike Holt, "Stumped by the Code? NEC Requirements for Identifying Circuit Conductors and More," EC&M, June 11, 2013, http://www.ecmweb.com/qampa/stumped-code-nec-requirements-identifying-circuit-conductors-and-more; National Fire Protection Association, NFPA 70: National Electric Code, http://www.nfpa.org/codes-and-standards/all-codes-and-standards/list-of-codes-and-standards/detail?code=70.

2. Restatement (Third) of Torts: Product Liability (A.L.I. 1998). Strict liability regimes, as opposed to fault based regimes like negligence, can be used to nudge design change—for example, the type and amount of activity level. If application designers were forced to internalize the costs of harmful data breaches, they might design their products so that they do not capture sensitive personally identifiable information like geolocation. See Danielle Keats Citron, "Reservoirs of Danger: The Evolution of Public and Private Law at the Dawn of the Information Age," *Southern California Law Review* 80 (2007): 241–297.

3. Ira S. Rubinstein and Nathaniel Good, "Privacy by Design: A Counterfactual Analysis of Google and Facebook Privacy Incidents," *Berkeley Technology Law Journal* 28 (2013): 1350.

4. Christina Mulligan, "What's the Best Way to Fix the Patent System's Problems?," *Cato Unbound,* September 15, 2014, https://www.cato-unbound.org/2014/09/15/christina-mulligan/whats-best-way-fix-patent-systems-problems.

5. See Paul N. Otto, "Reasonableness Meets Requirements: Regulating Security and Privacy in Software," *Duke Law Journal* 59 (2009): 342, which notes, "Compliance monitoring is a general problem facing software engineers that extends beyond the context of requirements originating in laws and regulations."

6. Paul Ohm, "The Argument against Technology-Neutral Surveillance Laws," *Texas Law Review* 88 (2010): 1685–1713.

7. See Michael Birnhack, "Reverse Engineering Informational Privacy Law," *Yale Journal of Law and Technology* 15 (2012): 28, which notes, "Time and again

we realize that a law that seemed to be technology-neutral at one point (usually the time of its legislation), is in fact based on a particular technology, albeit in a general manner. We often realize the technological mindset that is embedded in the law only once a new technological paradigm replaces the previous one." Instead, Birnhack argues that we should "reverse engineer" laws that regulate technology "to expose the law's hidden assumptions about the regulated technology, i.e., the law's technological mindset." Once we discover our hidden assumptions about the way technology works, we can craft laws within those limitations to achieve flexibility, innovation, and harmonization. See also Bert-Jaap Koops, "Should ICT Regulation Be Technology-Neutral?," in *Starting Points for ICT Regulation: Deconstructing Prevalent Policy One-Liners,* vol. 9, ed. Bert-Jaap Koops, Miriam Lips, Corien Prins, and Maurice Schellekens (The Hague: T.M.C. Asser Press, 2006), 77–108.

8. Paul N. Otto, "Reasonableness Meets Requirements: Regulating Security and Privacy in Software," *Duke Law Journal* 59 (2009): 314–315, asserts that "legal requirements governing security and privacy must take the form of broad standards rather than specific rules. Broad standards allow the law to capture moving targets."

9. As Deirdre K. Mulligan and Jennifer King, "Bridging the Gap between Privacy and Design," *University of Pennsylvania Journal of Constitutional Law* 14 (2012): 992, note, "Privacy regulators across the globe are increasingly demanding that FIPPs inform the design of technical systems. In the past, FIPPs have largely been discharged through the adoption of policies and processes within the firm: privacy has been the bailiwick of lawyers. Now, under the rubric of 'privacy by design,' policymakers are calling on the private sector to use the distinct attributes of code to harden privacy's protection."

10. As Florian Schaub, Rebecca Balebako, Adam L. Durity, and Lorrie Faith Cranor, "A Design Space for Effective Privacy Notices," paper presented at the Symposium on Usable Privacy and Security 2015, Ottawa, July 22–24, 2015, https://www.usenix.org/system/files/conference/soups2015/soups15-paper-schaub .pdf, note, "Existing frameworks and processes for building privacy friendly systems, such as Privacy by Design or privacy impact assessments, focus on the analysis of a system's data practices and less so on the design of notices. Even the OECD report on 'making privacy notices simple' basically states that one should design a simplified notice, conduct usability tests, and deploy it—the crucial point of how to design a simplified notice is not addressed." See also Organisation for Economic Co-operation and Development, *Making Privacy Notices Simple: An OECD Report and Recommendations,* OECD Digital Economy Papers 120 (Paris: Organisation for Economic Co-operation and Development, 2006).

11. Graham Greenleaf, *Asian Data Privacy Laws: Trade and Human Rights Perspectives* (Oxford: Oxford University Press, 2014), 60–61 (citing James Rule,

Douglas McAdam, Linda Stearns, and David Uglow, *The Politics of Privacy: Planning for Personal Data Systems as Powerful Technologies* [Westport, CT: Praeger 1980], 93).

12. Ibid. (quoting Rule et. al., 93).

13. Ibid., 61.

14. James Grimmelmann, "Privacy as Product Safety," *Widener Law Journal* 19 (2010): 820; Mulligan and Jennifer, "Bridging the Gap between Privacy and Design," 993.

15. James Grimmelmann, "Saving Facebook," *Iowa Law Review* 94 (2009): 1137–1206.

16. Sarah Spiekermann and Lorrie F. Cranor, "Engineering Privacy," *IEEE Transactions on Software Engineering* 35 (2009): 67–82. See also Sarah Spiekermann, *Ethical IT Innovation: A Value-Based System Design Approach* (Boca Raton, FL: CRC, 2015).

17. Restatement (Third) of Torts: Products Liability § 1 (A.L.I. 1998) ("One engaged in the business of selling or otherwise distributing products who sells or distributes a defective product is subject to liability for harm to persons or property caused by the defect.").

18. Modern notions of comparative fault allow for proportional recovery based on an allocation of fault. Restatement (Third) of Torts.

19. Grimmelmann, "Privacy as Product Safety," 820.

20. See Danielle Keats Citron, "Mainstreaming Privacy Torts," *California Law Review* 98 (2010): 1805–1852; and Grimmelmann, "Privacy as Product Safety," 814, which notes, "Despite their different historical roots and paths of development in the twentieth century, privacy law and product safety law fit squarely within the intellectual and doctrinal system of modern tort law." See also Eric Jorstad, "The Privacy Paradox," *William Mitchell Law Review* 27 (2001): 1511–1512; Benjamin R. Sachs, "Consumerism and Information Privacy: How Upton Sinclair Can Again Save Us from Ourselves," *Virginia Law Review* 95 (2009): 231–233; Sarah Ludington, "Reining in the Data Traders: A Tort for the Misuse of Personal Information," *Maryland Law Review* 66 (2006): 171–172; and Citron, "Reservoirs of Danger," 244.

21. As Grimmelmann, "Privacy as Product Safety," 816, asserts, "The duty to handle personal data securely has relatively little to do with how the data was acquired: the same concerns arise whether it is consciously entered into an online quiz or generated invisibly by a grocery-store scanner. Instead, the greatest—and, so far, largely untapped—potential of the product safety metaphor is on the front end."

22. Restatement (Third) of Torts: Products Liability § 2 (A.L.I. 1998).

23. Ibid.; emphasis added.

24. Grimmelmann, "Privacy as Product Safety," 821.

25. Restatement (Third) of Torts: Products Liability § 2(b) (A.L.I. 1998).

26. The Office of the Privacy Commissioner of Canada has issued a report critical of the notion of "consent" and requesting input on alternatives; see Office of the Privacy Commissioner of Canada, *Consent and Privacy,* May 2016, https://www.priv.gc.ca/en/opc-actions-and-decisions/research/explore-privacy -research/2016/consent_201605/.

27. Office of the Privacy Commissioner of Canada, "Commissioner Seeks Public Input on Consent," May 11, 2016, https://www.priv.gc.ca/en/opc-news /news-and-announcements/2016/an_160511/.

28. Restatement (Third) of Torts: Products Liability § 2 cmt. j (A.L.I. 1998) ("In general, a product seller is not subject to liability for failing to warn or instruct regarding risks and risk-avoidance measures that should be obvious to, or generally known by, foreseeable product users.").

29. See, e.g., Glittenberg v. Doughboy Recreational Indus., 491 N.W.2d 208, 216 (Mich. 1992) ("A warning is not a Band-Aid to cover a gaping wound, and a product is not safe simply because it carries a warning.").

30. Restatement (Third) of Torts: Products Liability § 2 (A.L.I. 1998).

31. Jessica Rich, "Working Together to Protect Consumers," paper presented at the National Association of Attorneys General Consumer Protection Conference, Washington, DC, May 19, 2014, https://www.ftc.gov/system/files /documents/public_statements/310541/140519naggremarks.pdf, notes that the FTC is "making it a priority to stop fraudulent and deceptive practices targeted at particular groups of consumers, including Spanish-speakers, seniors, financially distressed consumers, service members and veterans, and kids. As fraudsters and marketers increasingly target different segments of the market using highly personalized leads and profiles, we need to make sure we are reaching these populations in the most effective way possible."

32. Federal Trade Commission, In re Request for Information Regarding the Use of Mobile Financial Services by Consumers and Its Potential for Improving the Financial Lives of Economically Vulnerable Consumers, September 10, 2014, https://www.ftc.gov/system/files/documents/advocacy _documents/ftc-staff-comment-consumer-financial-protection-bureau -regarding-use-mobile-financial-services/140912mobilefinancialservices _update.pdf; Federal Trade Commission, "Georgia Board of Dentistry Proposal to Restrict Services by Dental Hygienists Would Harm the State's Most Vulnerable Consumers," January 5, 2011, https://www.ftc.gov/news-events /press-releases/2011/01/georgia-board-dentistry-proposal-restrict-services -dental; Federal Trade Commission, "FTC Acts to Halt Medical Plan Scheme That Targeted Vulnerable Consumers," October 10, 2012, https://www.ftc.gov /news-events/press-releases/2012/10/ftc-acts-halt-medical-plan-scheme -targeted-vulnerable-consumers.

33. Lesley Fair, "Full Disclosure," Federal Trade Commission, September 23, 2014, https://www.ftc.gov/news-events/blogs/business-blog/2014/09/full -disclosure.

34. Schaub et al., "A Design Space for Effective Privacy Notices."

35. In re DesignerWare, LLC, FTC File No. 112 3151, No. C-4390 (F.T.C. Apr. 11, 2013).

36. Complaint, FTC v. Neovi, Inc., No. 306-CV-01952-WQH-JMA (S.D. Cal. Sept. 19, 2006).

37. See Robert L. Rabin, "Enabling Torts," *DePaul Law Review* 49 (1999): 437.

38. Pierce v. Standow, 163 Cal. App. 2d 286 (1st Dist. 1958); Schneider v. Midtown Motor Co., 854 P.2d 1322 (Colo. Ct. App. 1992); Alexander v. Alterman Transp. Lines Inc., 387 So. 2d 422 (Fla. Dist. Ct. App. 1980); V.L. Nicholson Constr. Co. v. Lane, 150 S.W. 2d 1069 (Tenn. 1941).

39. Citron, "Mainstreaming Privacy Torts," *California Law Review* 98 (2010): 1836–1837.

40. Rich, "Working Together to Protect Consumers."

41. Restatement (Third) of Torts: Liability for Economic Harm § 9 (A.L.I. 2014).

42. FTC Statement on Deception," letter from James C. Miller III, chairman, Federal Trade Commission, to John D. Dingell, chairman, House Committee on Energy and Commerce, October 14, 1983, reprinted in In re Cliffdale Assocs., Inc., 103 F.T.C. 110, app. at 175–184 (1984) (decision and order), https://www.ftc .gov/system/files/documents/public_statements/410531/831014deceptionstmt.pdf. See also the letter from FTC commissioners to Senators Wendell H. Ford and John C. Danforth, December 17, 1980, reprinted in In re Int'l Harvester Co., 104 F.T.C. 949, app. at 1070–1076 (1984).

43. "FTC Statement on Deception," 175.

44. Satnam Narang, "Tinder Spam: A Year Later, Spammers Still Flirting with Mobile Dating App," Symantec, July 15, 2014, https://www.symantec.com /connect/blogs/tinder-spam-year-later-spammers-still-flirting-mobile-dating -app; Satnam Narang, "Tinder Safe Dating Spam Uses Safety to Scam Users out of Money," Symantec, July 21, 2016, https://www.symantec.com/connect/blogs /tinder-safe-dating-spam-uses-safety-scam-users-out-money.

45. Steven Melendez, "Tinder Bots Have Evolved to Mimic the Girl Next Door," Motherboard, February 10, 2015, https://motherboard.vice.com/en_us /article/nze9zm/tinder-bots-next-door.

46. Fabian, "Meet Ransom32: The first JavaScript ransomware," *Emsisoft Blog*, January 1, 2016, http://blog.emsisoft.com/2016/01/01/meet-ransom32-the-first -javascript-ransomware/.

47. See, e.g., 18 U.S. Code § 1030.

48. Federal Trade Commission, "FTC Charges Operators of "Jerk.com" Website with Deceiving Consumers," April 7, 2014, https://www.ftc.gov/news

-events/press-releases/2014/04/ftc-charges-operators-jerkcom-website-deceiving
-consumers.

49. Ibid.

50. Matt Blaze (@mattblaze), "WTF? Pennsylvania State Police license plate reader SUV camouflaged as Google Street View vehicle," Twitter, May 11, 2016, 8:05 a.m., https://twitter.com/mattblaze/status/730413475231617028; PA State Police (@PAStatePolice), "Matt, this is not a PSP vehicle. If this is LPR technology, other agencies and companies might make use of it," Twitter, May 11, 2016, 9:41 a.m., https://twitter.com/PAStatePolice/status/730437661 807284224.

51. Dustin Slaughter, "This Isn't a Google Streetview Car, It's a Government Spy Truck," Motherboard, May 12, 2016, https://motherboard.vice.com/en_us /article/bmvjwm/this-isnt-a-google-streetview-car-its-a-government-spy-truck.

52. See Janice Tsai, Serge Egelman, Lorrie Cranor, and Alessandro Acquisti, "The Effect of Online Privacy Information on Purchasing Behavior: An Experimental Study," *Information Systems Research* 22 (2011): 254–268; Serge Egelman, Janice Tsai, Lorrie Faith Cranor, and Alessandro Acquisti, "Studying the Impact of Privacy Information on Online Purchase Decisions," paper presented at the Workshop on Privacy and HCI: Methodologies for Studying Privacy Issues, CHI 2006, Montreal, April 22–27, 2006, http://cups.cs.cmu.edu/pubs/chi06.pdf; Serge Egelman, Janice Tsai, Lorrie Faith Cranor, and Alessandro Acquisti, "Timing Is Everything? The Effects of Timing and Placement of Online Privacy Indicators," paper presented at CHI 2009, Boston, April 3–9, 2009, which observes that consumers took into account privacy indicators, when available, when purchasing from websites; Julia Gideon, Lorrie Cranor, Serge Egelman, and Alessandro Acquisti, "Power Strips, Prophylactics, and Privacy, Oh My!," paper presented at the Symposium On Usable Privacy and Security 2006, Pittsburgh, July 12–14, 2006, which finds that privacy policy comparison information had an impact on non-privacy-sensitive purchases but more influence on privacy-sensitive purchases; and Lorrie Faith Cranor, "What Do They "Indicate?" Evaluating Security and Privacy Indicators, Interactions," *Interactions* 13 (2006): 45–57, which notes the disappointing effectiveness of privacy indicators because of the ease in fooling humans.

53. See Benny Evangelista, "Tweets Preserved for All Time Under Library of Congress Deal," *San Francisco Gate,* April 16, 2010, which notes, "The only exceptions are tweets from a small percentage of protected accounts."

54. Complaint at 4, In re Google Inc., FTC File No. 102 3136, No. C-4336 (F.T.C. Oct. 13, 2011), http://www.ftc.gov/sites/default/files/documents/cases/2011 /10/111024googlebuzzcmpt.pdf.

55. Complaint at 1, In re True Ultimate Standards Everywhere, Inc., FTC File No. 132 3219, No. C-4512 (F.T.C. March 12, 2015), https://www.ftc.gov/system/files

/documents/cases/150318trust-ecmpt.pdf; In re Stanton, FTC File No. 072 3165, No. C-4287 (F.T.C. Apr. 5, 2010).

56. Complaint at 1, In re Path, Inc., FTC File No. 122 3158, No. C-130448 (F.T.C. Feb. 1, 2013), https://www.ftc.gov/sites/default/files/documents/cases/2013 /02/130201pathinccmpt.pdf.

57. For more information about how subtle cues can affect our thoughts and behaviors, *see* Adam Alter, *Drunk Tank Pink: And Other Unexpected Forces That Shape How We Think, Feel, and Behave* (New York: Penguin, 2014).

58. Cigarette Rule Statement of Basis and Purpose, 29 FR 8324, 8352 (July 2, 1964).

59. "FTC Statement on Deception," https://www.ftc.gov/system/files /documents/public_statements/410531/831014deceptionstmt.pdf ("A misrepresentation is an express or implied statement contrary to fact. A misleading omission occurs when qualifying information necessary to prevent a practice, claim, representation, or reasonable expectation or belief from being misleading is not disclosed. Not all omissions are deceptive, even if providing the information would benefit consumers.").

60. Federal Trade Commission, *Mobile Privacy Disclosures Building Trust through Transparency* (Washington, DC: Federal Trade Commission, 2013), https://www.ftc.gov/sites/default/files/documents/reports/mobile-privacy -disclosures-building-trust-through-transparency-federal-trade-commission -staff-report/130201mobileprivacyreport.pdf.

61. Complaint at 7–9, In re Facebook, Inc., FTC File No. 092 3184, No. C-4365 (F.T.C. July 27, 2012), http://www.ftc.gov/sites/default/files/documents/cases/2012 /08/120810facebookcmpt.pdf.

62. Complaint for Permanent Injunction and Other Equitable Relief at 19, FTC v. Frostwire, LLC, No. 1:11-cv-23643 (S.D. Fla. Oct. 12, 2011), http://www.ftc .gov/sites/default/files/documents/cases/2011/10/111011frostwirecmpt.pdf.

63. Yang Wang, Gregory Norcie, Saranga Komanduri, Alessandro Acquisti, Pedro Giovanni Leon, and Lorrie Faith Cranor, "'I Regretted the Minute I Pressed Share': A Qualitative Study of Regrets on Facebook," in *Proceedings of the Seventh Symposium on Usable Privacy and Security* (New York: Association for Computing Machinery, 2011), https://www.andrew.cmu.edu/user/pgl/FB -Regrets.pdf. See also Kelly Moore and James McElroy, "The Influence of Personality on Facebook Usage, Wall Postings, and Regret," *Computers in Human Behavior* 28 (2012): 267–274, https://pdfs.semanticscholar.org/035f/eaca8 88c03c2112519fd10b346de50809fb4.pdf.

64. Stanford Persuasive Tech Lab, "Overview," http://captology.stanford.edu /about.

65. Nir Eyal, *Hooked: How to Build Habit-Forming Products* (New York: Penguin, 2014).

66. Natasha Dow Schüll, *Addiction by Design: Machine Gambling in Las Vegas* (Princeton, NJ: Princeton University Press, 2012)

67. Alexis C. Madrigal, "The Machine Zone: This Is Where You go When You Just Can't Stop Looking at Pictures on Facebook," *Atlantic,* July 31, 2013, http://www.theatlantic.com/technology/archive/2013/07/the-machine-zone-this -is-where-you-go-when-you-just-cant-stop-looking-at-pictures-on-facebook /278185/.

68. Ian Leslie, "The Scientists Who Make Apps Addictive," *Economist 1843,* October–November 2016, https://www.1843magazine.com/features/the-scientists -who-make-apps-addictive; Bianca Bosker, "The Binge Breaker," *Atlantic,* November 2016, http://www.theatlantic.com/magazine/archive/2016/11/the-binge -breaker/501122/.

69. See, e.g., Cass R. Sunstein, Christine Jolls, and Richard Thaler, "A Behavioral Approach to Law and Economics," *Stanford Law Review* 50 (1998): 1477, which explains, "Bounded rationality . . . refers to the obvious fact that human cognitive abilities are not infinite."

70. See Daniel Kahneman, *Thinking Fast and Slow* (New York: Farrar, Straus and Giroux, 2011); Dan Ariely, *Predictably Irrational: The Hidden Forces That Shape Our Decisions* (New York: HarperCollins, 2008); Daniel Gilbert, *Stumbling upon Happiness* (New York: Vintage, 2006).

71. S. Shyam Sundar, Jinyoung Kim, Andrew Gambino, and Mary Beth Rosson, "Six Ways to Enact Privacy by Design: Cognitive Heuristics That Predict Users' Online Information Disclosure," paper presented at CHI 2016, San Jose, CA, May 7–12, 2016, https://networkedprivacy2016.files.wordpress.com/2015/11 /sundar-et-al-final_chi-pbd-workshop-161.pdf.

72. S. Shyam Sundar, Hyunjin Kang, Mu Wu, Eun Go, and Bo Zhang, "Unlocking the Privacy Paradox: Do Cognitive Heuristics Hold the Key?," in *CHI 2013 Extended Abstracts* (New York: Association for Computing Machinery, 2013), https://pdfs.semanticscholar.org/8ea2/5edadef2ed8a5bb16bbf19117cffde84a 6ac.pdf.

73. Leslie, "The Scientists."

74. 12 U.S.C.A. § 5531 (West); emphasis added.

75. See Patrick M. Corrigan, "'Abusive' Acts and Practices: Dodd-Frank's Behaviorally Informed Authority over Consumer Credit Markets and Its Application to Teaser Rates, *N.Y.U. Journal of Legislation and Public Policy* 18 (2015): 127, which notes, "While shopping for the best offer, consumers may misperceive the real costs and benefits of a consumer product or service because of a lack of information about the product or service or due to a misunderstanding of the information available to them. The former is said to be a problem of imperfect information, while the latter is said to be a

problem of imperfect or bounded rationality. Problems of imperfect information are extrinsic to the consumer, while problems of imperfect rationality are intrinsic."

76. Ryan Calo, "Digital Market Manipulation," *George Washington Law Review* 82 (2014): 999.

77. Ibid., 1017.

78. Consider race-based targeting as a test case for problematic price and targeted advertising discrimination. See Alethea Lange and Rena Coen, "How Does the Internet Know Your Race?," Center for Democracy and Technology, September 7, 2016, https://cdt.org/blog/how-does-the-internet-know-your-race/.

79. Jeffrey Rachlinski, "Cognitive Errors, Individual Differences, and Paternalism," *University of Chicago Law Review* 73 (2006): 228. See also Jon D. Hanson and Douglas A. Kysar, "Taking Behavioralism Seriously: The Problem of Market Manipulation," *NYU Law Review* 754 (1999): 637; and Xavier Gabaix and David Laibson, "Shrouded Attributes, Consumer Myopia, and Information Suppression in Competitive Markets," *Quarterly Journal of Economics* 121 (2006): 506–511, which explains that firms can market goods with "salient" and "shrouded" attributes.

80. For a fascinating case study about the effect of default choices on avoiding fraud, see Robert Letzler, Ryan Sandler, Ania Jaroszewicz, Isaac T. Knowles, and Luke Olson, "Knowing When to Quit: Default Choices, Demographics and Fraud," October 8, 2014, https://www.fdic.gov/news/conferences/consumersymposium/2015/presentations/letzler.pdf.

81. Ryan Tate, Gregory Conti, Alexander Farmer, and Edward Sobiesk, "Evaluating Adversarial Interfaces: An Automated Approach," *IEEE Technology and Society* 35 (2016): 56–68.

82. See Gregory Conti and Edward Sobiesk, "Malicious Interface Design: Exploiting the User 271," paper presented at WWW 2010: The 19th International World Wide Web Conference, Raleigh, NC, April 26–30, 2010, http://www.rumint.org/gregconti/publications/201004_malchi.pdf, which argues that security and human-computer interaction committees need to come together to fix deceptive designs.

83. Gregory Conti and Edward Sobiesk, "Malicious Interfaces and Personalization's Uninviting Future," *IEEE Security and Privacy* 7 (2009), http://www.rumint.org/gregconti/publications/j3pri.pdf, 73.

84. Conti and Sobiesk, "Malicious Interface Design."

85. Tate et al., "Evaluating Adversarial Interfaces."

86. Troy Hunt, "Your Affairs Were Never Discreet—Ashley Madison Always Disclosed Customer Identities, July 20, 2015, https://www.troyhunt.com/your-affairs-were-never-discrete-ashley/; Lorenzo Franceschi-Bicchierai, "Who

Needs Hackers? You Can Already See Who's on Cheating Site AshleyMadison,"
Motherboard, July 20, 2015, http://motherboard.vice.com/read/who-needs
-hackers-you-can-already-see-whos-on-cheating-site-ashleymadison.

87. [Restatement,] Helicoid Gage Div. of American Chain and Cable Co. v.
Howell, 511 S.W. 2d 573 (Tex. Civ. App. 1974).

88. See Ben Wojdyla, "The Top Automotive Engineering Failures: The Ford
Pinto Fuel Tanks," *Popular Mechanics*, May 20, 2011, http://www
.popularmechanics.com/cars/a6700/top-automotive-engineering-failures-ford
-pinto-fuel-tanks/; and RAND Corporation, "Asbestos Litigation," http://www
.rand.org/topics/asbestos-litigation.html.

89. 15 U.S.C. § 45(n) (2012) (limiting the FTC's authority to declare act or
practice unlawful on unfairness grounds).

90. "FTC Policy Statement on Unfairness," appended to International
Harvester Co., 104 F.T.C. 949, 1070 (1984); see 15 U.S.C. § 45(n) (2012).

91. Harry Surden, "Structural Rights in Privacy," *Southern Methodist
University Law Review* 60 (2007): 1606.

92. Daniel J. Solove, "Access and Aggregation: Public Records, Privacy and
the Constitution," *Minnesota Law Review* 86 (2002): 1139.

93. Michael Hiltzij, "Should CalPERS Post Pensioners' Financial Data
Online?," *Los Angeles Times,* July 19, 2013.

94. danah boyd, "Facebook's 'Privacy Trainwreck': Exposure, Invasion, and
Drama," September 8, 2006, http://www.danah.org/papers/FacebookAndPrivacy
.html; Zeynep Tufekci, "Can You See Me Now? Audience and Disclosure
Regulation in Online Social Network Sites," *Bulletin of Science and Technology*
28 (2008): 20–36.

95. See Data Protection Working Party of the European Commission,
"Guidelines on Data Protection Impact Assessment (DPIA) and Determining
Whether Processing Is 'Likely to Result in a High Risk' for the Purposes of
Regulation 2016/679," Article 29, April 2017, ec.europa.eu/newsroom/document.
cfm?doc_id=44137.

96. See Danielle Keats Citron, "Spying Inc.," *Washington and Lee Law Review*
72 (2015): 1250, which notes, "Software secretly tracking a phone's activities exacts
profound costs to privacy while serving no legitimate purpose."

97. "mSpyVIP, Cell Phone Spy—mSpy Review," YouTube, December 15, 2012,
https://www.youtube.com/watch?v=YNbT0At4Tsg.

98. Brian Krebs, "More Evidence of mSpy Apathy over Breach," Krebs On
Security, May 27, 2015, https://krebsonsecurity.com/2015/05/more-evidence-of
-mspy-apathy-over-breach/.

99. See, e.g., Aspen Way Enters., Inc., F.T.C. File No. 112 3151, No. C-4392
(F.T.C. Apr. 11, 2013); CyberSpy Software, LLC and Trace R. Spence, F.T.C. File
No. 082 3160, No. 08-CV-01872 (F.T.C. Nov. 17, 2008) (alleging that selling

spyware and showing customers how to remotely install it on other people's computers without their knowledge or consent is an unfair and deceptive trade practice). See also Federal Trade Commission, "Spyware and Malware," www.ftc .gov/news-events/media-resources/identity-theft-and-data-security/spyware-and -malware.

100. Aspen Way Enters., Inc., F.T.C. File No. 112 3151.

101. 18 U.S.C. § 2511 (2012); S. REP. NO. 90-1097, at 2183.

102. Danielle Keats Citron, "Spying Inc.," 1265.

103. Privacy Rights Clearinghouse, "Data Breaches," http://www.privacyrights .org/data-breach.

104. Derek E. Bambauer, "Privacy Versus Security," *Journal of Criminal Law and Criminology* 103 (2013): 669.

105. Federal Trade Commission, "Commission Statement Marking the FTC's 50th Data Security Settlement," January 31, 2014, http://www.ftc.gov/system/files /documents/cases/140131gmrstatement.pdf.

106. See Woodrow Hartzog and Daniel J. Solove, "The Scope and Potential of FTC Data Protection," *George Washington Law Review* 83 (2015): 2230–2300; 16 C.F.R. § 682.3(a); 45 C.F.R. §§ 164.308–314; 16 C.F.R. §§ 314.3–314.4.

107. PCI Security Standards Council, "PCI SSC Data Security Standards Overview," https://www.pcisecuritystandards.org/security_standards/.

108. For more on this topic, see Natali Helberger, Frederik Zuiderveen Borgesius, and Agustin Reyna, "The Perfect Match? A Closer Look at the Relationship between EU Consumer Law and Data Protection Law," *Common Market Law Review* 54 (2017): 1427–1465.

5. A Tool Kit for Privacy Design

1. As Joshua A. T. Fairfield notes, "a corporate-drafted contract will still favor the corporation on balance, no matter what tools of interpretation or equity a court brings to bear. On the contrary, the modern tools of automated contract formation should be available to the consumer and corporation alike. Courts therefore can and should enforce consumer-offered contract terms—such as the preference not to be tracked—as part of a broader effort to restore balance to online contract law and the consumer information market." Fairfield, "'Do Not Track' as Contract," *Vanderbilt Journal of Entertainment and Technology Law* 14 (2012): 548.

2. In Re Google Inc. Cookie Placement Consumer Privacy Litigation, Case No. 1:12-md-02358 (D.Del.).

3. See Chris Jay Hoofnagle, Ashkan Soltani, Nathaniel Good, Dietrich J. Wambach, and Mika D. Ayenson, "Behavioral Advertising: The Offer You Cannot Refuse," *Harvard Law and Policy Review* 6 (2012): 277, which notes that "by

signing up for some 'free' offer, advertisers can link the information provided by the user to the existing cookies on that user's machine."

4. In re DoubleClick Inc. Privacy Litigation, 154 F. Supp. 2d 497 (S.D.N.Y. 2001).

5. Crystal N. Skelton, "Cookies, Promises, and California: Why the 3rd Circuit Revived Privacy Claims against Google," Ad Law Access, November 19, 2015, http://www.adlawaccess.com/2015/11/articles/cookies-promises-and-california -why-the-3rd-circuit-revived-privacy-claims-against-google/.

6. European Commission, Directive on Privacy and Electronic Communications (E-Privacy Directive) Directive 2002/58/EC (2002) (Amendments 2009). But see Joon Ian Wong, "Consenting to Cookies is Driving Europeans Nuts—A New Law Might Kill the Pop-ups," Quartz, January 12, 2017, https://qz.com /883232/eu-cookies-and-eprivacy-directive-the-proposed-regulation-moves -cookie-consent-to-the-browser/.

7. Complaint, In re Scanscout, FTC. No. 102 3185 (2011).

8. M. Ryan Calo, "People Can Be So Fake: A New Dimension to Privacy and Technology Scholarship," Penn State Law Review 114 (2010): 809–855; Kate Darling, "Extending Legal Protections to Social Robots: The Effects of Anthropomorphism, Empathy, and Violent Behavior Towards Robotic Objects," in Robot Law, ed. Ryan Calo, A. Michael Froomkin, and Ian Kerr (Cheltenham, England: Elgar, 2016), 213–232.

9. Harry Brignull, "Dark Patterns: Inside the Interfaces Designed to Trick You," The Verge, August 29, 2013, https://www.theverge.com/2013/8/29 /4640308/dark-patterns-inside-the-interfaces-designed-to-trick-you. See also Dark Patterns, http://darkpatterns.org/.

10. Tristan Harris, "How Technology Hijacks People's Minds—From a Magician and Google's Design Ethicist," Observer, June 1, 2016, http://observer .com/2016/06/how-technology-hijacks-peoples-minds%E2%80%8A -%E2%80%8Afrom-a-magician-and-googles-design-ethicist/.

11. Yael Grauer, "Dark Patterns Are Designed to Trick You (and They're All Over the Web)," Ars Technica, July 28, 2016, https://arstechnica.com/information -technology/2016/07/dark-patterns-are-designed-to-trick-you-and-theyre-all -over-the-web/.

12. Federal Trade Commission, "Putting Disclosures to the Test," https://www.ftc.gov/news-events/events-calendar/2016/09/putting-disclosures -test.

13. Joseph Turow, Michael Hennessy, and Nora Draper, The Tradeoff Fallacy: How Marketers Are Misrepresenting American Consumers and Opening Them Up to Exploitation (Philadelphia: Annenberg School for Communication, University of Pennsylvania, 2015), https://www.asc.upenn.edu/sites/default/files /TradeoffFallacy_1.pdf.

14. Defense Advanced Research Projects Agency, "DARPA 'Brandeis' Program Aims to Ensure Online Privacy through Technology," March 11, 2015, http://www.darpa.mil/news-events/2015-03-11.

15. Alex Hern, "US Government Increases Funding for Tor, Giving $1.8m in 2013," *Guardian*, July 29, 2014; KeriLynn Engel, "Follow the Money: How the US Government Funds Tor," Who Is Hosting This?, http://www.whoishostingthis .com/blog/2014/11/17/who-funded-tor/.

16. Sharon Solomon, "11 Essential Bug Bounty Programs of 2015," Tripwire, February 10, 2015, https://www.tripwire.com/state-of-security/vulnerability -management/11-essential-bug-bounty-programs-of-2015/.

17. Aaron Massey, "Technical Standards and Privacy Law" (unpublished manuscript, 2016).

18. Evan Selinger and Woodrow Hartzog, "Opinion: It's Time for an About-Face on Facial Recognition," *Christian Science Monitor,* June 22, 2015, https://www.csmonitor.com/World/Passcode/Passcode-Voices/2015/0622 /Opinion-It-s-time-for-an-about-face-on-facial-recognition; Natasha Singer, "Wrangling over 'Do Not Track,'" *New York Times,* July 15, 2013.

19. Other standards, such as the Platform for Privacy Preferences and Do Not Track, have had rockier roads to development and adoption. William Mc-Geveran, "Programmed Privacy Promises: P3P and Web Privacy Law," *NYU Law Review* 76 (2001): 1812–1854; Lorrie Cranor, Marc Langheinrich, Massimo Marchiori, Martin Presler-Marshall, and Joseph Reagle, "World Wide Web Consortium, The Platform for Privacy Preferences 1.0 (P3P1.0) Specification" (unpublished manuscript, September 28, 2001), http://www.w3.org/TR/2001/WD -P3P-20010928/; Joshua A. T. Fairfield, "Do-Not-Track As Default," *Northwestern Journal of Technology and Intellectual Property Law* 11 (2013): 580.

20. Massey, "Technical Standards and Privacy Law"; Roy T. Fielding and Richard N. Taylor, "Principled Design of the Modern Web Architecture," in *Proceedings of the 22nd International Conference on Software Engineering* (New York: Association for Computing Machinery, 2000), 407–416.

21. International Organization for Standardization, "ISO / IEC 27000 Family—Information Security Management Systems," http://www.iso.org/iso /iso27001.

22. Matt Blaze, Twitter, https://twitter.com/mattblaze/status /919932388548998928l (republishing Mathew Green, who wrote, "It's not a coincidence that IETF crypto protocols get a lot more review than IEEE ones, and most of the reason is that I can Google any RFC"); Dan Goodin, "Severe Flaw in WPA2 Protocol Leaves Wi-Fi Traffic Open to Eavesdropping," Ars Technica, October 16, 2017, https://arstechnica.com/information-technology/2017 /10/severe-flaw-in-wpa2-protocol-leaves-wi-fi-traffic-open-to-eavesdropping/.

23. Alan Travis and Charles Arthur, "EU Court Backs 'Right to Be Forgotten': Google Must Amend Results on Request," *Guardian,* May 13, 2014.

24. Rigo Wenning, "The ECJ Is Right, the Result Is Wrong," Internet-Law, May 14, 2016, http://www.internet-law.de/2014/05/the-ecj-is-right-the-result-is -wrong.html.

25. Jonathan L. Zittrain, *The Future of the Internet—And How to Stop It* (New Haven, CT: Yale University Press, 2008), 225–227.

26. White House Press Office, "Executive Order—Improving Critical Infrastructure Cybersecurity," *The White House,* February 12, 2013, https://www .whitehouse.gov/the-press-office/2013/02/12/executive-order-improving-critical -infrastructure-cybersecurity. The framework was developed in a series of multistakeholder meetings over the course of a year. NIST Cybersecurity Framework, https://www.nist.gov/cyberframework.

27. Massey, "Technical Standards and Privacy Law."

28. Nicole Perlroth and David E. Sanger, "Obama Won't Seek Access to Encrypted User Data," *New York Times,* October 10, 2015.

29. Harold Abelson, Ross Anderson, Steven M. Bellovin, Josh Benaloh, Matt Blaze, Whitfield Diffie, John Gilmore, Matthew Green, Susan Landau, Peter G. Neumann, Ronald L. Rivest, Jeffrey I. Schiller, Bruce Schneier, Michael Specter, and Daniel J. Weitzner, "Keys Under Doormats: Mandating Insecurity by Re-quiring Government Access to All Data and Communications," *Computer Science and Artificial Intelligence Laboratory Technical Report,* July 6, 2015, https://dspace .mit.edu/bitstream/handle/1721.1/97690/MIT-CSAIL-TR-2015-026.pdf; Matt Blaze, "A Key Under the Doormat Isn't Safe. Neither Is An Encryption Backdoor," *Washington Post,* December 15, 2015, https://www.washingtonpost.com/news/in -theory/wp/2015/12/15/how-the-nsa-tried-to-build-safe-encryption-but-failed/.

30. Perlroth and Sanger, "Obama Won't Seek Access," reports that "[Peter G.] Neumann and other top cryptographers and computer scientists argued that there was no way for the government to have a back door into encrypted communications without creating an opening that would be exploited by Chinese and Russian intelligence agents, cybercriminals and terrorist groups." See also Mark Hosenball and Dustin Volz, "Exclusive: White House Declines to Support Encryption Legislation—Sources," Reuters, April 7, 2016, http://www .reuters.com/article/us-apple-encryption-legislation/exclusive-white-house -declines-to-support-encryption-legislation-sources-idUSKCN0X32M4; and Andrea Peterson and Ellen Nakashima, "Obama Administration Explored Ways to Bypass Encryption," *Washington Post* September 24, 2015.

31. "The Computer Fraud and Abuse Act Hampers Security Research, Electronic Frontier Foundation, https://www.eff.org/document/cfaa-and-security -researchers; Aaron Alva, "DMCA Security Research Exemption for Consumer Devices," Federal Trade Commission, October 28, 2016, https://www.ftc.gov

/news-events/blogs/techftc/2016/10/dmca-security-research-exemption
-consumer-devices; Andrea M. Matwyshyn, "The Law of the Zebra," *Berkeley Technology Law Journal* 28 (2013): 223.

32. Joshua A. T. Fairfield, *Owned: Property, Privacy, and the New Digital Serfdom* (Cambridge: Cambridge University Press, 2017); Courtney Nash, "Cory Doctorow on Legally Disabling DRM (for Good)," O'Reilly, August 17, 2016, https://www.oreilly.com/ideas/cory-doctorow-on-legally-disabling-drm-for -good.

33. See David Thaw, "Criminalizing Hacking, Not Dating: Reconstructing the CFAA Intent Requirement," *Journal of Criminal Law and Criminology* 103 (2013): 907–948.

34. Fairfield, "'Do Not Track' as Contract."

35. See Tabreez Govani and Harriet Pashley, "Student Awareness of the Privacy Implications When Using Facebook," paper presented at the Privacy Poster Fair at the Carnegie Mellon University School of Library and Information Science, 2005; http://lorrie.cranor.org/courses/fa05/tubzhlp.pdf, which finds that 80 percent of the users surveyed for the study had not read Facebook's privacy policy; and Andy Greenberg, "Who Reads the Fine Print Online? Less Than One Person in 1000," *Forbes,* April 8, 2010, https://www.forbes.com/sites/firewall/2010 /04/08/who-reads-the-fine-print-online-less-than-one-person-in-1000 /#67474a2f7017, which notes that studies have found that only 0.11 percent of users will view a site's terms of service by clicking on a link.

36. Mary Madden and Aaron Smith, "Reputation Management and Social Media: How People Monitor Their Identity and Search for Others Online," Pew Research Center, May 26, 2010, http://www.pewinternet.org/Reports/2010 /Reputation-Management.aspx, which finds that "71% of social networking users ages 18–29 have changed the privacy settings on their profile to limit what they share with others online."

37. See Facebook, "Statement of Rights and Responsibilities," http://www .facebook.com/terms.php?ref=pf, which states, in the first term of the agreement, "Your privacy is very important to us," and refers users to Facebook's data policy; and Facebook, "Data Policy," https://www.facebook.com/about/privacy/, which informs users how Facebook uses and shares their information, along with giving extensive other terms.

38. See Joseph Turow and Chris Jay Hoofnagle, "The FTC and Consumer Privacy in the Coming Decade," paper presented at the Federal Trade Commission Tech-ade Workshop, November 8, 2006, http://www.law.berkeley.edu/files /FTC_Consumer_Privacy.pdf, which finds that only 1.4 percent of study participants reported reading the terms of standard-form electronic agreements often and thoroughly, 66.2 percent rarely read or browse these agreements, and 7.7 percent stated that they have never noticed or read them.

39. See Complaint at 2, 12, Del Vecchio v. Amazon.com, Inc., No. C11-366-RSL, 2011 U.S. Dist. LEXIS 138314 (W.D. Wash. Nov. 30, 2011) (describing users' use of privacy settings, and alleging that Amazon circumvented the settings established by users); and Complaint at 2, 7, Ferguson v. Classmates Online, Inc., No. 2:10-CV-00365-RAJ (W.D. Wash. Mar. 5, 2010) (alleging a claim for, among others, breach of contract for failing to keep confidential information protected by privacy settings).

40. For more on this issue, see Nancy S. Kim, *Wrap Contracts: Foundations and Ramifications* (New York: Oxford University Press, 2013); and Margaret Jane Radin, *Boilerplate: The Fine Print, Vanishing Rights, and the Rule of Law* (Princeton, NJ: Princeton University Press, 2013).

41. Restatement (Second) of Contracts § 2(1) (1981).

42. See Facebook, "Statement of Rights and Responsibilities," which outlines what permissions a user gives to Facebook in relation to the type of content the user provides.

43. Facebook, "Privacy Policy."

44. Fred Stutzman, Robert Capra, and Jamila Thompson, "Factors Mediating Disclosure in Social Network Sites," *Computers in Human Behavior* 27 (2011): 590–598.

45. Myspace, "Terms and Conditions," http://www.myspace.com/help/terms.

46. Facebook, "Statement of Rights and Responsibilities." Facebook's terms of use agreement contains numerous references to the ability to control who sees your information via privacy settings:

> [S]ubject to your privacy and application settings: you grant us a non-exclusive, transferable, sub-licensable, royalty-free, worldwide license to use any IP content that you post on or in connection with Facebook ("IP License"). . . . You can use your privacy settings to limit how your name and profile picture may be associated with commercial, sponsored, or related content (such as a brand you like) served or enhanced by us. You give us permission to use your name and profile picture in connection with that content, subject to the limits you place.

Yet, arguably, the default for some of the settings is contrary to the spirit of these terms. For example, the "Wall Photos" album is, by default, viewable by everyone. Facebook, "Who Can See My "Wall Photos" Album?," https://www.facebook.com/help/?faq=20139.

47. See Omri Ben-Shahar and Carl E. Schneider, "The Failure of Mandated Disclosure," *University of Pennsylvania Law Review* 159 (2011): 649–651.

48. Ibid, 651.

49. See Peter P. Swire, "The Surprising Virtues of the New Financial Privacy Law," *Minnesota Law Review* 86 (2002): 1264, which notes that "critics have

largely overlooked, however, important benefits from these notices. Perhaps most significantly, publication of the notices and the new legal obligation to comply with them have forced financial institutions to engage in considerable self-scrutiny as to their data handling practices."

50. See, e.g., Lukasz Jedrzejczyk, Blaine A. Price, Arosha K. Bandara, and Bashar Nuseibeh, "On The Impact of Real-Time Feedback on Users' Behaviour in Mobile Location-Sharing Applications," paper presented at the Symposium on Usable Privacy and Security 2010, Redmond, WA, July 14–16, 2010, http://oro.open.ac.uk/22571/1/RTF-SOUPS2010-camera-ready.0.1.pdf.

51. See M. Ryan Calo, "Against Notice Skepticism in Privacy (and Elsewhere)," *Notre Dame Law Review* 87 (2012): 1027, which notes, "Unlike traditional notice that relies upon text or symbols to convey information, emerging strategies of 'visceral' notice leverage a consumer's very experience of a product or service to warn or inform. . . . [F]or a variety of reasons, experience as a form of privacy disclosure is worthy of further study before we give in to calls to abandon notice as a regulatory strategy in privacy and elsewhere."

52. For example, people regularly misperceive the advertising industry's AdOption icon. See U.S. Committee on Commerce, Science, and Transportation, "The Need for Privacy Protections: Is Industry Self-Regulation Adequate?," hearing webcast, at 34:26.

53. Andy Greenberg, "Google's Chrome Hackers Are About to Upend Your Idea of Web Security," *Wired,* November 2, 2016, https://www.wired.com/2016/11/googles-chrome-hackers-flip-webs-security-model/.

54. Daniel E. Ho, "Fudging the Nudge: Information Disclosure and Restaurant Grading," *Yale Law Journal* 122 (2012): 574–688.

55. Information and Privacy Commissioner of Ontario, "Introduction to PbD," https://www.ipc.on.ca/english/Privacy/Introduction-to-PbD/.

56. Ann Cavoukian, "Privacy by Design: From Rhetoric to Reality," https://www.ipc.on.ca/wp-content/uploads/resources/pbdbook-from-rhetoric-to-reality.pdf, 192.

57. "Resolution on Privacy by Design," 32nd International Conference of Data Protection and Privacy Commissioners, Jerusalem, October 27–29, 2010, https://secure.edps.europa.eu/EDPSWEB/webdav/site/mySite/shared/Documents/Cooperation/Conference_int/10-10-27_Jerusalem_Resolutionon_PrivacybyDesign_EN.pdf.

58. David Goodis and Stephen McCammon, "Privacy by Design in Law, Policy and Practice," Presentation at the International Association of Privacy Professionals, Canada Privacy Symposium, Toronto, May 10, 2012, https://iapp.org/media/presentations/12Symposium/CS12_Privacy_by_Design_in_Law_Policy_Practice_PPT.pdf.

59. See Edith Ramirez, "Privacy by Design and the New Privacy Framework of the U.S. Federal Trade Commission," remarks at the Privacy by Design Conference, Hong Kong, June 13, 2012, https://www.ftc.gov/sites/default/files/documents/public_statements/privacy-design-and-new-privacy-framework-u.s.federal-trade-commission/120613privacydesign.pdf, which notes, "By signing onto the APEC Privacy Rules System, a company effectively agrees to abide by privacy by design."

60. Federal Trade Commission, *Protecting Consumer Privacy in an Era of Rapid Change: Recommendations for Businesses and Policymakers,* March 2012, https://www.ftc.gov/sites/default/files/documents/reports/federal-trade-commission-report-protecting-consumer-privacy-era-rapid-change-recommendations/120326privacyreport.pdf.

61. Ramirez, "Privacy by Design and the New Privacy Framework."

62. Complaint, In re Google Inc., F.T.C. File No. 112 3151, No. C-4336 (F.T.C. Oct. 13, 2011).

63. European Union, Data Protection by Design and Default, article 25, General Data Protection Regulation, https://gdpr-info.eu/art-25-gdpr/.

64. Lee A. Bygrave, "Hardwiring Privacy," in *The Oxford Handbook of the Law and Regulation of Technology,* ed. Roger Brownsword, Eloise Scotford, and Karen Yeung (Oxford: Oxford University Press, 2017), 754–775; Lee Bygrave, "Data Protection by Design and Default: Deciphering the EU's Legislative Require-ments," *Oslo Law Review* 1 (2017): 105–120.

65. David Wright, "Should Privacy Impact Assessments be Mandatory?," *Communications of the ACM* 54 (2011): 121–131, http://cacm.acm.org/magazines/2011/8/114936-should-privacy-impact-assessments-be-mandatory/fulltext; David Tancock, Siani Pearson, and Andrew Charlesworth, *The Emergence of Privacy Impact Assessments,* HP Laboratories, May 21, 2010, www.hpl.hp.com/techreports/2010/HPL-2010-63.pdf; R. Clarke, "Privacy Impact Assessment: Its Origin and Development," *Computer Law and Security Review* 25 (2009): 123–135.

66. See Federal Trade Commission, "Privacy Impact Assessments," https://www.ftc.gov/site-information/privacy-policy/privacy-impact-assessments.

67. See Joshua B. Bolten, "Memorandum for Heads of Executive Departments and Agencies: OMB Guidance for Implementing the Privacy Provisions of the E-Government Act of 2002," Executive Office of the President, September 26, 2003, http://www.whitehouse.gov/omb/memoranda/m03-22.html.

68. A. Michael Froomkin, "Regulating Mass Surveillance as Privacy Pollu-tion: Learning from Environmental Impact Statements," *University of Illinois Law Review* 2015 (2015): 1752.

69. Kenneth A. Bamberger and Deirdre K. Mulligan, "Privacy Decision-making in Administrative Agencies," *University of Chicago Law Review* 75 (2008): 75–107.

70. Ari Ezra Waldman, "Designing Without Privacy," *Houston Law Review,* March 31, 2017, https://papers.ssrn.com/sol3/papers.cfm?abstract_id=2944185.

71. Seda Gurses, Carmela Troncoso, and Claudia Diaz, "Engineering Privacy by Design," article presented at the Amsterdam Privacy Conference, October 23–25, 2015, https://securewww.esat.kuleuven.be/cosic/publications /article-1542.pdf.

72. See, e.g., Christopher Avery and Bryan Thompson, "California Beefs Up Encryption and Notice in Data Breach Law," Privacy and Security Law, October 19, 2015, http://www.privsecblog.com/2015/10/articles/marketing-and -consumer-privacy/california-beefs-up-encryption-notice-in-data-breach-law/.

73. As Adam J. Kolber, "Smooth and Bumpy Laws," *California Law Review* 102 (2014): 655, notes, "Modest differences in conduct can lead to wildly different legal outcomes. A person deemed slightly negligent when harming another may owe millions of dollars. Had the person been just a bit more cautious, he would owe nothing."

74. Neil M. Richards and Daniel J. Solove, "Prosser's Privacy Law: A Mixed Legacy," *California Law Review* 98 (2010): 1887–1924.

75. 17 U.S.C. § 512; 45 C.F.R. § 164.514.

76. 17 U.S.C. § 512.

77. Andrea Matwyshyn, "The Internet of Bodies," Ninth Annual Privacy Law Scholars Conference (PLSC), George Washington University, June 2–3, 2016, Washington DC (manuscript on file with author).

78. "The Evolution of Secure Things," Emergent Chaos, November 17, 2015, http://emergentchaos.com/archives/2015/11/the-evolution-of-secure-things .html.

79. Andy Greenberg, "Apple's 'Differential Privacy' Is about Collecting Your Data—But Not *Your* Data," *Wired,* June 13, 2016, https://www.wired.com/2016/06 /apples-differential-privacy-collecting-data/.

80. Restatement (Third) of Torts: Products Liability § 1.

81. Eric Jorstad, "The Privacy Paradox," *William Mitchell Law Review* 27 (2001): 1511; Benjamin R. Sachs, "Consumerism and Information Privacy: How Upton Sinclair Can Again Save Us from Ourselves," *Virginia Law Review* 95 (2009): 231.

82. Danielle Keats Citron, "Reservoirs of Danger: The Evolution of Public and Private Law at the Dawn of the Information Age," *Southern California Law Review* 80 (2007): 244, citing Rylands v. Fletcher, (1868) 3 L.R.E. and I. App. 330 (H.L.).

83. See James Grimmelmann, "Privacy as Product Safety," *Widener Law Journal* 19 (2010): 827, which notes that "products-liability law has its own doctrinal problems, such as the confused split of authority between risk-utility balancing and consumer expectations as the test for whether a design is defective. There is no good reason to import the full details of these doctrines, warts and all, into privacy law."

84. McGee v. Cessna Aircraft Co, 82 Cal. App. 3d 1005, 147 Cal. Rptr. 694 (1978), later app. 139 Cal. App. 3d 1–79, 188 Cal. Rptr. 542 (1983); Ryan v. Blakey, 71 Ill. App. 3d 339, 27 Ill. Dec. 540, 389 N.E. 2d 604 (1979).

85. Daniel Solove and Danielle Citron, "Risk and Anxiety: A Theory of Data Breach Harms, *Texas Law Review* 96 (forthcoming 2017), https://papers.ssrn.com /sol3/papers.cfm?abstract_id=2885638.

86. DesignerWare, LLC, FTC File No. 112 3151, No. C-4390 April 11, 2013, http://www.ftc.gov/sites/default/files/documents/cases/2013/04 /130415designerwarecmpt.pdf.

87. Complaint, FTC v. Neovi, Inc., No. 306-CV-01952-WQH-JMA (S.D. Cal. Sept. 19, 2006), https://www.ftc.gov/sites/default/files/documents/cases/2006/10 /060919neovicmplt.pdf.

88. Complaint at 10–11, FTC v. CyberSpy Software, LLC and Trace R. Spence, No. 6:08-CV-01872 (M.D. Fla. Nov. 5, 2008), https://www.ftc.gov/sites /default/files/documents/cases/2008/11/081105cyberspycmplt.pdf.

89. M. Ryan Calo, "Open Robotics," *Maryland Law Review* 70 (2011): 593–601.

90. See, e.g., Randall P. Bezanson, "The Right to Privacy Revisited: Privacy, News, and Social Change, 1890–1990," *California Law Review* 80 (1992): 1134, which notes that "the legal emphasis on controls over publication [should] be shifted to a duty of confidentiality imposed on those possessing private information"; Susan M. Gilles, "Promises Betrayed: Breach of Confidence as a Remedy for Invasions of Privacy," *Buffalo Law Review* 43 (1995): 14–15, which notes, "American law is in the process of recognizing three distinct theories—contract, fiduciary duty and perhaps tort—which can be used to found an action against a confidant who reveals information"; Andrew J. McClurg, "Kiss and Tell: Protecting Intimate Relationship Privacy through Implied Contracts of Confidentiality," *University of Cincinnati Law Review* 74 (2006): 887–940; Pamela Samuelson, "Privacy as Intellectual Property?," *Stanford Law Review* 52 (2000): 1125–1174, which urges the adoption of certain trade secrecy laws to protect personal information online; Steven A. Bibas, "A Contractual Approach to Data Privacy," *Harvard Journal of Law and Public Policy* 17 (1994): 591–605, which advocates a contractual solution to data and privacy problems; Scott L. Fast, "Breach of Employee Confidentiality: Moving toward a Common-Law Tort Remedy," *University of Pennsylvania Law Review* 142 (1993): 431–470, which argues that courts should provide a common law remedy for disclosures to third

parties in the employer-employee context; G. Michael Harvey, "Confidentiality: A Measured Response to the Failure of Privacy," *University of Pennsylvania Law Review* 140 (1992): 2392, which advocates for a legally enforceable duty of confidentiality that attaches when a person engages in an unauthorized publication of information; Alan B. Vickery, "Breach of Confidence: An Emerging Tort," *Columbia Law Review* 82 (1982): 1426–1468, which concludes that the basis for imposing liability for breach of confidence should be the disclosure of information revealed in the course of a nonpersonal relationship of a sort customarily understood to carry an obligation of confidentiality.

91. "Confidentiality," *Black's Law Dictionary,* 9th ed. Eagan, MN: West, 2009), 339.

92. Sissela Bok, *Secrets: On the Ethics of Concealment and Revelation* (New York: Vintage, 1982), 119.

93. See Daniel J. Solove and Neil M. Richards, "Rethinking Free Speech and Civil Liability," *Columbia Law Review* 109 (2009): 1669, which notes, "There are also other confidentiality rules not involving civil liability, such as criminal prohibitions on divulging certain kinds of confidential information, evidentiary privileges restricting testimony about confidential data, and statutory protections that limit the release of confidential information by certain companies or government agencies."

94. See, e.g., McClurg, "Kiss and Tell," 908–911, advocating the adoption of contract remedies for breach of implied or express confidentiality agreements.

95. See, e.g., Vickery, "Breach of Confidence," 1448–1452, examining the scope of the emerging tort of breach of confidence.

96. See, e.g., Federal Rules of Civil Procedure 26(c)(1), which authorize protective orders "to protect a party or person from annoyance, embarrassment, [or] oppression." See also Freedom of Information Act, 5 U.S.C. § 552(b)(6) (2006) (providing an exemption from the disclosure of personnel and medical files if the disclosure "would constitute a clearly unwarranted invasion of personal privacy").

97. See, e.g., Fair Credit Reporting Act, 15 U.S.C. §§ 1681 (regulating the collection, dissemination, and use of consumer information); Financial Services Modernization [Gramm-Leach-Bliley] Act of 1999, 15 U.S.C. §§ 6801–6809 (2006) (requiring financial institutions to provide each customer with a notification about her privacy rights at the time the consumer is established and annually thereafter); Video Privacy Protection Act of 1988, 18 U.S.C. § 2710(b)(2) (B) (2006) (preventing the disclosure of rental records of videos or other audiovisual materials); and Health Insurance Portability and Accountability Act of 1996, 42 U.S.C. §§ 1320d–1320d-8 (2006) (regulating the disclosure of information related to an individual's health care).

98. Gilles, "Promises Betrayed," 15.

99. Ibid.: "Express written contracts, binding the signer to hold information confidential, have long been used in the commercial area, particularly by employers to prevent employees from revealing business secrets."

100. See, e.g., Amy J. Schmitz, "Untangling the Privacy Paradox in Arbitration," *University of Kansas Law Review* 54 (2006): 1212–1253, which describes the value of confidentiality agreements in arbitration proceedings.

101. See, e.g., Laurie Kratky Doré, "Secrecy by Consent: The Use and Limits of Confidentiality in the Pursuit of Settlement," *Notre Dame Law Review* 74 (1999): 286, noting that courts permit confidentiality agreements to encourage parties to settle.

102. See, e.g., Samuelson, "Privacy as Intellectual Property?," 1152, explaining how a confidentiality agreement to protect trade secrets typically works.

103. See, e.g., Hammonds v. Aetna Cas. and Sur. Co., 243 F. Supp. 793, 801 (N.D. Ohio 1965) (holding that a contract between a doctor and a patient contains an implied condition for the doctor not to release any confidential information gained through the contractual relationship without the patient's permission); and Daniel J. Solove and Neil M. Richards, "Privacy's Other Path: Recovering the Law of Confidentiality," *Georgetown Law Journal* 96 (2007):123–182, discussing early cases where courts created a legal remedy for divulging confidential information based on implied contract.

104. See, e.g., Cohen v. Cowles Media Co., 479 N.W. 2d 387, 391 (Minn. 1992) (applying promissory estoppel where newspapers breached promises of confidentiality). Promissory estoppel is an equitable doctrine designed to enforce promises that are detrimentally relied upon even though the formal elements of a contract are not present. Woodrow Hartzog, "Promises and Privacy: Promissory Estoppel and Confidential Disclosure in Online Communities," *Temple Law Review* 82 (2009): 909.

105. See Gilles, "Promises Betrayed," 39. Gilles notes, "Where such a relation exists, a fiduciary is under a duty 'to act for the benefit of the other party to the relation as to matters within the scope of the relation.' This duty, often characterized as the 'duty of loyalty,' includes an obligation not to reveal information" (39–40). Like confidentiality agreements, the existence of a confidential relationship is a question of fact. Roy Ryden Anderson has found that "confidential relationships have been labeled 'fact-based' fiduciary relationships to distinguish them from formal [fiduciary relationships]." Although professional relationships such that of doctor and patient and attorney and client are the most common types of confidential relationships, courts have found many kinds of relationships to be confidential, including friendships, business relationships, and familial relationships. See Roy Ryden Anderson, "The Wolf at the Campfire: Understanding Confidential Relationships," *SMU Law Review* 53 (2000): 317.

106. See Gilles, "Promises Betrayed," 4–14, tracing the English breach of confidence tort and the American invasion of privacy tort to their common doctrinal ancestor; Harvey, "Confidentiality," 2392–2393, noting the breach of confidence doctrine in England and stating American courts' basis for rejecting it; and Richards and Solove, "Privacy's Other Path," 156–158, 180, discussing how American courts have largely ignored the breach of confidence tort. See, generally, Paul Stanley, *The Law of Confidentiality: A Restatement* (Portland, OR: Hart, 2008), which states the fundamental principles underlying the modern English law of confidentiality.

107. Alan E. Garfield, "Promises of Silence: Contract Law and Freedom of Speech," *Cornell Law Review* 83 (1998): 341.

108. See, e.g., Richards and Solove, "Privacy's Other Path," 178, noting that confidentiality law focuses on the source, rather than the content, of information; and Winn, "Confidentiality in Cyberspace: The HIPAA Privacy Rules and the Common Law," *Rutgers Law Journal* 33 (2002): 653–654, which notes, "Claims for invasion of privacy . . . are based on the misuse of the personal information due to the sensitive and private nature of the information. On the other hand, breach of confidentiality represents an injury to a relationship of trust between the injured person and the person who has misused the information."

109. See, e.g., Winn, "Confidentiality in Cyberspace," 657, which notes that "in the tort of breach of confidentiality, the unauthorized revelation of confidential medical information is protected without regard to the degree to which the information has been published to the general public." It is important to note that some conceptions of confidentiality will not protect information that is publicly available. See Patricia Sánchez Abril, "Private Ordering: A Contractual Approach to Online Interpersonal Privacy," *Wake Forest Law Review* 45 (2010): 713, which notes, "Fundamentally, a confidentiality agreement cannot shield information that is publicly available." Compare Smith v. Dravo Corp., 203 F.2d 369, 375 (7th Cir. 1953) (holding that an obligation of confidentiality can still exist even if information is publicly available if the discloser somehow saved the recipient time and effort in disclosing the information or presented the information in a more ready and usable form than what was publicly available).

110. See, e.g., Paul M. Schwartz, "Free Speech vs. Information Privacy: Eugene Volokh's First Amendment Jurisprudence," *Stanford Law Review* 52 (2000): 1561, arguing that fair information practices are a narrow exception to First Amendment limitations; Eugene Volokh, "Freedom of Speech and Information Privacy: The Troubling Implications of a Right to Stop People from Speaking about You," *Stanford Law Review* 52 (2000): 1122, concluding that much of American privacy law presents unavoidable First Amendment problems; Diane L. Zimmerman, "Requiem for a Heavyweight: A Farwell to Warren and Brandeis's Privacy Tort," *Cornell*

Law Review 68 (2000): 294, stating that many justifications of the Warren-Brandeis right of privacy "have often underplayed its serious constitutional problems."

111. Cohen v. Cowles Media Co., 501 U.S. 663, 670 (1991).

112. See Campell v. MGN Ltd., [2002] EWCA (Civ.) 1373 (2003) 1 Q.B. 633, 662 (England) (describing third party's duty of confidence when he receives information that he knows was disclosed in breach); Attorney Gen. v. Observer, Ltd., (1990) 1 A.C. 109 (H.L.) 268 (appeal taken from England) ("The duty of confidence is . . . imposed on a third party who is in possession of information which he knows is subject to an obligation of confidence."); and Winn, "Confidentiality in Cyberspace," 619, arguing that breach of confidentiality can provide an effective remedy for the improper disclosure of health information.

113. See, e.g., Attorney Gen. v. Observer Ltd., [1990] A.C. 109 (H.L.) 268 (appeal taken from England); Campell v. MGN Ltd., [2002] EWCA (Civ.) 1373, [2003] Q.B. 633 [662] (England); Paul Stanley, *The Law of Confidentiality,* 1–5; and Richards and Solove, "Privacy's Other Path," 178, which notes that "a third party can freely disclose private facts about a person as long as the third party did not learn the information from a confidant."

114. Rachel Thompson, "Snapchat Has Revolutionized Sexting, But Not Necessarily for the Better," *Mashable,* February 7, 2017, http://mashable.com/2017/02/07/snapchat-sexting-revolution/#rMSjQmat9aqT.

115. Food and Drug Administration, "Device Approvals, Denials and Clearances," http://www.fda.gov/MedicalDevices/ProductsandMedicalProcedures/DeviceApprovalsandClearances/.

116. Adam Therier, *Permissionless Innovation: The Continuing Case for Comprehensive Technological Freedom* (Arlington, VA Mercatus Center at George Mason University, 2016).

117. Lauren E. Willis, "Why Not Privacy by Default?," *Berkeley Technology Law Journal* 29 (2014): 131.

118. Bernard Harcourt, *Exposed: Desire and Disobedience in the Digital Age* (Cambridge, Harvard University Press, 2015). Perhaps in some circumstances lawmakers might find choice so coerced or invalid as to value privacy regardless of consumer preference. Anita Allen, *Unpopular Privacy: What Must We Hide?* (Oxford, Oxford University Press, 2011).

119. William McGeveran, "Friending the Regulators," *Arizona Law Review* 58 (2016): 959–1025.

6. Social Media

1. Neil M. Richards, "The Perils of Social Reading," *Georgetown Law Journal* 101 (2013): 689–724. William McGeveran, "The Law of Friction," *University of Chicago Legal Forum* 2013 (2013): 15–68.

2. See John Koetsier, "Facebook Goes all Twittery in Its New iOS 7 App Updates," VentureBeat, September 18, 2013, https://venturebeat.com/2013/09/18 /facebook-goes-all-twittery-in-its-new-ios-7-app-updates/, which notes, "The new Facebook app kills the one infinite scroll of the previous app, in a sense, by adding a row of never-moving icons to the bottom of every screen, to make the app 'easier to get around.'"

3. Amir Efrati, "Facebook Struggles to Stop Decline in 'Original' Sharing," The Information, April 7, 2016, https://www.theinformation.com/facebook -struggles-to-stop-decline-in-original-sharing; Erin Griffith, "Facebook Users Are Sharing Fewer Personal Updates and It's a Big Problem," Fortune, April 8, 2016, http://fortune.com/2016/04/07/facebook-sharing-decline/; Sarah Frier, "Facebook Wants You to Post More about Yourself," Bloomberg Technology, April 7, 2015, http://www.bloomberg.com/news/articles/2016-04-07/facebook -said-to-face-decline-in-people-posting-personal-content.

4. Frier, "Facebook Wants You to Post More about Yourself."

5. See Natasha Lomas, "Everything You Need to Know about iOS 8 Keyboard Permissions (But Were Afraid to Ask)," TechCrunch, October 4, 2014, https://techcrunch.com/2014/10/04/everything-you-need-to-know-about-ios-8 -keyboard-permissions-but-were-afraid-to-ask/, which notes that "if you provide Full Access to a third party keyboard you are technically giving that app the ability to capture and transmit your keystroke data (aka the stuff you type) elsewhere"; "Using Bitmoji in Snapchat," Bitmoji, https://www.bitmoji.com /support/ios.html; Eric Slivka, "iOS 8 Keyboards, 'Full Access,' and User Privacy," MacRumors, September 24, 2014, http://www.macrumors.com/2014/09 /24/ios-8-keyboards-full-access-and-user-privacy/.

6. Tristan Harris, "How Technology Hijacks People's Minds—From a Magician and Google's Design Ethicist," The Startup, May 18, 2016, https:// medium.com/swlh/how-technology-hijacks-peoples-minds-from-a-magician -and-google-s-design-ethicist-56d62ef5edf3#.svac5ux9h.

7. Woodrow Hartzog, "Don't Listen to Snapchat's Excuses. Security is its Job," Wired, October 14, 2014, http://www.wired.com/2014/10/the-snappening-is -not-your-fault/.

8. See danah m. boyd and Nicole B. Ellison, "Social Network Sites: Definition, History, and Scholarship," Journal of Computer-Mediated Communication 13 (2007): 210–230, http://www.danah.org/papers/JCMCIntro.pdf, which explains, "We define social network sites as web-based services that allow individuals to (1) construct a public or semi-public profile within a bounded system, (2) articulate a list of other users with whom they share a connection, and (3) view and traverse their list of connections and those made by others within the system. The nature and nomenclature of these connections may vary from site to site."

9. Bruce Schneier, "A Revised Taxonomy of Social Networking Data," Schneier on Security, August 10, 2010, https://www.schneier.com/blog/archives/2010/08/a_taxonomy_of_s_1.html. See also Bruce Schneier, "A Taxonomy of Social Networking Data," *IEEE Security and Privacy* 8 (2010): 88.

10. Steve Rosenbush, "Facebook Tests Software to Track Your Cursor on Screen," *Wall Street Journal,* October 30, 2013, http://blogs.wsj.com/digits/2013/10/30/facebook-considers-vast-increase-in-data-collection/; Jam Kotenko, "Facebook Officially Hits Stalker Mode, Wants to Watch Your Cursor Movements," Digital Trends, October 20, 2013, http://www.digitaltrends.com/social-media/facebook-wants-learn-mouse-hover-habits-site-officially-creepy-stalker-mode/.

11. Schneier, "A Revised Taxonomy of Social Networking Data."

12. Evan Selinger and Woodrow Hartzog, "How to Stop Facebook from Making Us Pawns in Its Corporate Agenda," *Wired,* July 1, 2014, http://www.wired.com/2014/07/facebook-partner-in-scheme/.

13. See Viktor Mayer-Schönberger and Kenneth Cukier, *Big Data: A Revolution That Will Transform How We Live, Work, and Think* (London: Murray, 2013), 91–94; Julie E. Cohen, "What Privacy Is For," *Harvard Law Review* 126 (2013): 1918, which notes, "Efforts to repack age pervasive surveillance as innovation—under the moniker 'Big Data'—are better understood as efforts to enshrine the methods and values of the modulated society at the heart of our system of knowledge production"; and Daniel J. Solove, "Introduction: Privacy Self-Management and the Consent Dilemma," *Harvard Law Review* 126 (2013): 1889, which notes, "Modern data analytics, which is also loosely referred to as data mining or 'Big Data,' can deduce extensive information about a person from these clues. In other words, little bits of innocuous data can say a lot in combination."

14. Facebook, "Data Policy," quoted in Andrew Chin and Anne Klinefelter, "Differential Privacy as a Response to the Reidentification Threat: The Facebook Advertiser Case Study," *North Carolina Law Review* 90 (2012): 1421.

15. Julia Angwin and Terry Parris Jr., "Facebook Lets Advertisers Exclude Users by Race," Pro Publica, October 28, 2016, https://www.propublica.org/article/facebook-lets-advertisers-exclude-users-by-race.

16. Scott Shane, "The Fake Americans Russia Created to Influence the Election," *New York Times* (Sept. 7, 2017), https://www.nytimes.com/2017/09/07/us/politics/russia-facebook-twitter-election.html; Scott Shane and Vindu Goel, "Fake Russian Facebook Accounts Bought $100,000 in Political Ads," *New York Times,* September 6, 2017, https://www.nytimes.com/2017/09/06/technology/facebook-russian-political-ads.html; Jonathan Zittrain, "Engineering an Election: Digital Gerrymandering Poses a Threat to Democracy, " *Harvard Law Review Forum* 127 (2014): 335–341.

17. Kashmir Hill, "Facebook User Unwittingly Becomes Sex Lube Pitchman Thanks To Sponsored Stories," *Forbes,* February 28, 2012, http://www.forbes.com /sites/kashmirhill/2012/02/28/facebook-user-unwittingly-becomes-sex-lube -pitchman-thanks-to-sponsored-stories/#49a9928d78cb. See also "The Most Humiliating Accidental Status Updates Ever Posted on Facebook," Some News, July 10, 2013, http://www.someecards.com/news/so-that-happened/the-most -humiliating-accidental-status-updates-ever-posted-on-Facebook/.

18. Alice E. Marwick and danah boyd, "I Tweet Honestly, I Tweet Passion-ately: Twitter Users, Context Collapse, and the Imagined Audience," *New Media and Society* 13 (2010): 114–133; Jenny Davis, "Context Collapse: A Literature Review," The Society Pages, January 10, 2013, https://thesocietypages.org /cyborgology/2013/01/10/context-collapse-a-literature-review/; danah boyd, "How 'Context Collapse Was Coined: My Recollection," Zephoria, December 8, 2013, http://www.zephoria.org/thoughts/archives/2013/12/08/coining-context-collapse .html.

19. See, e.g., Will Ripley, "Denver Man Fired for Complaining about Work on Facebook," 9News, May 7, 2013, http://www.9news.com/news/article/334929/222 /Denver-man-fired-for-complaining- about-work-on-Facebook: "I got to a point where I put a comment on Facebook that got me fired,' [employee] said. [Employee]'s coworker reported him to their boss." The Facebook Fired, https:// thefacebookfired.wordpress.com/, a site aggregating links to stories about employees fired as a result of postings made on Facebook and other social media; and Daniel Solove, "Employers and Schools That Demand Account Passwords and the Future of Cloud Privacy," Teach Privacy, June 3, 2013, https://www .teachprivacy.com/employers-schools-demand-account-passwords-future-cloud -privacy/.

20. "Depressed Woman Loses Benefits over Facebook Photos," CBC News, November 21, 2009, http://www.cbc.ca/news/canada/montreal/depressed-woman -loses-benefits-over-facebook-photos-1.861843; Ki Mae Heussner, "Woman Loses Benefits after Posting Facebook Pics," ABC News, November 23, 2009, http:// abcnews.go.com/Technology/AheadoftheCurve/woman-loses-insurance-benefits -facebook-pics/story?id=9154741.

21. See Airi Lampinen, "Practices of Balancing Privacy and Publicness in Social Network Services," in *Proceedings of the 16th ACM International Confer-ence on Supporting Group Work* (New York: Association for Computing Ma-chinery, 2010), 343, which notes, "Conventional privacy and computer security studies focus on threats and risks created by faceless third parties. In social media, end-user privacy concerns are more than before related to real second parties . . . people who are known also offline and who are anything but faceless.")

22. Maritza Johnson, Serge Egelman, and Steven M. Bellovin, "Facebook and Privacy: It's Complicated," in *Proceedings of the 8th Symposium on Usable Privacy and Security* (New York: Association for Computing Machinery, 2012), http://cups.cs.cmu.edu/soups/2012/proceedings/a9_Johnson.pdf, 2.1 (including in the "threats" category people purposefully posting content to harm the individual and a general concern over a lack of control over the actions of other users).

23. See Woodrow Hartzog, "Website Design as Contract," *American University Law Review* 60 (2011): 1635; and Allyson W. Haynes, "Online Privacy Policies: Contracting Away Control over Personal Information?," *Penn State Law Review* 111 (2007): 588.

24. See, e.g., The Facebook Fired (detailing reports of many social media users disciplined for their posts, many of which were reported by the user's social network connections); Geoffrey Fowler, "Three Facebook Privacy Loopholes," *Wall Street Journal,* October 12, 2012, http://blogs.wsj.com/digits/2012/10/12/three-facebook-privacy-loopholes/?mod=WSJBlog; and Will Oremus, "Could Your Crummy Klout Score Keep You from Getting a Job?," *Slate,* October 3, 2012, http://www.slate.com/blogs/future_tense/2012/10/03/online_privacy_can_employers_use_klout_scores_facebook_profiles_to_screen_applicants_.html, which notes, "There are also plenty of instances of workers being fired for Facebook posts even if their employers don't have access to their accounts."

25. Carl Franzen, "Facebook Surveying Users about Their Friends' Fake Usernames," Talking Points Memo, September 20, 2012, http://talkingpointsmemo.com/idealab/facebook-surveying-users-about-their-friends-fake-usernames.

26. See Yang Wang, Pedro Giovanni Leon, Xiaoxuan Chen, Saranga Komanduri, Gregory Norcie, Alessandro Acquisti, Lorrie Faith Cranor, and Norman Sadeh, "From Facebook Regrets to Facebook Privacy Nudges, *Ohio State Law Journal* 74 (2013): 1307–1335. This fact is often evident when employees are fired for complaining about their jobs to their Facebook friends, at least one of whom might be their boss.

27. According to Neil Richards, "Under a regime of 'frictionless sharing,' we don't need to choose to share our activities online. Instead, everything we read or watch automatically gets uploaded to our Facebook or Twitter feed." Richards, "Social Reading," 691. See also Somini Sengupta, "Private Posts on Facebook Revealed," *New York Times,* January 18, 2013, http://bits.blogs.nytimes.com/2013/01/18/private-posts-on-facebook-revealed/.

28. See, e.g., Joanna Stern, "Demanding Facebook Passwords May Break Law, Say Senators," ABC News, March 26, 2012, http://abcnews.go.com/Technology/facebook-passwords-employers-schools-demand-access-facebook-senators/.

29. See, e.g., John Browning, "Universities Monitoring Social Media Accounts of Student-Athletes: A Recipe for Disaster," *Texas Bar Journal* 75 (2012): 840; Sandra Engelland, "Keller District Officials Look to Extra Security, Monitoring Social Media to Prevent Pranks," *Fort Worth Star-Telegram,* May 28, 2013, http://www.star-telegram.com/2013/05/28/4888860/keller-district-officials-look .html; and Michael Hartwell, "Schools Monitor Students' Posts on Facebook, Twitter," *Fitchburg (MA) Sentinel and Enterprise* January 14, 2013, http://www .sentinelandenterprise.com/topstory/ci_22369565/schools-monitor-students -posts-facebook-twitter.

30. See, e.g., Benny Evangelista, "Social Media Monitored More by Law Enforcement," *San Francisco Gate,* August 13, 2011, http://www.sfgate.com /business/article/Social-media-monitored-more-by-law-enforcement-2335017 .php; Priya Kumar, "Law Enforcement and Mining Social Media: Where's the Oversight?," Internet Monitor, July 1, 2013, https://blogs.law.harvard.edu /internetmonitor/2013/07/01/law-enforcement-and-mining-social-media-wheres -the-oversight/; Paul Wagenseil, "British Cops Admit They Monitor Facebook, Twitter," *Tech News Daily,* June 27, 2013, http://www.technewsdaily.com/18448 -socmint-police-monitoring.html; and Barton Gellman and Laura Poitras, "U.S., British Intelligence Mining Data from Nine U.S. Internet Companies in Broad Secret Program," *Washington Post,* June 6, 2013, http://articles .washingtonpost.com/2013-06-06/news/39784046_1_prism-nsa-u-s-servers, which discusses leaked documents implying that the National Security Agency had direct access to Facebook servers). Compare Ted Ullyot, "Facebook Releases Data, Including All National Security Requests," Facebook Newsroom, June 14, 2013, http://newsroom.fb.com/News/636/Facebook-Releases-Data-Including-All -National-Security-Requests, which denies allegations of direct server access but discloses that U.S. government entities requested Facebook data between nine thousand and ten thousand times in the six months prior to December 31, 2012.

31. Mike Isaac and Sydney Ember, "Facebook to Change News Feed to Focus on Friends and Family," *New York Times,* June 29, 2016, http://mobile.nytimes .com/2016/06/30/technology/facebook-to-change-news-feed-to-focus-on-friends -and-family.html.

32. Ian Kerr, Jennifer Barrigar, Jacquelyn Burkell, and Katie Black, "Soft Surveillance, Hard Consent: The Law and Psychology of Engineering Consent," in *Lessons from the Identity Trail: Anonymity, Privacy and Identity in a Networked Society,* ed. Ian Kerr, Valerie Steeves, and Carole Lucock (New York: Oxford University Press, 2009), 5–22.

33. Gary Marx, "Surveillance and Society," in *Encyclopedia of Social Theory,* ed. George Ritzer, (Thousand Oaks, CA: Sage, 2005), 817. Soft surveillance, Marx

writes, is the use of "persuasion to gain voluntary compliance, universality, and . . . utilizing hidden or low visibility information collection techniques." See Gary T. Marx, "Soft Surveillance: The Growth of Mandatory Volunteerism in Collecting Personal Information—'Hey Buddy Can You Spare a DNA?,'" in *Surveillance and Security: Technological Politics and Power in Everyday Life,* ed. Torin Monahan (New York: Routledge, 2006), 37–56.

34. Will Oremus, "Facebook's 5 New Reactions Buttons: Data, Data, Data, Data, and Data," *Slate,* February 24, 2016, http://www.slate.com/blogs/future _tense/2016/02/24/facebook_s_5_new_reactions_buttons_are_all_about_data _data_data.html.

35. Federal Trade Commission, "Operators of AshleyMadison.com Settle FTC, State Charges Resulting from 2015 Data Breach That Exposed 36 Million Users' Profile Information," December 14, 2016, https://www.ftc.gov/news-events /press-releases/2016/12/operators-ashleymadisoncom-settle-ftc-state-charges -resulting.

36. Tim Jones, "Facebook's "Evil Interfaces," Electronic Frontier Foundation, April 9, 2010, https://www.eff.org/deeplinks/2010/04/facebooks-evil-interfaces.

37. Evan Seliger and Woodrow Hartzog, "Why Is Facebook Putting Teens at Risk?," Bloomberg October 24, 2013, https://www.bloomberg.com/view/articles /2013-10-24/why-is-facebook-putting-teens-at-risk-.

38. Jillian D'Onfro, "Mark Zuckerberg Promises That You'll Stop Getting So Many Candy Crush Saga Invites," Business Insider, October 28, 2015, http://www .businessinsider.com/facebook-ceo-mark-zuckerberg-on-game-invites-2015-10.

39. Harris, "How Technology Hijacks People's Minds."

40. Yang Wang, Gregory Norcie, Saranga Komanduri, Alessandro Acquisti, Pedro Giovanni Leon, and Lorrie Faith Cranor, "'I Regretted the Minute I Pressed Share': A Qualitative Study of Regrets on Facebook," in *Proceedings of the Seventh Symposium on Usable Privacy and Security* (New York: Association for Computing Machinery, 2011), https://www.andrew.cmu.edu/user/pgl/FB -Regrets.pdf; Kelly Moore and James McElroy, "The Influence of Personality on Facebook Usage, Wall Postings, and Regret," *Computers in Human Behavior* 28 (2012): 267–274, https://pdfs.semanticscholar.org/035f/eaca888c03c2112519fd10b3 46de50809fb4.pdf.

41. Marx, "Soft Surveillance."

42. Kerr et al., "Soft Surveillance, Hard Consent"; Nancy S. Kim, *Wrap Contracts: Foundations and Ramifications* (New York: Oxford University Press, 2013); Margaret Jane Radin, *Boilerplate: The Fine Print, Vanishing Rights, and the Rule of Law* (Princeton, NJ: Princeton University Press, 2013).

43. Harry Brignull, "Dark Patterns: Inside the Interfaces Designed to Trick You," The Verge, August 29, 2013, http://www.theverge.com/2013/8/29 /4640308/dark-patterns-inside-the-interfaces-designed-to-trick-you.

44. Yannis Bakos, Florencia Marotta-Wurgler, and David R. Trossen, "Does Anyone Read the Fine Print? Consumer Attention to Standard Form Contracts," *Journal of Legal Studies* 43 (2014): 1–35.

45. Debra Cassens Weiss, "Chief Justice Roberts Admits He Doesn't Read the Computer Fine Print," *ABA Journal,* October 20, 2010, http://www.abajournal .com/news/article/chief_justice_roberts_admits_he_doesnt_read_the_computer _fine_print/. Chief Justice Roberts also stated that standard-form agreements were a problem without a clear answer.

46. Kim, *Wrap Contracts.*

47. Ibid.

48. Hartzog, "Website Design as Contract."

49. Facebook, "Data Policy," https://www.facebook.com/full_data_use _policy.

50. 306 F.3d 17 (2d Cir. 2002).

51. Ibid., 23.

52. Adam Alten, *Drunk Tank Pink: And Other Unexpected Forces That Shape How We Think, Feel, and Behave* (New York: Penguin, 2014).

53. danah boyd, "Facebook's Privacy Trainwreck," *Convergence: The International Journal of Research into New Media Technologies* 14 (2008): 13–20; Zeynep Tufecki, "Can You See Me Now? Audience and Disclosure Regulation in Online Social Network Sites," *Bulletin of Science, Technology and Society* 28 (2008): 20–36.

54. Woodrow Hartzog and Evan Selinger, "Obscurity: A Better Way to Think About Your Data Than 'Privacy.'" *Atlantic,* January 17, 2013, https://www .theatlantic.com/technology/archive/2013/01/obscurity-a-better-way-to-think -about-your-data-than-privacy/267283/.

55. Kaveh Wadell, "Should Border Agents Scroll through Foreigners' Facebook Profiles?," *Atlantic,* June 29, 2016, https://www.theatlantic.com /technology/archive/2016/06/should-border-agents-scroll-through-foreigners -facebook-profiles/489353/.

56. Biz Stone, "Tweet Preservation," Twitter Official Blog, April 14, 2010, https://blog.twitter.com/2010/tweet-preservation; Michael Zimmer, "The Twitter Archive at the Library of Congress: Challenges for Information Practice and Information Policy," *First Monday* 20 (2015), http://firstmonday.org/article/view /5619/4653.

57. Alex Hern, "Facebook Is Chipping Away at Privacy—And My Profile Has Been Exposed," *Guardian,* June 29, 2016.

58. Federal Trade Commission, "Snapchat Settles FTC Charges That Promises of Disappearing Messages Were False," May 8, 2014, https://www.ftc.gov /news-events/press-releases/2014/05/snapchat-settles-ftc-charges-promises -disappearing-messages-were.

59. Inti De Ceukelaire, "Why You Shouldn't Share Links on Facebook," *Quartz*, June 29, 2016, http://qz.com/715019/why-you-shouldnt-share-links-on-facebook/.

60. John Ellis, "Coalinga Grad Loses MySpace Rant Lawsuit," *Fresno Bee*, October 12, 2010, http://www.fresnobee.com/2010/09/20/2085862/ex-student-loses-myspace-rant.html#storylink=mirelated.

61. Ibid.

62. Pietrylo v. Hillstone Restaurant Group, No. 06-5754 (F.S.H.), 2008 WL 6085437 (D.N.J. July 25, 2008).

63. Ibid., *1.

64. Woodrow Hartzog, "Don't Listen to Snapchat's Excuses: Security Is Its Job," *Wired*, October 14, 2014, https://www.wired.com/2014/10/the-snappening-is-not-your-fault/.

65. Steven Loeb, "Heyward: Whisper Is "The Safest Place on the Internet," *Vator*, October 4, 2014, http://vator.tv/news/2014-10-04-heyward-whisper-is-the-safest-place-on-the-internet#WtOpEKs2f4PfzMO9.99.

66. Woodrow Hartzog, "Promises and Privacy: Promissory Estoppel and Confidential Disclosure in Online Communities," *Temple Law Review* 82 (2009): 891–928.

67. Woodrow Hartzog, "The Privacy Box: A Software Proposal," *First Monday* 14 (2009), http://firstmonday.org/ojs/index.php/fm/article/vie%20w/2682/2361.

68. Of course, the broader concept of confidentiality is not completely absent from online disputes. Explicit confidentiality agreements have an undeniable presence in online privacy disputes in the form of claims for violations of privacy policies and the reliance on terms of use to justify refusals to disclose information about Internet users. But these agreements do not define the entire boundaries and expectations inherent in all online relationships. Indeed, given that virtually no one reads or understands online boilerplate, these agreements likely do not even scratch the surface the true expectations and perceptions of Internet users.

69. boyd and Ellison, "Social Network Sites."

70. In re Easysaver Rewards Litigation, 2010 WL 3259752 (S.D. Cal.); Google, Inc. v. Traffic Info, LLC, 2010 WL 743878 (D. Or.); Best Western Int'l v. Furber, 2008 WL 4182827 (D. Ariz.); London v. New Alberton's, Inc., 2008 WL 4492642 (S.D. Cal.); Watson v. Public Serv. Co. of Colo., 207 P.3d 860 (Colo. Ct. App. 2008); Pisciotta v. Old Nat. Bancorp., 449 F.3d 629 (7th Cir. 2007); Southwest v. Boardfirst, LLC, 2007 WL 4823761 (N.D. Tex.). It is worth noting that these cases all involve commercial, not social, disputes.

71. See, e.g., Andrew J. McClurg, "Kiss and Tell: Protecting Intimate Relationship Privacy through Implied Contracts of Confidentiality," *University of Cincinnati Law Review* 74 (2006): 887–940; and Patricia Sánchez Abril, "A (My)

Space of One's Own: On Privacy and Online Social Networks," *Northwestern Journal of Technology and Intellectual Property* 6 (2007): 77.

72. Hartzog, "Don't Listen to Snapchat's Excuses."

73. Michael Connell, "You Are Not Very Incognito in Incognito Mode," *Computerworld,* April 4, 2017, http://www.computerworld.com/article/3186941/web-browsers/you-are-not-very-incognito-in-incognito-mode.html.

74. Danielle Citron, *Hate Crimes in Cyberspace* (Cambridge, MA: Harvard University Press, 2014).

75. Ibid., 4–5.

76. Ibid, 5.

77. Ibid, 239–240.

78. Katherine Schaeffer, "Yak Flak: How Should Schools Respond to Students' Anonymous Speech?," Student Press Law Center, September 18, 2015, http://www.splc.org/article/2015/09/yak-flak.

79. Gabby Hinsliff, "Play Nice! How the Internet is Trying to Design Out Toxic Behavior," *Guardian,* February 27, 2016.

80. Kashmir Hill, "Blocking People on Twitter Now Just Mutes Them (Update: Psych!)," *Forbes,* December 12, 2013, https://www.forbes.com/sites/kashmirhill/2013/12/12/blocking-people-on-twitter-now-just-mutes-them/.

81. Samantha Allen, "How Facebook Exposes Domestic Violence Survivors," *Daily Beast,* May 20, 2015, http://www.thedailybeast.com/how-facebook-exposes-domestic-violence-survivors; James Vincent, "Facebook Tells Users They Can't Hide From Searches," *Independent,* October 11, 2013.

82. Mary Anne Franks, "The Many Ways Twitter Is Bad at Responding to Abuse," *Atlantic,* August 14, 2014, https://www.theatlantic.com/technology/archive/2014/08/the-many-ways-twitter-is-bad-at-responding-to-abuse/376100/.

83. Ibid.

84. Ibid.

85. Evan Selinger, "When Nudge Comes to Shove," *Slate,* July 7, 2013, http://www.slate.com/articles/health_and_science/new_scientist/2013/07/nudge_critiques_is_nudging_behavior_unethical_infantilizing_coercive_or.html.

7. Hide and Seek Technologies

1. Kevin Rothcock, "Facial Recognition Service Becomes a Weapon against Russian Porn Actresses," Ars Technica, April 26, 2016, https://arstechnica.com/tech-policy/2016/04/facial-recognition-service-becomes-a-weapon-against-russian-porn-actresses/?comments=1.

2. Neil Richards, "The Dangers of Surveillance," *Harvard Law Review* 126 (2013): 1934–1965.

3. Aarti Shahani, "Smartphones Are Used to Stalk, Control Domestic Abuse Victims," NPR, September 15, 2014, http://www.npr.org/sections /alltechconsidered/2014/09/15/346149979/smartphones-are-used-to-stalk-control -domestic-abuse-victims.

4. See Julie Cohen, "Privacy, Visibility, Transparency, and Exposure," *University of Chicago Law Review* 75 (2008): 190, addressing the "nature of the spaces constituted by and for pervasive, continuous observation. Those spaces are characterized by what I will call a condition of exposure. The term "condition" is intended to signify that exposure is not a given but rather a design principle that in turn constrains the range of available behaviors and norms. Neither privacy law nor privacy theory has recognized an interest in limiting exposure uncoupled from the generally acknowledged interest in limiting observation, and in general we lack a vocabulary for conceptualizing and evaluating such an interest."

5. See John Kelly, "Cellphone Data Spying: It's Not Just the NSA," *USA Today,* June 13, 2014, http://www.usatoday.com/story/news/nation/2013/12/08 / cellphone-data-spying-nsa-police/3902809, which notes, "Armed with new technologies, including mobile devices that tap into cellphone data in real time, dozens of local and state police agencies are capturing information about thousands of cellphone users at a time, whether they are targets of an investigation or not."

6. See Rishi Iyengar, "New FBI Software Can Process up to 52 Million Facial Images," *Time,* September 17, 2014, http://time.com/3389559/fbi-facial -recognition-software-interstate-photo-system-ips-next-generation -identification-ngi, which notes, "A Freedom of Information Act lawsuit filed by the foundation in April revealed that the system could process up to 52 million facial images, including millions of pictures taken for noncriminal purposes."

7. See Devlin Barrett, "U.S. Spies on Millions of Drivers," *Wall Street Journal,* January 26, 2015, http://www.wsj.com/articles/u-s-spies-on-millions-of -cars-1422314779, which notes that "The Justice Department has been building a national database to track in real time the movement of vehicles around the U.S., a secret domestic intelligence-gathering program that scans and stores hundreds of millions of records about motorists, according to current and former officials and government documents."

8. See Tom Loftus, "Concerns Rise about Growing Use of Domestic Drones," *USA Today,* July 18, 2013, http://www.usatoday.com/story/tech/2013/07 /18/drone-concerns-rules-regulations/2552999, which explains that "government agencies and universities can apply to the FAA for a certificate of authority to fly a drone—large or small. Commercial drone usage is prohibited now but is expected to take off after September 2015, a deadline Congress gave the FAA to create a plan to integrate unmanned aircraft into the airspace." See also Dan

Roberts, "FBI Admits to Using Surveillance Drones over US Soil," *Guardian,*
June 19, 2013, http://www.theguardian.com/world/2013/jun/19/fbi-drones
-domestic-surveillance, which notes that "the potential for growing drone use
either in the US, or involving US citizens abroad, is an increasingly charged issue
in Congress, and the FBI acknowledged there may need to be legal restrictions
placed on their use to protect privacy."

9. As Mary-Ann Russon, "Are Flying Drones a Peeping Tom's Dream Tool?,"
International Business Times, June 11, 2014, http://www.ibtimes.co.uk/are-flying
-drones-peeping-toms-dream-tool-1452278, notes, "Fears are growing that
helicopter drones could be used to sexually harass women and take secret
photographs of them."

10. See Andrew Guthrie Ferguson, "Personal Curtilage: Fourth Amendment
Security in Public," *William and Mary Law Review* 55 (2014): 1290; Joel R.
Reidenberg, "Privacy in Public," *University of Miami Law Review* 69 (2014): 143;
Helen Nissenbaum, "Privacy as Contextual Integrity," *Washington Law Review*
79 (2004): 156; Christopher Slobogin, "Making the Most of United States v. Jones
in a Surveillance Society: A Statutory Implementation of Mosaic Theory," *Duke
Journal of Constitutional Law and Public Policy* 8 (2012): 4; Jeffrey M. Skopek,
"Reasonable Expectations of Anonymity," *Virginia Law Review* 101 (2015): 691,
which notes, "The problem with the public exposure and third party doctrines is
not only that they fail to recognize that a piece of personal information can be
protected in varying degrees. . . . In addition, and more fundamentally, they
conflate two distinct forms that this protection can take: privacy and anonymity." See also Andrew E. Taslitz, "The Fourth Amendment in the Twenty-
First Century: Technology, Privacy, and Human Emotions," *Law and Contemporary Problems* 65 (2002): 169; Brian J. Serr, "Great Expectations of Privacy:
A New Model for Fourth Amendment Protection," *Minnesota Law Review* 73
(1989): 597–598; Margot E. Kaminski, "Regulating Real-World Surveillance,"
Washington Law Review 90 (2015): 1113–1165; and David Gray and Danielle
Citron, "The Right to Quantitative Privacy," *Minnesota Law Review* 98 (2013):
62–144.

11. 489 U.S. 749 (1989). In the domain of cybersecurity, obscurity has a
technical meaning as well. There it involves "hiding information": concealing
vulnerabilities, so that others cannot take advantage of those weaknesses, and
"deliberately suppressing general information about a system to make things
more difficult for adversaries, hackers, and third parties to discover flaws in a
system." Edward Amoroso, *Cyber Attacks: Protecting National Infrastructure*
(Burlington, MA: Butterworth-Heinemann, 2012: 171).

12. See U.S. Dep't of Justice v. Reporters Comm. for Freedom of the Press,
489 U.S. at 750 (recognizing a strong privacy interest in maintaining the
"practical obscurity" of a rap sheet).

13. Ibid. ("[T]he privacy interest in maintaining the rap sheet's 'practical obscurity' is always at its apex while the FOIA-based public interest in disclosure is at its nadir.").

14. Ibid., 770.

15. See, e.g., Woodrow Hartzog and Frederic D. Stutzman, "The Case for Online Obscurity," *California Law Review* 101 (2012): 21–24, discussing the reluctance of courts to expand upon the "practical obscurity" concept articulated in *Reporters Committee*.

16. Ibid., 21–22: "Beyond a general sense that shared or available information does not always constitute public information, courts have had a difficult time expanding on the concept."

17. See Woodrow Hartzog and Evan Selinger, "Surveillance as Loss of Obscurity," *Washington and Lee Law Review* 72 (2015): 1343–1387.

18. Paul Ohm, "Good Enough Privacy," *University of Chicago Legal Forum* 2008 (2008): 1–63.

19. Neil Richards, *Intellectual Privacy: Rethinking Civil Liberties in the Digital Age* (New York: Oxford University Press, 2015); Julie Cohen, *Configuring the Networked Self: Law, Code, and the Play of Everyday Practice* (New Haven: Yale University Press, 2012).

20. Daniel Meissler, "Obscurity Is a Valid Security Layer," https://danielmiessler.com/study/security-by-obscurity/#gs.QHA8qvc.

21. Ira S. Rubinstein, "Regulating Privacy by Design," *Berkeley Technology Law Journal* 26 (2011): 1413.

22. Of course, paywall technologies are both controversial and subject to circumvention. But increasing the labor required to access information is another way to lower the probability of discovery. See, e.g., "5 Ways to Get Around the New York Times Paywall," Make Use Of, March 30, 2011, http://www.makeuseof.com/tag/5-ways-york-times-paywall/.

23. There are privacy implications regarding the use of cookies, but these threats are better addressed by other strategies within privacy by design and are beyond the scope of this article. See, e.g., Ashkan Soltani, Shannon Canty, Quentin Mayo, Lauren Thomas, and Chris Jay Hoofnagle, "Flash Cookies and Privacy" (unpublished manuscript, August 11, 2009), http://papers.ssrn.com/sol3/papers.cfm?abstract_id=1446862; and Joseph Turow, Jennifer King, Chris Jay Hoofnagle, Amy Bleakley, and Michael Hennessy, "Americans Reject Tailored Advertising and Three Activities That Enable It" (unpublished manuscript, September 29, 2009), http://papers.ssrn.com/sol3/papers.cfm?abstract_id=1478214.

24. See, e.g., Lior Strahilevitz, "A Social Networks Theory of Privacy," *University of Chicago Law Review* 72 (2005): 919–988.

25. See Mary Madden and Aaron Smith, "Reputation Management and Social Media." Pew Research Center, May 26, 2010, http://www.pewinternet.org /Reports/2010/Reputation-Management.aspx, which finds that "more than two-thirds (71%) of social networking users ages 18–29 have changed the privacy settings on their profile to limit what they share with others online."

26. See, e.g., Loporcaro v. City of New York, 2012 WL 1231021 (Apr. 9, 2012) ("When a person creates a Facebook account, he or she may be found to have consented to the possibility that personal information might be shared with others, notwithstanding his or her privacy settings, as there is no guarantee that the pictures and information posted thereon, whether personal or not, will not be further broadcast and made available to other members of the public.").

27. See, e.g., Frederic Stutzman and Woodrow Hartzog, "Boundary Regulation in Social Media," in *Proceedings of the ACM 2012 Conference on Computer Supported Cooperative Work* (New York: Association for Computing Machinery, 2012), 769–778.

28. See, e.g. Jonathan Zittrain, "Privacy 2.0," *University of Chicago Legal Forum* 2008 (2008): 102, which notes, "Today, nearly all Web programmers know robots.txt is the way in which sites can signal their intentions to robots, and these intentions are voluntarily respected by every major search engine across differing cultures and legal jurisdictions."

29. Ashley Poland, "Can You Restrict Ages on Tumblr?," eHow, June 29, 2011, http://www.ehow.com/info_8665566_can-restrict-ages-tumblr.html.

30. "Why Page 2 of the Search Results if the Best Place to Hide a Dead Body," Digital Synopsis, http://digitalsynopsis.com/tools/google-serp-design/.

31. See, e.g., Claire Garvie, Alvaro Bedoya, and Jonathan Frankle, "The Perpetual Line-Up: Unregulated Police Face Recognition in America," Georgetown Law Center on Privacy and Technology, October 18, 2016, https://www .perpetuallineup.org/; and Megan Geuss, "Facebook Facial Recognition: Its Quiet Rise and Dangerous Future," *PC World,* April 26, 2011, https://www .pcworld.com/article/226228/Facerec.html.

32. Garvie et al., "The Perpetual Line-Up."

33. "Augmented Reality," Mashable, http://mashable.com/follow/topics /augmented-reality/. See also Scott R. Peppet, "Freedom of Contract in an Augmented Reality: The Case of Consumer Contracts," *UCLA Law Review* 59 (2012): 676–745.

34. Ryan Singel, "YouTube Offers Face-Blurring Tool to Protect Dissidents," *Wired,* July 18, 2012, https://www.wired.com/2012/07/youtube-face-blurring.

35. For more on this topic, see the effort of a group of computer security academics advocating an exemption to the anticircumvention provisions of the DMCA for security research in Andy Greenberg, "It's Finally Legal to Hack Your

Own Devices (Even Your Car)," *Wired*, October 31, 2016, https://www.wired.com
/2016/10/hacking-car-pacemaker-toaster-just-became-legal/; and Aaron Alva,
"DMCA Exemption For Consumer Devices," Federal Trade Commission,
October 28, 2016, https://www.ftc.gov/news-events/blogs/techftc/2016/10/dmca
-security-research-exemption-consumer-devices.

36. A. Michael Froomkin, "The Metaphor Is the Key: Cryptography, the
Clipper Chip, and the Constitution," *University of Pennsylvania Law Review* 143
(1995): 713.

37. Froomkin, "The Metaphor Is the Key," 712 notes, "Secrecy is a form of
power. The ability to protect a secret, to preserve one's privacy, is a form of
power.' The ability to penetrate secrets, to learn them, to use them, is also a form
of power. Secrecy empowers, secrecy protects, secrecy hurts. The ability to learn
a person's secrets without her knowledge-to pierce a person's privacy in secret-is
a greater power still."

38. For more information regarding compromise in the encryption debate,
see Justin (Gus) Hurwitz, "Encryption Congress Mod (Apple + CALEA),"
Harvard Journal of Law and Technology 30 (2017): 355–424.

39. Eric Geller, "A Complete Guide to the New 'Crypto Wars,'" The Daily
Dot, May 5, 2016, https://www.dailydot.com/layer8/encryption-crypto-wars
-backdoors-timeline-security-privacy/; Electronic Frontier Foundation, "The
Crypto Wars," https://www.eff.org/document/crypto-wars; Brian Barrett, "The
Apple-FBI Battle Is Over, but the New Crypto Wars Have Just Begun," *Wired*,
March 30, 2016, https://www.wired.com/2016/03/apple-fbi-battle-crypto-wars
-just-begun/.

40. Matt Blaze, Testimony to the U.S. House of Representatives Committee
on Energy and Commerce, Subcommittee on Oversight and Investigations,
Hearing on "Deciphering the Debate over Encryption," April 19, 2016, http://docs
.house.gov/meetings/IF/IF02/20160419/104812/HHRG-114-IF02-Wstate-BlazeM
-20160419-U3.pdf, notes, "The most basic problem with third-party access
cryptography is simply that we do not fully understand how to design it securely.
Any key escrow or lawful access cryptography system, by its very nature,
increases its number of points of failure. Unfortunately, we do not understand
the problem well enough to even precisely quantify how this reduces security, let
alone identify a safe level for this reduction." See also Matt Blaze, "Protocol
Failure in the Escrowed Encryption Standard," in *Proceedings of the 2nd ACM
Conference on Computer and Communications Security* (New York: Association
for Computing Machinery, 1994), 59–67.

41. Froomkin, "Metaphor"; Hurwitz, "Encryption Congress"; Whitfield Diffie
and Susan E. Landau, *Privacy on the Line: The Politics of Wiretapping and
Encryption* (Cambridge, MA: MIT Press, 1998), 66–68.

42. Paul Ohm, "Good Enough Privacy," *University of Chicago Legal Forum* (2008): 1–63; Justin (Gus) Hurwitz, "Encryption Congress Mod (Apple + CALEA)," *Harvard Journal of Law and Technology* 30 (2017) :356–424.

43. Kim Zetter, "The FBI Drops Its Case against Apple after Finding a Way into That Phone," *Wired,* March 28, 2016, https://www.wired.com/2016/03/fbi -drops-case-apple-finding-way-iphone/.

44. House of Representatives Judiciary Committee, "Hearing Wrap Up: House Judiciary Committee Examines Encryption," March 2, 2016, https:// judiciary.house.gov/press-release/hearing-wrap-up-house-judiciary-committee -examines-encryption/.

45. Government's Reply in Support of Motion to Compel and Opposition to Apple Inc.'s Motion to Vacate Order, In re the Search of an Apple iPhone Seized during the Execution of a Search Warrant on a Black Lexus IS300, California License Plate 35KGD203 (Mar. 10, 2016), http://www.scribd.com/doc/303738452 /Gov-t-Response-to-Apple.

46. Peter Swire and Kenesa Ahmad, " 'Going Dark' versus a 'Golden Age for Surveillance,' " Center for Democracy and Technology, November 28, 2011, https://fpf.org/wp-content/uploads/Going-Dark-Versus-a-Golden-Age-for -Surveillance-Peter-Swire-and-Kenesa-A.pdf.

47. Hayley Tsukayama, "How Closely Is Amazon's Echo Listening?," *Washington Post,* November 11, 2014, https://www.washingtonpost.com/news/the -switch/wp/2014/11/11/how-closely-is-amazons-echo-listening/.

48. Jaikumar Vijayan, "DOJ Seeks Mandatory Data Retention Requirement for ISPs," *Computerworld,* January 25, 2011, https://www.computerworld.com /article/2512742/data-privacy/doj-seeks-mandatory-data-retention-requirement -for-isps.html?page=2; Nancy Libin and Jim Dempsey to Interested Persons, "Re: Mandatory Data Retention—Invasive, Risky, Unnecessary, Ineffective," memorandum, June 2, 2006, https://www.cdt.org/files/privacy/20060602retention.pdf.

49. See, e.g., Alexis Madrigal, "A Privacy Manifesto in Code: What if Your Emails Never Went to Gmail and Twitter Couldn't See Your Tweets?," *Atlantic,* April 4, 2012), https://www.theatlantic.com/technology/archive/2012/04/a -privacy-manifesto-in-code-what-if-your-emails-never-went-to-gmail-and -twitter-couldnt-see-your-tweets/255414/; and Electronic Frontier Foundation, "HTTPS Everywhere," https://www.eff.org/https-everywhere.

50. Alexander Howard, "White House Mandates HTTPS by Default for Federal Websites," *Huffington Post,* June 9, 2015, http://www.huffingtonpost .com/2015/06/08/https-federal-websites_n_7539164.html.

51. Kate Conger, "Apple Will Require HTTPS Connections for iOS Apps by the End of 2016," *TechCrunch,* June 14, 2016, https://techcrunch.com/2016/06/14 /apple-will-require-https-connections-for-ios-apps-by-the-end-of-2016/.

52. Michael Horowitz, "Lenovo Collects Usage Data on ThinkPad, Think-Centre and ThinkStation PCs," *Computerworld,* September 22, 2015, http://www.computerworld.com/article/2984889/windows-pcs/lenovo-collects-usage-data-on-thinkpad-thinkcentre-and-thinkstation-pcs.html.

53. Cory Doctorow, "Chrome Update Turns Browsers into Covert Listening Tools," Boing Boing, June 24, 2015, http://boingboing.net/2015/06/24/chrome-update-turns-browsers-i.html.

54. Katie Rogers, "Mark Zuckerberg Covers His Laptop Camera. You Should Consider It, Too.," *New York Times,* June 22, 2013, http://www.nytimes.com/2016/06/23/technology/personaltech/mark-zuckerberg-covers-his-laptop-camera-you-should-consider-it-too.html.

55. Federal Trade Commission, "Retail Tracking Firm Settles FTC Charges It Misled Consumers about Opt Out Choices," April 23, 2015, https://www.ftc.gov/news-events/press-releases/2015/04/retail-tracking-firm-settles-ftc-charges-it-misled-consumers.

56. Soltani et al., "Flash Cookies and Privacy."

57. Farai Chideya, "The Facebook of the Future Has Privacy Implications Today," The Intercept, September 17, 2015, https://theintercept.com/2015/09/17/facebook/.

58. "What They Know," *Wall Street Journal,* http://www.wsj.com/public/page/what-they-know-digital-privacy.html; Ania Nussbaum, "7 Ways You're Being Tracked Online (and How to Stop It)," *Wall Street Journal,* August 4, 2014, http://blogs.wsj.com/digits/2015/08/04/7-ways-youre-being-tracked-online-and-how-to-stop-it; Jennifer Valentino-DeVries, "What They Know about You," *Wall Street Journal,* July 31, 2010, http://www.wsj.com/articles/SB10001424052748704 93930457539904184993 1612.

59. Danielle Citron, "Spying, Inc.," *Washington and Lee Law Review* 71 (2015): 1243–1282.

60. Anil K. Jain and Ajay Kumar, "Biometrics Recognition: An Overview," in *Second Generation Biometrics: The Ethical, Legal and Social Context,* ed. Emilio Mordini and Dimitros Tzovaras (Dordrecht, Netherlands: Springer, 2011), 49–79, http://biometrics.cse.msu.edu/Publications/GeneralBiometrics/JainKumar_BiometricsNextGeneration_Overview.pdf; Jim Giles, "Cameras Know You by Your Walk," *New Scientist,* September 19, 2012, https://www.newscientist.com/article/mg21528835-600-cameras-know-you-by-your-walk/.

61. Federal Bureau of Investigation, "Next Generation Identification (NGI)," https://www.fbi.gov/services/cjis/fingerprints-and-other-biometrics/ngi; Garvie et al., "The Perpetual Line-Up."

62. Aviva Rutkin, "Facebook Can Recognise You in Photos Even If You're Not Looking," *New Scientist,* June 22, 2015, http://www.newscientist.com/article

/dn27761-facebook-can-recognise-you-in-photos-even-if-youre-not-looking
.html#.VYmbS_nBzRZ.

63. Cyrus Fariar, "We Know Where You've Been: Ars Acquires 4.6M License
Plate Scans from the Cops," Ars Technica, March 24, 2015, http://arstechnica
.com/tech-policy/2015/03/we-know-where-youve-been-ars-acquires-4-6m
-license-plate-scans-from-the-cops/.

64. American Civil Liberties Union, "You Are Being Tracked," https://www
.aclu.org/feature/you-are-being-tracked.

65. Kaveh Wadell, "How License-Plate Readers Have Helped Police and
Lenders Target the Poor," Atlantic, April 22, 2016, http://www.theatlantic.com
/technology/archive/2016/04/how-license-plate-readers-have-helped-police-and
-lenders-target-the-poor/479436/.

66. Dave Mass and Cooper Quentin, "EFF: We found 100+license plate
readers wide open on the Internet," Ars Technica, October 28, 2015, http://
arstechnica.com/tech-policy/2015/10/lprs-exposed-how-public-safety-agencies
-responded-to-major-vulnerabilities-in-vehicle-surveillance-tech/.

67. Justin Peters, "Why Would Anyone Want a Drone to Follow Them
Around All the Time?," Slate, January 14, 2016, http://www.slate.com/blogs
/future_tense/2016/01/14/lily_drone_follows_owners_around_all_the_time_why
.html.

68. Daniel Demay, "Amazon Nets Patent for Mini Police Drones," KOMO
News, October 28, 2016, http://komonews.com/news/tech/amazon-nets-patent
-for-mini-police-drones.

69. Justin Peters, "Judge Dismisses Case against Man Who Shot Down a
Drone over His Property," Slate, October 28, 2015, http://www.slate.com/blogs
/future_tense/2015/10/28/case_against_william_merideth_for_shooting_down
_a_drone_is_dismissed.html; Margot Kaminski, "Enough with the 'Sunbathing
Teenager' Gambit," Slate, May 17, 2016, http://www.slate.com/articles/technology
/future_tense/2016/05/drone_privacy_is_about_much_more_than_sunbathing
_teenage_daughters.html.

70. M. Ryan Calo, "The Drone as Privacy Catalyst," Stanford Law Review
Online 64 (2011), https://www.stanfordlawreview.org/online/the-drone-as
-privacy-catalyst/.

71. Kaminski, "Enough with the 'Sunbathing Teenager' Gambit."

72. Ibid.

73. Bruce Schneier, "Your TV May Be Watching You," CNN, February 12,
2015, http://www.cnn.com/2015/02/11/opinion/schneier-samsung-tv-listening/.

74. Eliot C. MacLaughlin, "Alexa, Can You Help with This Murder Case?,"
CNN, December 29, 2016, http://www.cnn.com/2016/12/28/tech/amazon-echo
-alexa-bentonville-arkansas-murder-case-trnd/.

75. Stacey Gray, "Always On: Privacy Implications of Microphone-Enabled Devices," Future of Privacy Forum, April 2016, https://fpf.org/wp-content /uploads/2016/04/FPF_Always_On_WP.pdf.

76. Kate Cox, "All Those Smart Devices That Listen To Your House May Be Unlawfully Violating Kids' Privacy," Consumerist (May 26, 2016), https:// consumerist.com/2016/05/26/all-those-smart-devices-that-listen-to-your-house -may-be-unlawfully-violating-kids-privacy/.

77. Tom Scocca, "The New iPhone Is Set to Record You, Whether You Ask It to or Not," Gawker, September 10, 2015, http://gawker.com/the-new-iphone-is-set -to-record-you-whether-you-ask-it-1729857048.

78. "Body Worn Camera Laws Database," National Conference of State Legislatures, http://www.ncsl.org/research/civil-and-criminal-justice/body-worn -cameras-interactive-graphic.aspx.

79. Elizabeth Joh, "Beyond Surveillance: Data Control and Body Cameras," Surveillance and Society 14 (2016):133–137.

80. Elizabeth Joh, "The Undue Influence of Surveillance Technology Companies on Policing," New York Law Review Online (forthcoming 2017), https:// papers.ssrn.com/sol3/papers.cfm?abstract_id=2924620.

81. Jamie Condliffe, "AI Has Beaten Humans at Lip-Reading," MIT Technology Review, November 21, 2016, https://www.technologyreview.com/s/602949 /ai-has-beaten-humans-at-lip-reading/.

82. Jeff John Roberts, "Twitter Warns Developers about Misusing Data," Fortune, November 22, 2016, http://fortune.com/2016/11/22/twitter-data -surveillance/.

83. Rebecca C. Hetey and Jennifer L. Eberhardt, "Racial Disparities in Incarceration Increase Acceptance of Punitive Policies," Psychological Science 25 (2014): 1949–1954; Garvie et al., "The Perpetual Lineup."; Julia Angwin, "Machine Bias: There's Software Used across the Country to Predict Future criminals. And It's Biased against Blacks," Pro Publica, May 23, 2016, https://www.propublica.org /article/machine-bias-risk-assessments-in-criminal-sentencing; Solon Barocas and Andrew D. Selbst, "Big Data's Disparate Impact," California Law Review 104 (2016): 671–732.

84. David Segal, "Mugged by a Mug Shot Online," New York Times, October 5, 2013, http://www.nytimes.com/2013/10/06/business/mugged-by-a-mug -shot-online.html; Ingrid Rojas and Natasha Del Toro, "Should Newspapers Make Money off of Mugshot Galleries?," Fusion, March 9, 2016, http://fusion.net /story/278341/naked-truth-newspapers-mugshot-galleries/.

85. See William McGeveran, "The Law of Friction," University of Chicago Legal Forum 2013 (2013): 18, which notes, "In the physical world, too much friction can impede movement or even start fires, but too little would cause objects to slide off tables and cars off roads. The key to online disclosures also

turns out to be the correct amount of friction, not its elimination." See also Neil M. Richards, "The Perils of Social Reading," *Georgetown Law Journal* 101 (2013): 692, which posits that "social reading and frictionless sharing menace our intellectual privacy."

86. Segal, "Mugged by a Mugshot"; "Mug Shot Website Fallout Raises a Bigger Question," Bloomberg, October 7, 2013, http://www.bloomberg.com/news /articles/2013-10-07/mug-shot-website-fallout-raises-a-bigger-question.

87. 868 N.Y.S. 2d 470 (N.Y. Sup. Ct. 2008).

88. Ibid., 479 ("The Internet has no sunset and postings on it will last and be available until some person purges the Web site, perhaps in decades to come.").

89. Ibid., 473–474.

90. Ibid., 480.

91. Ibid., 481.

92. Ibid., 480 ("It is the scope and permanence of public disclosure on the Internet by a government agency that distinguishes the County's 'Wall of Shame' from traditional and regular forms of reporting and publication such as print media.").

93. Brian Merchant, "Your Porn Is Watching You," Motherboard, April 6, 2015, http://motherboard.vice.com/read/your-porn-is-watching-you.

94. Ibrahim Altaweel, Maximilian Hils, and Chris Jay Hoofnagle, "Privacy on Adult Websites," paper presented at the Workshop on Technology and Consumer Protection, colocated with the 38th IEEE Symposium on Security and Privacy, San Jose, CA, May 22–24, 2017.

95. Lorenzo Franceschi-Bicchierai, "Shazam Keeps Your Mac's Microphone Always On, Even When You Turn It Off," Motherboard, November 14, 2016, https://motherboard.vice.com/read/shazam-keeps-your-macs-microphone -always-on-even-when-you-turn-it-off.

96. Danielle Keats Citron, "Reservoirs of Danger: The Evolution of Public and Private Law at the Dawn of the Information Age," *Southern California Law Review* 80 (2007): 243.

97. Paul Ohm, "Don't Build a Database of Ruin," *Harvard Business Review,* August 23, 2012, https://hbr.org/2012/08/dont-build-a-database-of-ruin.

98. See Catherine Crump, "Data Retention: Privacy, Anonymity, and Accountability Online," *Stanford Law Review* 56 (2003): 191–229.

99. Court of Justice of the European Union, "The Court of Justice declares the Data Retention Directive to be invalid," Press Release No 54/14, April 8, 2014, http://curia.europa.eu/jcms/upload/docs/application/pdf/2014-04/cp140054en .pdf; Electronic Privacy Information Center, "Data Retention," https://www.epic .org/privacy/intl/data_retention.html.

100. Joel R. Reidenberg, "The Data Surveillance State in the United States and Europe," *Wake Forest Law Review* 49 (2014): 605.

101. Ibid.

102. General Services Administration, "Privacy Impact Assessment: Data Leakage Prevention Content Filtering," October 17, 2011, http://www.gsa.gov /portal/mediaId/125018/fileName/PIA_GSA_DataLeakagePrevention _WebVersion.action; Christoph Eckstein, "Preventing Data Leakage: A Risk Based Approach for Controlled Use of the Use of Administrative and Access Privileges," SANS Institute, August 10, 2015, https://www.sans.org/reading-room /whitepapers/dlp/preventing-data-leakage-risk-based-approach-controlled-use -administrative-36202.

103. Paul M. Schwartz and Edward J. Janger, "Notification of Data Security Breaches," *Michigan Law Review* 105 (2007): 913–984.

104. Malena Carollo, "Why Webcam Indicator Lights Are Lousy Privacy Safeguards," *Christian Science Monitor,* July 13, 2015, http://www.csmonitor.com /World/Passcode/2015/0713/Why-webcam-indicator-lights-are-lousy-privacy -safeguards.

8. The Internet of Things

1. Vibrundies, http://www.vibrundies.com/.

2. Harry Yorke, "Grieving Family's Horror as Hardcore Pornography Played at Funeral for Father and Baby Son," *Wales Online,* January 27, 2016, http://www .walesonline.co.uk/news/wales-news/grieving-familys-horror-hardcore -pornography-10797800.

3. Lorenzo Franceschi-Bicchierai, "Smart Fridge Only Capable of Displaying Buggy Future of the Internet of Things," Motherboard, December 11, 2015, http://motherboard.vice.com/read/smart-fridge-only-capable-of-displaying -buggy-future-of-the-internet-of-things.

4. Nick Statt, "Nest Is Permanently Disabling the Revolv Smart Home Hub," The Verge, April 4, 2016, http://www.theverge.com/2016/4/4/11362928/google -nest-revolv-shutdown-smart-home-products.

5. Reuters, "The Internet of Things: By 2020, You'll Own 50 Internet-Connected Devices," *Huffington Post,* June 22, 2013, http://www.huffingtonpost .com/2013/04/22/internet-of-things_n_3130340.html; OECD Insights, "Smart Networks: Coming Soon to a Home Near You," January 21, 2013, http:// oecdinsights.org/2013/01/21/smart-networks-coming-soon-to-a-home-near-you/. See also Dave Evans, "The Internet of Things: How the Next Evolution of the Internet Is Changing Everything," Cisco, April 2011, http://www.cisco.com/c /dam/en_us/about/ac79/docs/innov/IoT_IBSG_0411FINAL.pdf.

6. Maria Farrell, "The Internet of Things—Who Wins, Who Loses?," *Guardian,* August 14, 2015, https://www.theguardian.com/technology/2015/aug/14/internet -of-things-winners-and-losers-privacy-autonomy-capitalism.

7. Sarah Halzack, "Privacy Advocates Try to Keep 'Creepy,' 'Eavesdropping' Hello Barbie from Hitting Shelves," *Washington Post,* March 11, 2015, https://www.washingtonpost.com/news/the-switch/wp/2015/03/11/privacy -advocates-try-to-keep-creepy-eavesdropping-hello-barbie-from-hitting-shelves/; Kashmir Hill, "Parents Are Worried About the New WiFi-connected Barbie, But Should They Be?," Splinter, January 6, 2016, https://splinternews.com/parents-are -worried-about-the-new-wifi-connected-barbie-1793853908.

8. Scott Peppet, "Regulating the Internet of Things: First Steps toward Managing Discrimination, Privacy, Security and Consent," *Texas Law Review* 93 (2014): 85–176.

9. Ibid.

10. Kashmir Hill, "Fitbit Moves Quickly After Users' Sex Stats Exposed," *Forbes,* July 5, 2011, https://www.forbes.com/sites/kashmirhill/2011/07/05/fitbit -moves-quickly-after-users-sex-stats-exposed/#2bf8c6754327.

11. Meg Leta (Ambrose) Jones and Kevin Meurer, "Can (and Should) Hello Barbie Keep a Secret?," paper presented at the IEEE International Symposium on Ethics in Engineering, Science, and Technology, Vancouver, May 13–14, 2016.

12. Peppet, "Regulating the Internet of Things."

13. Bruce Schneier, "The Internet of Things That Talk About You Behind Your Back," Schneier on Security, January 16, 2016, https://www.schneier.com /blog/archives/2016/01/the_internet_of.html.

14. Federal Trade Commission, "FTC Issues Warning Letters to App Developers Using 'Silverpush' Code," March 17, 2016, https://www.ftc.gov/news -events/press-releases/2016/03/ftc-issues-warning-letters-app-developers-using -silverpush-code.

15. Schneier, "The Internet of Things."

16. Federal Trade Commission, "FTC Issues Warning Letters."

17. Samuel Gibbs, "Toy Firm VTech Hack Exposes Private Data of Parents and Children," *Guardian,* November 20, 2015, http://www.theguardian.com /technology/2015/nov/30/vtech-toys-hack-private-data-parents-children.

18. John Leyden, "One Ring to Own Them All: IoT Doorbell Can Reveal Your Wi-Fi Key," The Register, January 12, 2016, http://www.theregister.co.uk/2016/01 /12/ring_doorbell_reveals_wifi_credentials/.

19. Andy Greenberg and Kim Zetter, "How the Internet of Things Got Hacked," *Wired,* December 28, 2015, http://www.wired.com/2015/12/2015-the -year-the-internet-of-things-got-hacked/.

20. Lorenzo Franceschi-Bicchierai, "A GPS Tracker for Kids Had a Bug That Would Let Hackers Stalk Them," Motherboard, February 2, 2016, http:// motherboard.vice.com/read/a-gps-tracker-for-kids-had-a-bug-that-would-let -hackers-stalk-them.

21. Greenberg and Zetter, "How the Internet of Things Got Hacked."

22. Dave Evans, "The Internet of Things [Infographic]," Cisco, July 15, 2011, http://blogs.cisco.com/diversity/the-internet-of-things-infographic.

23. Omner Barajas, "How the Internet of Things (IoT) Is Changing the Cybersecurity Landscape," Security Intelligence, September 17, 2014, https://securityintelligence.com/how-the-internet-of-things-iot-is-changing-the-cybersecurity-landscape/(citing Dave Evans, "The Internet of Things: How the Next Evolution of the Internet Is Changing Everything," Cisco, April 2011, http://share.cisco.com/internet-of-things.html); Daniel Miessler, "HP Study Reveals 70 Percent of Internet of Things Devices Vulnerable to Attack," HP, July 29, 2014, http://h30499.www3.hp.com/t5/Fortify-Application-Security/HP-Study-Reveals-70-Percent-of-Internet-of-Things-Devices/ba-p/6556284#.U_NUL4BdU00.

24. Miessler, "HP Study."

25. Trevor Timm, "The Government Just Admitted It Will Use Smart Home Devices for Spying," Guardian, February 9, 2016, http://www.theguardian.com/commentisfree/2016/feb/09/internet-of-things-smart-devices-spying-surveillance-us-government; bracketed text in the original.

26. See, e.g., "Lack of Database and Password Security Leaves Millions of Users Exposed," Duo December 15, 2015, https://duo.com/blog/lack-of-database-and-password-security-leaves-millions-of-users-exposed; and J. M. Porup, "'Internet of Things' Security Is Hilariously Broken and Getting Worse," Ars Technica, January 23, 2016, http://arstechnica.com/security/2016/01/how-to-search-the-internet-of-things-for-photos-of-sleeping-babies/.

27. Lorenzo Franceschi-Bicchierai, "Hacked Toy Company VTech's TOS Now Says It's Not Liable for Hacks," Motherboard, February 9, 2016, http://motherboard.vice.com/read/hacked-toy-company-vtech-tos-now-says-its-not-liable-for-hacks.

28. Ibid.

29. See e.g., Yash Kotak, "5 Reasons Why My IoT Startup Failed," VentureBeat, June 16, 2015, http://venturebeat.com/2015/06/16/5-reasons-why-my-iot-startup-failed/; and Nat Garlin, "Quirky Files for Bankruptcy, Will Likely Sell Its IoT Company Wink in the Next 60 Days," The Next Web, September 22, 2015, http://thenextweb.com/insider/2015/09/22/quirky-bankruptcy/.

30. See, e.g., Peppet, "Regulating the Internet of Things."

31. MIT Information Systems and Technology, "Why Patch?," https://ist.mit.edu/security/patches.

32. Parc Lawrence Lee, "How the 'Internet of Everyday Things' Could Turn Any Product into a Service," VentureBeat, February 7, 2015, http://venturebeat.com/2015/02/07/how-the-internet-of-everyday-things-could-turn-any-product-into-a-service/.

33. See, e.g., Brian Krebs, "IoT Reality: Smart Devices, Dumb Defaults," Krebs on Security, February 8, 2016, http://krebsonsecurity.com/2016/02/iot-reality-smart-devices-dumb-defaults/; Brian Krebs, "This Is Why People Fear the 'Internet of Things,'" Krebs on Security, February 18, 2016, https://krebsonsecurity.com/2016/02/this-is-why-people-fear-the-internet-of-things/; and Kashmir Hill, "The Half-Baked Security of Our 'Internet Of Things,'" *Forbes,* May 27, 2016, http://www.forbes.com/sites/kashmirhill/2014/05/27/article-may-scare-you-away-from-internet-of-things/#3e6ec4ab23dd, which quotes designer Artem Harutyunyan: "The reason why [Internet of Things] vendors are not doing security better is that it's cheaper not to do it. It's expensive to build security in. The shopper in Best Buy will buy the camera for $40 not the one that's $100. She doesn't know or care about the security. There will be more and more hacks, not just of cameras but of lots of things. Eventually it will make people care, and it will be more expensive to be insecure than secure." (Bracketed text in the original.)

34. See, e.g., Brian Krebs, "The Lingering Mess from Default Insecurity," Krebs on Security, November 12, 2015, http://krebsonsecurity.com/2015/11/the-lingering-mess-from-default-insecurity/, which notes, "As the Internet of Things grows, we can scarcely afford a massive glut of things that are insecure-by-design. One reason is that this stuff has far too long a half-life, and it will remain in our Internet's land and streams for many years to come. . . . Mass-deployed, insecure-by-default devices are difficult and expensive to clean up and / or harden for security, and the costs of that vulnerability are felt across the Internet and around the globe."

35. Rakesh Sharma, "A New Perspective on the Internet Of Things," *Forbes,* February 18, 2014, http://www.forbes.com/sites/rakeshsharma/2014/02/18/a-new-perspective-on-the-internet-of-things/#53652d3d267c.

36. Krebs, "IoT Reality."

37. Craig Williams, quoted in Krebs, "IoT Reality."

38. Krebs, "IoT Reality."

39. Dan Goodin, "Why the Silencing of KrebsOnSecurity Opens a Troubling Chapter for the 'Net," Ars Technica, September 23, 2016, https://arstechnica.com/security/2016/09/why-the-silencing-of-krebsonsecurity-opens-a-troubling-chapter-for-the-net/. Zombie devices are those that are still operational but no longer being supported by their creators.

40. Goodin, "Why the Silencing of KrebsOnSecurity Opens a Troubling Chapter for the 'Net."

41. Krebs, "IoT Reality."

42. Emerging Technology from the arXiv, "First Wi-Fi-Enabled Smart Contact Lens Prototype," *MIT Technology Review,* July 29, 2016, https://www.technologyreview.com/s/602035/first-wi-fi-enabled-smart-contact-lens

-prototype/; Jennifer Langston, "Interscatter Communication Enables First-Ever Implanted Devices, Smart Contact Lenses, Credit Cards That 'Talk' Wi-Fi," UW Today, August 17, 2016, http://www.washington.edu/news/2016/08/17/interscatter -communication-enables-first-ever-implanted-devices-smart-contact-lenses -credit-cards-that-talk-wi-fi/; Daniel Clery, "Could a Wireless Pacemaker Let Hackers Take Control of Your Heart?," *Science,* February 9, 2015, http://www .sciencemag.org/news/2015/02/could-wireless-pacemaker-let-hackers-take -control-your-heart; Andrea Matwyshyn, "Internet of Bodies," paper presented at Privacy Law Scholars Conference, George Washington University, Wash- ington, DC, June 2, 2016.

43. James Maude, quoted in Jaikumar Vijayan, "If You're Reading This with Internet Explorer, Stop in the Name of Security," *Christian Science Monitor,* January 13, 2016, https://www.csmonitor.com/World/Passcode/2016/0113/If-you-re -reading-this-with-Internet-Explorer-stop-in-the-name-of-security.

44. Federal Trade Commission, "ASUS Settles FTC Charges That Insecure Home Routers and 'Cloud' Services Put Consumers' Privacy at Risk," Feb- ruary 23, 2016, https://www.ftc.gov/news-events/press-releases/2016/02/asus -settles-ftc-charges-insecure-home-routers-cloud-services-put; Federal Trade Commission, "FTC Approves Final Order Settling Charges against TRENDnet, Inc.," February 7, 2014, https://www.ftc.gov/news-events/press-releases/2014/02 /ftc-approves-final-order-settling-charges-against-trendnet-inc.

45. See James Grimmelmann, "Privacy as Product Safety," *Widener Law Journal* 19 (2010): 816, which notes that "the database-centric Fair Information Practice approach has been the basis for most of the information privacy law the United States actually has."

46. Federal Trade Commission, "Start with Security: A Guide for Business," June 2015, https://www.ftc.gov/system/files/documents/plain-language/pdf0205 -startwithsecurity.pdf.

47. See, e.g., Woodrow Hartzog and Daniel J. Solove, "The Scope and Potential of FTC Data Protection," *George Washington Law Review* 83 (2015): 2230–2300; and Kristina Rozen, "How Do Industry Standards for Data Security Match Up with the FTC's Implied "Reasonable" Standards—And What Might This Mean for Liability Avoidance?," International Association of Privacy Profes- sionals, November 25, 2014, https://iapp.org/news/a/how-do-industry-standards -for-data-security-match-up-with-the-ftcs-implied-reasonable-standards-and -what-might-this-mean-for-liability-avoidance.

48. Peppet, "Regulating the Internet of Things."

49. I Am The Cavalry, "About," https://www.iamthecavalry.org/about /overview/: "The Cavalry is a grassroots organization that is focused on issues where computer security intersect public safety and human life. The areas of

focus for The Cavalry are medical devices, automobiles, home electronics and public infrastructure."

50. On the five-star rating system, see J. M. Porup, "'Internet of Things Security Is Hilariously Broken and Getting Worse," Ars Technica, January 23, 2016, http://arstechnica.com/security/2016/01/how-to-search-the-internet-of -things-for-photos-of-sleeping-babies/.

51. Julia Layton, "How Digital Rights Management Works," How Stuff Works, January 3, 2006, http://computer.howstuffworks.com/drm1.htm.

52. Chris Hoffman, "Is DRM a Threat to Computer Security?," Make Use Of, June 12, 2014, http://www.makeuseof.com/tag/drm-threat-computer-security/.

53. Cory Doctorow, "You Can't Destroy the Village to Save It: W3C vs DRM, Round Two," Electronic Frontier Foundation January 12, 2016, https://www.eff .org/deeplinks/2016/01/you-cant-destroy-village-save-it-w3c-vs-drm-round-two.

54. U.S. Department of Homeland Security, *Strategic Principles for Securing the Internet of Things (IoT)* (Washington, DC: U.S. Department of Homeland Security, 2016), https://www.dhs.gov/sites/default/files/publications/Strategic _Principles_for_Securing_the_Internet_of_Things-2016-1115-FINAL. . . . pdf.

55. Ibid.: "User names and passwords for IoT devices supplied by the manufacturer are often never changed by the user and are easily cracked. Botnets operate by continuously scanning for IoT devices that are protected by known factory default user names and passwords. Strong security controls should be something the industrial consumer has to deliberately disable rather than deliberately enable" (5–6).

56. Ibid.: "Many IoT devices use Linux operating systems, but may not use the most up-to-date operating system. Using the current operating system ensures that known vulnerabilities will have been mitigated" (6).

57. Ibid.: "For example, use computer chips that integrate security at the transistor level, embedded in the processor, and provide encryption and anonymity" (6).

58. Ibid.: "Understanding what consequences could flow from the failure of a device will enable developers, manufacturers, and service providers to make more informed risk-based security decisions. Where feasible, developers should build IoT devices to fail safely and securely, so that the failure does not lead to greater systemic disruption" (6).

59. Raluca Ada Popa and Nickolai Zeldovich, "How to Compute with Data You Can't See," IEEE Spectrum, July 23, 2015, https://spectrum.ieee.org /computing/software/how-to-compute-with-data-you-cant-see.

60. Federal Trade Commission, "Commission Statement Marking the FTC's 50th Data Security Settlement," January 31, 2014, http://www.ftc.gov/system/files /documents/cases/140131gmrstatement.pdf.

61. See Hartzog and Solove, "The Scope and Potential of FTC Data Protection," 2246nn80–83; 16 C.F.R. § 682.3(a); 45 C.F.R. §§ 164.308–314; 16 C.F.R. §§ 314.3–314.4; Danielle K. Citron, "The Privacy Policymaking of State Attorneys General," *Notre Dame Law Review* 92 (2017): 747–816

62. U.S. Department of Homeland Security, *Strategic Principles*, 12.

63. Aaron Perzanowski and Chris Jay Hoofnagle, "What We Buy When We 'Buy Now,'" *University of Pennsylvania Law Review* 165 (2017): 316–378.

64. Bruce Schneier, "I've Seen the Future and It Has a Kill Switch," *Wired*, June 26, 2008, https://www.wired.com/2008/06/securitymatters-0626/.

65. Ibid.

66. U.S. Department of Homeland Security, *Strategic Principles*, 12.

Conclusion

1. See, e.g., American Civil Liberties Union, "Privacy and Surveillance," https://www.aclu.org/issues/national-security/privacy-and-surveillance; Owen Bowcott, "EU's Highest Court Delivers Blow to UK Snooper's Charter," *Guardian*, December 21, 2016, https://www.theguardian.com/law/2016/dec/21/eus-highest-court-delivers-blow-to-uk-snoopers-charter; and Ashley Gorkey and Patrick Toomey, "President Obama Will Soon Turn Over the Keys to the Surveillance State to President-Elect Trump," American Civil Liberties Union, November 21, 2016, https://www.aclu.org/blog/speak-freely/president-obama-will-soon-turn-over-keys-surveillance-state-president-elect-trump.

2. Dan Goodin, "Why the Silencing of KrebsOnSecurity Opens a Troubling Chapter for the 'Net," Ars Technica, September 23, 2016, http://arstechnica.com/security/2016/09/why-the-silencing-of-krebsonsecurity-opens-a-troubling-chapter-for-the-net/.

3. Claire Garvie, Alvaro Bedoya, and Jonathan Frankle, "The Perpetual Line-Up: Unregulated Police Face Recognition in America," Georgetown Law Center on Privacy and Technology, October 18, 2016, https://www.perpetuallineup.org/; Julia Angwin, "Machine Bias," Pro Publica, https://www.propublica.org/article/machine-bias-risk-assessments-in-criminal-sentencing; George Joseph, "Exclusive: Feds Regularly Monitored Black Lives Matter since Ferguson," The Intercept, July 25, 2015, https://theintercept.com/2015/07/24/documents-show-department-homeland-security-monitoring-black-lives-matter-since-ferguson/; American Civil Liberties Union, "Unleashed and Unaccountable: The FBI's Unchecked Abuse of Authority," September 2013, https://www.aclu.org/sites/default/files/assets/unleashed-and-unaccountable-fbi-report.pdf; and Sarah Brayne, "Surveillance and System Avoidance: Criminal Justice Contact and Institutional Attachment," *American Sociological Review* 79 (2014): 367–391 (reviewing how surveillance and criminal justice contact, which

tends to be concentrated on minorities and the poor, breeds distrust and "system avoidance."

4. Dylan Byers, "Exclusive: Russian-bought Black Lives Matter Ad on Facebook Targeted Baltimore and Ferguson," *CNN*, September 28, 2017, http://money.cnn.com/2017/09/27/media/facebook-black-lives-matter-targeting/index.html; Manu Raju, Dylan Byers, and Dana Bash, "Exclusive: Russian-linked Facebook Ads Targeted Michigan and Wisconsin," *CNN*, October 4, 2017, http://edition.cnn.com/2017/10/03/politics/russian-facebook-ads-michigan-wisconsin/index.html; Jonathan Zittrain, "Facebook Could Decide an Election Without Anyone Ever Finding Out," *New Republic*, June 1, 2014, https://newrepublic.com/article/117878/information-fiduciary-solution-facebook-digital-gerrymandering.

Acknowledgments

Even books with only one author are collaborative projects. I am so very grateful for the support and thanks of those who helped me with this project.

The fact that I am even a law professor in the first place is due to the care and diligence of a number of mentors, many of whom I am fortunate enough to call friends. Doris Compere taught an aimless, nervous fourteen-year-old the importance of eloquence and clarity in language and what it means to nurture a passion. Alex Bolla guided a naive law student through a gauntlet of academic challenges and career choices. Cathy Packer taught a PhD student who was accustomed to drafting dense legalese how to write in a more clear and meaningful way and how to seriously approach being an academic. And most relevant to the topic of this book, many years ago Daniel Solove saw potential in an enthusiastic but very undeveloped student who was passionate about privacy. His friendship, advice, and encouragement have been invaluable and instrumental not just in this book but in my entire career; he is a model of a teacher, mentor, and friend, and I give him my deepest thanks and appreciation.

I am incredibly grateful for the people at Samford University's Cumberland School of Law. As a student at Cumberland, I was taught how to think critically, how to value justice, and what it means to truly serve as one's counsel. To John Carroll and the faulty at Cumberland, thank you for making me a law professor. Your ceaseless support and friendship are the models of collegiality. To my students at Cumberland, I learned so much from you; thank you for your unending enthusiasm, curiosity, and good cheer. I will always be a proud Cumberlander. Special thanks to Cumberland Dean Corky Strickland, who gave me the time, space, and resources I needed to complete this book, and Associate Dean Brannon Denning, who read every single word of drafts of this book and provided invaluable feedback with record speed. And now, I am indebted to Deans Jeremy Paul and Carla Brodley and the faculty at Northeastern University School of Law and College of Computer and Information Science for inviting me to join their community. Thanks to the passionate students at Northeastern who consistently remind me of the virtue, joy, and responsibility of studying the law. I have already benefited enormously from being a part of these communities and am so excited for the future.

I am deeply indebted to the thoughtful, kind, and supportive community of privacy and technology scholars in the United States and around the world. Special thanks to my longtime collaborators and those who fundamentally influenced the structure and substance of this book—namely, Ryan Calo, Danielle Citron, Josh Fairfield, Chris Hoofnagle, Margot Kaminski, Ian Kerr, Bill McGeveran, Mark McKenna, Paul Ohm, Neil Richards, Evan Selinger, and Fred Stutzman. Many other people are deserving of special mention—too many, in fact, for the few pages allotted to an acknowledgments section. Although I am only listing their names, I extend deep gratitude to Alessandro Acquisti, Lisa Austin, Derek Bambauer, Julie Cohen, Greg Conti, Lorrie Cranor, Kate Darling, Will DeVries, Dave Fagundes, Jim Foster, Jonathan Frankle, Batya Friedman, Amy Gajda, Sue Glueck, Nathan Good, Jennifer Granick, Gehan Gunasekara, Joe Hall, Gus Hurwitz, Meg Jones, Kate Klonick, Sapna Kumar, Karen Levy, Aaron Massey, Andrea Matwyshyn, Emily McReynolds, Christina Mulligan, Deirdre Mulligan, Temple Northup, Frank Pasquale, Julia Powles, Omair Qazi, Joel Reidenberg, Jessica Roberts, Ira Rubinstein, Cameron Russel, Zahr Said, Paul Schwartz, Lisa Shay, Jessica Silbey, Ashkan Soltani, Zeynep Tufekci, Greg Vetter, Ari Waldman, Paul Wamsted, and Felix Wu.

I greatly benefited from the comments I received when presenting my ideas, as well as portions of the manuscript, at conferences, workshops, and symposia hosted by Cornell University's Law School and Department of Information Science; Fordham Law School's Center on Law and Information Policy; the University of Houston Law School; Maryland Law School; Melbourne Law School; the Samuelson Law, Technology & Public Policy Clinic at Berkeley Law School; Microsoft; the Asian Privacy Scholars Network Conference hosted at the University of Auckland; and the annual Privacy Law Scholars Conferences at The University of California–Berkeley and George Washington University.

Special thanks go to Natasha Duarte, who worked with me for years as an exceptional student, and whom I am proud to now call a friend. She completed a masterful edit on an early draft of the entire book. A number of Cumberland and Notre Dame Law students have helped me with my research over the years; special thanks to Kate Clark, Megan Fitzpatrick, Jonathan Green, Branden Moore, Carmen Weite, and Lydia Wimberly Messina.

I owe an immense debt to my family. My grandmothers Ruby and Eloise and my grandfathers, Woody and Jim, shaped me more than they knew through lessons and by example. My cousin Ellis, who is more like my brother, and my Aunt Deenie instilled so much confidence in me that I foolishly thought writing a book would be a breeze. My sister Deenie kept my skills sharp and my spirits up, even during midnight existential crises. And of course, my parents, Rickey and Debbie. The lessons they have taught me and the support and love they have given me could fill volumes, but over the years I have truly appreciated this: My parents taught me to be kind. They taught me to be brave. They taught me to ask questions. The spark necessary to give rise to a book began with them.

My wife and kids are the reason this book exists. My children were endlessly patient as I worked, and their enthusiasm for my project kept me going when I was flailing and exhausted. Will was always eager to read a few draft pages, particularly the ones with curse words. Romy was always eager to read a few draft pages, even though she couldn't yet read. But their largest direct contribution to this book was the perspective they provided and the ample evidence of the need for trust, obscurity, and autonomy as children grow up in a digital world. Let's just say I'm glad they've yet to figure out how to create their own YouTube channel (as far as I know).

My wife, Jen, the love of my life, has been my most steadfast supporter, most willing proofreader, and best friend. I cannot thank her enough for giving me everything I needed to complete this book. I am so grateful to be her teammate in this grand adventure.

Credits

Hacked Canadian baby monitor feed by Ars Technica via Shodan search engine, published in J. M. Porup, " 'Internet of Things' Security is hilariously broken and getting worse," Ars Technica (Condé Nast, January 23, 2016).

User interface, Snapchat, Snap, Inc., published in Federal Trade Commission, In re Snapchat, Inc., File No. 132-3078, Docket No. C-4501 (Washington, DC: FTC, December 23, 2014).

Fake Microsoft Windows registration verification wizard, DesignerWare LLC, published in Federal Trade Commission, In re DesignerWare, LLC, File No. 112-3151, Docket No. C-4390 (Washington, DC: FTC, April 15, 2013).

Padlock icons. Google Chrome; Twitter, Inc.; Facebook, Inc. Google is a registered trademark of Google, Inc., used with permission.

Mutant Font by Agência Africa for Amnesty International, "Mutant Wavy" variation.

Casual user interface for Carnegie Mellon University questionnaire. Courtesy of Alessandro Acquisti, Carnegie Mellon University.

Formal user interface for Carnegie Mellon University questionnaire. Courtesy of Alessandro Acquisti, Carnegie Mellon University.

On / Off Toggle button, iOS, Apple, Inc.

Privacy submenu, Facebook, Inc.

"Find Friends" prompt screen, Snapchat, Snap, Inc., published in Federal Trade Commission, In re Snapchat, Inc., File No. 132-3078, Docket No. C-4501 (Washington, DC: FTC, December 23, 2014).

"The privacy notice design space." Reprinted from Florian Schaub, Rebecca Balebako, Adam L. Durity, and Lorrie Faith Cranor, "A Design Space for Effective

Privacy Notices," *Symposium on Usable Privacy and Security (SOUPS) 2015*, July 22–24, 2015, Ottawa, Canada. Figure 1. Courtesy of Lorrie Faith Cranor, Carnegie Mellon University.

Spam bot on Tinder, detected by Symantic, published in Satnam Narang, "Tinder: Spammers Flirt with Popular Mobile Dating App," *Symantic Official Blog*, (Symantic, Inc., Jul. 1, 2013). Figure 5.

Ransom32 discovered by Emisoft, from "Meet Ransom32: The first JavaScript ransomware," *Emsisoft Blog* (January 1, 2016). Courtesy of Emsisoft Ltd.

User interface, Path, Inc., published in *United States v. Path, Inc.*, File No. C13-0448 JCS (N.D. Cal. Jan. 31, 2013), FTC File No. 122-3158 (Washington, DC, February 8, 2013), Exhibit A.

"OUSD Policies Signature Page," *Student Registration Packet, 2016-2017*, Oakland Unified School District (Oakland, California: OUSD, 2016).

Privacy Settings (January 2015), Facebook, Inc.

Disclaimer, Q-tips Cotton Swabs, Unilever. Photo by the author.

Facebook Sponsored Story, with link to Amazon.com, from Nick Bergus, "How I became Amazon's pitchman for a 55-gallon drum of personal lubricant on Facebook," (nbergus.com, February 23, 2012). Courtesy of Nick Bergus.

Index

Double-weight
serial
of
duplet
cuvers